Oleg Cassini

IN MY OWN FASHION

An Autobiography

SIMON AND SCHUSTER

NEW YORK

Designed by Eve Kirch
Manufactured in the United States of America

1   3   5   7   9   10   8   6   4   2

Library of Congress Cataloging-in-Publication Data
Cassini, Oleg, date.
In my own fashion.

Includes index.
1. Cassini, Oleg, date.   2. Costume designers—
United States—Biography.   I. Title.
TT140.C37A3   1987   746.9′2′0924 [B]   87-13046
ISBN 0-671-62640-X

Chapter opening photographs and sketch are from the author's collection except for the following: chapters 3 & 11 (photo only), UPI/Bettmann Newsphotos; chapter 4, AP/Wide World Photos; chapter 5, Culver Pictures; chapter 9, Ed Quinn, Black Star Photographs; chapter 12, courtesy Eugene McGrath, *Connaissance des Arts.*

To Laurie Lister, whose dedication, energy, and talent made this book impossible . . . and possible.

Photographs

16-page section of photographs, following page 160

CHAPTER

1

I have always loved the way she looked . . . fresh, but not quite innocent: tall, with red hair, freckles, and blue eyes. She seemed thin, but actually had a fine figure, delightfully round. Her name was Nina. She was perhaps eighteen, and Danish. She was everything to me: mysterious, alluring, affectionate, soothing, and—regrettably—my younger brother's wet nurse.

I was three at the time and badly in need of soothing. In fact, I was perpetually disconsolate. Our family lived in Copenhagen, where my father was first secretary of the Russian embassy. Each day the king of Denmark would ride past our window on his horse. He wore a blue uniform with a single row of buttons and silver trim, and I saluted as I had been taught. The king presented a fine figure, but a false sense of permanence. I did not know those were difficult times for kings.

I wasn't aware of the news from home, the last totterings of our poor czar, Nicholas II. Our sweet, sheltered world was about to change drastically, forever, but I was only three—and have only wisps of memory from that time. I do not remember our world collapsing. I do remember the king of Denmark and, of course, Nina.

What a comfort she was! I had been a difficult child from the first, a blue baby—cyanosis, the malady was called—subjected regularly to the tortures of boiling mustard baths to improve my circulation. A nervous and finicky child, I am told; allergic to cow's milk, unable to keep most food down. I was thin, sickly, my coloring an unstable array of primary

13

hues: blue, red, yellow—never pink. Nina was pink. In addition to the attentions bestowed upon my lucky brother, she had the responsibility of putting me to sleep—a difficult project; a lesser woman would have found it impossible. But Nina had her ways, soothing me through the massage of a certain sensitive part of my body, rubbing me against her . . .

But what is that? Why is Mother screaming? Why is Nina crying? It is a sad truth that I was caught in the act years before I quite knew what the act was. I would be caught many other times in my life—so often, in fact, that I sometimes wonder if the need to be caught was a secret program on my part.

But Nina, Nina was gone—dismissed by my protective mother, who had performed that most common of matronly contortions, metamorphosing from outrageous young flirt to Victorian prude via the miracle of childbirth. Mother taught me manners, made certain that despite our straitened circumstances, I knew I was born a gentleman, and a count. An aristocrat. She convinced me of my talent; she encouraged me to believe that I had a place among the finest people of society. But she was rather squeamish about sex.

Nina was the first *scandale*, but not my first conquest. I was adored by women, I must confess. This was, however, nothing to be proud of: because of my catalogue of ills, I required their constant attentions (not my favorite strategy with women, but one that I would employ from time to time in later life). There was Mother, who must have dissipated her youth on me. There was Nurse Farrell, my English nanny; and Maroussia, my Russian wet nurse.

Nurse Farrell was shriveled and starched, very formal in the English manner, olive skin, yellow teeth—an austere, forbidding presence, but passionately devoted to me. Indeed, she was engaged in a quiet, fierce competition with Maroussia, a competition she believed she'd won the day I swallowed the needle.

I was less than a year old. Nurse Farrell awakened my mother in the middle of the night and told her that I had a needle in my stomach. "How did this happen?" Mother demanded.

"Maroussia allowed him to play with it," Farrell said.

Maroussia wept and denied the charge, but I was rushed to a hospital and, oddly enough, a needle *was* in my stomach, about to pass into my intestines. An operation was necessary to remove it; I still have the scar. Nevertheless, Mother believed Maroussia and decided to fire Farrell, but the nurse begged to stay. She said that she loved me so much she would work for nothing: at least the price was right.

Well, I don't know, but that is the way the story was told by my mother—to comfort me, I suspect, to make me feel important in those early years after all had been lost and stories, our glorious past, were all we had.

The stories, the countless, endless stories of times that are unimaginable now, of a majestic opulence, a lineage descending from the Crusaders on one side and the Teutonic knights on the other—these were my inheritance, along with the noble but suddenly anachronistic title of Count. The stories ranged from family myths and legends passed down through the generations to more recent, documented triumphs. An ancestor on my father's side had been a knight named Von Loiew (meaning "lion" in German), captured by Poles at the Battle of Grünwald; a descendant of his, Loiewski Bjela, had been king of Poland for a day. From the earliest recollection, I was aware—I was, indeed, suffused with the knowledge— that I was descended from knights, from noble, fighting stock.

More recently, my maternal grandfather—Arthur Paul Nicholas, marquis de Capizzucchi de Bologna, count de Cassini—had been a famous Russian diplomat, the czar's minister to China, and then Russian ambassador to the United States during the administrations of Presidents William McKinley and Theodore Roosevelt. Arthur Cassini had signed the Treaty of Portsmouth, ending the Sino-Japanese War—and was honored by having both Port Arthur in Asia and Port Arthur in Texas named for him. Arthur Cassini's stern portrait, in splendid uniform, with monocle and medallions, stares down from the wall of my living room, a constant reminder of the bizarre twists of my fate: if history had not taken its left turn in 1917, my place would have been as an officer in the Chevaliers Gardes, the best of the four regiments of guards cavalry.

My parents had expected a military career for me. It was one of only three creditable professional activities for a Russian nobleman (the others were the diplomatic corps or an academic position, though that was less prestigious). A commission in the Imperial Guards was secured from birth; Father ordered my name inscribed on the rolls, a traditional course of action for members of our caste. My future was thus assured: at seventeen, I would become a member of the *corps des pages* (cadets in training) and then, after several years, join one of the regiments of the horse guards, regiments whose duty it was to serve as the last line of defense, to defend the czar himself. Members of the guards were expected to be master horsemen, swordsmen, chess players . . . and also, I assume, passionate lovers, linguists, dancers (of the traditional Russian national dances, of course), gourmets; in my child's mind, the horse guards were the most dashing fellows imaginable. Their position was, obviously, a great *social* as well as military honor. A member of the guards was a gentleman; he was invited to all the great balls; he lived a life of honor and grace. And what uniforms they had! They were spectacular: a golden helmet and cuirass, a white tunic, blue trousers with a red stripe, and tall leather boots.

How odd that I became a designer instead. Yes, it is true that I have dressed (and undressed) some of the more significant women of the twentieth century. I have been of service to American royalty, the Kennedys. I have done well in business. I have had a life filled with romance, excitement, and glamor. But I am plagued by the insignificance of it all when compared with the family heritage, the role I might have played, the life I might have led.

I was born in Paris on April 11, 1913. The doctor arrived in a carriage after midnight. He wore a top hat, white tie and tails, white gloves, and spats, an appropriately formal costume for the circumstances of my birth, which took place in a splendid apartment on the Rue de General Lambert, several blocks from the Tour Eiffel and the Seine. I am told that I was born in a gold and white bed draped with pink silk; pleated pink silk on the walls and pink carpeting. I arrived—blue (to set off all that pink?)— at 2:00 A.M., an hour that became one of my favorites in later life. My godmother was the renowned beauty Princess Olga Paley.

My father was employed, at the time, in the pursuit of pleasure; that was his occupation. He was Count Alexander Loiewski, the son of a very successful Russian lawyer who specialized in finding lost heirs to great fortunes. He was short, about five feet eight inches, with handsome, even features that I did not inherit. He spent much of his time either eating or preparing to be fed. He would consult with restaurants about their menus in advance and then loiter three or four hours over a meal, return home for a nap, and awaken in time to eat again. His other primary occupation was going to the tailor, an event of the utmost seriousness: fittings might continue for hours. He was quite a dandy and practically lived at Charvet in Paris, where he bought shirts and ties. His shoes were made by Loeb, and his suits by Brandoni of Milan. He owned several hundred shirts, all of them silk in various colors. Later, in the 1960s, when I created a revolution in men's fashion by reintroducing colored shirts, it was from memories of Father's wardrobe. He would send these shirts, fifty at a time, to London for laundering. He also claimed to own 552 ties.

I am assured by Mother that the eating sprees indeed took place; she was slim, she says, until Paris. I remember distinctly, too, my father's wonderful clothes . . . but it is hard for me to square the serious, defeated man I knew with the voracious frivolity he displayed in Paris. He was a learned man, a scholar, a linguist versed in Oriental languages and philosophy—an ambulatory encyclopedia. He could respond to any question, and yet, sadly, he was entirely unfit for life after the revolution. A very fastidious man, a fanatic about hygiene, always formally dressed, even in our most desperate moments of poverty. If he removed his jacket, it was replaced by a silk robe. He was a man of great dignity, even in despair.

The Paris period ended abruptly soon after my birth when Grandfather Clement Loiewski reluctantly concluded that, with World War I on the horizon, the German government was not going to satisfy the debt on an enormous, complicated inheritance case that he had been pursuing for seven years—and decided to relieve his misery by shooting himself, in Leipzig. He left a fortune in Russian property, but not enough to support Father's French appetites. We returned to Russia in June 1913, and Father studied for the foreign service examinations. It was assumed that he would pass these easily, and he did.

Mother hated Russia. The weather was always so cold, and the people drank excessively. She hated the overheated rooms. To her last days, her only dream was Paris. Even after many successful years in Italy, she would say, "The minute I arrive in Paris, I breathe again." French was the primary language spoken in our family. I learned Russian in Russia, Danish in Denmark, Italian in Italy, English from Nurse Farrell and American movies; but, as it was for all those of our caste throughout Europe, French was always the language of choice.

My first days of life coincided with the last days of the class of privilege, a group that achieved its apotheosis just prior to World War I but is only a memory now. Our family status was assured by our listing in the Fifth Book of Russian Nobility, in which the foreigners who had been granted titles by the czar were recorded. This meant instant acceptance among our peers in London, Paris, Rome, Munich, and other meeting places of the elite. We were citizens of all Europe, and like many other Russians of that time and class, my parents, especially Mother, seemed to prefer residence anywhere in Europe to home.

Apparently, my reaction to St. Petersburg was similar to Mother's but more drastic. My health became more precarious. The doctors recommended that I be moved to a more healthful environment, and so we repaired to the Loiewski country estate in Pavlovsk, just outside the city. It was a large villa with a verandah in front and white columns, a marvelous park, and over twenty thousand hectares of terrain and landscaped gardens.

It was there that I had my first encounter with the military. The villa was located near the barracks of one of the Imperial Guards regiments that I was intended to join. Very early, I knew all the ranks and how to salute properly. Mother recalls that I would salute the Chevaliers Gardes when my uncle, Colonel George Mengden, led them from their barracks on parade, in gleaming blue, white, and gold. Later, in Sevastopol (Father was stationed there during World War I), I saluted a regiment of troops and, apparently, was mistaken in my sailor suit for the czarevich, for the troops saluted me in return.

Sevastopol was one of many stops for my family during the war. I do not remember them all. Father served in a series of diplomatic posts, in Sevastopol, Reni, Bucharest. We were in perpetual motion, traveling on trains—I remember the soothing sound of the wheels—special trains with servants, as many as twenty trunks, Mother's dogs (borzois named Tristan and Isolde, and, later, poodles); there were, no doubt, troop movements less complicated than our family's relocations.

My brother, Igor, was born in Sevastopol in 1915. He was blessed with a sunny disposition and luxurious curls. We were opposites, known as *Jean qui ris* and *Jean qui pleure* ("Jean who laughs" and "Jean who cries"). His career, my parents believed, was to be in the diplomatic service. He and I were, from the very beginning, terrible rivals and dearest friends.

My first real memories date from this period of constant travel. I remember crossing the frozen Gulf of Bothnia, from Finland to Sweden, in a troika. Were we fleeing the revolution? I think not. I think we were on our way to Copenhagen to rejoin Father, taking the northern route to avoid the fighting in Europe. It was at night; Mother, Gigi, and I, covered by heavy furs. I remember the smell of the furs and the horses, and small glowing lights in the distance. Mother said that they were the eyes of wolves. For some reason, she was frightened. When we arrived in Sweden at dawn, she kept repeating, "How lucky, how lucky!"

I remember, too, when the Kronstadt sailors shot my cousin Uri. The Kronstadt Revolt occurred in June of 1917. It marked the beginning of the Russian Revolution, after the czar had been defeated at the battles of Königsberg and Tannenberg—one million Russians had been killed by

Hindenburg. The Russian troops marched home; the navy revolted first, having been promised amnesty, splitting into the White and the Red. When the White navy returned, all of the officers were shot.

I don't know why our family was in Pavlovsk at the time; we should have been in Copenhagen. Perhaps we had returned, fearing for Grandmother Eugenia Eugenievna's safety, as she had remained in Russia with Father's sister to oversee the family's properties. But there we were, and I remember the mutinous sailors bursting into the garden as we were about to go down for tea. I watched from a window above, in horror, as my cousin went out to talk with them. Uri was perhaps seventeen then, in the bottle-green uniform of the *corps des pages*. The uniform was what did him in. The sailors were killing everyone in uniform. They took him to the back patio and shot him like a dog. I was not allowed to see the body, but I was stunned by this.

In Copenhagen, wisps of memory entwine into a solid braid: there was Nina and, in the first stirrings of consciousness, the sense that all was lost. My uncle, George Mengden, was dead, killed by his own troops. There was confusion, and tears, and arguments. Mother and Father argued constantly, Father saying, "I must go back. I will be dishonored if I don't go and fight; I will not be a man. We must save Russia from the Bolsheviks."

Mother pleaded with him. His first duty was to his family. He was leaving her alone with two children and no money. Later she would recall, "For every blow of fortune, Sacha had the same remedy: join Admiral Alexander Kolchak in Siberia."

I remember him leaving. He was preparing his equipment to leave for Siberia to join the White armies. He had uniforms and boots specially made for the Siberian climate. I remember the boots in particular—I have always loved boots, and his were knee length, lined with tiger skin. Remarkable boots. But then Father was gone.

I have delayed describing Mother. I am unsure how to go about it. I refuse to blather as so many others do: "My mother was an extraordinary woman" or, worse, "My mother was a *saint*." That would be so common, and Mother would never approve. Still, I must say that she did live a very dramatic life, and, in the years after we were cast adrift by the revolution, her sole purpose became the promotion of her two sons. She lived for us, a sacrifice one tends to appreciate more in retrospect; at the time, it sometimes seemed harsh and claustrophobic.

Mother was the product of a rather strange alliance. There was Grandfather, Count Arthur Cassini, the last in a line of Triestine Italians who served the czars (a family tradition that dated, along with the title, from a battle for Malta in the late eighteenth century). For generations the first-born Capizzucchi-Cassini son would travel north to be educated at the Imperial Lyceum in Moscow and then enter the czar's service.

And then there was Grandmother, Stephanie ("Dada") Van Betz. She was titled, too, though not quite in the same way as Arthur Cassini: she was "the White Cat," a vaudeville performer of the very first rank, a singer invited, on occasion, to give command performances for royal courts. It was during one such evening in St. Petersburg, sponsored by Grand Duke Vladimir, that Arthur Cassini first heard Dada Van Betz sing and was smitten, as she was.

Their romance progressed secretly. Cassini had been married once before, to a niece of Prince Gorchakov, who had grown tired of Grandfather's infidelities and gambling (with her fortune) and divorced him, returning to St. Petersburg, where she apparently told all to the empress. The divorce, and Grandfather's subsequent tracking of a pretty singer across Europe, did little to enhance his diplomatic career. (That he was allowed to remain in the service at all was probably a tribute to his enormous talents.)

In any case, a public marriage to the White Cat might have been the last straw. So Arthur Cassini married Dada privately, morganatically, in 1880. Two years later my mother, Marguerite Cassini, was born and an elaborate charade ensued. When Grandfather was named ambassador to China, Mother traveled as his "niece," and Grandmother as her governess. In 1898 Grandfather was posted to Washington—the czar's first ambassador there—and President McKinley insisted that the ambassador's pretty niece serve as official hostess for the embassy. Mother subsequently became one of the more notable and popular young belles of the capital, along with her good friends Alice Roosevelt (President Theodore Roosevelt's daughter), Helen Hay (later Mrs. Payne Whitney), and Cissy Patterson.

Mother was a trendsetter in those days, in fashion and society. She designed all her own clothes (not unusual for someone of her class; Marie Antoinette did the same), and had them executed by a battery of seamstresses. From photographs, it appears Mother's strategy was to emphasize her tiny waist; she introduced a cummerbund look that became quite the thing in turn-of-the-century Washington. She enjoyed audacity; she was a glorious flirt. She was one of the first women to smoke cigarettes in public; and perhaps the very first to win an automobile race: from Washington to Chevy Chase, at breathtaking speeds of up to fifteen miles per hour. Years later, Franklin Roosevelt, Jr., told me, "You know, my father had a crush on your mother." He was one of many, apparently. Another was Cissy Patterson's brother Joe, later the publisher of the New York *Daily News*.

In 1900, finally, Grandfather confessed to the czar that Mother was his daughter, not his niece, and she became Countess Cassini, a hereditary title created by imperial ukase, eventually passed on to my brother and me.

Mother was not a classic beauty, though she certainly was very attractive; she had the devil's beauty, as much a consequence of her personality as her looks. She had delicate features and eyes. She had a velvety voice (indeed, she had spent years trying to repeat her mother's success as a singer) and, most remarkable, was able to speak English, French, German, Mandarin Chinese, and Russian, all without an accent. She was weaker in Italian, a language she was forced to learn later in life.

I am introducing Mother at a turning point in her life—autumn 1919 —the moment she was forced to sink or swim. Her husband had gone off to the war. She had no means of support, except the proceeds from a Fabergé cross and other jewels, family heirlooms. (The proceeds weren't much, as it happened; with the deluge of Russian artifacts on the market at the time, the "priceless" could be had cheap.) She also was burdened by two squalling children suffering, she believed, from whooping cough—and for the first time, no servants.

Mother had as little training for practical life as Father, but she did have a fierce instinct for survival. Fearing that our whooping cough might be something worse, she immediately took us to Switzerland, to the wonderful village of Montreux, on Lake Geneva, where a pulmonary specialist gave us a clean bill of health . . . and Mother had to face the much more serious problem of what to do next. Later, she would say there were times she wanted to throw herself off a mountain; my brother and I saw only her cheerful persistence. To me, Mother was ever the optimist, palpably alive, always bubbling with ideas, observations, jokes, proposals, orders.

We lived in a pensione at first; Mother cooked spaghetti for us on a hot plate. Soon, though, she began to encounter old friends in the streets of Montreux, which seemed awash with exiles—as did all of Europe. Grand Duchess Helen (of Russia) was there with her husband, Prince

Nicholas of Greece; indeed, the king and queen of Greece lived in temporary exile at Lucerne. There was a steady stream of American tourists as well, including socialites like Ruth Hanna (Senator Mark Hanna's daughter) and Martha Hoy, whom Mother had known in better days.

These friends encouraged her to pursue a career in fashion. She had no training in the field, nothing except an innate sense of style. She knew the secret of good fashion: how to be daring in ways that are not inappropriate. She was instinctively bold, always introducing new styles as she had so successfully in Washington, D.C. Now, in Montreux, with money borrowed from Queen Sophie of Greece, she opened a small boutique in the Grand Hotel where she sold hats and handbags, plus a line of children's clothes (sometimes modeled by the young Greek princesses), and other charming items. Grand Duchess Helen helped as well, sitting in the shop and encouraging customers, a titled saleswoman. The business was a modest success.

One day Mother encountered Prince Constantine Cantacuzene on the street. The Cantacuzenes were among the five or six richest families in Russia . . . and now they had nothing but a house, a villa they had given to a faithful servant years before. Arriving in Montreux, the family found the servant, who insisted not only that they resume residence there but also that he resume his former role. And so they had a magnificent house in Glion, the village above Montreux in the mountains, but no money; we had a little money, but no place to live. Mother and the prince struck a bargain. We moved into their marvelous villa. It was a huge stone edifice with at least forty rooms.

I remember Prince Cantacuzene as a fierce-looking man, the sort of face you would find on an icon. He had a black Vandyke beard and ferocious features, a bald head and a stern, dignified bearing. I could imagine him as an ancient knight of Byzantium brandishing a sword. However, I often saw him engaged in more modest activities, carrying trunks about for my mother's boutique. She would say to me, "Look, Olie, at what a real gentleman will do. A real gentleman is willing to work, to even carry a suitcase."

My brother and I were not interested in work. We stayed away from the shop. We were off cavorting in the mountains, almost always by ourselves. Mother was constantly pushing us toward sports. She was worried about my sickly appearance and thought that strenuous exercise would improve my health. She was convinced, not unreasonably, that we would have to be strong to survive in this frightening new world we had inherited.

Through all this, we heard nothing from Father. Kolchak was killed in Siberia, the White armies routed. More than a year passed, and still no word. Finally, one day Mother arrived home in tears. Father had been located in Japan, in Yokohama. She had sent him money. He was coming home.

This homecoming was to be another turning point. Mother expected him to return, take charge, resume his former role as head of the family and breadwinner. But that didn't happen. He returned broken, unable to make the adjustment to the new world, unable to even admit that the old world was lost. To the end of his life, he would see the Bolsheviks as a temporary aberration; they couldn't last. He was certain we would return to Russia eventually, restored to dignity. In the meantime, he would remain a gentleman. Mother later recalled that he arrived in Montreux in September 1920 "in fine shape, with a dozen trunks of beautiful new shirts, ties, socks, pajamas, suits."

Fighting ensued. Mother accused Father of delaying his return. She said he'd been having an affair in Japan with a Frenchwoman (Father insisted the woman was Russian). She wanted him to go to work; he resisted. I remember one fight in particular: Mother had found him a job with a Swiss bank. Father was appalled.

"I am no bank teller!" he shouted. "I will not consider such a position. Never!"

He added, for good measure, that he had decided to round up his old colleagues and mount another military challenge to the Bolsheviks. He dreamed of this, but he knew that all was lost. He was tortured by it. I once saw him slap himself across the face and say, "At thirty-two, Alexander the Great had conquered the world. Here I am, at thirty-nine, and look . . ." And then he began to beat his head against the wall.

Gigi and I pressed Father for details of the war. He would not speak much of the fighting, although he did tell of seeing a man sliced diagonally from shoulder to waist by a cossack's saber. He was more willing to use his experience to impress certain lessons upon us, like the importance of cleanliness; he often told of how he insisted on taking a bath every day at the front in Siberia, even when the temperature was fifty below zero and he had to bathe in snow. Father's stories, and the image of him as a military man, had an enormous impact on Gigi and me. We began a collection of toy soldiers that became a lifelong project; and I became fascinated with uniforms, weapons, and armor. I collected pictures of regimental garb (to this day, the walls of my home are covered with prints of men in uniform). Later this would have a profound influence on my designs; I would introduce a modified military look in ladies' fashions—double rows of large buttons, color combinations of bottle green and scarlet and navy blue. It became an important theme in my work.

Father's stories were fascinating to me, but Mother was frustrated by his preoccupation with the past. It was clear to her now that she would have to support the family. The boutique was successful, but not very lucrative. She decided to move us to Greece, where King Constantine was about to be restored to the throne, and prospects were bound to be better. Queen Sophie also encouraged her to come to Greece.

And so, in February of 1921, we left Montreux by train, stopping in Milan, where Mother encountered yet another old friend, Count O'Sullivan, who advised her against Greece. The monarchy was precarious (indeed, it soon toppled); better to go to Florence, a city Mother had always hated, where she might open a boutique that would cater to the American tourist trade. The count gave Mother the name of a valuable contact there, Countess Arturo Fabricotti.

Our arrival in Florence, the city where I would spend the rest of my youth, was memorable. Father met a Russian emigré at the train station, a wild, smelly vegetarian named Kurt Ovchinikof. They immediately fell into noisy gossiping and plotting (the counterrevolution, always). Father may have been quite inept in other areas, but he had an uncanny ability to find Russian emigrés within minutes, it seemed, of his arrival in any new place.

Mother, meanwhile, dragged Gigi and me off on a sightseeing tour: statues, monuments, ancient bridges, a city made of stone. Our last stop was a small church in the Piazza Antinori, which for some reason was very crowded. We were pushed about; it was very uncomfortable. Just as we were leaving, there was a tremendous explosion. It seemed the building would collapse. There was screaming and panic. We were pushed down a staircase by the mob—it was almost fun at the time, all the running and excitement. Later we learned that a bomb had gone off; several people had been killed. And this was how we found out that Italy was practically at war. The Communists and Mussolini's Fascists were fighting for power. There were murders in the streets. You would spot people running, people being beaten. On several occasions I saw the Fascists force castor oil, which had an immediate, explosive effect, down a Communist's throat in the street. At least, I assumed they were Communists.

My reaction to these things—the bomb in the church, the violence in the streets—was a kind of outward numbness, more curiosity than fear, but I think, too, a kind of residual anxiety. I was a nervous child; I had seen terrible things, from the earliest memories of my cousin Uri being shot. I had only known uncertainty. Obviously these things had an impact on my personality . . . and the confusion, too, about who we were. We were very important, of course. "Remember," Mother would always say, "you are *Loiewsk-Cassinis*. You are gentlemen." And yet, we had no money. We were very poor. We were better *and worse* off than other people; my self-image fluctuated accordingly.

All of this was very difficult for a high-strung child to understand, and became more so when Mother insisted on sending me immediately to a Jesuit school, without any knowledge of Italian. That was Mother's way: throw them in the icy water and they will learn how to swim. In this case, the water was particularly frigid.

The Collegio della Querce was located in a remodeled fifteenth-century villa on top of a hill, surrounded by high walls and beautiful pine trees. It became a prison to me. My teacher there was named Don Luigi. He wore an impressive, nicely cut (I was already conscious of such things) black robe, an effect that was marred by his terrible dandruff and unshined shoes. I tried to cultivate his favor by smiling sweetly, feigning attention when I could barely understand what was being said. (Even if I *had* understood Italian, I would have been only slightly more successful; I was an ardent daydreamer; I had perfected the science of being able to sleep in class with my eyes open.) In any case, Don Luigi found me out soon enough.

One day he called me to the front of the room and asked me several questions. I was terrified, and lost control of my bladder; worse, some of the effluent dripped onto his cassock. He was so angry that he took me by the hair and beat my head against the wall. This, of course, caused something of an uproar in the class. I became an obvious target for ridicule by my classmates.

The beatings continued regularly. Don Luigi would take me into his private room, bang my head against the wall, whack my fingers with a ruler, and threaten me: "Don't tell anyone about this or there will be very big trouble."

There was hardly a danger of that. I was afraid to tell Mother; she would think me a sissy, a complainer. I lived in fear for months. It began to affect my health. I was losing weight, I had trouble sleeping, my eyes were red. When I finally broke down and told Mother, I must say she never hesitated (this would be true all our lives; she always believed us, always took up our cause and defended us). She marched right up to the school, complained bitterly about the priest, and took me out of there. She placed me in a more lenient school, run by the Scalopian friars. Despite my Roman Catholic education, our family continued as intermittently attentive members of the Greek Orthodox church. Father would bring Gigi and me to church on occasion, to remind us of our roots.

Mother, meanwhile, was busily making a success of herself in Florence. Her good fortune began with a remarkable coincidence: Countess Fabricotti turned out to be Cornelia Roosevelt Scovel, an old friend from Washington. She was happy to help get Mother started.

Countess Fabricotti ran a fashionable boutique on the Via Tornabuoni. The family owned a magnificent Palladian-style marble villa, one of the finest homes I've ever seen. It seemed a park within the city: 15 acres of landscaped gardens; ponds, flowers, birds and sculpture; a grand marble staircase leading to the villa itself, which must have had 60 rooms. Mother was as impressed as I, remarking on the fabulous furniture.

We were invited there for tea, and it was decided that Mother's first project would be a line of hats that the countess would feature in her boutique. These did not turn out very well; they fell apart in the wind (Mother often had excellent ideas, but little notion how to execute them). Still, Countess Fabricotti did not give up on her. The next project was a collection of dresses, variations on what Mother considered the most appealing Paris fashion, and this turned out more successfully.

It was during this time that I experienced one of the few unqualified triumphs of my young life. Mother insisted that Igor and I be raised as gentlemen, and gentlemen simply *must* know how to ride. We were acquainted by then with every Russian nobleman in the city, most of whom were chauffeurs. The most dashing was Prince Djorjadze, a noted horseman, who knew of a stable where I might learn to ride.

A most remarkable thing happened then: I was placed on a horse and given a few rudimentary instructions. The riding master said, "Little boy, you must keep your heels down and straight, your weight forward . . ." —the basic things one is taught—and very quickly I was not only riding but *galloping*. I felt very comfortable astride.

The riding master said to my mother, "I've never seen anything like it. This boy has never ridden before?"

"Never in his life," Mother said.

"Well," said the riding master, "there is not much I can teach him. He can ride."

And my father began to laugh. He said, "See, I told you—an Indian. He was an Indian. . . ."

In an earlier life, he meant. Father was turning into quite a mystic. He believed in reincarnation and the transmigration of souls. (I suppose his life was such a disappointment that he had to believe it would eventually take a more triumphant form of expression.) He always told me that I'd once been an American Indian, probably a chief, and I was much taken by this. I loved to listen to Father talk about religion and mysticism, about anything, really. When he wasn't preoccupied with his bad fortune, he would tell us stories of traveling around the world, to Brazil on a tramp steamer, to the Far East . . .

Usually, though, he ignored my brother and me. He had lost his pride, his position, and his money. Mother was so totally involved in her work that she'd become a noncompanion to him—and he was still a young man. Their sexual life was over. She didn't want more children. Her disinterest was very clear to us: she seemed to flinch, to pull back when he tried to make contact. "No, no, Sacha," she would say, "not that, not that." Father was infuriated by this, and became rather jealous, because Mother was still quite an attractive woman.

Mother apparently still had a high opinion of her looks, too. She fell for one of the oldest tricks in the book, and hired a local "filmmaker" to make a short movie, a vanity film, featuring her as a vamp. This would be presented to a producer in Rome, who might hire her for one of his projects. I thought it was *revolting:* a heavily bearded Italian Romeo—the producer played the hero—pursuing my mother on the grounds of the Fabricotti villa. The plot was something like that of *Lady Chatterley's Lover*, without the pornography. I was horrified when this man kissed Mother. Father was, too. They fought about it; he thought she was wasting money and making a fool of herself, as indeed she was.

Father had more cause to be jealous, I suspect, of a rather dashing Italian cavalry officer named Ferrucci, who often came to visit Mother. He would arrive on a bicycle, with his sabre strapped to the handlebars. One time, Ferrucci and several fellow officers were having a cocktail party with Mother and some of her friends. Father arrived, sat down in a chair, and stared furiously at everyone without saying a word. This cast something of a chill on the party, and the guests soon left. A terrible fight ensued. My parents fought often—she knew just how to cut him; his temper was explosive—but this was more severe, Father following her from room to room screaming, finally to the kitchen, where he grabbed her by the throat. Gigi and I were terrified, and in my panic, I picked up a plate and hit him on the head with it. This brought Father to his senses, and embarrassed, humiliated, he released her.

In retrospect, I have more sympathy for my father than I did at the time. He was frustrated, and ashamed of his role. But in those days, he seemed just a monster; poor Mother was the victim, and our allegiance was only to her.

That summer, 1922, Mother decided to send Father, Gigi, and me off to the seacoast while she prepared her collection and found us a new apartment. She rented several rooms for us in a small caretaker's cottage in the *pineta*—the pine forest—near Viareggio. It was the first of many summers we would spend in that area, a wilderness then (an overcrowded resort now). In later years, Mother would rent wonderful villas at Forte dei Marmi, and we would have Emilio Pucci and Gianni Agnelli for playmates. The Agnellis, who owned Fiat, had a majestic, rather exotic tent erected on the beach. The tent itself was made entirely of tooled morocco leather; inside, it looked like a scene from the *Arabian Nights*, decorated in pillows and rugs. It was always a wonderful treat to be invited for lunch there, after a morning of running on the beach, jumping in the waves with Gianni (who was a few years younger than I).

The first summer, with Father, in the caretaker's cottage, was somewhat less luxurious—and more confusing, as life with him always was. He hated the sun and refused to go outside. He hated even more the notion of being nursemaid, and found the merest domestic chores impossible to perform. He raged and raged, once forcing me out at night to retrieve a toy cane I'd left at a friend's house. I didn't want to go; I was frightened of the dark, but more frightened of Father, as was Gigi, who joined me standing outside until the screaming stopped. At other times, though, Father, calm and collected, would give us the benefit of his learning, telling us stories of Taras Bulba, the Russo-Turkish War, and Alexander the Great, filling our heads with history, creating in me a profound love for the past that continues to this day.

We returned to a new life in Florence that fall. Mother's business was a success. Her idea was a simple one: she would go to Paris twice a year, look at the collections, take the best designs, and produce them more cheaply in Florence. She also introduced the idea of showing her line on live models, as they did in Paris, a custom that became an event in Florentine society (especially with the large numbers of American tourists wandering through Europe in those days of the Roaring Twenties). In short, her business boomed.

We also returned to a spectacular, if somewhat bizarre, new home: a triplex apartment in a fashionable neighborhood on the banks of the Arno, the Viale Amerigo Vespucci. The place had been decorated by a Russian girl Mother found who called herself "La Bartsova" and had designed sets for Diaghilev; she favored a dramatic palette of reds, purples, and pinks. The room I shared with Gigi, for example, had red walls with white cornices upon which she had painted red poppies. The curtains were thick white linen, also embroidered with poppies. The carpet was pure white (for a day or two). As a final touch, La Bartsova had scattered expensive Lenci dolls about—dolls wearing the native dress of various countries; Gigi and I later diverted ourselves by massacring the dolls, cutting off their heads and tossing them into the Arno, which flowed just beneath our window.

Gigi and I were inseparable, and rather notorious. We were "the Little Cossacks," real battlers from the very start. We resumed the Russo-Turkish War, using Nahad Bey, the mild, overweight son of the local Turkish consul, as a stand-in for the entire infidel army. Gigi attacked from one side, I from the other; we gave him a tremendous beating, ruining his sailor suit.

Our favorite game was cowboys and Indians. I designed costumes for both of us, my first effort in this area (I was the Indian, of course), and we engaged in other costume dramas as well. For a time, we pretended to be beggars: we stood on the street near our home, wrapped in rugs, our faces smeared with dirt, raising money for the movies. This continued until Mother, mortified, caught us.

In time, both of us would engage—enthusiastically—in a costume drama of a more portentous sort: we were *balilla*, members of the Fascist Youth. This was required training for all schoolchildren, and—I must admit—rather exciting for us, although, in truth, it was merely a sort of Boy Scouts with a martial twist. We played soldier on Sundays, and were told we were being prepared to fight communism. This was very important to me. The Communists, after all, had taken everything from our family.

The other great attraction was the uniform: black shirt, green shorts, and a little black beret. I also had black boots made to order. It was fun to be done up so elegantly, although, even then, I was able to see through the propaganda we were being fed: here we were, the *front line* of defense against communism, and completely inept. I was a squad leader, and it was impossible to get my ten boys to march correctly; they wandered all over the place. I knew that if *we* were going to defend Italy, the country was in serious trouble. As time went on, the propaganda became heavier and more strident; in the early days, though, Mussolini seemed quite a hero. He had defeated the Communists and restored order, he was fighting the Mafia, and—of course—the trains were running on time. All the best people in society supported him.

And then, too, the Fascists taught me how to ski. They encouraged athletic competition. There were ski races on weekends in the winter, and my brother and I became quite adept. The sport was just growing popular outside Scandinavia; the techniques and equipment were still rather primitive, as was the dress. Mother got me up in a Russian fur hat, a bulky sweater, and a Scotch plaid jacket, which was fine. Down below, though, there was trouble. The pants were made of military cloth and absorbed water, as did the boots, which I suspect were made from papier-mâché. Within minutes my feet were frozen. It wasn't a very comfortable experience, yet it was certainly exhilarating.

We would be loaded into open trucks and taken to Abetone, in the Apennines, which is only a few hours' drive from Florence now, but in those days took most of the day. We would ski for a few hours, then pile back into the trucks, still sweaty, for the long drive home. This was not the most healthy situation, but it made a man of you—and the Fascists were very concerned about that.

I was always running; I never walked. I couldn't stand still. I loved to run and jump and explore . . . and this habit nearly caused a tragedy when I was eleven years old. It happened one afternoon after school. I was going to a small, short-lived tearoom my father had opened with his friend Kurt, called The Daisy (for years after, Father was known in Florence as Signor Daisy). I would go there often to eat cakes. This particular day I was running along the street, which was under construction. There was a pile of big granite blocks—paving stones—a mountain, a challenge for me. I stormed the mountain, and it collapsed, toppling me into the excavation. An enormous stone fell on top of me, hitting my leg just above the knee, severing the muscles, touching the bone. There was a lot of blood, and yellow—the muscle itself—oozing out, an incredible sight. I was half delirious.

A metropolitan guard saved me. He picked me out of the hole, commandeered a taxi, and took me to the nearest hospital, which happened to be the best in Florence, San Giovanni di Dio. They rushed me to the operating room, intending to amputate (this was before the era of wonder

30

drugs; tetanus was a mortal danger). They put a block of wood, wrapped in gauze, in my mouth for the pain—and that was all.

But just as the doctor was about to commence, Mother erupted into the room. Someone had seen me hurt and notified her. I remember realizing she was in the room, and the pain was excruciating, and not being able to say anything because of this block of wood in my mouth, tears rolling down my cheeks—but also, through the haze of delirium, realizing that Mother was *arguing* with this doctor. "We amputate," he'd said.

"I'd rather have him dead than without a leg," said Mother.

The doctor was insistent, and so Mother slapped him. This, apparently, got his attention. A second doctor was called in for consultation. He said that if gangrene did not set in, the chances of keeping the leg were fair; the healing process would be very lengthy, though.

I spent the next year in bed, in mortal fear that the doctor would come and chop off my leg. The doctor did come, every day, to check the wound—a painful process; the wound was a monstrous thing to look at— and every day there was the chance that he would say, "Okay, forget it. We have to amputate." I wasn't allowed to move. They had sewn things together, and the situation was very delicate. After a while, though, it was clear that the danger had passed. I would keep my leg, but the recuperation was far from over. It seemed to last forever.

That year in hibernation had, I think, a profound effect on my personality. I stopped running and became more reflective. I began to read omnivorously, especially history. I learned the history of Russia and Italy. I loved to read about the Crusades and the knights, chivalry and honor. I became fascinated by costumes and the symbolism of dress. My favorite topic was the American Indian. My reading began with James Fenimore Cooper and went quickly on to more weighty, factual material. I came to know them all: the Comanches, who were excellent horsemen; the rugged, handsome Navajos; the elegant Crow, who were the dandies of the Plains; and the noble, doomed Sioux, who were my favorites. They were my world for that year.

I emerged from my confinement as someone might enter the sunshine from a dark room: blinded, disoriented, exhilarated. I was both ahead *and* behind my classmates in schoolwork; tutors were necessary now—especially in mathematics, a subject whose existence I would only deign to acknowledge later in life.

Our family's life was different now, too. We were quite wealthy; Mother's business was bringing in two million lire per year (twenty-four lire to the dollar in those days). We moved to a magnificent villa on the Viale dei Mille; it had twenty-five rooms, a park, stables, and a small platoon of servants. Both my brother and I had ponies, which we would ride in the Cascine. We went to school each day in an English buggy: varnished black wood and leather, silent rubber wheels, pulled by a gray pony—a very distinctive arrival.

Mother bought a country estate as well, in Riboia, on top of a hill surrounded by forty-four hectares of the finest Chianti grapes; the famed Antinori vineyards were our neighbors. Mother insisted that I participate in the wine-making process, and I'll never forget the tactile, squishy bliss of stomping our grapes barefoot with the peasants, although I was somewhat perplexed: *Here we are, walking on these grapes with our dirty feet*, I thought. *Who will ever drink it?* The house itself was cool, breezy; the floors were terra-cotta quarry tile; there was a fifteenth-century chapel. We spent weekends there and summers at Forte dei Marmi. We had three cars: a Stutz, an Alfa, and a Fiat.

This was the period, too, of intense instruction in how to be a gentleman. Mother insisted that we take boxing, fencing, and piano lessons; semiclassical dance lessons from the famous master Dalcroze (I wasn't bad); and tap-dancing lessons from a black man who had appeared in the Folies-Bergère (I was the best in my class). Already a good athlete, playing soccer and running track in school, I was also an adept caricaturist, doodling instead of paying attention in class, and Mother thought I had artistic talent.

And yet, even with all these skills, I was plagued by feelings of uncertainty, of inferiority. I was very slender, and seemed young for my age; it would be years before I grew into my facial features. I remember walking along the street in my best suit one Sunday, feeling pretty good, jaunty, and some guy shouting from a tram, "Hey, Pinocchio!"

I was perhaps twelve; there were others my age rapidly becoming men. I was among the shortest in my class, and still very much a boy.

A tutor was hired to help me become a man, and this gentleman, Colonel Zboromirski, had a profound influence on my life. He had been an officer in the Preobrazenski Regiment of the Imperial Guards and carried himself accordingly. A tallish, stocky man with cropped graying hair, a great handlebar mustache, and blue eyes with long lashes, he stood very erect, and moved and spoke ve-ry de-lib-er-ate-ly. That was one of the things I liked best about him. I was still a rather nervous sort, and Mother, arriving like a freight train, barking orders, could make me jump.

But Zboromirski, a human sedative, would calm her immediately: "Counnnntesssss, Counnnntessss, pleeeaaase, pleeeaaase . . ."

I was ready to follow him anywhere; I think he felt strongly about me, too . . . a father/son relationship. I often thought, *This is the kind of man I'd like to be when I grow older.* Certainly I didn't want to be like Father, who lost his poise in the most trivial of domestic crises. I wanted to be a man of action, a daring man like the heroes I'd read about: Ivanhoe, d'Artagnan, Richard the Lion-Hearted. A man who could face all calamities with a smile. Even Mother would say, "Do not be like your father." And Zboromirski had a very impressive air of grandeur and dignity.

He lived on the Viale dei Mille with us, and helped preside over the elaborate ritual that was dinner. Gigi and I would, of course, have to change our clothes, from knickers and argyles into a shirt and tie, and bathe. Zboromirski would inspect our hands and make sure we had brushed our teeth.

At dinner, polite conversation was required. Each of us had to report what we'd done that day. Zboromirski gave instructions during the meal: "Oleg, don't ever speak with food in your mouth. That is not done," and "Don't make noises when you drink your wine. You sip the wine. Taste it." And more subtle things: "After dinner, when you are having your cigar, don't bite it—*flirt* with it."

During the day, he favored, as was the fashion among Russian gentlemen, English tweeds and a pipe, the country-squire look. "Style is very important, Oleg," he would say. "Your clothes and appearance are crucial to your position in the world—but, equally important, when you are well-dressed, you *feel* better, more confident and assured about yourself."

He would instruct me in the obvious points of etiquette—standing up when a lady entered the room, tipping your cap—as well as more complicated situations. What do you do if you accompany a young lady to a party and she abandons you for another gentleman?

"You challenge him to a duel," I'd say, suffused as I was with the spirit of chivalry. "A fistfight."

"No, no," Zboromirski would reply, gravely. "A gentleman should do this: he surely should not beat this man; he should have the greatest revenge—polite, cool indifference. On the other hand, what you say might also be true: if the gentleman were to challenge you directly, you must never, never adhere to the Christian belief of turning the other cheek. That is for weak people. You cannot allow a direct challenge to go unanswered; an affront demands a reaction—and don't listen to women when they try to dissuade you from fighting. You must defend your honor."

Most important, Zboromirski's notions of honor and etiquette flowed directly from a strong moral sense. "It is not enough simply to have manners," he said. "You must have manners of the heart."

My first real opportunity to test Zboromirski's gentlemanly strategies with women came during the summer of 1927, when Mother took the family for a season of French society at Deauville. Picture this: I am fourteen, testing the waters at a tea dance in the famous casino, dressed in a marvelously cut blue blazer (made to order by my tailor), white flannel pants, white silk shirt, regimental striped tie, my hair plastered down— Argentine style—with *gomina*. I am trying to seem very grave, in the manner of Zboromirski. The orchestra is playing a tango, very popular then. I don't really know how to dance a tango, but no matter: I am a wolf on the prowl. I see a beautiful girl talking to a friend. She is taller than I by a head, and older; she has a short haircut, very fashionable. Her name, I later learn, is Jeannette Harrang. She is, I believe, fair game.

I ask her to dance: *"Mademoiselle, voulez-vous danser avec moi?"* in my perfect French.

"Porquoi pas?" She shrugs. I ignore her lack of enthusiasm and lead her onto the floor. Now the challenge: how does one do this? I walk rhythmically in straight lines. We literally square the floor. After a few minutes of this, she says, *"Merci beaucoup,"* politely, with a nod, and returns to her friend.

I am terribly pleased with myself. I decide to stick around, try another girl. I spot one, and as I walk toward her—a path that takes me past Jeannette Harrang—I hear her say, "Oh, not again, not that little shit."

Crushed. Ah well.

The summer of 1927 was when I decided to learn how to triumph socially—not just succeed, but triumph. Jeannette Harrang was a friend of Olga and Carlos Gómez, the children of the Venezuelan dictator. I was in love with Olga, my first real crush. I was determined to have her, even if she stood a head taller and regarded me only as a little friend of her younger brother.

Juan and I did Deauville together. He was fourteen, too, and drove a Rolls-Royce. We would go to the casinos and order champagne and caviar. Mother did not mind these extravagances: anything was all right if it was done with the right people. We had a great many adventures that summer; I learned a lot about myself. It was a turning point, of sorts.

One thing I learned was that I was not afraid in a fight. Gigi, my cousin Lello, and I were walking home from the beach one afternoon when we were set upon by caddies from the golf course. These were tough young boys; they pushed us against a wall. Lello began to cry, and they, in the inimitable fashion of bullies everywhere, picked on him to slap around. I was having none of this. I grabbed an iron from one of their bags and slashed at them, like a knight in a duel. They were routed, to my amazement. But, more important, I realized something: I had had the strength of many. I had been without fear. Somehow, half crazed, I had induced a state of autohypnosis—a trance—that enabled me to perform without feeling anything.

This was also the summer when Mother began to realize that I had a talent that might prove of some use to her. There were costume parties for children at the casino, and I would design the clothes for my brother and cousin. There was a contest one week, and my efforts—Russian costumes, fur caps, leather boots—won the first prize. These were actually designed by me and made by a seamstress under my direction. Mother was pleased, but more impressed by the results from a Paris fashion show I attended with the Gómez children. It was a Lucien Lelong presentation, and, apparently, I enjoyed it so much that I decided to sketch what I saw. I did this on the spot, quickly and, apparently, very accurately. Mother was amazed; even more remarkable, she included the dresses I sketched in her new collection. She said that I had the ability to understand a dress in one glance.

Later, she would send me to Paris, where, posing as an Italian fashion reporter, I would go to the major shows and sketch all the latest fashions for her. I was very happy to be able to help Mother in that way; it would be fair to say that my interest in fashion stemmed from that impulse.

And from one other: I loved women, the way they looked and moved. I was preoccupied by them. I would always be interested in women—how to make them look good, how to please them. I designed as a connoisseur. This desire to please had its roots, I think, in the long strolls Olga Gómez and I would take on the boardwalk of Deauville. I realized that I was starting with certain physical disadvantages and would have to work harder than other boys to succeed. My fantasy was to do this through athletics, to be a champion tennis player. I saw my first tennis match that summer and I was impressed by the innate elegance of the sport, the formal dress, the graceful movements. This memory would lead me, several summers later, into a frantic program of tennis practice . . . and eventually to ranked status and many tournament victories as a player in Italy.

In Deauville, though, I had no such laurels and had to rely on other, more subtle means to hold Olga's attention. Just to keep her walking along the boardwalk with me—there was no real chance for anything more than that—I had to keep her entertained. I had to learn how to talk to her about things *she* was interested in; I had to make her laugh. These seemed rudimentary enough skills at the time; later, I would realize that most men courted women by talking about *themselves*. My success with women —and, perhaps, as a designer—flowed from my willingness to concentrate on what pleased them. In love, as in the rest of life, hard work pays off.

Mother noticed my strenuous efforts. She issued warnings: "*Cochons!* Pigs! Men are nothing but pigs! You see these men in the wheelchairs on the boardwalk? Do you know *why* they're in wheelchairs? Because they're *pigs!* They made love to too many women. All men are pigs. Your father was a pig . . . you will be one, too!"

Not yet, not yet, Mother. But soon . . .

CHAPTER
2

B ut not quite so soon as I might have hoped.

It was not for lack of effort. I was well schooled in the traditions and alleged prerogatives of European aristocracy—and one of the more hallowed, if questionable, traditions was the surreptitious utilization of servants—ancillary love. In short, I developed a mild crush on one of the maids.

Her name was Lucia, and she had an exotic assortment of neo-Oriental, southern Italian features. She had dark, curly hair, full lips, perfect teeth, and she smelled good. I suspect she smelled so good because of all the soap she used when she showered, an act I had once managed to reconnoiter.

In any case, I made my artless approach one day when she was making beds. She was not entirely unresponsive. She was wearing one of those wonderful little uniforms: white cap, white apron, black dress . . . which I unbuttoned and was rummaging beneath—when *Mother* and Zboromirski walked in.

Mother's reaction was predictable: it was as if I'd been dismembering the maid, rather than just exploring her. She went berserk; I was a pig, just like my father. A sex maniac! Zboromirski tried to placate her: "Countess, Countess, calm yourself. This is not so bad. This is not so bad."

Mother was not to be placated, though. She fired the girl, sent me to my room . . . and followed me there, forcing me to get down on my knees and pray to God for forgiveness. I was humiliated and, despite my best intentions, began to cry pitifully. I believe I began to distance myself from Mother's influence then. I was beginning to think for myself, and I knew that what I'd done hadn't been so horrible.

Zboromirski visited me after Mother left. He sat down on my bed and patted my head. "Don't cry, Oleg," he said. "These things are perfectly normal, and understandable. I did it myself."

And then this kind man—he was smoking a cigarette in a holder that day—placidly began to explain to me the etiquette of the situation. My urges were natural, part of the cycle of life, but it was best not to exercise them with a chambermaid. He went on sonorously about the proper relations between masters and servants.

The colonel managed to convince Mother to reinstate the maid, who remained a source of libidinal anguish for me until I realized that she was seeing the postman, whereupon I angrily renounced my feelings for her.

This incident was Zboromirski's swan song with us. Soon after, he went to Switzerland and never returned. He met a woman there and married her. I remember our farewell. "Good-bye, Oleg," he said. "There is something that I want you to remember, and that is the old Russian peasant proverb: 'Life is like a large pie made of shit, of which we must eat a slice every day.' " I must say that I miss Colonel Zboromirski to this day.

I was still having difficulties in school, especially with mathematics. I was attending the Licea Galileo, a public school with very high scholastic standards. It was classical education, literally. The emphasis was on Greek, Latin, and memorization of the classics. I had little ability or interest in rote learning.

And now Mother hired Beppe Donati, the most successful academic tutor I would ever have. A graduate of the University of Florence with a romantic, dramatic turn of mind, he was thin, with blue eyes and a long nose—the sort of face commonly found in Renaissance paintings—and teeth blackened from constant smoking. Donati gave me an examination and then suggested to Mother, "Countess, let's try an experiment. Give me this boy and I will advance him three years in one. Let's take him out of school. I'll work with him eight hours a day. After a year he will pass his examinations and be admitted to the university."

Somehow, Donati understood that I would respond to such a challenge. He had a rather curious teaching method. If he saw I was getting tired with one subject, he'd move me on to another. From Greek to Latin to history to geometry. And we would play games. He had two wooden swords made and we dueled in the park. He would be Achilles and I Hector. He would ask me questions, and if I couldn't answer, he'd hit me with the sword; if I answered correctly, I scored on him.

The result was that I did pass the examinations, not with flying colors, indeed only with some luck. I had never been very good at memorizing, and part of the exam was a recitation—one hundred lines from Dante, Caesar, or one of the other classics. I began, *"Omnia Gallia est . . . ,"* etc., etc. I was about ten lines into it when I ran out of gas, but the master, bored, no doubt, after a long day of listening to recitations, engaged one of his colleagues in conversation while I repeated the same lines over and over. Finally, he waved a hand: "Fine, fine, well, at least you have a good memory."

There was another, symbolic graduation still to be celebrated and here, too, professional tutoring was required. In Florence at that time there were two bordellos—Saffo and La Rina—that served as educational institutions and also social clubs for young gentlemen of standing, as well as for town notables, including the mayor. (In the smaller towns, even the village priest might stop in occasionally for a cup of coffee.) They were places where one might go to play cards, have a drink, or simply socialize; there was no pressure to patronize the girls, who circulated in a casual state of undress or draped themselves languorously on couches. At that time, the Italian government controlled and licensed all bordellos, and regular medical checkups were required. Later, when the Merlin Law (which closed the bordellos) was passed, the incidence of venereal disease skyrocketed a hundredfold. They were peasant girls mostly, a few of them foreigners, and quite clean; some were very alluring.

My indoctrination occurred at La Rina, which was named for its procuress, a Greek woman whom you were expected to treat with respect, as an equal. The facility was decorated as one might hope—rococo, heavily draped, and mirrored.

I arrived there one evening with five or six friends, bragging and talking loudly to camouflage my near-panic. I was seventeen years old. We ordered coffee, and the girls wandered over desultorily for inspection. As the moment of truth approached, I stopped bragging and became quiet, withdrawn. We were expected to choose, and I was paralyzed. I couldn't . . . I didn't want to *offend* any of those young women by not choosing them—and then one of them (the prettiest of the lot, I thought) came over and chose *me*. Her name was Ramona: she was a brunette, with blue eyes. She led me off to her cubicle . . . and I couldn't deliver the goods. I was so nervous.

Ramona was very kind to me then. She said, "Don't worry. It happens to everyone. You're just a little nervous. You're thinking about it too much." True enough, but I was more than just a *little* nervous and quite incompetent. Finally, she said, "I'll tell you what: come back tomorrow morning—on me. You'll be my guest."

I was elated by this and rejoined my friends, bragging, naturally, about my triumphant success. I might even have bragged that she invited me back for more. In any case, I returned there the next day and this time was able to perform. Ramona and I were friends now; it was no longer merely a financial transaction.

Still, the episode bothered me and I asked Father about it. He laughed, told me not to worry, and said that a similar thing had happened to him. "Only a bestial man can always be successful," he said, "because for him sex is no more significant than eating a dish of spaghetti."

And I must confess, throughout my life, even though I could perform impressively at times, it was only under perfect romantic conditions— only when there was a sense of mystery, allure, challenge. Indeed, my love affairs often proceeded *despite* the initial physical contacts, rather than because of them; later, as my confidence grew, so would my prowess. I was never one of those who, during the sexual revolution, proclaimed that this was just another biological function. To dismiss something so curious, so intimate, to toss it off as mere biology seemed the height of folly. The actual mechanics of love were never as interesting to me as the events that led up to it. The art of the seduction was always far more fascinating than the ultimate result. There were infinite subtleties and challenges in the manner of the chase. Indeed, fifty years later I can remember the strategies and events of my amorous campaigns like a career military man, but I could not care less about the precise results.

From my earliest days, I would prepare myself with a certain furious enthusiasm before going out on a date. I was priming myself for victory in the most significant of arenas; everything was at stake. I wanted to present an unfailingly romantic image; in later years, if I spent a night with a woman, I had to be perfect when she opened her eyes in the morning . . . and so I would perform these ablutions, bathing myself in Atkison cologne, which I carried in the shaving kit I made sure always to have with me.

I'm not sure why all this was, and is to this day, necessary, but I suspect it had to do with my aesthetic sense, the conviction that unless I was absolutely perfect, at the top of my game, no woman of consequence would ever be interested in me.

And even then, with every hair in place, I sensed that I faced an uphill struggle. I never enjoyed the bliss of the handsome; girls didn't swoon at the sight of me. I had to work for what I got in those early days. I had to be clever.

The top quarry then was American girls, college girls—so fresh and informal in their sweaters and skirts, so unlike their Italian counterparts. Italian girls were much more circumspect, very concerned about their reputation, very strictly chaperoned. A stray word, a rumor could ruin them (as I soon would learn). A liaison with an Italian was serious business, and therefore foolhardy; but the American girls were just passing through, a last season studying art before returning home to marry. If I worked at it, I could be part of their Florentine education.

I had one strategy that was foolproof and, I must admit, brilliant. It worked this way: I would go with several friends to the part of town where the American girls usually walked. Invariably, we would find a group of three or four strolling down the street, and deploy ourselves. My friends would walk after them, making tasteless comments and assorted salacious noises. The girls, or their chaperone, would try to shoo away these louts, who would become even more obnoxious. And then, suddenly, *I* would appear, challenging the miscreants, chasing them off. At which point I would approach the chaperone and say, "Excuse me, dear lady. I am ashamed to be an Italian when these hoodlums act this way. Permit me to accompany you back to the hotel, to protect you from further insults." And the reaction, of course: "How nice. Oh, how nice to find a gentleman here."

I'd walk them back, to the Grand Hotel or the Hôtel de la Ville if they were well off. As a reward, they might invite me for tea, or just thank me profusely. And then I would say, "If you would permit me, in view of this marvelous chance meeting, perhaps I could invite the young ladies to dinner. I will be pleased to chaperone them; I know you must be tired." You would be surprised how often this offer was accepted, always with a caveat, of course: "They must be back by midnight. We must be in the museum at eight tomorrow morning!"

That evening I would take the girls to a certain nightclub—my favorite was a place called Rajola, where there was live music (I learned the rumba there)—and we would be met by my fellow conspirators, the ones who'd been harassing them on the street. Meeting the girls at night would be their payoff. And do you know, the girls almost never recognized them! It always worked.

There were, to be sure, more forthright ways of meeting American girls. Two or three of the finishing schools in villas on the periphery of the city would, on occasion, invite some of us for tea dances. We would meet the girls at the dances, and then arrange to see them after hours. It was all very dramatic, very romantic. The villas had walls topped with broken glass. We would hammer down the glass and scale the walls at midnight; the girls, impressed by our daring, would bestow appropriate favors.

My daytime activities usually began with classes in the morning. At noon we would gather at the Café Doney, located on the Via Tornabuoni, the most elegant street in Florence (Mother's business was located in a five-story building across the way), for a small sandwich and an Americano (gin and bitters), followed by several hours of digestion, reflection, and observation. We paid great critical attention to every passing girl, foreign and domestic. The Italians suffered terribly in our evaluations; we were convinced they were less desirable, perhaps because of the difficulties they posed for us. The best we could hope for with an Italian girl was a "raincoat" date, a chaperoned trip to the movies, to which the boy would bring a raincoat, beneath which various manipulations would occur while stern countenances were maintained for the benefit of the chaperone.

In any case, we were convinced that Italian men were better-looking than their female counterparts, although both men and women devoted much time to making themselves more presentable. We dressed impeccably. We talked about fashion continually. To dress well was a ritual and a passion; to dress well was like being in love. We shopped. We spent whole afternoons shopping, but not as it is done today. It was an entirely different sort of experience—Socratic, almost *religious*, an extended negotiation over the most basic details: fabric, cut, stitching. We were the architects of our appearance; we supervised each new suit the way an architect guides the construction of a building. If I was going to have a new pair of shoes made, I would visit Gucci the cobbler—who later achieved international success, but at that time had only a small shop in Florence—and he would produce various leathers for me, which we would consider together. We would then discuss style and construction, for he made the best moccasins in Italy; several weeks later, a finished pair of made-to-order shoes would be delivered. This was also true of Zanobetti, who sold fine Borsalino hats and silk shirts, and Franchi the tailor (I bought two conservatively cut suits a year), and Old England, where we purchased sweaters and tweeds, the *only* ready-to-wear items we bought. We did nothing in life as well, or as studiously, or as carefully, as we dressed.

I suppose the reason we went to such great lengths to entertain ourselves was that there wasn't much else to do in Florence. It was a dead, stone, fifteenth-century city, little more than a museum maintained, like Venice, for the benefit of tourists. The pace of life was quite leisurely, especially for a university student, as I was. It wasn't unusual for students of the best families to dawdle along until age twenty-seven or so, taking a class here and there, then be married and pursue the even more leisurely life of a gentleman in society. This was the life that would be mine if I remained in Florence.

In late afternoon when the weather permitted, I would go to the tennis club and put in a few hours on the courts. I hadn't been playing long, but was already the ranking player at the club. I'd learned my tennis during the course of a summer when I was sixteen and we were at Forte dei Marmi. I had an American girlfriend that year, Baby Chalmers, very blonde and healthy, and seaworthy as well. She and I would go off in the little *pattino* boats that tourists considered so picturesque, but that were actually quite utilitarian. We'd engage in naval maneuvers far enough from shore to be discreet. This was very satisfactory until one day I noticed a black hulk bobbing in the water nearby—her mother, Mrs. Chalmers, swimming out to chaperone.

In any case, Baby Chalmers was very American, very athletic, and very beautiful. One day we were walking in the *pineta*—the pine forest— and we came upon the tennis court. The owner, whose name was Franceschi, was there, and Baby asked to play with him. I watched and then Franceschi suggested we visit the tournament at Viareggio, and that tournament settled it. I remembered the feelings about tennis I'd had at Deauville: it was simply the most elegant sport. I *had* to be a tennis player. I told Mother, "I have to be a tennis player." And immediately she bought Gigi and me racquets and found us an old German instructor.

In truth, though, we taught ourselves. We played every day for hours. We threw ourselves into it, and were playing in tournaments within a year. Mother was very pleased. She'd say, "With a tennis racquet and a dinner jacket, you'll be able to go anywhere in life."

Mother was beginning to wear out the old aphorisms. Her business was in deep trouble, and it began to seem once more that wisdom was all she'd be able to leave to us. In part, the failure was beyond her control. The American Stock Market Crash of 1929 had robbed her of many clients; the great wave of tourism was ebbing. But she was also a terrible businesswoman, very careless, too trusting—especially of an accountant, who absconded with all the receipts one year. The business didn't exactly crash; it fell with the teasing, airborne coquetry of a feather. The villas were sold; we moved into another triplex, an extravagant place by American standards, filled with fifteenth- and sixteenth-century furniture. We continued to dress well (Italians never paid their tailor bills in any case, a tradition that later caused me much consternation). We continued to pretend to be rich, and to appear so for all the world. But, finally, Mother admitted defeat—much to our surprise; it was so out of character for her —one day at the train station. I think we were going off to Forte dei Marmi and she said, "It's over. The business has collapsed. From now on, you boys will have to make it on your own."

I remember thinking, *If Mother, with all her energy and optimism, has failed, how will I ever make it? Where will I get the energy?*

For all that, though, Mother maintained a furious optimism on our behalf. We were still gentlemen, she insisted, still Cassinis. The absence of money was only a temporary inconvenience. It would come. Meanwhile, we mustn't give in to our straitened circumstances. We must continue as before . . . and playing tennis was very important in that respect. Indeed, Mother knew precisely what she was talking about. My ability with a tennis racquet opened many doors throughout my life. Wherever I traveled, all I had to do was find the best club, introduce myself as a ranked player, and then prove it on the court, and I'd be welcomed as an equal.

Being older and stronger than Gigi, I usually beat him, but his youth proved advantageous in one respect: He was young enough to be picked for the Italian junior national team. I was ranked among the top ten in Italy, but suffered from a certain inconsistency. I would play poorly in one match—usually those scheduled in the morning, given my social proclivities—and triumph unexpectedly in the next. I had no idea how to prepare myself for a contest. I was considered a spoiler, but nonetheless won thirteen major tournaments. My strengths as a player were speed and guile, willpower more than strength.

I played tennis, in fact, as I lived: I ran and ran. I ran my opponents

46

silly. I ran *myself* silly, always running when others walked. I ran through the streets of Florence (and, later, New York) forty years before jogging became an American obsession. I ran because I was impatient, and because I enjoyed it. I ran the four hundred meters on the university track team; I ran continually when playing soccer with "Boys" of Fiorentina—one of the finest teenage teams in the nation. I ran from home to school, from class to class, from store to store. I could not run when skiing, but I trudged and that also helped build my stamina. There were no lifts in those days. You walked up the mountains. You wrapped skins around your skis and walked for hours to get into position for your *one* run of the day. It was a far more strenuous sport than it would become.

I skied on the university's varsity team, usually placing in the top three or four in my two events, which were the downhill and the fifty-kilometer run. Each year, there were national collegiate championships. I remember one in particular that took place when I was eighteen. Teams from all the major universities took a train to Asiago, a famous resort in the Dolomites. In the downhill, I finished eighth among several hundred contestants.

The trip to Asiago was memorable also for a practical joke played on Emilio Pucci, who has been a lifelong friend of mine and, of course, a fellow designer. Emilio was always the butt of jokes in those days. He was tall, gangly, loose-jointed, as if he were made of rubber. He was very self-conscious, creative in his manner, and difficult to rile, which made getting his goat something of a challenge. One night, several of the fellows on the team (not me) filled a sock with excrement and placed it next to Emilio's head on the pillow; we were awakened by screams the next morning—somehow Emilio had gotten himself entangled in the sock, and the stuff was all over his face and hair.

This was an accurate reflection of our maturity in those days. We were young and well-off; the world seemed a fine place. . . . I think back on those carefree days with wonder, knowing that most of those pranksters would die horribly in the next ten years: Paolo Carena, Renzo Gilioli, Paolo Farina, dying in Russia from typhus; Count Roberto Frassineto, Count Angi Freschi, shot down over the Mediterranean . . . and so many, many more. The heart of my generation would be eviscerated by the war. Our naughty innocence seems so fleeting, so poignant now.

Emilio made it through, of course, and later developed into a very fine skier. My own skiing was interrupted for thirteen years when I left Italy for America, but it was a logical companion to tennis in my youth.

Tennis was a warm-weather sport—there were no indoor courts, and I required physical activity year-round.

Tennis led directly to my first great romance, my first great campaign for a woman. I was eighteen, still taking courses at the university at the time. Her name was Lucy Winslow. She was an American, very beautiful and very wealthy. Her father had made a fortune in shoemaking machines in Massachusetts. She appeared at the tennis club in Florence one day, the very picture of radiant American healthiness. She was tall, with red hair, blue eyes, and freckles. She also had an overpowering, brilliant smile. I do not know why this was, but American girls always were given away by their teeth, which seemed larger, brighter, and sometimes even more numerous than the Italian ones. In any case, it was the teeth that caught my eye, flashing courtside, and then I assessed the rest of the package and decided: *I must meet this girl and get to know her*.

This was a brazen and completely unrealistic goal. Lucy was in her early twenties and already a divorcée. Her parents had recently bought a villa in Florence and were planning a long European sojourn, perhaps to give her time to catch her breath before resuming the hunt for an appropriate American catch. I, on the other hand, might charitably have been described at that moment with the German expression *backfisch*—neither fish nor fowl. My mother put the best face on it: "You are not yet a handsome man; you are too young for your looks. You will grow into your features as you get older, after you turn forty, and you will continue to grow handsome even as those who seem so attractive to you now grow fat and ugly."

This was cold comfort. Forty seemed a long way off, and Lucy was accompanied by a breathtaking entourage that included her handsome brother, his wife (who looked quite a bit like Katharine Hepburn), and Lucy's date, a local fellow named Aldo Settepassi, whose primary distinction was his rather unlikely Nordic appearance. There seemed a small army of other men, most of them ten years older than I, competing for her attention. What did I have to offer against that? Only fantasy.

I was so unlikely a suitor that Lucy remained unaware of my intentions until, I suspect, the very moment of my triumph. She didn't perceive me as a threat; she therefore was open to my connivings. It would have been impossible for me to ask her for a date, so I became a daytime presence in her life. I invited her to play tennis with me, to have lunch, to take walks. I don't think anyone took such good care of her. It's like that famous line, I think it was Aly Khan's, when he was asked what is the most important quality of a great lover: "Availability," he said. Time is a real luxury, and I lavished it upon Lucy day after day. I'd watch her at night at the Rajola, dancing so closely with Aldo, and I'd steam, quietly. I lay in wait, patiently. I heard the way other men talked to her: about themselves, their prospects, their work. I talked to her about her freckles. I said silly things; we laughed a lot. Eventually, I made my move.

I borrowed a friend's car one evening and invited her out. Lucy and I were friendly enough by then that she felt quite comfortable with me, more comfortable, in truth, than I felt, since I knew what my intentions were. I *had* to make a move that night: another platonic encounter and we were in danger of remaining mere friends for life. A bold move was indicated. A bold move, however, is not necessarily an honorable one. I wasn't going to take any chances. I settled upon one of the oldest and most persistently successful strategies: I got her good and drunk, while slyly watering the palms with my own drinks.

And so it was no problem inviting her home to meet my family, who happened to be away at the shore, alas. There was a wonderful alcove just off the living room, with a huge red velvet couch covered with zebra skin and Persian throw pillows; a very dramatic, medieval place to make love. I was still quite inexperienced as a lover, but apparently sufficiently skilled to leave a favorable impression with her, an impression that lingered—luckily, perhaps remarkably—past her hangover.

We became lovers then, and more. We talked seriously—at least, *we* thought we were talking seriously—about getting married. She assumed I was a wealthy young man, and so there was no question of what I would *do* for a living, although she did ask me what my plans for the future were, a question I found it easy to avoid. Our best topic of conversation was her, in any case.

To all the world, and most especially to her parents, I remained nothing more than an innocent companion of Lucy's, a pal. There was no suspicion. This was all to the good. When her parents decided to go to England for a while, it was easy for Lucy to ask to bring along her young playmate. And so I became part of the Winslow traveling party, a guest in the classic, half-timbered country cottage they rented in Chobham-Woking, a small village near London.

One evening, however, the Winslows announced their intention to go to the theater. Lucy and I excused ourselves, preferring to remain home, and set upon each other immediately, passionately, on the living room floor . . . for a moment or two until her father and brother returned, having forgotten the tickets, and found us there in the midst of the most ecstatic operations. This was becoming a rather unfortunate pattern in my life.

Suffice it to say, I was asked to leave. Immediately I was allowed to dress, but nothing more. "Write! Write!" I implored her, as I was hustled out the door. "I will, I will!" she cried. (Years later, I bumped into Lucy, still radiant, in Los Angeles and she claimed that she did write, but the letters apparently were intercepted. I never received one.)

I was left standing outside her gate, with only enough money to get to London.

I spent a miserable evening there, walking the streets alone, trying to figure out how to get home, wondering what would become of me now. And then, disconsolate, I ran into someone I knew.

It was Beppe Bellini, who was not only a member of the tennis club and a noted art collector, which explained his presence in London, but also the landlord of the building in which my parents lived. He laughed when I told him of my predicament, and loaned me money for the trip home. It was the first time I ever flew in an airplane.

Back home, I faced the question Lucy Winslow had asked and I had not answered: what *were* my plans for the future?

I studied political science at the University of Florence, with the idea of perhaps becoming a lawyer, but that seemed an impossibly boring prospect. And then there was the question of my "talent," my ability to draw. I took several courses at the Accademia di Belle Arti, and my sketching was considered technically quite good. I spent many hours at the Galleria degli Uffizi, formerly a Medici palace, which goes from one side of the Arno River to the other and contains more than four hundred yards of galleries. I practiced my hand copying the Old Masters. I would be caught up in the work, mesmerized by the brilliance of such artists as Botticelli, Giotto, Raphael, Uccello, Fra Filippo Lippi, and Michelangelo.

During that period, I decided that I should learn to paint. I studied briefly with Sensani and later with De Chirico. Giorgio De Chirico was a very great painter, one of the leaders of the Surrealist movement. His manner was brusque, as if he had no time to waste. He spoke little, saying something like "Paint this flower or this leaf, but first, *sketch* it." He told me, "I have spent all my life—even while sleeping—thinking about painting." He said that I might have the talent to become a painter, but that I lacked the temperament entirely. "You can't paint," he said, "and play tennis three hours a day."

I was interested in the arts but more in the art of living. Which left fashion, which in the broadest sense is our oldest art. But there was Father, stern, ineffectual, entirely disappointed that his son would be interested in something so . . . well, unorthodox. I agreed with him, in a way. On the other hand, there was Mother, pragmatic, supportive, thrilled that I not only understood what she did, but also could help by going to Paris and sketching the collections. It was true, too, I must admit, that I'd always had an interest in costume, in decor, in *appearances*. I did have the talent, even though I might denigrate it. I understood clothes. I appreciated the fine fabrics. And I lived a life where fashion thrived.

My ability manifested itself when, in 1934, I won five first prizes at an international fashion competition, Mostra della Moda, in Turin: for a number of sketches and for "most creative presentation," an evening dress painted in dramatic colors on aluminum foil. There was money—five thousand lire—attached to these prizes. I began to wonder if I might be able to make a living at design.

I'd already made several successful trips to Paris on Mother's behalf, and now she arranged for me an introduction to the great couturier Jean Patou, actually to Baron Hugo Oddo, who was Patou's social secretary. Oddo introduced me to the great man. Indeed, that very night I accompanied Patou, Oddo, and several obviously wealthy women to the Lido. I was awestruck, and did not say very much; I watched the show, and felt rather provincial. I might be quite the dashing man-about-town in Florence, but this was Paris, and I was eighteen.

It was a great honor to be associated with Patou, even if the job I was soon given was just about the lowest on the totem pole. I was one of half a dozen sketch artists. We worked in a large white room; I had a desk near the window. Sometimes we would be asked to go to the library and research a period in history or the costumes of a certain region—say, the Caucasus—and come up with ideas; more often we would be given the silhouette, the fabric, the colors and told, "Let's see what you can come up with." When the sketches were done, they would be handed to an elderly woman, the *première*, who would then select some to be shown to Patou.

He was an awesome figure, a tallish man with gray hair, ruddy complexion, even features, even temperament, cold and polite. He often wore bow ties. I was never important enough to sit down and have a conversation with him, but I did see him review my sketches on several occasions: quietly, dispassionately, nodding his head when he saw something he liked. A successful sketch might be changed, modified three or four times before it was pinned upon the wall by the *première*.

As for the rest of it, living away from home for the first time—in *Paris*, no less—was not as enjoyable as I might have hoped. Mother had arranged a room for me with a destitute family of Russian refugees on the Rue de Vaugirard, which was far from the center of nightlife. These people expected me to be present for dinner at seven. They expected me to be in bed by midnight. They lectured me when I failed to live up to these responsibilities, threatening to tell my mother that I was living a dissolute life. But I hated listening to their typical Russian émigré talk about the past. So I wandered the streets, dining on bananas, arriving home just before their curfew. In all, it wasn't a very glamorous or exciting time.

And it didn't last very long. After I'd been employed for several months by Patou, France passed a law forbidding foreign workers. As I had been born in Paris, I had the option of claiming French citizenship, but that might have meant military service at that time. I wasn't very happy in Paris anyway, and I certainly wasn't ready to make so serious a choice as nationality (after all, I was more Russian and Italian than French; plus, from my earliest days in talking with Mother, I'd harbored the dream of going to America).

I returned home to Florence without regret, perhaps not fully aware of the importance of my decision: I had decided to make a career for myself in fashion. At the time, it must be understood, Paris *was* fashion. Couture did not exist elsewhere. There were no great American designers, and certainly no Italians. There wasn't even an Italian word for "designer"; a man who created clothes was called a *sarto*, a tailor. I found that very annoying. Fashion in Italy meant businesses like Mother's, which copied the latest from Paris. There was also a lot of private work: rich girls would see something in *Vogue*, clip it out, take it to a seamstress, a *sartina*, and get a reasonable facsimile. And so, when I decided in 1933 to start my own small house of couture, on the Via Frattina in Rome, inspired by what I had learned at Patou, it was something of a gamble and an innovation.

Mother sent me off with her blessings. I continued to spend time in Florence, and often used her sample hands to put together clothes I designed. Patou and most of the other great couturiers could build a dress from start to finish: sketch, drape, cut, sew. I had learned the rudiments of those skills from Mother's production manager, but I had little interest in practicing them. I didn't want to cut my own fabric or make my own patterns. I wasn't so much interested in technique or theory. For a master like Lucien Lelong, the woman was just an element in the design; for me, it was more personal—I designed for particular women. I wanted to show *them* off to their best advantage. In Rome especially, the women were more important than my "concepts."

And I had the opportunity to design for the *crème de la crème* of Roman society, including Mussolini's daughter Edda Ciano (an unexceptional girl but for her father). Many of these were girls I'd met during my summers at Forte dei Marmi, where the best people from all over Italy had mingled. Indeed, I had a rather strange connection to my first real client in Rome, an absolutely stunning girl named Nadia Berlingieri. I had once fought a duel over her sister, Lola.

That had happened during the summer of 1930. It was the result of an incident in a popular club called the Capannina. I had played in the tennis tournament at Viareggio that day, one of the most important in Italy, and I suppose I was feeling full of myself. I spotted Nadia and her older sister, Lola, sitting at a table with Lola's fiancé, Prince Alighiero Giovanelli. These girls were half Roman and half Russian and among the most beautiful in society. Just sensational: Nadia looked something like Ava Gardner. But it was the older sister whom I asked to dance.

I was known as a very good dancer, and in Italy, dancing is often a suggestive act. And so, there I was in the middle of the floor with this beautiful, engaged girl and suddenly Giovanelli pushed me aside and slapped me across the face.

This was a classic challenge, of course. Everyone had seen it. I might have punched him in the nose right then and there, but that would have been ungentlemanly. A response, however, was mandatory.

I went to a friend, an older man, Marchese Ludovico Antinori, and asked him to be my second. He tried to dissuade me, saying I wasn't eighteen, the "legal" age for a duel. Of course, duels were illegal in Italy; he was talking about the *traditional* minimum age. I was adamant, though. I really wanted to have at this Giovanelli; I wanted blood.

Eventually Antinori agreed, and arranged for one of his friends also to be a second. He then contacted Giovanelli, who reluctantly agreed. We were to meet at dawn in the *pineta;* it was to be a duel with swords, to the first blood (duels to the death hadn't been fought in years).

I spent the evening before the duel drinking brandies to steel my heart and dull the pain. Most painful of all was the expense. I had learned why only gentlemen fought duels: no one else could afford them. You had to buy splendid gifts for your seconds, because they were risking arrest, and you also had to shell out a princely sum for the doctor. It was traditional—and also prudent—to hire a professional instructor the evening before, and practice your strokes; this was also quite expensive.

And so we met at dawn in the *pineta*, and my bravado melted a bit in the morning chill, facing an opponent with a weapon. I remember seeing Giovanelli there before me and wondering, *How did I get myself into this?* I didn't want to hurt him, I certainly didn't want to lose my life over something so frivolous. I realized that even though a nick, a mere scrape would be sufficient to end the affair, a false step could cause a mortal wound. As it happened, I nicked him first—in the forearm, a flesh wound. He apologized then, I accepted, and we became friends again. Indeed, in the grand tradition, we made quite a show of appearing arm in arm (he with a slightly bandaged forearm) at the finest café in town.

Italians love drama, the dramatic gesture, the gentlemanly show. News of this duel spread through Italy overnight, and it did *wonders* for my reputation.

So I was known to the young women of Italy. I was a curiosity: a gentleman who fought duels, played tournament tennis, was called "the Matchstick" because of his temper, and also designed ladies' clothes. How odd. How unusual. I was particularly friendly with three sisters, the Cerianas, and the Serra di Cassano family. The Cerianas were very well placed in society. They were among my first and best-known clients, but I do think my very first was Nadia Berlingieri, the younger sister of Lola, who had caused the duel.

One day I had lunch with Nadia. She was ravishing, the best-looking girl in Italy: dark hair, blue eyes, a tiny waist. If she agreed to wear my clothes, everyone would follow her. I told her my plans and asked if I could design something for her, for free. Well, of course: the price was right.

What I did for her was very dramatic. It was an homage to our common Russian heritage, and to the life I might have led: a cossack's uniform. It was a suit with a three-quarter-length cassock top in elegant black wool, double-breasted with black leather buttons, large buttons. (A favorite fashion accent of mine: later, on Seventh Avenue, some would call me Mr. Button; later still, I would make dramatic use of large buttons in the clothes I designed for Jacqueline Kennedy.) It was tight to the waist, tucked there and flared out, taking advantage of her figure. The skirt was tight, tight to the knees. There were accessories, too: a black Russian-style fur hat, and boots. High black leather boots I'd designed and contracted out to a bootmaker; no one had done this before.

She loved it. She paraded down the Via Veneto in it one evening, and all her friends asked, "Who did this for you?" And I was made. I was made.

I was . . . still a curiosity, though. A gentleman *and* a designer? The idea was to be as lighthearted about it as possible, to make it seem only a diversion, something I did for the pleasure of it. I became known to the young ladies of that very elite circle as a Dr. Feelgood of couture, someone they could go to for advice on how to dress, a good luncheon companion, lots of laughs. It was a remarkable experience. I saw a side of women that I'd never known before, the most intimate side imaginable. There was the physical intimacy, of course: I would be dealing with their bodies, fitting the clothes. But more important than the physical intimacy was the psychological: I had to analyze their assets and give advice on how they should present themselves to the world. I was dealing with a form of knowledge that most men don't even know exists. I had the power to envision women as they wanted to be seen; to help them create fantasies about themselves. This was a position of great privilege that I had to be careful not to exploit. There was a sexual tension. But it was curious: once I'd designed for a woman, I usually knew so much about her that the mystery was gone from it. It was much easier to date a woman and *then* design for her than vice versa. This put me into a troubling situation, since most of the girls for whom I was designing were just the sort of women I was seeking to date.

But a gentleman *and* a designer? I needed the money. I needed the money badly. The problem was, as I knew from personal experience on the other side of the equation, Europeans were very bad when it came to paying their tailors. They might gather all the bills together and pay them once a year; then again, they might not. This would not do. There were times when I would hand-deliver the finished product, pretending to be a messenger from the Cassini Studio, and insist that Mr. Cassini's instructions were to be paid right then and there. Immediately. Surprisingly, this often worked; at least, I was never found out.

A gentleman *and* a designer? Well, my position was ambiguous at best, especially with the other young men in society. They were alternately suspicious about what I was doing with their sweethearts during the day (the hours for serious philandering in Rome at the time were 4:00

to 6:00 P.M.) and derisive: why would a young man of good standing interest himself in ladies' clothes?

(At that time, the leaders in Roman society were of the great families, such as Borghese, Colonna, Massimo, Orsini—some of whose lineage descended from the days of the Roman Empire. They were all friends of mine, and knew of my family background; and knew that the Cappizucchi/ Cassini palace in Rome, now owned by Count Pecci Blunt, had once belonged to my family.)

I had a very active social life. I was out most every night. A typical evening would begin with a cocktail party—an elaborate affair, sometimes black tie. One would meet friends at these parties; we would gather into groups, and then go out to a dinner party, a ball, a café, or a club.

I remember walking into one such party after having been away from Rome for a while: I'd often spend time in Florence with my parents and old friends. In any case, as I walked in, I saw two fellows chatting. One was Belmonte, whom I knew; the other was new to the scene. I nodded to Belmonte and continued on, but I overheard the new fellow asking about me, "Who is he?"

"Oh, him," Belmonte said. "He's a nonentity. A *sarto.*"

I turned around and said to Belmonte, "I heard that!"

"So what of it?"

"I'll tell you what of it," I said. "It'll probably be the first time in your life that a *sarto* will give you a thrashing. I'm giving you the option. You wait for me outside after this party. If you don't, I'll brand you for what you really are: a coward."

I actually said such things in those days. Rather melodramatic, to be sure—but his comment had cut to the heart of all the doubts I had about myself. In any case, I continued on at the party, lighthearted, making my jokes, entertaining the girls. Then some of us decided to leave, and I said to Giulianella Ceriana, "You must excuse me a moment. I have a job to do before we go."

"How long will it take you?" she asked.

"Oh, a very short time. You can be present."

We went outside and there was Belmonte, leaning against the fender of a car with his arms crossed, a smirky expression on his face, which made me hate him all the more. I challenged him; he did not respond. I went toward him, but he would not fight. So I slapped him across the face —one, two . . . and still he would not take the bait. I turned to Giulianella and said, "Now I can tell the world I'm dealing with a coward."

And I turned and marched off with great aplomb, believing my reputation enhanced. I might be a *sarto*, but I wasn't someone you wanted to mess with.

My behavior may be forgiven as youthful impetuosity, but there was more to it than that. This was just the beginning of a pattern that would continue all my life, a curious form of expression for a gentleman, and one that I should explain more fully right here and now.

I fought for three reasons. The first has already been mentioned: I fought for respect. Most of my friends in Rome were in the military or diplomatic service, or, more likely, so wealthy that they did not require employment. To the world, I was a couturier, an honorable profession but an unlikely one for someone of my background; I had to be sure that people realized this didn't signal the sort of sensitivity that is often mistaken for weakness. It was almost a genetic requirement that I be taken seriously.

Ah, genetics: that was the second reason. Fighting was bred in my bones. I came from a warrior class. My ancestors, on both sides, had been warriors from the steppes of Asia, Mongol horsemen, cossacks, or Italian crusaders. It is often forgotten that today's aristocrats are descended from the medieval knights. Titles were conferred on those who distinguished themselves militarily; later, in the Middle Ages, this class would devolve into landholders and courtiers. My ancestors had excelled in combat; and the urge to fight, I believe, was imprinted in my genetic material.

I cannot prove my point scientifically, only through my behavior in combat—the preternatural calm that settled upon me the first time I fought, when I battled the caddies in Deauville, and in every subsequent fight; the sense I always had when fighting that I was behaving in a way that was preordained, and right somehow. I know that I have, throughout my life, prospered only when I thought strategically, believing each day was a battle to be fought and not merely another interlude at the office. I know too that the knowledge of my heritage, the blood of my ancestors coursing through my veins, has always given me the confidence to rebound from disappointments and fight another day.

The other reason I got into so many fights was a bit more modern. I had seen a lot of cowboy movies. I had the sense that real men settled their differences with their fists, and later, when I arrived in Hollywood, I was very surprised to discover that the fellows who played the belligerent heroes on the silver screen suffered from the same delusions as I. There was more brawling in Hollywood than anyplace I've ever been: the fighters were people like Errol Flynn and John Huston. It was a town that bought its own romance, a romantic *codíce di duello* that I was more than willing to adopt.

"Where's the *sarto?* Where's the *sarto?*"

Why did they have to call me that? Even when I designed the clothes for a big-budget Italian movie, the name of which, fortunately, I am unable to recall, I was still a tailor. "Where's the *sarto?*" they would run about the set screaming, making my blood run cold.

I'd gotten involved in this venture through the duke of Laurino, who was a bona fide duke, a very elegant man, but impoverished and working as an assistant producer of sorts. I'd met him at the Hotel Excelsior, on the Via Veneto, which was where movie people hung out in those days. He said, "Cassini, why don't you design for pictures?"

But of course. Hollywood had always been my dream, which did not distinguish me from half the young men and women in Italy. I think we took that vision, that image of Hollywood glamor, more seriously even than Americans.

"Very well, I will call you on my next picture," he said.

And he did. (Looking back on this experience, I realize that it caused me a great deal of anguish when I actually did reach Hollywood: whenever someone said "We'll call you," I always assumed they would. But this was not Hollywood. It was Italy.) I couldn't tell you what the picture was about, because I never saw a full script, just a scene here and a scene there, out of sequence. All the technical departments were a shambles, but most particularly wardrobe. I kept trying to get information from Laurino, but all he'd say was "We'll see, we'll see."

Working this way, a disaster was inevitable, and it came the day before the big scene, the ballroom scene, was to be shot. "Well, where are the dresses?" the director asked.

"What dresses?"

Forty dresses for the ballroom scene.

"But I was never told."

Laurino was screaming, "You know you were told. You know you were told!"

"I am not interested in your excuses," the director said. "We shoot tomorrow."

Laurino and I proceeded to commandeer a studio car and chase about from shop to shop buying fabric—satins, velvets—by the bolt, hundreds of yards of material and a great quantity of pins. We found an old seam-

58

stress in the wardrobe department and we worked all night, draping the fabric, the *sartina* carrying out my instructions and Laurino on his knees with pins in his mouth. We did them all the same style, simply, draped like saris, pinned together (luckily there was no dancing in this ballroom scene, and nobody was wearing a magnet).

The director said, "Well, you see, I knew you could do it."

Laurino never forgot this. I would see him for years afterward in Europe and he would never fail to remind me, "Remember our ballroom scene?"

A series of events began to unfold then which ultimately led to my departure for America. Italy was becoming a much less pleasant place for both gentlemen and designers. The country was at war in Africa, Mussolini was suffering from rampaging grandiosity, and a campaign was on to destroy all the non-Italian influences that had permeated the culture. American music, for example, was considered "African" and degenerate. Nightlife of any sort was being discouraged. The patriotic Italian stayed home and made babies. Even the idea of wearing a dinner jacket had become un-Fascist, un-Roman (the notion of recapturing the glory that was Rome was the centerpiece of the Fascist delusion), a vaguely unpatriotic act.

One night I was coming out of the Hôtel Ambassadeurs, on the Via Veneto, which had one of the better swing bands in town, and was walking down the Via Veneto with a friend named Francesco Bitossi, who was an officer in the colonial service. We were wearing dinner jackets, talking quietly, bothering no one, when the metropolitan police stopped us and asked for documents. I had none; I'd never felt the need to carry any.

I told the police my name was Oleg Loiewski Cassini, that my family lived in Florence and that I had an address in Rome. Apparently, the "Loiewski" sounded suspicious or the dinner jacket looked suspicious. Pierre Laval, the French premier and Fascist sympathizer, was in town that weekend and the police were taking no chances. They said, "You'd better come with us."

Bitossi had his colonial-service identification and, instead of defending me, meekly said he'd call me the next day. I asked him to come along, just in case. But no, he went home and I went to the police station, where they took my shoelaces, belt, and necktie—suicide precautions—and threw me into a real dungeon. A very high room, filthy, with a wooden bench and a wooden toilet. The smell and cold were horrifying. The walls were covered with excrement. I stood in the middle of the room, shivering—it was a cold night and all I had was the damn dinner jacket. I screamed at the jailers, I insulted them, I gave them the names of people to call, important people, names they knew. I threatened them, told them they'd be sorry. They laughed, or didn't hear me.

I stood there, straight up, in the middle of this dungeon cell, for three days without sleeping. I would not allow myself to lie down in filth or lean against it. I was paralyzed with disgust, simply horrified, amazed. Could this be happening to me? I remember thinking about the Carthaginians, who tortured prisoners by keeping them awake until they died. I was not given the opportunity to make a phone call, and Bitossi never called to find out what had happened to me.

I was arrested on a Friday, and it wasn't until Monday morning that I was brought before an official, who apologized. "We know you're of good standing," he said. "This was an unfortunate mistake. The visit of Laval made us security-conscious, but you shouldn't go out without your papers."

I was furious, but too exhausted to say or do much about it. I made a lame stab at a speech. "Well, if this is the way you're going to treat people who've lived here for years," I said, "then this is not a fit place to live."

So I left with my dignity, but was forced to part with my dinner jacket, which was so permeated with the fetid smell of the jail that I had to throw it out. I was also forced to part, finally, with any illusions I'd had about Mussolini, and what he was doing in Italy. I knew then that it was going to end badly, and I began to think about acting on a long-standing dream: America.

I must say that I cannot imagine why, after this incident, I would ever want to have anything to do with the cursed Bitossi, but shortly thereafter he and I took the same train to Florence together. This was to be a grand occasion for me. While designing for the girls in Rome, I'd also been sending sketches up to Mother in Florence. Her business was dead at this point, but she still had fine craftsmen at her disposal and she supervised the creation of my designs. We'd built quite a line. I was bringing it to Florence now for a show that was to be my formal debut as a designer and Mother's last hope to keep some sort of business afloat.

Bitossi and I took a taxi together to the station, where I was to get our tickets and he was to make sure that the luggage was put on the train.

It was about an hour out of Rome that I felt a twinge. I just wanted to be sure the large trunk carrying the collection had made it onto the train—and, of course, it hadn't. Bitossi, who was maddeningly nonchalant about the whole business, hadn't superivsed the loading carefully enough. I wanted to kill him. I wanted to kill myself for leaving the collection, a year of my life's work, in his care. Why hadn't I sent him to get the tickets and taken care of the unloading myself? That was one of the thoughts that kept running through my mind—that and what would be the most efficacious way to commit suicide.

I sent wires back to Rome at the first stop. Later, we learned that the trunk had stood in the middle of the street for an hour or so; finally a little boy had come, walked by it several times, then summoned a friend, and they had carried it away.

Mother met us at the train station. She was jubilant. The show was arranged, everyone would be there . . . and then I told her, and I saw in her eyes how much she had been counting on this, what a terrible blow this was. And indeed, it was the end for us in Florence. A few months later Mother closed her business, sold most of her possessions, and came with Father to join me in Rome.

Well, these were setbacks, but there was still hope. I had my business in Rome, my social standing . . . and prospects. One of the most intriguing prospects was a girl named Helena Parodi Delfino. She was an attractive but not quite beautiful girl, with a strong face, a good figure, and millions and millions and millions of dollars, which made her more attractive to everyone. Her family was known in shipping and steel, and the sheer weight of their power had made them known in society as well. But they were not of aristocratic background, and so there was an attractive prospect here. We each had something to offer the other. I had a title that would be refurbished by her fortune; in European society at the time, this was considered a fair exchange. It certainly seemed the logical thing to do; my friends encouraged it, but I was reluctant. I needed something more in such a match: love, as I would realize all my life.

I had met Helena at an embassy party, and soon we were considered something of an item. She was a fine girl, make no mistake, and quite a poker player. She loved to gamble. Everything between us was proceeding quite smoothly until I stupidly involved myself in a scandal that caused me to be exiled, completely blackballed from Italian society.

What happened was this: A lovely girl named Donnina Toeplitz arrived from England for her debut in Rome. She was seventeen, the daughter of an English movie mogul—a partner in Toeplitz/Korda Films—and she was simply breathtaking. She had brown hair, enormous brown eyes, a lovely figure, and a lively personality. Everyone was crazy about her.

Parties heralded her arrival in town. At one of these parties I managed to engage her interest. I suggested we visit the best fortune-teller in Rome. I've never really believed in such things, but this sorceress was all the rage and it was an offbeat date, a way of keeping the flirtation going.

The fortune-teller lived in a nondescript apartment in Trastevere. Her reputation was strong enough that she didn't have to resort to crystal balls and other mystical mumbo-jumbo. She achieved triangulation of the future by reading your palm, reading the cards, and making a horoscope. I will never forget what she told me that day: she said I would not marry the girl I was with, but would be forced to take a long journey over the sea. Eventually, she said, I would be married twice to women who were more famous than I, and there would be many years of struggle, but eventually I would be successful and better known than either of my wives.

This gave me pause, but would not have much impact until later, as the events in my life evolved precisely as the woman predicted. At the time, I was convinced that I would marry Donnina.

Several days later, a group of us—chaperoned, of course, by the formidable Marchesa Guglielmi, with whom Donnina was staying—went off to Roccaraso, a ski resort near Rome, for the weekend. Helena could not make it, since she was helping to plan one of the grand balls her family would throw from time to time at their palazzo. This left me a clear field with Donnina, and our flirtation now became much more advanced. She would visit my room each night after everyone was asleep, and stay till early morning. Her visits were not entirely innocent, but not quite conclusive, either. Unfortunately, these nocturnal visits did not go unnoticed. A member of our party was the noted gossip Pierà Bourbon Del Monte, a sarcastic, fat, jolly fellow who managed to set a land-speed record for the dissemination of damaging rumor as soon as we returned to Rome. Within hours, Helena had summoned me: she had to see me immediately. And so I went, immediately.

Helena proceeded to accuse me of behaving scandalously with Donnina over the weekend and said, "I will not have that woman in my house. I'm calling her right now and telling her not to come."

I protested on Donnina's behalf. I said she was innocent, that if anything had happened, I was completely to blame; and that if she were to be disinvited, I certainly would not be able to attend, either.

I did not attend the Parodi ball, nor did Donnina, a circumstance that only intensified the gossip. It became the talk of the city. I had compromised a young woman of standing. It is difficult to imagine, from our present-day vantage point, how serious an issue this was for the Italian aristocracy in 1936; indeed, even at the time, I found it hard to believe that I had committed an unpardonable transgression. But, apparently, I had. It was extremely distressing and unfair, especially to Donnina. I decided to contact Donnina's chaperon to see if there was anything that could be done to remedy the situation.

She agreed to give me an audience. I prepared for it solemnly: I put on my best dark-gray flannel suit, a creamy, off-white silk shirt, a black tie, black shoes. The meeting took place in her parlor, a large, echoey room filled with seventeenth-century furniture. The marchesa was appropriately severe in appearance: pale skin, black hair, flashing black eyes. She was dressed in black velvet, with a white lace collar, and seated on a very large red sofa. I was seated in front of her, in a silent frenzy. She said, "You have ruined this girl."

I said, "It was all very innocent, Marchesa."

"It's the scandal of Rome. Her father is coming here tonight, and I am recommending that he take her back to England."

"Marchesa," I said, "this is out of proportion to anything that happened. Is there anything I can do to remedy this? I could apologize, but that would not be considered sufficient. I could offer to marry her, but you would not approve. What would you have me do? Disappear? Commit suicide? No crime has been committed. There is only the appearance of impropriety and a lot of idle gossip."

Given the options I had presented, the marchesa chose my disappearance: "I think it would be best if you were never seen again."

I could not take this seriously. But I soon began to notice that I was, in fact, disappearing. I made an effort to meet with Donnina's father, and I did offer to marry her. He told me I could "jolly well go to hell." Then there was a party at the French embassy which I was pointedly not asked to attend. Ciprienne Charles Roux, the daughter of the French ambassador, had disinvited me.

Worst, though, Count Kikki Leonardi—a good friend—visited and suggested that it might not be a bad idea to leave town. I took this *very* seriously, since Leonardi was an unofficial representative of the cream of Roman society. He was part of a group that included the princes Orsini, Borghese, Massimo, Barberini—as I have said, the very best families, and friends of mine. Without their support, I couldn't survive in Rome.

Given my sense of drama, this solution was not entirely unappealing.

The only thing I really had in Italy was my acceptance in society. Without that, I had no career, no real future, no prospects. I decided that the romantic gesture would be to leave, go to America, make my fortune and return to Rome years later, victorious, like the Count of Monte Cristo. I had been thinking of America the year before, after my mistaken arrest. However, in playing poker with friends, I had lost my entire stake for the New World, and I had to wait. But the episode with Donnina most definitely precipitated my departure.

Donnina, now Countess Cicogna, and I have maintained our friendship through several decades, by the way. "For four weeks after we were discovered," she told me, "I wasn't allowed out of my room, even for meals." Today, she happens to be one of the most in-demand ladies in international society—her wit, looks, and elegance are legendary. We remain friends to this day.

My American fantasy was propelled by several other events. My brother had recently returned from a year in the United States, at the University of Georgia. He had been offered a fellowship there, teaching French and Italian, and coaching the tennis team. He and Emilio Pucci returned on the same boat from America dressed identically in camel coats and porkpie hats, white shoes and gray flannel suits. I could not imagine a more elegant look. They brought home records, the latest music. I remember listening to "Moon over Miami," again and again. Igor brought me a hat and a pair of white shoes as gifts—college clothes. This reinforced the vision of the New World I'd had since my days chasing American girls in Florence. America was just one big college campus (with, perhaps, a few wild Indians remaining out West) with beautiful blonde girls in camel coats who would meet you at the boat and then invite you to dance (the "dip" was all the rage) and play tennis, and where jobs were easily available. My imagination was inflamed. And Igor did nothing to discourage me; indeed, he planned to join me in New York after a last year at the university.

I made arrangements to go. The previous summer, I'd met an American businessman named Victor Ridder at a tennis tournament in Venice. He owned some German-language newspapers in New York (his company would merge and become Knight/Ridder), and invited me up if I ever came to America and needed assistance. Of course, he assumed that I was a wealthy young Italian and that the assistance would be social rather than financial . . . and so when I wrote to him asking if I could use his name as my guarantor on the immigration form, he agreed. Since I'd been born in Paris, I could be included in the French quota and accepted immediately into the United States. I bought a first-class ticket to sail on the *Saturnia*, of the Italian line, in early December 1936.

Mother was quite concerned about all this. She'd remained in correspondence with some of her old American friends from Washington. One of them, a Mrs. Hadley, wrote to her: "Don't send your boy to this country. American men are tough and competitive, and he'll never make it. He hasn't got a ghost of a chance."

She was concerned about other things as well. The Italian government had imposed currency restrictions and would allow you to take only $100 from the country. So that was all the money I had, going to the Promised Land, that and letters of introduction from my mother to her old friends, plus a tennis racquet, a dinner jacket, and a quantity of hope. It seems incredible, but I was not aware that America was in the midst of an economic depression. But then, all my information had come from movie theaters, not newspapers.

Mother accompanied me to Naples. She was sad, and crying, but she also encouraged me. Everything was going to be all right. I was sure everything would be fine. I was all set for America: I had a gray flannel suit, a navy shirt, a white tie, white shoes, a camel coat, and a brown porkpie hat. This was, after all, the American uniform. Thus armed, I could not help but succeed—and succeed immediately, as everyone who went to America did.

I remember Mother standing on the dock as the *Saturnia* departed, waving furiously, calling up to me: "Remember, you are a Cassini! Always remember: *Loiewski-Cassini!*"

I arrived in New York in mid-December 1936. It had been a difficult passage, very stormy. The *Saturnia* arrived several days late, and at night. The city appeared, from a distance at least, to have none of the grace or charm of Rome. It seemed overwhelming; I had not imagined the buildings would be so tall. I had not imagined the snow, which was very bad that year. There was a fleeting moment of doubt; New York was, perhaps, not the place I'd expected. I watched it warily as we drew up to the dock. It was a jungle of cement. There were thousands and thousands of lights in the windows of the skyscrapers. They gave me a feeling of desolation and anonymity. Would I be just another little man, working in one of those huge structures? How would I ever make an impact in a place so big, so majestic and cold? Suddenly I realized that I was very scared.

Despite the rough seas, I'd had a good crossing. I avoided seasickness, won the Ping-Pong tournament, and passed the time in a halfhearted romance with an American girl, whose mother delighted in trying to dash my hopes. There was a depression on, she kept saying. American boys from the top colleges were working as messengers for Western Union, if at all. "What makes you think you're going to do so well?"

"But of course, I'll do very well," I said. I had always done well, moving in the best circles in Florence and Rome, regardless of whether my family had money or not. I assumed it would be the same in America. I assumed the leaders of society would recognize me immediately: "Ahh, here's Oleg. He's arrived, and not a moment too soon. We've needed him all this time. Anyone for tennis?"

I'd certainly spent my money as if I believed they were coining it in the streets! I lived it up on ship, bought everyone drinks. I had only $25 of my $100 when we docked.

Well, the immensity of the city gave me pause. Clearly, my arrival had not been a major event in the history of the place. But there wasn't time to be anxious. I was still glowing from the excitement of seeing the Statue of Liberty and the skyline, and now there was customs and immigration. It was very late when that was done, and a kind Italian-American doctor offered to drive me to my hotel.

I was staying at the Plaza.

Mother told me it was the only place to stay. Her friend Mrs. James Black owned a piece of the hotel and would take care of me. The Plaza was one of the few architectural sights that weren't disappointing in New York. (I was especially dismayed by the residences. I couldn't understand why very wealthy people would live in such unimportant-looking little houses. Where were the palazzi?) In any case, I checked in at the Plaza and asked, "Is Mrs. Black in?"

"No," the clerk said, "Mrs. Black is not in."

The next day, I made an appointment with my sponsor, Mr. Ridder, and wandered about the city, mildly disappointed that everyone was not wearing a gray flannel suit and white bucks. Looking at the men, I remembered my brother's advice about getting a haircut: Americans wore their hair much shorter than Europeans at that time. I would meet with Ridder about my prospects and then be shorn. Again I asked for Mrs. Black and the clerk said no.

The trip to Ridder's office the following morning was an adventure: I took the subway downtown, to the Brooklyn Bridge. Ridder's office was near there, and he welcomed me with open arms . . . and why not? He'd met me in the most elegant circumstances; he could only assume that I was a young *homme du monde*. My presence in his office was flattering; we flattered each other. He was honored that I'd come to him for advice; I was honored that he saw fit to give it. He took me to lunch at a German restaurant. He thought my plan to continue as a designer was a good one. "But first, you must travel, see the country," he said. "You must go to California and visit my friends the Basil Rathbones." It occurred to me that Mr. Ridder had a somewhat unrealistic view of my finances.

But then, another thought. He was, after all, my sponsor. Perhaps he was going to advance me the money to travel about the country. He didn't make any offer, but I assumed this was merely an exploratory lunch. I assumed that events would unfold in the continental manner, slowly, politely. I returned uptown for my haircut.

And there, in the barbershop, my American fantasy began to disintegrate. The barber asked, "Fringing?" I said yes. "Cologne?" Yes. "Massage?" Yes. "Manicure?" Of course. The bill: $2.50. I was astonished. This was ten times more than I'd ever paid for a haircut in Italy. I figured they'd spotted me for a foreigner and were taking advantage. I ran into the street and grabbed a policeman: "They're robbing me," I screamed. The policeman came in with me. The situation was explained, and he said, "No, they are perfectly right." I was dumbfounded.

Perhaps it was the haircut that triggered my worry, but I decided to find out just when Mrs. Black would be returning to the Plaza. I had been asking for several days now, and the clerk had been looking in his book and saying, "No, no Mrs. Black."

And, of course, it happened that Mrs. Black would not be returning to the Plaza anytime soon, or perhaps ever again. She had sold her interest in the place fifteen years earlier.

Now I was in a serious panic. I would have to pay my hotel bill. A first-class hotel bill. I would also have to find another place to stay. I called Mr. Ridder and asked for another appointment. Our second meeting was quite different from the first.

Here was a tremendous problem. Tact had to be set aside. I told him the truth: I had no money, and I couldn't stay on at the Plaza, and I needed a place to stay, and he had to help me find a job right away. There would be no trips to California.

His face changed then. It turned red. His anger was only temporary, because he would later invite me to his house for the holidays—he was, in fact, a remarkably kind man. But his immediate reaction was dismay: he had an Italian problem on his hands. And so he said, resignedly, "I will give you a hundred dollars, which should take care of your hotel bill, and I'll also give you a due bill for another hotel for two weeks. And I will introduce you to the one contact in your field that I have, the vice-president of Saks Fifth Avenue. And this is all I will do. The job you'll have to get on your own merit."

The hotel he sent me to was the Broadway Towers, a miserable place on the West Side. (A "due bill," I discovered, meant that the hotel had advertised in Mr. Ridder's paper and never paid; it offered, instead, payment in kind: two weeks free.) I spent two of the most awful weeks of my life there. I was in a panic night and day. The furniture in my room was horrible, and smelled of old cigars. The room was stifling hot, and so I kept the windows open all the time.

I had nothing to do, no one to talk to. Mother had given me letters of introduction to her old friends, like Mrs. Payne Whitney, which I delivered dutifully (nicking an edge of my card to indicate that I had made a personal call), but no one was home. They were all off for the Christmas holidays. Mr. Ridder had warned me, too, "Don't even think about looking for a job until after the holidays. No one will see you."

I had nothing to do but walk about in the knee-deep snow, which ruined my black suede shoes and necessitated more pants pressing than I could afford, and deliver my letters, look at ads for jobs, and go to the movies, which were very inexpensive, or the burlesque, which I'd never seen before. I ate in drugstores. I remember that this too was a depressing experience. The first time I sampled one of these places, the soda jerk pointed his finger at me and said, "Hey, buddy, whaddaya want?" I was shocked. When I went to a restaurant in Italy, they would immediately recognize my position in society and called me Excellency or Count. I was used to servants treating me with deference and respect. I had moments of doubt, thinking *Is it my fault? Maybe I don't look like a gentleman anymore.* I was still at a loss to understand American informality.

And also, it appeared, American cuisine. Once, upon entering a drugstore, I had seen the specials posted up on the wall, and one of them was the "hot fudge sundae." It sounded to me like a warm American dish, and I was eager to try it—it was cold and snowing outside. I ordered it immediately and to my surprise, a mountain of ice cream with chocolate sauce arrived—certainly not what I expected, and certainly not warm!

Two weeks passed, and nothing changed. When my due bill at the Broadway Towers elapsed, I had no choice but to check into the YMCA on West Sixty-third Street. It was Christmastime—I remember this very well, because they were singing carols in the lobby and serving tea and cookies. I became a devoted caroler, living on tea and cookies for several days.

This was pathetic, of course, but I was not entirely disheartened. In those first days, I gambled on pleasure. I had a list of beautiful American girls I had compiled in Florence and Rome. But they had seen me in only the best circumstances; their assumptions were the same as Victor Ridder's. A more prudent man might have waited until he was better situated, but I contacted them immediately. They were, by and large, pleased to hear from me ("Oh, divine! You're in town") and several even turned out to be willing to overlook my tight circumstances. I remember a wonderful evening dancing at the Commodore Hotel with Ann McAdoo from Baltimore, who had dark eyes and exquisite long blonde hair. She was the heiress to the Bromo-Seltzer fortune. The Tommy Dorsey band performed. The experience was so pleasurable that I've quite forgotten how, or whether, I paid for it. Such moments kept me going in the midst of my despair. Perhaps Mother was right: a dinner jacket was all that was needed.

Other dates didn't work out so well, though. I called one young lady who'd known me from my best days in Rome, when I was invited to all the right parties. I called her from the YMCA, alone at Christmastime, and asked her out. She accepted immediately, and volunteered to pick me up in her car. "Where are you staying?" she asked. I told her. There was a long pause on the other end. Perhaps she thought it was some sort of joke. When she arrived that evening, her mood was quite cool. She knew she had made a mistake, and suggested now that we go to the Cotton Club, which had moved down to Broadway from Harlem and become something of a tourist trap. Later, when I learned the ways of the city, I realized this was a snub. Normally, she'd go to the Stork Club. But Cab Calloway was playing that night and I loved to dance, and I tried to keep the cost of the evening down by not drinking anything, and I allowed myself to think that even in these very adverse circumstances, I might still triumph . . . until the bill came. It was $15. How could this have happened? There was a cover charge, I was told. A cover charge? The concept was new to me. I made no effort to hide my dismay, and the evening fizzled. The girl dropped me at the YMCA and I didn't see her again for many years.

That evening took a lot out of me, financially and emotionally. The ridiculous optimism I'd had about America was now replaced by the darkest pessimism. I had made a terrible mistake, one that could not be rectified. I couldn't imagine going back to Italy. The humiliation would be overwhelming. I seriously considered suicide. I spent New Year's Eve alone in my room at the YMCA while the city swirled around me greeting 1937. It had been twenty years since the Russian Revolution. Mother had salvaged the family honor for a time, but now it was our turn—Igor's and mine—and I wasn't doing very well at it. Count Cassini of the YMCA. I was just beginning to discern the scorn Americans had for impoverished nobility.

My dejection was complete. I walked the city, staring at my feet, depressed, disconsolate, unable to look other men in the eye, staring at the gutter (where I was convinced I would now end up). It was this very process of ambulatory dejection that may have been my salvation. I was walking near the Plaza Hotel one day, eyes downward, when I saw some money on the ground. Quite a bit, in fact. I scooped the bills up: $175 in all, a large windfall.

This encouraged me tremendously. I believed it was a sign from the gods—and indeed, it was a turning point of sorts for me. I could eat half decently now, and face the world with confidence. The holidays were over, and I contacted Mr. Ridder's friend at Saks, who in turn introduced me to the store's chief buyer, Mr. Roy.

Mr. Roy was a dapper, perfumed, short but handsome man, with a wonderful personality and extravagant jewelry. He asked me about my background and I exaggerated a little bit. I had been an associate of Patou, a full-fledged designer who worked on the collection. I showed him sketches, which he thought were good. "Oh, yes, I know who you are," he said, "I've seen you in the bar at the Ritz many times."

Well, I'd been there *once*, but I wasn't about to disabuse him of the idea that I was a debonair young international sophisticate. And he gave me the names of several fashion houses to contact. "Ask for a hundred and fifty dollars a week, because they won't respect you if you ask for less," he said. "And don't worry, I'll back you up."

Indeed, he called Germaine Monteil right then and there to arrange an appointment for me. Her office was only a few blocks from Saks, and I went straight over.

Unfortunately, Monteil was a real professional and she saw immediately that I knew nothing of the *prêt-à-porter* system in America. She and her husband had been in the dress business for many years (this was well before they struck it rich in cosmetics), and she knew just what she was looking for. She examined my sketches and said, "Oh, yes, very good, but what is your practical knowledge of ready-to-wear? Can you drape? Can you prepare things for fittings? Because I need someone who can take sketches I send from Paris and translate them into clothes."

Well, in a matter of minutes, it was perfectly clear that I could be of no use to her. She gave me an hour of her time—perhaps out of deference to Roy—and then sent me on my way. "You are a good designer," she said, "but you're not practical enough. You don't know anything about Seventh Avenue and what a wholesale collection is. You have no experience, and I don't have the time to teach you right now."

This was right on the money, of course. I had, at the time, a vague notion that in America you sold to stores like Saks, rather than to individuals. But that was all.

My next stop was across the street, at the firm of Jo Copeland, which was quite successful at the time. I was interviewed there by Miss Copeland and her partner, a Miss Sadofsky . . . and apparently Mr. Roy had created a very favorable impression on them for me, because their questions were rather perfunctory. Later on, I realized why. They assumed I was a "friend" of his, and figured it would be smart business to hire a young designer who was so powerfully close to a top buyer, no matter what I did in the collection.

In fact, they hired me on the spot for $100 per week, a large sum. They showed me a bare room that was to be my designing quarters, and Miss Copeland, who was a handsome, well-dressed, rather cool woman, said, "You will start work on Monday. I'm going to Nassau and won't be back for a while, but you get started and make yourself at home."

I rushed back to Mr. Roy, thanked him profusely, and then raced to a telegraph office to send a communiqué of victory to my family: "Great success. Please come."

In the days that followed, I left the YMCA and moved into a very lovely little apartment with a garden on East Sixty-second Street. I was now as high again as I'd been low before. I wrote home that I was making more than the president of an Italian bank (which was true). No one in Italy made $100 per week; you could get a six-course meal there for 75 cents. A top man's shirt cost a dollar. Soon I received word from my family. Igor, emboldened by my success, would soon be joining me—to be followed, in a few months, by Mother and Father.

I spent the next three weeks sketching. I worked nine to five, sketching. I did nothing else. I never saw a piece of material, or any of the other employees. I didn't know what was expected of me, so I kept sketching.

Finally, Miss Copeland returned from Nassau. She looked at my work and said nothing, and I began to wonder what was happening. I never met the piece-goods man (the person who bought fabric) or any of her other assistants; I never was asked to a fitting. More weeks passed. The collection was assembled, and I wasn't even invited to see it.

Mr. Roy, of course, was. As it happened, he didn't like it very much. He asked. "Which of these are Cassini's?" They made excuses: it was too early, or perhaps too late; they didn't have time to put me to work on anything; I was being trained for the next collection.

I knew nothing of this for several weeks, until the day the orders from Saks came in, which happened to be the very day that Igor was scheduled to arrive from Italy. The orders were disastrous, for Copeland and for me. She and Miss Sadofsky called me in and said, "We're very sorry, but we no longer require your services."

For a moment, I was unable to understand. "But," I spluttered, "don't you think you should give me a chance?"

No, they couldn't. Business wasn't very good (especially from Saks). They were very sorry. I was numb. I tried not to appear upset and to show some dignity, but I was dead inside. My great moment of triumph, meeting Gigi at the boat, had turned to dust.

I went immediately to see Mr. Roy, who was dumbstruck. He said, "How could they fire you? You haven't designed anything yet." And then: "Well, don't worry, I'll send you to some other people." His tone was less warm, though. He was still friendly, but I could tell that he was thinking, *Let's hope this boy doesn't become a problem for me.*

Igor received the news with equanimity, as always. He was less temperamental than I, eternally optimistic, full of confidence. It was a great comfort to be with him. He shrugged off my disaster. "You'll get another job, and I'll get a job, too." He was thrilled to be back in America. He was thrilled with our apartment. He remained smiling, hopeful, and even-tempered in the weeks that followed, even as we were reduced to one meal a day—frankfurters, at Nedick's—and subjected to a series of humiliations.

Igor had brought with him a jeweled miniature of Nicholas II, one of the last of our family treasures, which the czar himself had given to our grandfather, Ambassador Cassini. It had been festooned with diamonds, but Mother sold them one by one during our dark years in Switzerland. Igor took it to a store called À la Vieille Russie, which specialized in Russian *objets*, and sold it for $500 with an option to buy it back for $1,000 within a year. Of course, we never did buy it back. Who knows what it would be worth today?

We lived off that money for a time. There was no real work to be found. It was the height of the Depression; people were selling apples on street corners and going to soup kitchens for a free meal. Mr. Roy's contacts proved not very useful—or perhaps it was I, who barely knew the difference between wholesale and retail, who was not very useful. I was a naive, overpolite boy trying to find my way in the pushiest, most cynical of all possible worlds. There were times I would be told, "Well, we have no work, but those are nice sketches, can we buy a couple?" I would sell them for a dollar each. There were times when I'd say to Igor, "I'd sell my soul to the devil for a guaranteed hundred and fifty a week for the rest of my life."

We went everywhere looking for help. We went to the Italian consulate, where several fellows I'd known from the university were working in the diplomatic service. I had a long conversation with one of them: Aldo Loni, the vice-consul, whom I'd known well enough in Florence not to like. I was more respectful now, perhaps reminiscing about the time I'd beaten up his brother, and then allowing that I was going through a rough patch here in New York. "Well, my good fellow," he said, savoring his revenge, "that is too bad . . . but you must realize that what you were in Italy means nothing here. You might think you can just go to Newport and play tennis in high society, but you can't. You are nothing here. Too bad."

"You *cafonaccio!*" I said to him. It was the worst Italian insult, difficult to translate—it is something beyond a phony, perhaps a cross between a phony and a parvenu, maybe a little worse. "You were born a *cafone* and you will die a *cafone*. I will show you how wrong you are."

In fact, he *was* wrong—especially about the tennis. Igor and I visited the West Side Tennis Club at Forest Hills one day, introduced ourselves as ranking Italian players, and were asked to prove ourselves in a doubles match. We polished our opponents off easily enough and were invited to become junior members. The dues weren't bad, but we probably would have joined even if they had been. This was our only link to the glamorous world we assumed was our natural habitat. Given our dreary reality at that point, there was an almost dreamlike quality to our immediate acceptance on a tennis court.

Indeed, playing tennis was far more pleasant than scuffling for work, and I proceeded to spend much of the summer playing in small tournaments around New England, including Newport. Room and board usually were provided; I convinced myself that it would be difficult to find a good job in the summer in any case.

Igor, more practical and even-tempered always, wasn't holding out for a *good* job. He did anything that came along. He sold stockings, and tomato paste. He literally worked night and day: at night, as a proofreader for the Italian newspaper *Il Progrèsso*; and during the day, as a clerk in a travel agency. Mother had arrived in March. She seemed a bit disoriented, I thought, and worried about the prospect of starting all over yet again.

Father followed her a month later. He had remained in Rome to

dispose of the apartment and sell the furniture. He did this, apparently
trading it all (except his trunks full of clothes, of course) for a hot plate—
Father became incomprehensible when asked to recount financial transactions, so we were never quite sure. In any case, he walked down the
gangplank of the ship, the hot plate proudly cradled in his arms. He would
be no more successful finding productive labor in New York than he had
been anyplace else.

Mother found a cramped, depressing apartment in Yorkville, on the
then unfashionable far upper East Side; she filled it with ponderous, unattractive (but valuable) Victorian pieces, gifts from an old friend of hers
in Washington. It was a very demoralizing place, the sort of neighborhood
where men sat on the stoops in their undershirts, and children screamed
and ran about banging garbage cans. Even in our worst times, we'd never
lived so modestly before.

We lived there together for a time, although I escaped the worst of
the summer heat by playing tennis. Mother tried finding work for Igor
through her old suitor, Joseph Patterson—then the publisher of the New
York *Daily News*—but he snubbed her (Mother implied that this was
because she had spurned his offer of matrimony thirty-five years earlier).

Mother never really stopped trying, but she became increasingly distressed. The idea that she might not be a success in America, the scene of
her greatest social triumphs, was unthinkable, an impossible thing for her
to face. Of course, she hadn't yet tried Washington, the city where she'd
particularly been known. It was a matter of pride: when she returned
there, she wanted to do it in style. (I suspect there was some fear involved, too: what if she were not to be well received in Washington?)

Igor and I prevailed upon her. She had to try her contacts in Washington. And so she did, and immediately the world brightened for us. It
had been thirty-five years, but Washington apparently hadn't forgotten
Mother's reign at the Russian embassy. Her old pal Cissy Patterson, the
recalcitrant Joe Patterson's sister, promised work for Igor at her paper,
the Washington *Times-Herald*, and a warm welcome for Mother in society
as well. It was the sort of greeting we'd all been waiting for: "Ah, Marguerite, you're back! We've missed you."

In any case, the family packed up and left for Washington in the fall
of 1937, leaving me in New York, still hoping to find my way as a designer.

The tide began to turn when I once again bumped into Beppe Bellini,
my savior in the Lucy Winslow affair. He was in town dealing Italian
antiquities from a suite at the Ambassador Hotel—a European-style es-

tablishment on Park Avenue. Bellini assumed I was as well connected in New York as I'd been in Florence, and would invite me to informal cocktail parties he'd have for prospective clients and other old acquaintances from the Continent. One of these was Ernesto de Angeli, the heir to an Italian munitions fortune, who was supposedly a student at Yale but spent most of his time on the prowl in café society. He was a handsome fellow, quite clever with the girls, and he introduced me around.

De Angeli kept an apartment on the East Side, and I was able to store some of the family's possessions with him, including a portrait of Mother by John Singer Sargent. It was a full-length portrait, painted most likely when Mother was a girl in Washington; she wore a black dress with white tulle on the shoulders and her hair pulled back. I am ashamed to admit that while I admired the work, I had no comprehension of its value . . . and so, I was not alarmed when it was lost, seized with all of de Angeli's possessions by the landlord when Ernesto returned to Italy without having paid several months' rent.

De Angeli introduced me to Adelaide Moffet, who was something of a celebrity in New York society at the time. She was an ex-debutante . . . and a chanteuse. She performed each night with the orchestra at the Ambassador, largely on the strength of her social standing, I suspect. The situation was quite extraordinary, even if her voice wasn't. Society girls didn't work in those days. Adelaide, however, wasn't one to let convention ruin her fun. She was striking, with dark hair and enormous dark eyes, though perhaps a little too voluptuous. She was very lively and had lots of friends; in a way, almost a copy of the classic Peter Arno cartoon debutante. She and I hit it off immediately, a nice, light, sophisticated affair. She was recently widowed. Her husband had been the handsome, wealthy, and profoundly alcoholic Winky Brooks, who had fallen (or perhaps been pushed) from a window a year earlier. It had been quite a scandal, in all the papers; but the rich seemed to have a penchant for melodrama in those days. Adelaide managed to overcome her grief somehow, and had taken up first with de Angeli and then me, as well as with Franklin Roosevelt, Jr., who was married and lived in Charlottesville, Virginia, where he was attending law school.

It was all very civilized: Adelaide introduced me to Roosevelt over drinks at the Sherry Netherland one evening. He was a big, good-looking fellow, a classic American sort, with all his father's charm. He looked at me in a condescending way and said to her, "You like them skinny, don't you." Ah well, laughter, laughter . . . we were all good chums, weren't we (I didn't like it). But this galoot—actually, we later became friendly—lived elsewhere and wasn't much of a threat, although he did have a terrible habit of calling her late at night and chattering for hours and hours.

There were many advantages to dating Adelaide, not the least of which was a complimentary dinner at the Ambassador each night, between her shows. Afterward, we would go to the Stork Club, which was, of course, *the* place to be seen in those days, along with El Morocco. I became known at both places, which operated like private clubs; and so I became part of café society—even if no one was quite sure what I'd *done* to merit such status. Through Adelaide, I met some of the most important people in New York at the time, young ladies who were tired of the close-cropped, foursquare, unrelievedly collegiate young gentlemen from Yale and Princeton who populated that scene, girls who were looking for something more exotic, and sophisticated, and continental. The idea that I could attract such girls became a crucial part of my life.

I felt I *needed*, for my own self-respect, to be seen with the loveliest girls in the city, the girls who decorated the banquettes at the Stork in their black cocktail dresses and pearls (dinner jackets were *de rigueur* for men). The Stork was where the debutantes and the postdebs and the models would go; it had the feel of an Ivy League supper club, although the atmosphere was more elegant. The main room was a safe, chaperoned sort of place, well lighted, with lots of candelabra and mirrors; the girls loved dancing (there were two bands, American and South American, continuous music), and watching themselves in the mirrors as they danced. But there was another, smaller room off the bar, known as the Cub Room. It was lined with photographs and presided over by Walter Winchell, who was the emperor of the place. Only the most important people were seated there.

The Stork was as much controlled by Winchell as it was by Sherman Billingsley, the man who owned it . . . Billingsley, the former bootlegger from Enid, Oklahoma. A subdued, cordial man with clear blue eyes and a fascinating smile, he seemed, I thought, almost bemused by the success he enjoyed. He knew the advertisements he received from Winchell's column were crucial, and so he paid court to the king, could often be found sitting next to him, acceding to his whims. For a time, Winchell banned me from the Stork. I never knew why. But I had my revenge years later, when I arrived in town with Gene Tierney and Billingsley sent notes to the hotel practically begging us to drop by. When we finally did, after a diplomatic interval of several days, a photograph of us was taken and hung on the wall of that room with the immortals.

El Morocco, by contrast, was a naughtier sort of place. It was darker, gaudier—blue-and-white zebra-stripe banquettes, white palm trees everywhere, and dark blue walls with little stars, representing the desert night, I suppose. It was presided over by John Perona, also a former bootlegger, who held court at a round table, surrounded by his buddies. Actors like Errol Flynn and Bruce Cabot could often be found there, and others, less celebrated people like me. Perona and I hit it off from the start; he liked me because I was Italian and I would show up with top girls and important people like the Rhinelander-Stuarts . . . and that was entertainment of a sort for the crowd. If I didn't have a date, I was always welcome at his table. He was a powerful man, with enormous arms and hands, like Popeye the Sailor, tiny slits for eyes, and slicked-down hair; you could see that, unlike Billingsley, he might have been a pretty dangerous fellow during Prohibition, but he was always extremely kind to me.

In truth, I felt more comfortable at El Morocco. It attracted a more sophisticated, continental crowd. I might meet the right sorts of girls at the Stork, but I would take them to El Morocco once we got past the initial pleasantries and I wanted to send a message. El Morocco was where one *ended* the evening, and Perona tried to make sure it was as late as possible, always encouraging his friends to stay on and keep him company, "Shall we have a risotto or some pasta?" he might say at two or four o'clock in the morning. How could one refuse? Indeed, between Perona and Adelaide Moffet, along with my other friends in society, I was kept very well fed during this time. It was rare that I had to pick up a check. No one seemed to notice this or mind very much. I was considered a gentleman in society, and Mother was right: a gentleman was always welcome. To all appearances, I was as well off as Ernesto de Angeli, who was a multimillionaire.

But I languished by daylight, despite my late-night celebrity. Seventh Avenue was proving to be a revolving door. I worked several weeks for a man named William Bass, and also several months for an ex-pugilist named Rothenberg. It had reached the point that, like everyone else in those post-Depression times, I was continuously looking for work, even when employed, because I always expected to be fired.

It was about the time I was working for Rothenberg that I finally managed to secure a job that lasted for more than a few months. It was not much of a position. In fact, it was something of an embarrassment: I was hired by an elderly gentleman, a Mr. Bouslogue, who was convinced that his wife was the world's foremost designer. He was an elegant fellow who spoke and dressed well, and had bought a marvelous building on Fifty-seventh Street to display his wife's work. But the clothes were early Theda Bara. Thirty years out of date: tea gowns, at-home dresses with yards and yards of chiffon, and furs. It was a vanity operation, an anachronistic fashion concept.

I was hired, ostensibly, as a young designer-collaborator. Actually, though, Mr. Bouslogue expected me to bring my friend in as customers. He and his wife were old enough to have heard of my mother's exploits in Washington, and they figured I would have powerful connections in New York society. "I'm not interested in having you hang around here all the time," he said. "Go out. Meet people. Have lunch, have dinner. Bring your friends around."

I was paid $80 a week to do this. I had no qualms about being paid the money, but I still had hopes of becoming a great designer in my own right, and tried to convince the Bouslogues that if they wanted to attract a younger clientele, debutantes and so forth, they should let me design a collection. Madame Bouslogue, a fierce-looking woman with white hair parted in the middle like a Sioux, would have none of it, though. *She* was the designer. I let her be a genius and collected my pay.

I don't think I brought them much business. Victor Ridder, my patron, came through for me once more. His wife visited the studio, and spent thousands of dollars on some very ugly fashion. I would also, from time to time, encourage some of the girls I knew to drop by. "Where are *your* dresses?" they would ask (within earshot of Mrs. Bouslogue, I hoped).

In early 1938, though, I received a better offer.

Terry Schey was a typical Stork Club debutante, a tall girl, pretty, rather brash, and a bit too skinny—not a romantic interest of mine, but a friend. One night, she said, "You know, you and I should go into business together."

"Oh, but of course," I said.

But, sure enough, an invitation to meet her father came. He was a very successful textile manufacturer, with a beautiful home on Park Avenue. He was also a classic Middle European type, an Austrian, always dressed very formally in a dark jacket and pin-striped pants. I found him very polite, very courtly, and I think he appreciated who I was. He had me for tea. "You know, my daughter is up to no good," he said, sitting there in an old-fashioned stiff collar and monocle, looking very much like the prime minister of some Balkan country. "She goes to parties and to the Stork Club and she does nothing useful. She has talked a lot about you. Perhaps there could be an arrangement. We could create a business for her, a fashion studio, and you would be her partner."

I had the distinct impression, as we spoke, that he was not so much interested in a business as in a possible son-in-law. I said, "You are very kind, sir, but you must realize I haven't the resources for such a venture."

"Yes, yes," he said, "I will provide the financial backing. You will provide the inspiration and the customers. We will be equal partners."

He offered me a salary of $40 per week and a percentage of the profits. This was half what I'd been making, but there seemed quite a bit of potential: I would have the opportunity to design and create my own fashion concepts, thereby building my own label and trademark. It would be something like what I'd done in Rome, for the same sort of clientele, only on a grander scale, with a staff—a secretary, a salesperson, a *pre-mière*, four sample hands—and a very *appropriate* studio on Madison Avenue, between Fifty-ninth and Sixtieth streets, a studio with a show-room, a workroom, and an office for me, an office with a large sofa.

The sofa was particularly important. Forty dollars per week was not much to live on; indeed; I'd had a somewhat nomadic existence on twice the salary. Ernesto de Angeli and I had shared a room at the Ambassador for a time, an arrangement that shattered rather dramatically one evening over competing claims of privacy (neither of us enjoyed being locked out when the other had a guest; when de Angeli had guests three evenings in a row, and prevented me from an intriguing engagement the third night, I became quite agitated). From there, I'd moved on to the Wyndham. But it would be silly to keep a hotel room on $40 per week, especially when there were a sofa and a shower at the office.

And so, Oleg, Inc., was launched. Announcements were mailed. There was a cocktail party. All the most fashionable girls came, and more than a few of them bought clothes. They bought one dress each. We offered creativity, individualized vision, and custom fitting, but our prices were three times as high as the better stores', and in America, younger woman, no matter how wealthy, were less of a market for made-to-order couture than their mothers. Ultimately, we could not compete, but no matter. We were launched, and optimism soared at first. Miss Schey even came to work on something resembling a regular basis. She was, in fact, shamed into it by my exhausting schedule. "You're always here!" she said. "How can you be out all night dancing and still be here first thing in the morning?"

The other employees were similarly impressed. They would arrive at the studio and find me asleep on the couch, obviously having worked all night. And hard work it was! Grueling work. This may seem silly, but I'm not kidding. I was still living one day at a time, and I felt compelled to triumph every night. The pressure created a great anxiety in me. I would spend two hours each evening, from six to eight, on my calendar, making phone calls, setting up dates two weeks in advance, reconfirming others. *Nothing* was left to chance. I lived under the tyranny of the "date": In Italy, everything had been so casual. There would be early-evening cocktail parties; groups would form and go out together. In New York, people *dated*. Even if it didn't work out, you were stuck with the girl for the night . . . and I couldn't bear the thought of a wasted evening, a failure.

Dating imposed certain financial obligations as well. I would always try to plead a business meeting, or some such thing, for early in the evening so that I wouldn't be expected to spring for dinner. When dinner was unavoidable, I would go to Luisa's, a small Italian place in the East Sixties, where I knew the owner and she would often let me run a tab. I tried to keep a strict budget: no more than $5 per night, which meant a few drinks at the Stork or El Morocco, and then what? Well, perhaps: "I've just designed a dress that would look *perfect* on you. I have it over at the studio. . . . Well, we could go there right now, if you like. . . ." I'd still have to take the girl home afterward (we couldn't be found there in the morning). I cannot count the number of taxis I hailed at dawn. Very romantic, but exhausting. If I was lucky, I might be able to sneak a couple of hours more alone on the sofa, and then it would be, "Good morning, Mr. Cassini!"

I was killing myself with this. I became addicted. Each new evening required some new conquest or perhaps a new contact made. The pressure, the folly! I had to perform or my reputation would suffer, I thought, and there would be whispers, because I knew that girls talked. I became obsessed by potency, and fortified myself with oysters and other aphrodisiacal foods. In short, I was seized by a kind of madness. I felt I was in a competition to the death against those handsome, solid American men who had homes, who had families, who had fortunes. If a beautiful girl, a top, powerful girl like Adelaide Moffet or Georgia Carroll or Kay Aldrich, showed an interest in me, rather than in one of those others, I would have had my high for the day and could move on to the next one. "But you are crazy," Terry Schey said, "living like this."

"It's very difficult," I allowed. "But I don't expect a long life."

And I proceeded, in my exhaustion, to come very close to committing social and intellectual suicide. In a matter of days, during the summer of 1938, I met and married Merry Fahrney.

It began with a call from one of Mother's friends, Baroness Maria Persico. She had been a great Hungarian beauty, married to an Italian and divorced, and was now working at Bergdorf Goodman as a sales representative. She called me and said, "A customer of mine, a very beautiful girl, extremely wealthy, who has a weakness for titled Europeans, has seen you dancing at El Morocco and would like to meet you."

The baroness and her escort, an empty suit named Post, accompanied me to the lady's apartment, a gigantic place on Fifth Avenue in the Seventies—rather bare, though, I remember thinking. It was as if someone had recently moved in, or just departed. There was a large sofa, and a baby-grand piano, and a crystalline bar, and a Kashmir carpet of beige and blue, but no art. The walls were bare. It was all very staid, very formal. A butler offered us champagne. We sat there and talked, and waited. I was uncomfortable; this was very impolite. But then I didn't realize we were being set up for a grand entrance.

Suddenly the door opened and I saw a girl with red hair, very pale, about five foot five in very high heels, wearing nothing but a white satin negligee and a fur boa. She was smoking a cigarette in a long holder. She was very pretty, but it all seemed manufactured. She wore a good deal of makeup, and long lashes that couldn't possibly be real; her hair looked shellacked in place. She had none of the casual beauty that I liked; indeed, she seemed almost Oriental in the formality of her presentation—a red-haired Japanese from a Kabuki show.

"Merry Fahrney," she said portentously, extending her hand to be kissed.

I thought, *What a phony.*

She sat with us, drinking champagne. She ignored me at first, directing her attention to the baroness. She might have asked, "And are you enjoying New York, Count Cassini?" She called me Count, always. Gradually, she turned her attention to me. We talked, and the baroness and

Post discreetly took their leave after a while. Merry's conversation was very jumpy, from one topic to another, always dropping a lot of names, talking about Biarritz and polo ponies, and all.

She said, "Count Cassini, aren't you playing polo now?"

"Ha, ha," I laughed. "But, Miss Fahrney, I haven't had the opportunity. I have been working."

"Oh," she said. "Well . . . *working*. It's such a terrible thing for a man. My good friend Barbara Hutton never allows her husbands to work."

"Yes, of course," I agreed (a basic rule in such conversations: always agree when you are disagreeing). "But even in Europe the situation has changed and men have to work, particularly when they don't have much money."

"How dull," she said. "How dreadfully dull. And how American! How dreadfully American of you, Count Cassini!"

"Well, yes, to be sure," I said, thinking of how wonderful it would be if my life even remotely resembled the one she imagined for me. "But in Rome you must do as the Romans do."

"I'm giving a party at El Morocco tonight," she said abruptly. "Will you join us?"

And so it began. There wasn't much chemistry between us, it seemed. I called the baroness the next day and told her so. "Anyway, I don't think she seemed particularly interested in me. There were no signs of approval," I said.

"I know she likes you," the baroness replied. "She's impressed. Pursue her; she's a divine girl."

I would arrive at Merry's apartment at 8:00 P.M., wait several hours for her to prepare herself, and then we would go to El Morocco with a large group of people, maybe ten or twelve. I paid the first two nights, exhausting all of my resources. "You know, this is a very hard thing for me to discuss," I told her, "but you see, I was restricted in the amount of money I could bring from Italy, and I cannot go every night to these places. In any case, I would like to take you to some small restaurant, a place we can talk. We've never done that, you know. I pick you up. We go out, with all these people around, and I don't know what I'm doing there. I feel like a fifth wheel."

"Oh, how silly of me," she said. "Think nothing of it. Oh, these terrible restrictions of money. How boring. I keep having trouble with my trust funds, too. Let me take care of the bill when we go out with my group. They are my friends. I invited them."

Well, that was very kind of her. I must say that in all this there was nothing particularly romantic going on; she didn't seem at all interested in that side of things. But the situation was progressing nonetheless. I played in a tennis tournament at Newport one weekend and she was there —and very impressed, of course. My position in society was reinforced in her mind. We had dinner that night, and drank a lot of champagne. She flattered me. She told me that I deserved to live like a count, that I deserved a string of polo ponies and all the accoutrements of nobility. She was, I would later realize, campaigning for me in much the same manner as I campaigned for women, with one very important difference: she had no genuine feeling for me; I was just another scalp. I would never have treated a woman that way. No: Merry Fahrney was one of only a few purely evil people I've met in my life.

I was intrigued by her, but not entirely swept off my feet. I had my doubts. I discussed them with Mother, who came to New York for a few days at about that time, as she often did, to check on my progress in life. I told Mother about my budding romance with Miss Fahrney. Apparently, she was able to read between the lines. She sensed the match was wrong. She opposed it vehemently. "Don't sacrifice yourself," she said. "I hope you're not being dazzled by her money, because no matter how hard you think things are now, no matter how dark, you will come back. You're so young. Everything that seems impossible to conquer now will be very easy later."

I wish I'd listened to her, but I was at that moment in the throes of a malignant psychological condition that, in its more benign form, is often described as love. I never felt anything so positive as love for Merry Fahrney, but I did experience the dark side of that emotion: bedazzlement. She was twenty-five years old, very rich, and very beautiful. I was falling for her.

One evening early in September she announced: "I have an idea, a *wonderful* idea. We're going to get married."

I remember thinking, *Well, there it is. Make your decision.*

She didn't leave me much time to think. "I have it all set up. We're going to Maryland. I have a plane. We're eloping."

I called my brother, who agreed to meet us at the airfield and act as my best man. I called Mother, who said, "Well, you know your mind. I hope it works out."

Merry flew the plane. It was my first experience in a small aircraft and I felt rather ill. I did not know then that she'd caused the death of a pilot in an air calamity in 1931. There were, in fact, a great many things I didn't know about Merry Fahrney at that point. I knew that she was rich, that she had inherited millions from a patent cough syrup her grandfather, Dr. Parker Fahrney, of Chicago, had developed. I knew that she'd been married to Baron Arturo Berlingieri, a cousin of Nadia Berlingieri, whom I'd dressed in Rome. They had divorced, she said, because Berlingieri had been a brute. That was all I knew, although I would soon learn more.

We were married September 2, 1938, by a justice of the peace in Elkton, Maryland. We rode the night train home to New York in silence. She seemed spent, as if she'd just made love—this act of bravado, this elopement, was ecstasy of a sort for her. She even smoked cigarettes, one after another, with the casual arrogance of the carnally satisfied. I, on the other hand, was quite dejected. I felt used. The horror of the situation now dawned on me. I was married to this chain-smoking girl with whom I'd never had a decent conversation. She was now Countess Cassini. We arrived in New York at first light and went to her apartment, where, exhausted, we went off to separate bedrooms. That was our honeymoon.

The next morning, it was in all the tabloids: "Madcap Merry Fahrney, the Cough Syrup Heiress, Weds Fourth!"

Fourth? As it happened, Berlingieri hadn't been the first but the third. There had been a childhood sweetheart, Hugh Pickering, whom she had divorced but who was still hanging around, much to my dismay, a frequent visitor to the apartment. Then there was Frank van Eiszner, also a childhood friend, whom Fahrney had married in a drunken stupor (the marriage was later annulled on those grounds). It was a moment of weakness after her true love of the moment, "Count" George DiGeorgio, had been deported back to Chile. DiGeorgio was known in the gossip columns as "the phony count," and there had been quite a scene at the boat when he left the country, Merry Fahrney begging and crying for clemency from the immigration officials. Even the *New York Times* had seen fit to record that event . . . and also, two days later, Fahrney's marriage to Eiszner. She would testify that she could not recall any detail of that marriage, or the serious car wreck that followed in which several people were killed. She awoke in the hospital, still pining for her phony count.

After the annulment, she had found Berlingieri. But, as she and I would both learn in the weeks to come, she had not disposed of him adequately. A judge in Chicago ruled that she'd never been legally divorced and was, in fact, a bigamist. She was Baroness Berlingieri *and*

Countess Cassini, at least until another court reversed the ruling of the first.

Well, there was not too much to our marriage. We made love once or twice, indifferently; she was concerned about mussing her hair, or her makeup, or something. And there was not much opportunity for romance, because we slept in separate rooms and she never awakened until five in the afternoon, at which time her various retainers and hangers-on would begin to drift in: Baroness Persico was a regular; and Hugh Pickering, the first husband; and Lowell Birrell, her attorney; and Sonny Griswold, a social butterfly of the time. They fluttered around her; I was expected to flutter as well.

I remember trying to make the grand romantic gesture on one occasion. I entered her bedroom very dramatically, uninvited, hoping to circumvent the retinue. She was there, somewhere beneath the mask and the layers of cold cream. I was daunted, but pressed on. I went to the bed, pulled down the covers; she was wearing a silk negligee and long, dark gloves. This was intriguing. I tried to rouse her. I took her by the arms . . . and cold cream spurted up, out of the gloves. I retreated, defeated.

She insisted that I quit my work. "I cannot be married to some little designer," she said. "You must have a string of polo ponies. You must be out playing polo."

I told her that I needed some means of making money, some regular salary, and needed to continue my fashion business. She said, "Well, if you must have a business, it should be a big one, not some ridiculous little thing like this situation with Schey. You must forget that. It's just too unimportant."

I went to Mr. Schey and told him that I could no longer continue. I was very embarrassed—this was one man who'd had faith in me and I'd let him down. He was a good sport about it, though. He understood, but I was beginning to understand as well. I was desperately afraid that this tabloid marriage had made me something of a joke. It began to seem that I'd sold my birthright and joined the ranks of the professionally foolish, the titled nonentities. Merry Fahrney was now Countess Cassini, but I was just another part of the retinue, and, I later realized, a rather boring member of the group at that. Always complaining, taking everything so *seriously*, wanting to start my new "big" business she had spoken of, moping about the apartment instead of going off to play polo somewhere.

And still, every evening, it was off to El Morocco—a joyless exercise, it had become. The marriage had changed nothing in Merry's life. The routine was exactly the same.

I would be served breakfast each day, but there would be no lunch (the mistress of the house was asleep, in any event). I was too embarrassed to ask the cook or one of the servants for something to eat. If I'd been another sort of man, I might have gone on a shopping spree, charging everything to my wife (indeed, it later came out that Sonny Griswold was charging his wardrobe to Merry Fahrney). But I never took a dime from her. This went on for weeks. My self-image was as low as it had been at the YMCA.

Finally, I confronted her: "We must make some sort of arrangement. I have to speak to your attorney about setting up this new big business. I need to work to make some money."

This interview took place in her bedroom. She was seated on the bed. She said to me, "I understand completely. I've got the money for you. I have all the money you will ever need or deserve."

She opened the drawer to her night table and she took out a handkerchief and threw it at me; it was filled with pennies that she had collected. She threw these pennies at me and said, "There is all the money you need."

I was stunned. I'd never been so insulted. I was in a white rage. It finally—*finally*—was apparent that she had absolutely no feeling for me, had married me only for the title (later, she'd say that she had done it to trade up, from Baroness to Countess), and that I'd been the biggest fool imaginable. I said, "I hate you for this. You're empty and evil. I'm leaving. I'm getting out of here, and I'm never coming back."

Well, I never did go back . . . but I wasn't quite finished with Merry Fahrney, either.

I fled to Washington, to my family. They lived in a three-bedroom apartment off Connecticut Avenue, in a state best described as modest gentility. Igor, now the junior society columnist for the Washington *Times-Herald*, was still the family's primary means of support, and, much to his credit, he made me feel welcome. "It's a bad situation," he said, "but don't worry. It'll pass." Mother, too, consoled me. She always believed that life was a series of errors, very few of which were irreparable. She believed, too, that her sons would eventually triumph. It was the most important thing for her.

No, that's not quite true. At that moment, Mother had something more. She had regained her former status in Washington. Her old friends

—the "cave dwellers," as they were called—had not forgotten her. Cissy Patterson had given Igor a job (the quid pro quo was Mother's memoirs, however). Eve Merriam, now Washington's greatest hostess, made sure that not only Countess Cassini but also her sons (and, yes, her husband, too) were invited to all the best parties. It wasn't hard for me to lick my wounds in such circumstances. Washington was a more courtly place then, not the dull warren of bureaucracy that we know today. It moved at a slower pace than New York; it was less sophisticated, perhaps, but more polite. In any event, Merry Fahrney had given me all the "sophistication" I could handle. I was relieved to move, once again, in a more mannered atmosphere.

The social life in Washington actually very much reminded me of Europe, and Rome in particular; it had the style of an international capital, a melding of society, diplomacy, and politics. There were embassy balls most evenings; white tie and tails were required. Guests would be announced as they arrived; there were formal dinners I attended for as many as one hundred guests. I moved easily among these people, and became friendly with the diplomats from Italy, of course, but also with those from countries as diverse as Germany, Poland, and the Philippines. It was at a Polish embassy party that I met Prince Alek Hohenlohe and his wife, Peggy Biddle Schultz, both of whom would become close friends of mine and, a decade later, business partners.

The Biddles, the Mellons, the cream of American society attended these embassy parties, and on weekends they returned the favor, inviting the various diplomats and politicians (and the Cassinis, as well) to their Virginia estates for fox-hunting. I rode with them on occasion, and more frequently after the war, when I had a stable of horses and hunted most weekends, everywhere from Virginia to Long Island. Their hunts were formal, elegant affairs, the riders always well mounted and attired in hunting pink; the ritual usually included a hunt breakfast and—always—cocktails; fox-hunting men were the hardest-drinking group of fellows I've ever encountered.

Mother was quite friendly with Evalyn Walsh McLean, who had a famous estate just across the Potomac. Mrs. McLean owned the Hope diamond and sometimes wore that enormous blue stone at parties (but always in the company of two detectives). I once attended a ball where Mrs. McLean's daughter, who was also called Evalyn, wore the diamond; she soon married Senator Reynolds, an older, courtly Southern gentleman. This was very much the sort of society in which Jacqueline Kennedy was raised, and which she hoped to reestablish in Washington when her husband was elected president in 1960.

There was still the chronic problem of what to do with myself professionally, however; my social life seemed to exist on a different level of reality from my workaday existence.

I became a teacher at a fashion "institute" on Connecticut Avenue, the sort of place that flourishes in any American city large enough to have a critical mass of young women who imagine themselves stylish dressers and, therefore, candidates for careers in fashion. There is nothing much that can be done for such girls, and I certainly, given my experience, was the last person who might have had any practical advice to impart. However, I could teach them how to sketch, and I did.

For a time, too, I contributed a daily cartoon to Igor's society column, which was called "Petit Point." This ended abruptly with a cartoon entitled "Ballski at the Polski Embassiski," in which the Polish ambassador, Jerzy Potocki, was portrayed dancing with a noted Washington matron of great girth. This mild jest caused the first edition of the *Times-Herald* to be pulled from the newsstands. Mrs. Patterson, who had been married to a Polish nobleman and retained a weakness for the breed, sent profuse apologies to the ambassador, along with my head on a platter.

Igor's job was spared, but he too found it difficult not to have fun at the expense of the grandees of Washington society. His light, sardonic tone offended some of the young cavaliers of Virginia, who were also dismayed that the beautiful Southern belle Austine "Bootsie" McDonnell, from Warrenton, Virginia, favored Igor's company over theirs. On the evening of June 24, 1939, several of the Warrenton Country Club's finest lured Igor into the parking lot, banged him on the head, took him for a drive, and tarred and feathered him. It proved a major, though rather uncomfortable, boost for his career. He filed the story of the kidnapping from his hospital bed. Gossip columnists everywhere—Walter Winchell, Cholly Knickerbocker (then written by Maury Paul)—rose to his defense. He was given a promotion, and set on a course that would lead to his succeeding Paul as Cholly Knickerbocker (the generic name for the Hearst newspapers' society columnist) after the war.

I could not match Igor's professional success, but I wasn't doing too badly in Washington society, either. I had found myself another debutante-chanteuse, an extremely attractive girl named Peggy Townsend. She performed at the Hotel Roger Smith, and dreamed of going to Hollywood . . . and certainly had the looks for it: she was a tall brunette, with long legs, an extraordinary figure, very dark eyes, and a turned-up nose. She started me thinking seriously about going to Hollywood too, a lingering dream from my earliest moviegoing days in Florence.

Washington had been a wonderful respite after the Merry Fahrney episode, but I couldn't see myself hanging on forever as a sketching instructor at a fashion institute.

Actually, the Merry Fahrney episode wasn't quite over yet. She kept calling me in Washington, trying to convince me to return. I wasn't about to do that, but I finally agreed to meet with her in New York to discuss what was to be done about the marriage.

I traveled there with Tommy Krock, the son of the *New York Times* Washington correspondent. I didn't want to be alone. We stopped by Fahrney's apartment in late afternoon, and she said that a room had been arranged for me at the Lowell Hotel. "I know you wouldn't want to stay *here*," she added, "even though I'm still hoping for a reconciliation. In fact, I'm sailing for Europe and I hoped perhaps to convince you to come along."

"Well, I don't see much chance of that," I said. "But I would like to talk with you, to come to some resolution about this marriage."

"Very well," she said, and suggested that I meet her for dinner.

She was at her most charming that night. It was, in fact, one of the few quiet evenings we ever spent together. She asked me to go to Europe with her; I said no. I told her that I didn't think it would work out between us, and that the best course of action would be a divorce.

"All right," she said, "but I must insist on a New York divorce."

I was very much opposed to this. In those days, a New York divorce required proof of brutality or moral turpitude. I was not yet an American citizen, and a charge of moral turpitude might get me deported. "I'll give you a New York divorce only after I become a citizen," I said.

"Oh, absolutely not," she replied. If it was to be over, she wanted it to be over immediately.

I suggested a Reno divorce then, and she seemed to agree. "Well, if that's the way it has to be . . . I'm sorry it didn't work out."

She was quite nice, very friendly throughout. I found myself forgiving her for all the abuse, for throwing the pennies at me, although I was not so smitten that I'd want to try living with her again. I said to her, "You're a good sport. It's really civilized that we can talk like this and be friends again, even if we'll no longer be married."

Toward the end of dinner, my friend Krock arrived and she was polite to him as well. Finally, she said, "Excuse me, but I must go home and pack for Europe. Why don't you stay here and have a few drinks. I must be on my way."

I was in a relaxed mood by then. Everything was working perfectly. I'd get my divorce with a minimum of anguish. Krock and I ordered brandies, and as we were talking, a beautiful girl walked in, sat down, ordered a drink, and asked the maitre d', "Has Mr. Jameson called?" The answer was negative, and she seemed perturbed. Krock kept looking toward the girl, and said, "Why don't we ask her for a drink?"

The maitre d' returned then and told the girl that a call *had* been received: the gentleman's plane was delayed and he wouldn't be arriving. She appeared upset, so we did the chivalrous thing and asked her to join us. We had several drinks together there and a few more back at the hotel. I was thinking about the divorce and Peggy Townsend and Hollywood, and was not much in the mood for a casual liaison; anyway, Krock seemed far more interested in the girl. I decided to call it a night, returned to my room, and went to sleep.

I woke up suddenly about an hour and a half later, sensing there was someone in the room. There was: the girl from the restaurant. She was in a negligee, getting into my bed . . . and the door was open, and there were flashbulbs, and Merry Fahrney was there with her first husband, Pickering, and several other people.

"What are you doing?" I said, pulling Fahrney aside. "We agreed to a divorce. Why are you doing this?"

"I'm going to get rid of you," she said. "I'm sending you back where you came from. I'll smear you across the front page of every newspaper in the country, you rotten . . ."

This was simply incredible. I'd been such a sucker. She had prepared it all, getting adjoining rooms at the hotel, connected by an interior door. I'd made the situation more difficult by not inviting the girl in, but she'd taken care of that easily enough. She had me; it was, I must admit, a brilliant frame-up.

Well, I was a mess. I didn't know what to do. All my plans had to be delayed until this matter was handled—and delayed they were, for almost a year. The incident in the hotel room occurred on July 19, 1939; the divorce trial didn't begin until late January 1940. I was intent on fighting it all the way: I would do everything necessary to avoid a charge of adultery (moral turpitude). Krock suggested a lawyer, who demanded hundreds of dollars for a retainer, and then did just about nothing to help me.

Actually, I nearly managed to break the case wide open that summer. I went to Saratoga for the thoroughbred racing in August with some friends. One night, Eddie Ely, a tall Egyptian who was a good friend of mine, and I were in a club when I saw her: the girl who'd set me up. She was dancing with a guy, and when they sat down, Eddie and I approached.

"Remember me?" I said.

She was shocked. Her date said something like, "Hey buddy, what do you want?"

"Keep your mouth shut," I said to him, quietly, firmly. "This young lady is in deep trouble. If you want to be in deep trouble too, keep talking."

He looked at the girl, then at Eddie, who was doing his best to seem enormous, and hopped up from the table with the nimble terror of an obviously married man, and scrammed.

"Look," I said to her, "you've ruined me. If you have any decency, you'll agree to sign a paper admitting that this was a frame-up."

She nodded. "This *has* been bothering me," she said. "I'll do what you want. I'll go to New York and meet with your attorneys and sign an affidavit."

"Right now?"

"All right," she said, "but first I'd like to go to my room and change my clothes."

Eddie and I went with her there and waited outside the room. We waited ten, fifteen minutes; a half-hour. We banged on the door, and of course she was gone, out the bathroom window.

The trial approached. I feared deportation. I was willing to do anything to defend myself—and readily accepted the offer of Merry Fahrney's disaffected Filipino butler, Fidel "Luke" Lukhan, to testify that he'd seen her *en flagrante* with six other men during the time we were allegedly married, including Hugh Pickering, Lowell Birrell, and Sonny Griswold, whom the tabloids would describe as tousle-haired (and who, as I mentioned, charged his wardrobe to Merry Fahrney).

The tabloids had a great deal of fun with the trial. It was the biggest society news in New York in early February 1940. This was nothing new for Merry Fahrney, who would continue to have her name dragged through the mud for the rest of her unhappy life (I was number four of nine husbands, who later included a Nazi sympathizer and a Swedish waiter). It was, however, a most humiliating experience for me, one that would haunt me and be used against me for years. The case was heard in a day; my attorneys refused to allow me to say a word, to my dismay. The judge, Aaron Levy, gave his decree a week later. I figured that my Filipino would neutralize her frame-up. He didn't. The judge ruled in Merry Fahrney's favor: "Whether the marriage [was] a provident one, or what inspired it, is utterly beside the point at this time. . . . It would prove equally futile at the moment to consider whether cultured and well-bred American womanhood should join in marital status with titled persons from abroad. . . . What is of moment is the charge that the defendant misconducted himself at the hotel of his abode. The evidence fully sustains this."

Judge Levy, whose xenophobia should be quite apparent from the quotation above, went on to describe my countercharges as "unworthy of belief."

Perhaps, but why did no one—my lawyer, for example, I now realize—inquire of Miss Fahrney how she happened to be looking in the keyhole of my room at the Lowell Hotel?

At the time, I wondered if Judge Levy's rather odd behavior had its roots in something more venal than a simple distrust of foreigners: to put it bluntly, there were rumors that the judge was on the take; that he'd been paid off by Merry Fahrney. There was nothing that could be done about it; they were just rumors. However, in November 1952 Judge Aaron Levy was called before the New York State Crime Commission to explain the rampant patronage on his staff, including jobs that were provided for ten friends of his son-in-law and a member of his household staff who was, according to the *New York Times*, "unequipped for such legal duties." More to the point, Judge Levy was asked to explain the source of $80,561 found in his accounts at that time. He couldn't, and resigned in disgrace from the bench soon after. When I got the news, I cried bitter tears. I had waited so long to be exonerated.

In retrospect, it seems clear that I was railroaded by an unscrupulous woman and a crooked judge. No one believed my innocence. My public reputation had been severely damaged; I had been made to seem foolish, trivial. The headline in the *Daily News* said it all: "Court Rids Merry of Naughty Count."

Miss Fahrney, by the way, was quoted as saying: "I'm sick and tired of being called a madcap. I'm really a very sensible person."

And I was a naughty count, an "international itinerant," according to another paper. It was an absolute nightmare (though not my worst scenario: I was not deported). Mother had accompanied me to the Foley

Square courthouse; she stood by me, as always, but I had let the family down. I had made the Cassinis seem foolish. And there was no forgiving that. I certainly never forgave Merry Fahrney.

Her life went downhill precipitously in the years that followed our divorce. She died miserable, and anonymous, and alone in Houston, Texas.

CHAPTER
4

My life had been delayed long enough by this embarrassing divorce; I was eager to get on with it, to try my hand in Hollywood. I intended to leave immediately by car, but Mother insisted that I not go alone. Who knew what dangers would be lurking—cowboys, Indians, rattlesnakes—in the Wild West? She wanted Father to accompany me.

He didn't like the idea at all. His spirit of adventure had withered, and he had no interest in traversing the continent in a third-hand Ford. But Mother didn't waver, and we were helpless to protest. We said goodbye in the traditional Russian manner: a moment of silence, with everyone holding hands, concentrating on a happy voyage.

My goal was to get to California as quickly as possible. I wanted to hook up with Igor, who was honeymooning in Los Angeles with his wife (Igor had married Bootsie McDonnell in April 1940, and the wedding/work trip had been a gift from Cissy Patterson); Igor would be in touch with people who might be helpful to me—after New York, I figured I'd need all the help I could get.

So, immediately, in Virginia, the car broke down. We waited three hours for it to be fixed. I drove most of the night to make up the time. And then, in Tennessee, a major automotive problem: two and a half days waiting for repairs. And a third breakdown in the Rockies somewhere. Father was no help in all this; he was oblivious—to the country, the people, the scenery. At one point, we stopped for a meal at a little Mexican restaurant in Arizona.

"I will have fish," Father said.

"Do you think it's wise?" I asked. "We are in a Mexican restaurant in the middle of the desert. There's no fish here. Why not have some chili?"

He insisted on the fish . . . and was, of course, violently ill the rest of the trip, moaning in the back seat with a wet handkerchief covering his face. And thus, my arrival in dreamland: in a precarious old jalopy with Father sick to death in the back seat.

But we were in *Hollywood:* a magical place, filled with perfect-looking people. Los Angeles was still a small town then; the air was fresh and clean, and smelled of gardenias and orange blossoms, the weather remarkable, the traffic minimal, the flowers lush and fragrant . . . the girls beyond belief. They ambled along Sunset Boulevard as if it were a Seventh Avenue runway, displaying their wares with a somewhat studied abandon, hoping against hope to be discovered by some errant producer. This was the era of the apocryphal story about Lana Turner getting "noticed" while sitting at the counter in Schwab's drugstore, and the town was just awash with stunning specimens, winking and pooching their mouths, strutting and preening like a misplaced flock of flamingos in heat. They came from all over the country, all over the world. I had expected beautiful girls in Hollywood, but the number—there always seemed to be three for every man—and the sheer beauty were enough to make any red-blooded fellow light-headed.

Igor and Bootsie were staying in an apartment on Fountain Drive at a residential hotel called, appropriately, the Garden of Allah. It was done in Spanish Colonial style, which I thought quite marvelous, and had a swimming pool. Their honeymoon trip was almost over. They would soon be returning to Washington, but the apartment was leased for several weeks more, so Father and I were set for a while.

The very first evening, we went to a party at Ciro's, which was the West Coast equivalent of El Morocco (and about the only nightclub that was any good—Hollywood was too small and too hard-working to support more than one). The party that night was being given by Rex St. Cyr, who was very rich and something of a professional host, a male Elsa Maxwell, and Igor introduced us: "My brother is staying on here. I hope you'll add him to your list of friends."

St. Cyr nodded, and invited me to circulate, and in the next few hours I met several of the people who would start my Hollywood education. There was the actress Wendy Barrie, a very attractive girl (I did not know she was the girlfriend of the mobster Bugsy Siegel, or I would have been more circumspect). I also met Hal Roach, who owned one of the smaller studios, and his daughter, Maggie; and John Metaxas, a charming Greek fellow whom I'd met once in New York and who now appointed himself my adviser. "Don't waste your time on pretty girls here," he said. "They grow like grass. Concentrate on the *important* pretty girls—like Hal Roach's daughter—the ones who can help you."

Metaxas was married to a very attractive and wealthy woman, who proceeded to invite me for dinner with Maggie Roach at their house several days later. We had a pleasant meal, and then John and his wife feigned fatigue while I asked Maggie to come dancing with me at Ciro's.

This seemed a stroke of good fortune—my first Hollywood date. But I soon learned that dating in Hollywood was a bizarre, stylized ritual conducted mostly for the benefit of professional onlookers. It turned into a boring evening. My date kept waving at people she knew, who would then visit our banquette. She invited one and all to a big party she was giving, everyone except me. Surely, I thought, she would get around to me eventually, but the evening wore on—and then ended—and no invitation. I was flabbergasted by her bad manners, and wondered how I would get along if such was the custom of the place.

The meeting with her father at the Roach studios was little better. I was ushered into his large office, and he was very friendly at first, talking about Ciro's and St. Cyr and all, but I moved the conversation to the heart of the matter. "Mr. Roach, I am a designer," I said. I told him my background. "I'd like very much the opportunity to show you my work."

His attitude changed immediately. I could see it in his eyes: *Ah, here's another one who just wants work.* He said, "Well, we don't use many designers with the kind of pictures we make, Westerns and such. Although we will be looking for someone to do clothes for Carole Landis, whom we've just signed. I'll certainly get in touch with you about that," and he told his secretary, "Remind me to call Mr. Cassini."

I had managed to reach the age of twenty-eight without ever having heard the expression "Don't call us, we'll call you," and I actually expected him to call me. I spent the next several weeks waiting for the call. I waited in my room at first, yearning for the sun and the swimming pool. Father didn't mind staying inside all day—he hated the sun—but I couldn't trust him to answer the phone. The idea of responding in English (a language he barely acknowledged for many years) and taking down a phone number was just too much for him. But to remain inside all day was impossible for me, and so Father would yell down to me at the pool—"*Oleg!*"—whenever the phone rang, and I would rush up to find him holding the instrument at arm's length as if it were a small, rabid animal. Invariably the call would be for Igor or Bootsie, or a wrong number. My phone call never came.

I was growing depressed again. Was this going to be another disappointment? There didn't appear to be many design jobs in town. There were only four major studios: Paramount, Twentieth Century-Fox, MGM, and Warner Bros. The others—Columbia, RKO, Roach, and so on—were too frugal to be very clothes-conscious. Costumes were an afterthought in most movies, certainly in all "B" pictures. The clothes for most Westerns and pirate movies and so forth came straight from central wardrobe; only a very few, stylish films with big stars had clothing that really was *designed*. It seemed impossible to have a permanent position in this industry.

Father and I left the Garden of Allah after our two weeks had elapsed. We took up residence in a depressing little place near the Twentieth Century-Fox studios. I was beginning to wonder if Hollywood, this earthly paradise of beautiful women, was a mirage created by a vengeful god to punish me for my stupidity in the Merry Fahrney affair. It shimmered seductively, just beyond my grasp.

One day, though, Wendy Barrie invited me to join her at the West Side Tennis Club in Cheviot Hills, where she was a member. This was a popular hangout for movie people, and quite a pleasant place: you could see the rolling countryside all around (nowadays the area is an eruption of skyscrapers). I noticed Errol Flynn and Gilbert Roland on the courts that day; and you could often find top directors, actors, and agents playing there. Later, I would learn that real tennis status in Hollywood meant an invitation to the regular Sunday matches at Jack Warner's or one of the other private courts; those who hung out at the club, especially on weekdays, were unemployed—temporarily, perhaps—or underemployed young agents—like Ray Stark, a stocky, strong, ruddy blond fellow, who was a very energetic tennis player and had a great sense of humor. He was called "Rabbit" because he scurried about. We became fast friends, and when the time came, I asked him to be my agent. In later years, of course, he would become one of Hollywood's most powerful producers.

In any case, Wendy Barrie and I played mixed doubles that day. Once again, my skill was recognized and I was welcomed as an equal. In fact, I was invited to join the club—a *free* one-month trial membership, which I was happy to accept.

I played lots of tennis the next few weeks, but not much else happened. Father and I were flat broke. In fact, I was forced to do something that only the truly desperate contemplate in Los Angeles: I sold my car. I knew I couldn't survive for very long in Hollywood that way; it was like being lost in the desert without a camel. I needed action, and fast . . . and once again tennis came through for me.

It was the very day I sold the car, or perhaps the day after. I was asked to be part of a round-robin tournament at the West Side Tennis Club. It was the sort of event most good players shun like death. You have to play with real hackers and it's not good for your game. But I had nothing better to do, to say the least, and, halfheartedly, agreed to play. I was coupled with a gray-haired, distinguished-looking gentleman, a nice fellow and a fair weekend player. He turned out to be unobtrusive enough to allow me to get us into the finals, and then win the championship.

The gentleman had never had a victory like this before, and he was overwhelmed with gratitude. He invited me to have a drink at his home and meet his wife. I still knew nothing about him except his name. He wanted to know all about me, though, so I told him the family history, and how I'd come to Hollywood to be a designer, but jobs were scarce. I admitted the situation was becoming difficult.

"Oh, my," he said, "I wish I'd known this a couple of days ago. I'm an administrative manager over at Paramount, and we've been looking for a designer. We have Edith Head, but she can't do everything. Look, do you think you could put some sketches together by tomorrow for Fred Richardson, who's the head of wardrobe? He's testing some people for the job, using the script for a Claudette Colbert movie."

I called Ray Stark and said, "Could you drive me over to Paramount right now? I might have a shot at a job." It was late Sunday afternoon, but he was happy to do it. He was just starting as an agent; in fact, he didn't have any clients. He had gotten a foot in the door at the Sokolow Agency because he was married to the daughter of Fanny Brice and Nicky Arnstein; it was assumed that he had connections. As it happened, his enormous energy and enthusiasm made the need for "connections" superfluous. Later, after Gene Tierney and I married, Ray and Fran Stark would be among our closest friends. Fran was a very charming and funny woman who quite resembled her mother. Ray introduced me to his mother-in-law early in our friendship. Fanny Brice was one of the first people in Hollywood to really encourage me. "Stick with it," she said. "Don't worry. You're going to do very well here."

The job at Paramount would be my first real chance to prove her right. Ray and I dashed over to the studio and met with Richardson, even though it was Sunday afternoon. He was very kind, but said there were many people who'd already submitted their work and I'd have to have my presentation ready by ten the next morning. The job was to replace Omar Khayam, a very well-known designer. There were thirteen scenes that would require changes of clothes, thirteen sketches to be done that night. I thanked Mr. Richardson, borrowed some sketch pads from him because the stores were closed, then raced home, told Father to start making coffee, and went to work. I worked all night. By midnight I had completed only five sketches and was beginning to think I'd never make it. I was sure I'd read the script too hurriedly to have a real sense of the character, but I knew who Claudette Colbert was and I designed for her. It was a movie about fashion (never actually made) and the clothes were supposed to be glamorous, which was to my advantage. I worked all night, knowing that I was competing for a position—a full-fledged unit designer, not an assistant—that came along only once every few years. This was going to be *it* for me in Hollywood; I couldn't afford to wait until the next one came around. I worked, laced with caffeine, blurry-eyed, numb, half crazed, but also with a growing confidence that, at the very least, the thirteen sketches would be completed on time.

The last one was done at 9:00 A.M. Ray Stark picked them up and took them to Paramount. It was more impressive, we believed, to have the agent make the presentation (I was in no shape to talk coherently at that point, in any case). Despite my fatigue, I was too nervous to sleep. I sat there in a stupor, the caffeine racing through me. Father paced like a cat. He'd been up most of the night with me, making coffee, doing his best (and hoping, no doubt, that I'd get the job so he could go home). The phone rang at noon. It was Stark.

"You got it," he said. "Two hundred fifty a week. They want you to report right away."

What a magnificent day! The sun was shining, the birds singing . . . well, of course, every day was like that in Los Angeles, but it seemed the first time I could really appreciate it. Two hundred fifty dollars a week! A seven-year-option contract! It was a big day for Ray, too; he could go back to the agency and say, "I signed Oleg Cassini," whom no one had ever heard of, but no matter. It was a start for both of us—and we celebrated that day. We talked and laughed and dreamed about the future. I took positive action as well. Ray drove me to the local Mercury dealer, where I bought a *very* sporty convertible with wood paneling on the sides, a very "in" car in those days. Now, finally, I was ready to have some fun in Hollywood. I was ready to make up for lost time.

But first, work. This was no insignificant job. I was given a suite of offices, including a fitting room lined with mirrors and a reception area for my secretary. The first day, I was led on a tour of the studio's design resources. There were rooms filled with hundreds of thousands of dollars' worth of materials, and warehouses where costumes, everything from cowboy outfits to the togas used in Cecil B. De Mille's biblical epics, were kept. It was all very impressive. I was introduced to the redoubtable Edith Head, who in turn introduced me to all the seamstresses—a gesture of hospitality, it seemed, but really an opportunity to size me up.

"Your success will depend on your ability to impress the producers of our films with your sketches," Richardson told me. "Your problem is that Edith Head has been here since the year one and knows just what is required in most cases."

As it happened, Edith Head was one of the most talented politicians I've ever encountered. She was a short woman with a long nose, dark glasses, a Prince Valiant hairdo, black, black hair, a small, tight mouth, and clever little eyes. She was an uninspired but competent designer: her answer to every fashion question was the shirtwaist. It was her specialty, and her limit. On the other hand, she was a fabulous talker. She spoke a curious language, a cross between Hollywoodese and fashionese (I was learning that there were many languages in America, most of which were ways to say nothing while sounding expert). She could really sell her ideas to producers. "This will shoot very well, very rich . . . you can tell this girl is wealthy, but not ruthless. She has good taste. You can just *see* her polite Southern background, can't you?"

There was no way I could do that, and so I concentrated on learning the basics of designing clothes for films. My couture experience and strong sketching ability helped immeasurably here. The object was not merely to create a dress that would enhance the actress but to enhance the way she looked on camera, a much trickier proposition. Luckily, I'd always had an innate technical ability to analyze a woman at first glance, to understand how her body worked; I could sense, too, what *she* considered her strongest attributes. Actresses were more obsessed by this than other women, of course. They knew their best sides and angles, the ways they photographed most effectively. It was crucial that I understand these things immediately and communicate my knowledge; then the actress and I could become co-conspirators in a game of *trompe l'oeil*. To design for films was to create optical illusions.

For example, I served as sarong-maker for Dorothy Lamour on a film called *Aloma of the South Seas*. She was beautiful in a sultry way, and alluring, certainly, but the camera would treat her unkindly unless the designer helped to create a mild optical illusion. Miss Lamour was rather short-waisted, with hips that came up very high and angularly; by lowering her waist to give the appearance of a longer torso, by draping and using a softer fabric, I could emphasize her bustline, which was one of her more attractive features.

I designed not only the sarongs for *Aloma* but also the loincloths for Jon Hall and Phil Reed. This was one of my more embarrassing moments in Hollywood. Measurements had to be taken. I had an assistant do the actual work, while I averted my eyes and attempted to engage the actors in a discussion of manly things.

The most persistent problem a designer faced in Hollywood was a famous one: actresses photographed about ten pounds heavier than they actually were, and you always had to be conscious of trying to make them look thinner. There were several ways to achieve this effect. Working with Madeleine Carroll, who was quite elegant but appeared a bit chubby at times on camera, I used soft fabrics like velvet in dark shades on top, and then a tight, elasticized black matte waist for contrast, to create an exaggerated sense of slimness.

There were other technical tricks I had to learn. Most of the pictures were black-and-white in those days, and a little touch of white around the neck made the face photograph better. Also, one had to be aware that true white and black were taboo: cameramen would scream, especially over true black, which absorbed too much light, they said. The trouble was that dresses made of off-white and off-black often appeared muddy, indistinct. There was a tightrope to be walked.

The most important shots were the close-ups: clothes were most often seen from the waist up, and that's where you had to concentrate; an elegantly detailed skirt was almost superfluous. One person who took exception to this rule was Katharine Hepburn; she was shot full length more than any other major star of that era, because she insisted on it. Luckily, she had Adrian, the designer I admired most in Hollywood, working with her. He was perhaps the only member of our profession powerful enough to impose his taste on a director (Edith Head might have also been, but she was a politician first and chose to acquiesce).

Still, the most difficult part of the job *was* the politics, the vast number of people you had to please. The producer, the director, the star, the cameraman, the star's dresser and hairdresser (who always had something to say), the star's agent or boyfriend, the president of the studio—the list was endless. Most of these people had no fashion sense; least of all, the stars. A new dress would render them nervous, fluttery, looking to their hairdressers and retainers for some reaction, even after our conspiratorial relationship was established. Silence or, worse, a nasty crack could mean death for a designer. As a result, I was never more charming than on the set, especially with hairdressers.

The first major producer I managed to win over was Arthur Hornblow, who was a cultured man and didn't see me as some insidious foreigner. I had already designed the clothes for one film, a very slight college comedy, when he asked me to work on *I Wanted Wings*, an aeronautical big-budget mishap, noteworthy only for the debut of a young starlet named Veronica Lake, whose blonde peekaboo hairstyle created a sensation across the country. With all due modesty, I must admit: I created that look . . . and it happened quite by chance.

Hornblow already had introduced me to the female star of the film, Constance Moore, and I'd done some work with her. Now he wanted me to meet the second lead. I went to his office and found a short, rather mousy girl with an enormous bust. She had blonde, straight hair, tiny arms, and a tiny waist. She seemed scrawny except for the bust . . . and an oddly healthy blush to her. "Well, what do you think?" Hornblow said, as if he were showing me a new car. At which point the girl's blush became a flush and she raced to the bathroom, sick to her stomach.

I thought she was nervous, but the bust, the flush, and the sickness were all signs of a particular condition: Veronica Lake was pregnant.

She returned to the office, disheveled. Her hair was mussed, a strand hanging down in front of one eye. I thought, *This is interesting.* I played with it some. Eventually, we had her wear it very long and simple, which was the way debutantes were wearing it that year, a very classy look. I also dressed her in sweaters to emphasize the bustline and narrow waist.

I think Edith Head was worried about this. She had envisioned me as a designer for only "B" pictures; she called me the "junior designer," which was inaccurate. Her position certainly was secure, but she was always wary. She was afraid that I'd convince some of the more powerful stars at Paramount to have me design for them. She understood the sexual politics better than I; she figured I would use charm and intimacy to gain influence. But when I had lunch with someone like Madeleine Carroll, *work* was nowhere near the top of my agenda, and that is something Edith Head would never have understood. Though she was married, work was the only item on hers. She arrived at daybreak each morning and was the last one to leave at night.

I, on the other hand, was celebrating my first bit of good fortune. My career sometimes took a back seat to the pursuit of happiness even when work was as gratifying as playing Pygmalion to Veronica Lake.

I shared a small house on Cherokee Lane in Coldwater Canyon with the agent Bill Josephy. It was a period of unmitigated girl-chasing. Bill was a tennis player, and a good-looking fellow. We were always in competition over women. Not over the same girls, since there were more than enough to go around; no, it was more a question of who could show up with the better-looking date at Ciro's on Saturday night. My primary source for "horseflesh" (a derogatory term, I admit, but generic at the time) was the commissary at Paramount, where the starlets would parade about at lunch each day, hoping to catch a producer's eye. It must have been terrible to be a starlet: so beautiful, so close to the pot of gold and yet so far away, so demeaned, so "available" if the advertising department needed someone to entertain a visiting executive. Starlets were not considered very important by the studios; it was assumed that each was there for any boss who wanted her. And so, they would be more than happy when I'd invite them for an actual night on the town, to be seen at Ciro's on a Saturday night. I dated girls like Susan Hayward and Ellen Drew, who worked in "B" pictures during that time, but later went on to better things; I dated more than a few others who sadly never made it.

Josephy and I, along with several other agents, actors, and eligible young bucks, constituted the Hollywood "Wolf Pack." There was a group of us—Franchot Tone, John Barrymore, Pat De Cicco, occasionally Errol Flynn, Bruce Cabot, and I—who would frequent Earl Carroll's theater, where there was a Las Vegas-style floor show with some of the most beautiful girls in town, girls who were more than happy to go out with us after the show. We were constantly on the prowl; status came from the women you were seen with (in the real Hollywood, the Hollywood of the moguls and stars, the Hollywood I'd later become part of with Gene Tierney, the Wolf Pack was considered a sideshow). To be seen with an actual star was the *ne plus ultra*; stardom trumped beauty every time in the world of the Wolf Pack. I must admit I wasn't immune to this disease. I felt a real sense of accomplishment when I could read in the gossip columns: "Betty Grable and Oleg Cassini tripping the light fantastic at Ciro's . . ." It was music to my ears.

Actually, Betty Grable and I *did* trip the light fantastic at Ciro's, and it was a real coup. She was new in town, and hot as a pistol, having made quite a sensation in *Du Barry Was a Lady*. She was one of the three or four best dancers I've ever met, which was all we had in common, really. She loved to dance and so did I, and we did—very publicly, very obviously, very well—at Ciro's. Beyond that, she was a simple hamburger-and-milkshake type of girl, not very sophisticated but very sweet and very pretty.

This was a classic Hollywood romance: there wasn't much to it. We were seen together, and it was noted in the columns. For those on the Hollywood periphery, as I was at the time, the reality was: *I am mentioned, therefore I am*. It was entirely career-oriented, almost a business, and I had a good deal of success at it, because I wasn't at all shy about asking even the top stars out for an evening. You'd be amazed how many nights a beautiful star like Lana Turner spent at home waiting for the phone to ring. Sometimes, in desperation, they would demand that their agents take them out, and it would be: "Carole Landis [or whoever] seen dancing with Bill Josephy at Ciro's . . ." More often than not, though, romances would be fulminated by the studios—"Tyrone Power seen with Sonja Henie." And, more often than not, they were publicity ploys or smoke screens. It was truly amazing how little sex was involved in all these steamy romances; certainly there was none between Betty Grable and me, but there was a lot of ink.

Indeed, I was becoming better known as a man-about-town than as a designer. I was, in fact, profoundly *unknown* as a designer because of a mistake my agent had made: he had neglected to stipulate screen credit in my contract. I learned about this in the most mortifying way, at the premiere of my first film, a silly college picture. Betty Grable was my date that night, and I suppose I pumped the movie up a bit. In any case, the credits rolled and my name was not there. And I was mortified. Betty was embarrassed for me, but took it well. She was a pro. I had trouble sleeping that night. I tried to call Ray Stark, but couldn't find him. The next day, I immediately went to see Richardson at the studio. "Look," I said, "I went to see the picture last night and I didn't get any screen credit."

"You didn't ask for it," he said. "It's not in your contract."

So I called Stark and said, "You're supposed to be an agent . . ."

"I was so excited," he said, "I forgot."

There was nothing we could do about it. I fought and fought for credit on *I Wanted Wings*, but it was not forthcoming . . . and this, I think, was the beginning of the end for me at Paramount.

Everyone at Paramount, including Richardson, was feeling a bit antsy at the time because Henry Ginsburg had just been brought in as studio head. He was supposed to be a tough guy, a new broom who was going to sweep the place clean. And, in my inimitable moonstruck fashion, I immediately placed myself in the path of the whirlwind.

The conflict was over a girl named Pat Dane. She was a fiery brunette with beautiful eyes, dark hair, and very white skin. She was a terrific dancer, and swore like a grenadier—great fun. All the bachelors in town were after her. I managed to convince her to go out with me one afternoon when I was playing tennis at Arthur Lyons' house. He was Jack Benny's agent and very big at the time. I approached Pat Dane after the match, and she said, "I can't have dinner with you, but maybe we can get together after."

I was elated. I went to the address she gave me at the appointed time and rang the bell. No answer. I rang several times . . . and who should come to the door?

"Yes?" Henry Ginsburg inquired, quietly but imperiously.

"Is this number . . . well, no, I must have the wrong address," I stumbled, retreating.

"Yes, you must," he said. "But let me give you a word of advice, Cassini. For a man on his way up, you're entirely too much discussed and too much in the papers. I sometimes wonder how you can do all these things at night and still give us a good day's work at the studio."

"Energy, sir," I said. "Energy."

One of my very good friends at the time was the English actor Richard Greene, who starred in many movies and later played Robin Hood on television. He was dating a popular English actress named Virginia Field. One day at the West Side Tennis Club, he said to me, "Listen, old chap, I'm going back home and I think you and Virginia would hit it off quite well. Why don't you ring her up? You have my blessing."

So I called her. "Could I take you out to dinner tonight?" I asked. "Not to celebrate, but to regret our mutual friend's departure."

Actually, we celebrated quite a bit. We danced, drank champagne, and discussed the intricate rituals of the Greek Orthodox Church for many hours. I noticed she had a small sore on her face; two or three days later, I noticed a similar one on mine. It became larger. I shaved, and it became larger still; within a week, it looked like the left side of my face had been mangled by a wild animal. I went to the studio doctor, and he told me that it was impetigo: "Very contagious," he said, "but not dangerous. You have to keep it breathing, uncovered."

I couldn't do that and be "seen," though. I was still dating Grable, still dancing with her at Ciro's (my right cheek—my dancing side—was unaffected, luckily). I put on a bandage and told her I'd hurt my face in an auto accident. I thought this was working until I called her one day to find out where to pick her up for a date we'd arranged.

"You're not picking me up at all," she said.

"Why?"

"I don't want to discuss it with you. We're through."

"We're through? But this is the most ridiculous thing. Why are we through?"

"I don't want to discuss it. Good-bye," and she hung up.

I had no idea what was going on. I wasn't all that unhappy, but I was annoyed. I tried to call her two or three times, but she wouldn't even come to the phone. It wasn't until several years later that I found out what had happened. My friend the actor Victor Mature was at the bottom of it all.

He was up-and-coming at the time, looking for a date who could help him get some publicity. He was scheduled to do a picture with Grable and figured she was just the girl. He called her and said, "I must talk to you about something very serious. It could save your life."

She invited him over, and he told her: "You're going out with a man who is very sick. You've noticed the bandage on Oleg's face?" Grable nodded gravely. "*Syphilis*," Mature intoned. "His family has had it for years. It's the talk of Europe. Everyone knows the Cassinis have syphilis."

And that was that. The big oaf admitted this to me when we served together in the coast guard during the war. In any case, I wasn't particularly upset about the end of this "romance." Events were moving quickly. I was making lots of friends, especially among the continental set. I became friendly with a family of five Egyptian brothers, the Hakims, who produced films in Hollywood and all over the world. My favorite was Raymond Hakim, a big, handsome guy who had the same taste in women as I. We would go to the track together, to Santa Anita, with a third fellow, named Roger Valmy (everyone called him "Frenchie"), who was an excellent handicapper.

Santa Anita was a strange, wonderful place in those days; Damon Runyan might have imagined it. The crowd consisted—in equal parts, it seemed—of touts, hustlers, Hollywood people, sports figures, and the hoi polloi. I remember meeting the well-known welterweight boxer Jimmy McLarnen there, and having a series of conversations with him about diet.

Actually, diet was one of my favorite topics of conversation—not because I wanted to lose weight (I was always slim), but as a matter of philosophy, a concern about what I was investing in my body. I've made a lifetime study of other people's approach to the subject, and Jimmy McLarnen's was one of the most unique. Each day he would eat something different, but only that thing. He might eat meat—*all day*, exclusively. He might eat eggs or vegetables or carbohydrates or fish. He wouldn't mix, though, and he worked it on a seven-day cycle. He claimed you could lose ten pounds doing this in two weeks.

My own dietary habits were less strict, of course, but not all that different in philosophy from McLarnen's. I saw my stomach as a pocket, and would visualize the various foods mixing down there. I had a vague sense that certain combinations worked better than others. I'd never eaten much meat: the meat in Italy was poor quality to begin with, and quite expensive. I ate what I loved—pasta, fresh fruits and vegetables, some cheese, never any dessert. I ate in moderation, always remembering the dismay I felt watching my father indulge himself with his favorite heavy, creamy dishes. Later, various American doctors would make fortunes writing books that counseled the diet and exercise regimen of my Italian youth.

Robert and Raymond Hakim invited me for New Year's Eve at their house that year. "Bring the prettiest girl you can," Raymond said, "but I bet my date will be prettier."

In the meantime, I went to a dinner at the home of Constance Moore and Johnny Maschio in honor of Gene Tierney, who had just arrived in town, fresh from a big success on Broadway in *The Male Animal*. Darryl F. Zanuck had convinced her to sign a huge contract at Twentieth Century-Fox ($1700 a week), and everyone was talking about her. My date that night was a tall, rather spectacular-looking redhead from the Earl Carroll show who was not a brain surgeon.

I met Gene Tierney over cocktails. She was stunning. It is difficult to describe just how breathtaking she was. Photography never really did her justice. She had soft, golden skin; it seemed to glow. And her eyes: very light, green-blue, magical. The effect on me was visceral, magnetic. Gene was wearing a simple black dress with a string of pearls. She had shoulder-length brown hair that curled at the ends. There was not an angle in her face that was not perfect, although her teeth were slightly bucked—which only added to her allure, as far as I was concerned. Without that slight imperfection, she would have appeared unreal, so completely beautiful as to seem synthetic, and therefore uninteresting. She was about five foot seven, with broad shoulders, an elegant body, long limbs. Spectacular. She had that Connecticut finishing-school accent, reminiscent of Katharine Hepburn's . . . but she was younger than Hepburn and more beautiful.

I tried to pretend it was very, very casual. I didn't make a beeline toward her or try to force myself in any way. There were twenty-four for dinner—Veronica Lake was there with her husband, an art director at MGM—and I was seated far from Gene. We didn't really speak until afterward. She was sitting in a corner; I approached her there. I said to her, "I read somewhere that you went to school in Switzerland, at Brillanmont. I spent part of my childhood near there. I understand you speak French."

We spoke French. She was quite fluent. "I haven't spoken French in so long," she said, delighted. "How very nice it is to meet someone here who is civilized."

She told me how disappointed she was in Hollywood—no one talked about anything but the movies. I told her how I loved to take long walks alone on the beach, and how I'd missed—since Europe—talking about philosophy. I was doing fine.

The other men at the party were nonplussed, watching me in helpless awe as I stole a march on the catch of the day, in French.

At which point my date emerged from the kitchen with a beer in one hand and a banana in the other. I had forgotten about *her*, but played it cool. "Hello," I said. "Would you like another banana?"

"Where did you find her?" Gene asked, in French.

"Well, you know," I said, "she has a heart of gold."

We continued our conversation. When I began to sense that she was really becoming interested in me, I said good-bye. I knew she was going to be very important to me and I was already thinking strategically. I asked her phone number and she gave it. I did not tell her when I was going to call, only that I would. I left the party early, depositing my beer drinker along the way, walking on air. Gene would later say that her first impression of me was that I was the most dangerous-looking character she'd ever seen. In this case, looks did not deceive.

I waited several days, and called her just before New Year's Eve. We spoke in French again, a polite, vague conversation: how nice it was to meet her, how I hoped I would have the pleasure of becoming her friend, blah, blah, blah . . . I was letting the conversation languish, letting her think it was just a social call, letting her grow a little disappointed, and then I said, "Oh, by the way, I'd like you to do me a favor."

"Of course."

"I'd like you to come out with me tomorrow night, New Year's Eve. I can't imagine a better way to start the year."

"But you are calling so late," she said, having been caught off guard in just the way I'd hoped—breathlessly. "I already have a date. I don't really see how I could. I would love to, if I could. But I can't."

There is a wonderful English expression: "In for a penny, in for a pound." "Ah, but when there is a moment like this in life," I said, "one must have the courage to eliminate any obstacle. I do not mean to say that spending New Year's Eve with me would be the most important thing in *your* life, but it would be the most important thing in *mine*. It all depends on the nature of your feelings. If this means nothing to you, by all means go—keep your date. I will stay home. I will stare out the window," I said, laughing a little, playing with this. "But if you do have feelings for me, you must be prepared to be . . . original! There are moments in life when one must be strong, *cruel*, if need be, brazen, audacious . . ."

"You're really impossible," she said, laughing. "I'll see what I can do. Call me in two hours."

I did, on the dot. "Well, I think we will see each other tomorrow night," she said. "I told my date that something very serious had come up that I could not explain on the phone."

Very casually, I said, "How good of you. We'll have a lot of fun."

"Where are we going? How shall I dress?"

"We're going to a wonderful party," I said. "Black Tie."

I was in seventh heaven! Delighted! Gene was the sort of girl I might have met back East or, before that, in Rome. I was flattered that she had picked me out, that, unlike so many of the frantic strivers and deal makers in Hollywood, she knew the more polite world of European society and recognized that I was a displaced part of it. I sensed from the start that she understood me; this boosted my confidence enormously. Anyway, I spent hours preparing myself for our date the next day. Everything would be just right—my shoes shined to a turn, my black tie crisply knotted. I would be perfect for her.

She was not perfect for me. She was wearing a rather remarkable ensemble of her own design, voluminous folds of gray chiffon that managed to camouflage her beauty entirely. I said to her, "Now, we're going to start everything right. The most important thing is not to lie to each other. I don't like your dress. I want you to go change."

"*Why?*"

"Too fussy. You're so beautiful. Anything superfluous detracts from it."

She wasn't too happy about it, but she went and changed, and we proceeded on to Hakim's house, which was a splendid Spanish Colonial mansion on Sunset, a very impressive place to take her, and she was thrilled. As we approached the door, she had that dazzling smile, that classic smile she never lost. And then, as Raymond opened the door, the smile froze and immediately I sensed what had happened.

The date she'd broken had been with Raymond Hakim.

In that instant at the door, I remembered talking to him earlier that day, telling him I'd have quite a surprise for him that night. And his telling me that his date hadn't felt very well, but he'd been lucky enough to make a last-minute date with Ellen Drew. "Oh, I know her from Paramount," I'd said. "She's lovely."

Now, at Hakim's door, I wondered why I hadn't put two and two together and realized that we were faced with a potential disaster. It must have been a terrible blow to him. I don't know how I would have responded. But certainly not in my wildest imaginings could I have come up with a response as suave as his. He was magnificent. Very cool. He merely smiled wickedly and said to Gene, "Oh, how wonderful that you could come after all. You must be feeling better."

He nodded to me, as if I'd merely escorted Gene to the party for him, and took her by the arm, making a grand entrance with her, so it would seem clear to everyone assembled—it was dinner for one hundred—that she was his date.

He sat Ellen Drew next to me at the table. I thought she was a charming girl, and under other circumstances I would have been delighted, but I was annoyed. I'd been outfoxed. For a time, I was so furious that I could barely speak. But then I began to pull myself together. I said to myself: *I have to beat this man. He's been so shrewd. This is going to be a long battle; it won't be decided over dinner. So back to the drawing board, and make sure it ends well.*

And, from across the table, I began to get some understanding looks from Gene, sitting next to Hakim, as if to say, *How did we get ourselves mixed up in this?* Gradually, I regained my assurance, and flirted outrageously with Ellen Drew because I could not show myself to be upset or peeved—that would be too great a victory for Hakim. I was determined not to come in second best in this contest. So I played my role, and people thought I was madly in love with Ellen Drew. However, I was preparing to strike. I would have my revenge.

After dinner, I approached Gene and said, "In twenty minutes, pretend you are going upstairs to the ladies' room, then take the back staircase and meet me outside."

"Can we do that?" she asked. "It's so impolite."

"Trust me," I said.

Hakim didn't make things easy. He buzzed around us like a mosquito . . . but the plan worked perfectly. We went to Ciro's, and something indescribable happened to us there, on the dance floor. Something magical. It was what I'd dreamed about all my life: a *coup de foudre,* a bolt of lightning. She was radiant, just glowing, the most marvelous girl imaginable, the fairy-tale love; and we floated, surrounded by magnificent people in beautiful clothes. I wanted the moment to last forever. I was intoxicated with her; she didn't seem to be having a bad time, either.

But my battle with Hakim was not yet over. He soon arrived at Ciro's, still smiling, still smooth, with Ellen Drew, and he said, "Well, it was so clever of you to come ahead and reserve a table for us." And then he proceeded to dance with Gene.

It was just a gesture, though. Hakim sensed what I knew: I had won, and won big. After a while, I said to Gene, "Let's go for a drive and talk."

We went for a drive, which ended at my little house on Cherokee Lane, which she thought was charming. Without saying very much, we both knew that something very serious was happening between us. Later, we went to a club that was open all night, and danced until 9:00 A.M. Then we had breakfast, still in our evening clothes, and talked.

Somewhere in there, perhaps over breakfast, we decided to elope. I had fallen for her completely. It might have been the only time in my life that I allowed myself to be so overwhelmed, to surrender unconditionally. She was so beautiful; I had lost control and succumbed to a pure romantic impulse. Gene seemed as infatuated as I . . . but then, she was only nineteen. Still, this was more than just youthful folly. There was—*even then,* at the very beginning—an unspoken understanding between us that would ripen into love over time.

I suppose she saw me as a sophisticated older man, a man of the world who might protect her in the jungle of Hollywood. So much of love is intuition. That morning, we allowed ourselves to believe that this was *it* for us.

We told each other our life stories over breakfast. I told her what my family represented, what I was—both the good and the bad. By the end of breakfast, she knew about the family "fortune" and about Merry Fahrney. By the end of breakfast, too, I knew that we had to elope or I'd be facing another Donnina Toeplitz situation. Her family seemed too strong, and she respected them too much. Her father was a powerful fellow, the president of an insurance company in New York, who controlled her finances through a corporation called Belle-Tier; her mother, Belle Tierney, was chaperoning her in Hollywood. They lived together in a little house on Doheny Drive. Her sister was the "prettiest," her brother the "sharpest," her father the "most clever businessman." She was just a good kid who loved her family.

"How do you think they'll react to me?" I asked.

"I don't think there's anything they *couldn't* like—except perhaps the question of money. But you're a working man. They'll respect that."

But I knew better. What would *I* do if I were the father of this girl who had the potential to be the hottest property in Hollywood? What would I do if she told me she was going to marry the "naughty count" who, less than a year earlier, had been involved in New York's messiest divorce? I had a very strong sense that if I didn't get her to the altar immediately, I would lose her to the family.

"What I want to do," I told her, "is just go home, change your clothes, give some excuse to your mother, and we'll go to the airport."

I dropped her at her place at 10:30 A.M., picked her up an hour later down the block, out of sight, and we drove to the airport. I had chartered a plane with the help of Bill Josephy, whom I'd awakened from a stupor. I said, "Wake up, you're going to be the best man at a great marriage." When I told him who it was, he almost fainted.

"Jesus," he said. "You work fast."

It was like winning the Irish Sweepstakes. It was better than that. We were in love.

119

We went to the airport New Year's Day, 1941. Rain had been predicted, and by the time we got there, it was falling heavily. We waited, but the rain grew worse and I began to fret. The fatigue was beginning to tell on both of us. Gene was cold, shivering. The memory of our beautiful night together was beginning to fade; elopement was seeming more and more precipitous to her. She said, "Don't you think we should at least talk to Mother?"

"Absolutely not," I said, struggling to control my temper. I had a gathering sense, a dread, that it was over. Finally, we were told the plane could not take off, and I drove her home in silence. It was a terrible anticlimax. She was smiling at me, but it was different now. It was over, I thought. We had become strangers. My pride, which has always been a terrible factor in my life, took over. I said nothing. I drove her home.

Once there she said, "But it need not end this way. Let me talk it over with my family. They'll love you when they get to know you."

"No," I said, "I'll not go through anything like this. I refuse to have to explain myself to them, to explain the divorce and everything else. I will not go through it. So, if you want to see me again, if you believe in your feelings and instincts, call me. I will not call you."

I was exhausted, true, but there is no rational explanation for my behavior at that moment.

I was determined not to call her, and didn't. I sat by the phone, waiting for her to call me. It would have been much easier to pick up the phone and take control of the situation once more, but my pride still held sway. Eventually, she called me after a few days. We had lunch together, and she said the marriage had to be cleared by her family. "They've done so much for me; it's the least I can do."

I agreed to meet her mother, who had once been very beautiful and suffered from the persistent narcissism of the formerly attractive. She talked a great deal about herself; even when she complimented Gene, it was self-referential. "Some say," she said, laughing gaily, "the mother is even prettier than the daughter." I did not like this lady, and the feeling was mutual. She was working against me throughout, calling me a phony and unattractive. "Good-looking men fall for you left and right," she told Gene at one point. "Why are you so insistent on *him*?"

It seemed certain then that we had missed the boat. Gene was not entirely swayed by her mother, but enough doubts had been planted to make our romance less viable. We still saw each other, but they were Hollywood dates—big smiles for the camera. Rex St. Cyr gave a costume ball at Ciro's, and we went as a cossack and a Russian peasant girl. When we were together, all was well. We talked; there were flutters of that initial magic. But there was so much working against us—not just her family, but the studio as well. If Gene Tierney were to be married, Twentieth Century-Fox wanted a stardust romance with a bankable name, not some little-known continental designer. The publicity department fed her a steady stream of show-biz dates so that her name could appear in the columns: "Gene Tierney dancing the night away with Mickey Rooney . . ."

My name was appearing in the columns, too, but for the first time I was being attacked. Miss Hedda Hopper, who would have a great deal to say about me in the months to come, fired her opening salvo: I had designed clothes for Mussolini's daughter. And? So? The reasoning went something like this: "With all the talent we have here, why do we need a foreign designer, particularly one who was close to Edda Mussolini Ciano?"

The war was heating up then. America was being nudged toward belligerence, and I had mixed feelings. I had no love of fascism, especially of the German variety, but I did have a great many Italian friends who'd be fighting on the other side, and I had no great desire to forge an alliance with the Communists, who had stolen my family's destiny. It was during this time, I think, that I was involved in a very embarrassing scene in the Brown Derby—with one of the lesser Hakim brothers, Rafael, who claimed to be a black belt in judo. We were having lunch there, a regular event, with Peter Lorre, Jean Negulesco, and Gilbert Roland. I spotted an Italian friend and began to converse—in Italian—when Hakim rose to challenge me. "We don't want alien talk here," he said very loudly. The room fell silent. "I forbid you to speak in Italian."

"You idiot," I said. "Since when have languages had anything to do with wars?"

"Don't fool with me," he said, "because I'll give you a lesson here, in front of everyone."

"No one has ever succeeded in *giving me a lesson*," I said, "and you won't, either—judo or not. I'll continue to speak Italian as I please."

He backed down then, but the damage was done. I was identified as an Italian in the minds of many people in Hollywood, a vaguely suspicious allegiance in that overheated atmosphere. Meanwhile, Gene and I had stopped seeing each other. It wasn't a formal break, but the studio seemed intent on keeping her busy most nights with publicity dates. She was filming *Hudson's Bay*, with Paul Muni and John Sutton, during the day. Then, in March, I read that she had become engaged to Robert Sterling, a handsome young actor whom MGM was trying to promote. And so it was over. Just another Hollywood romance, I assumed. She was just another actress, momentarily playing a role: the young actress in love with a "dangerous foreigner." I'd been silly, I was certain, especially when I read that she was traveling East to ask her father's permission to marry Sterling.

The disappointment was allayed somewhat by the fact that I began to have a romance with one of the great beauties of Hollywood, Lady Sylvia Ashley, the widow of Douglas Fairbanks, who'd been in mourning for a year and was just then returning to the social world. She was a classic tall blonde Englishwoman who viewed the Hollywood parade with amused detachment; we pretended to be tourists together in that curious venue.

Sylvia Ashley constantly impressed me with her sophistication, and an almost exotic ability to make a man feel extremely important. At dinner parties, for example, she would cut, then roll and light my cigars; indeed, she provided them herself in an elegant leather case. I could see, from the way people looked at us as she made these stylish preparations, that they were fascinated by our relationship, the sensuous elegance that was so clearly implied.

At one dinner with Lady Ashley, I met Charlie Feldman, the head of Famous Artists, one of the biggest agencies in town, and his beautiful wife, Jean. I remember sitting there, talking with Lady Ashley and Jean Feldman, and thinking, *This is more like it.* Mrs. Feldman, in particular, was being very supportive. Her encouragement was welcome. I felt my stock rising.

And then, in May, Gene called. She called from New York, and sounded different, uncertain. Her faith in her father was shaken (I later learned that she'd discovered he was having an affair with his wife's best friend; he and Mrs. Tierney would soon divorce). This was something; Gene's father had always been the miracle man. He handled all her finances; she'd always maintained that he was making a fortune for her through the Belle-Tier Corporation. But she was seeing only a fraction of her salary; the rest was in his hands, and now that her faith was shaken, the entire apparatus began to tremble. Soon, Howard Tierney's world would come tumbling down.

And what about Bob Sterling? "It was so silly," she said. "I realized on the train that I love you. He was really just a child. I told him that I didn't think I could marry him, and he had tears in his eyes. A child!" she said, all of nineteen herself. "I *must* see you."

This was thrilling, because I didn't realize she still cared about me that much. "I'll tell you what," I said. "Come back here and we'll see. I make no promises, but we will talk about it and see if there is anything to be salvaged from this. I'm not sure. Let's talk about it."

She returned soon after, but I did not meet her at the airport. I waited until she had arrived home . . . and waited a bit more, then phoned and made arrangements for dinner. I was very formal. I was very stern.

"Can't we get back to the way things were?" she asked.

"Hmmph," I said. "I do not want to be disappointed or toyed with again. If time is required, it will be because I wish to take *my* time. If we are to resume, you must agree to certain things. You must not date anyone else, not even studio publicity dates. You must respect my wishes. If I wish to meet your parents, it will be done when I'm ready to do so." And on and on I went, laying out contractual terms. Apparently, though, she found this rather dictatorial form of courtship appealing, because we took up again, and this time for keeps.

As we got to know each other, my role changed. I became her protector and, to a certain extent, her nurse.

Gene was under enormous pressure. She looked and acted calmer than she actually was. The disintegration of her family, the pressure of work, the pressure of being a *star* at so young an age—all these took their toll. I don't think I sensed then the problems that would lead to her eventual nervous collapse. She just seemed very moody, and unsure of herself—but so was I. It was something we had in common.

Gene was shooting the movie *Belle Starr* that spring and had developed a strange malady, a condition called angioneurotic edema, that was thought to be some sort of allergy. Her eyes would swell up for no apparent reason; they would become red, puffy slits. Obviously she couldn't work looking like that. Batteries of allergists were called in. One gave her a shot of Adrenalin; another told Darryl Zanuck that it was a chronic condition, she would have it for life. There was talk of finding someone else for the picture. There was talk of canceling her contract. I tried to soothe her, and then I tried something else.

I sensed a deficiency in Gene's diet, possibly a food allergy. I believed her body was filled with poisons; the chemicals were interacting badly. I suggested a more rational diet, more fresh fruits and vegetables. I don't know if it was my nutritional advice or the constant support—I told her she looked beautiful even when her eyes resembled raw hamburger—but the condition disappeared in six days, and the film was completed.

And we began to whisper once more, over candlelight dinners in small, out-of-the-way restaurants, about getting married. Gene understood now that she could depend on me. I had helped her through a difficult time. Our emotional attachment had deepened in the process; it seemed clear that the surge of feelings we had experienced on New Year's Eve had been more than just momentary infatuation. Gene also saw, very clearly now, that her parents would never approve. And so we planned our elopement. The actual logistics weren't very difficult. Gene would tell her mother that she was going to the studio for a fitting; we would fly to Las Vegas instead. "I'll get Bentley to arrange for a justice of the peace," she said, referring to her attorney, Bentley Ryan. This was a mistake, but not a fatal one.

We eloped, finally, on June 1, 1941. The first part of our deception worked perfectly. We flew to Las Vegas, traveling incognito: I was Oleg Loiewski and she was Belle Starr. I don't know if it was the emotion, or tension, or what, but I became terribly airsick on the plane. I tried to hide it from Gene, but I must have looked like a lemon.

Meanwhile, both our studios, tipped off by Bentley Ryan, were making frantic efforts to find us. Paramount had sent a wire to my house, calling me in; when I arrived home the next day, I responded and found out that I'd been fired. I am certain that the elopement had something to do with this, although the official reason was my devotion to nightlife above and beyond the call of duty. No doubt Darryl Zanuck, at Twentieth Century-Fox, had requested my head from Henry Ginsburg; star-stealing was a capital offense in those days and the studio heads, always friendly competitors, kept in touch. After our late-night meeting at Pat Dane's house, Mr. Ginsburg was probably more than happy to oblige.

Twentieth Century-Fox was far more frantic than Paramount, of course. The studio was dead set against us: the idea of glamorous Gene Tierney marrying a foreign designer of ladies' clothing was just too complicated to sell the public. The Tierneys, whom Ryan had also tipped, weren't very happy either, especially Howard Tierney. If Gene were married, Belle-Tier's contract with the studio would be null and void (since she would no longer be a minor); a new arrangement would have to be negotiated, and he had good reason to fear that she would ask for the corporation to be terminated. In any case, all these people were trying to call the justice of the peace in Las Vegas, where we were to be married, but Gene—dear girl—insisted that the judge not answer the telephone until the service was completed. It rang throughout. Harry Brand, the chief of publicity at Twentieth Century-Fox, was very persistent. When the judge finally answered and handed Gene the phone, Brand said, "Gene, you can't do this."

"Harry," she said, "I've already done it."

"Well, in that case," he said, "don't move. I'll fly right out. We'll have champagne and a wedding cake at the Apache Hotel."

And reporters and photographers as well. Even an elopement could be milked for all it was worth.

In the first few hours after the ceremony, we called our parents. Mother was happy, but cautious. Gene's mother was unequivocal. When told that I was her new son-in-law, she said, "You can keep him," and hung up.

All things considered, Howard Tierney's reaction was the most interesting. "Well, you must be quite a man," he said to me. "I'm sure that anyone my daughter loves will be just fine with me. I'm looking forward to meeting you. . . . Oh, and by the way, I'll be sending you some documents to sign. Nothing crucial, just some agreements making you part of the Belle-Tier Corporation. It's for Gene's protection and her future—and yours, too, now that you're part of the family. But, more important, you have my blessing. I hope you will be happy together."

I was so surprised by his reasonable attitude that I almost—almost —was willing to take him at his word. By the very next day, though, I knew better.

On the following day, Mr. Tierney was quoted *on the front page* of the New York *Journal-American*: "I think Gene has gone Hollywood. . . . It's unfortunate she married a man of this fellow's notoriety."

And Mrs. Tierney: "Gene is just a misguided child. . . . She has been carried away by this suave man of the world."

That was the opening salvo, and rather mild compared with what followed. The campaign against the marriage was relentless in the next few weeks, building in intensity, growing less principled by the day. There were constant phone calls to Gene from friends, family members, distant relations. Why had she done this? Was she having second thoughts? It wasn't too late to get out. An annulment was possible . . . .

Gene handled the intrusions well; she was used to that sort of pressure. In those first days, she was intent on making my little house on Cherokee Lane (Josephy had moved out) into a honeymoon cottage. She was a fanatic and a talented decorator and would remain so throughout our marriage, painting, plastering, repairing furniture, hanging drapes. She was an antic putterer, and felt nervous when she wasn't *accomplishing* something. The first day, she went around the house organizing things like a mess sergeant. My mother had come out from Washington to meet my new wife, and she was impressed. "I see I'm not going to have to worry about you anymore," she said. "Finally you've got someone who's going to take care of things around here."

And *her* mother showed up that day as well, and found Gene already at work, paintbrush in hand. Belle Tierney was polite, in a clenched sort of way, and said that if Gene really was insistent on being married, perhaps she could do it properly. Her father wanted to talk to her about it. He wanted to meet her halfway, in Chicago.

Both Gene and I smelled a rat. Why not speak by phone? Why Chicago? I suspected an abduction and annulment were in the works, and Gene was inclined to agree. In any case, she didn't have time to go. She had to shoot the last few scenes for *Belle Starr* and then head off to the Arizona desert for *Sundown*, with George Sanders and Bruce Cabot. In a matter of hours, it seemed, she was gone, and I was left with the telephone, which seemed to carry only bad news. I would call her each night in Arizona, and often Bruce Cabot would answer the phone on the set and say, "Worried already, heh-heh?" Heh-heh.

Her brother, Butch, called one night. He was in California on business, or so he said. "You know, I'm inclined to really teach you a lesson," he said. He suggested we meet at a gymnasium for a gentlemanly sparring session.

"The hell with the gloves and the gym, Butch," I said. "C'mon over here. We'll do it in the street."

Young Tierney, surprised by my enthusiastic response, begged off. But I was feeling angry and frustrated, ready for a fight. My whole life suddenly seemed a shambles: I had no job, my wife was off in the desert making a movie, and a real smear campaign was being mounted against me, orchestrated, I suspected, by the Tierneys. The rumor mills, as they say, worked overtime; the gossip was brutal, sleazy beyond words:

What did he have, this "pale . . . Russian dress designer" (as I was described in the *Journal-American* and, no doubt, the other Hearst newspapers), to sweep such a sweet young thing, a society girl from Connecticut, off her feet? Was he some sort of Svengali? Was it another case of a debutante being taken for a ride by a titled foreigner? What was I after? The money? (What money? Gene was a young star at that point, making a weekly salary; and the day before we eloped, I insisted on signing a pledge renouncing a "community-property" settlement if we were ever divorced.)

The speculation seemed endless. Within weeks, the Hearst writer Adela Rogers St. Johns did a long profile of me—for which I wasn't interviewed—and rehashed the Merry Fahrney affair in great detail.

But what was it, really? What was the cause of these attacks against me?

I believe it was a question of power. Twentieth Century-Fox had a nice, docile, malleable, and potentially enormous young star in Gene Tierney; it had a successful business relationship with Belle-Tier. That relationship had been dissolved by our marriage. The contract was null and void. I was not only a publicity disaster—why couldn't she marry someone more obvious and American, like Tyrone Power?—I was a danger. No doubt they feared that I would become a professional husband (a fairly common Hollywood phenomenon in those days, and since) with nothing better to do than cause problems for them. The studio was worried, and worked furiously to break up the marriage. "Nineteen-Year-Old Seduced by Man of World" was a plausible cautionary tale to sell the American public. The strategy was to discredit me in Gene's eyes. A concerted effort was made to prevent me from finding work as a designer.

This was confirmed years later by none other than Darryl Zanuck. We had become good friends, and were having dinner at the Bistro Righi in Paris with Juliette Greco, and he said to me, "Oleg, it was nothing personal. Gene was an important property. We could have given you work, but that would have made your life easier. We decided to boycott you in the hope that if we made the marriage more difficult, Gene would lose interest in you."

It is a cliché that Hollywood was a small town in those days, but it is true. Zanuck was in touch with my old friend Ginsburg at Paramount, and Jack Warner, Louis B. Mayer, and Harry Cohn as well. The message was clear: if Gene Tierney's own studio didn't want her husband hired, then nobody else should, either. Working hand in glove, they gave me a very tough year. But I survived, and so did the marriage, and when it became apparent that neither Cassini nor the marriage was going away, the boycott was lifted.

My troubles, and the studio's, were nothing compared with those of Howard Tierney, though, and this is why: He had ransacked Belle-Tier. It had no assets. His insurance business had foundered, and he'd spent all the money he was supposed to have invested for his daughter.

Gene found this out in the course of a messy suit and counter-suit about the validity of her old contract. She won in court, but lost: her father was exposed. Soon after, he divorced Gene's mother and married Helen Burdick, the wealthy divorcée (and close friend of Belle Tierney's) with whom he'd been having an affair.

The effect of all this on Gene was shattering. She had loved and respected her father so much; the idea that he'd been using her was too painful to contemplate. Her attitude toward all men changed, I believe. She became more suspicious and withdrawn, which made life difficult for me as time went on.

At first, though, we retreated into our own little world, a retreat imposed in part by the Hollywood establishment, which ignored our marriage and ostracized us for a time. But it was a voluntary withdrawal as well, a time to recover from the shocks and disasters that had befallen us. We joked about it. Dinner was "Our Crowd" most nights—Gene and me and Butch, our German shepherd.

Our retreat was physical as well as social. We soon found a secluded ten-acre plot of land on Mulholland Drive, at the top of Coldwater Canyon. There were two houses on the property, and a spectacular view. We were surrounded by a reservoir and city-owned parkland. The only other house nearby was Gregory Peck's, off to the left, but it was hidden; our view was perfect, pristine. We might easily have been in the middle of Idaho. It cost a mere $10,000 (and was sold four years later for $125,000). We lived in the cottage at first while the main house was being renovated. Gene decorated it with Early American antiques, her favorite style; lots of little doodads and chintzes with tiny flowers, and maple furniture. It was a very charming place, and idyllic.

What was it like to be married to a major movie star? We read a lot. Gene was a true perfectionist, *very* conscientious about learning her lines. That was how we'd spend our evenings when she was working (and she always seemed to be working; one year she had six films playing simultaneously on Broadway). We would spend hours and hours—all our free time, it seemed—studying her scripts.

She would come home from the studio at about eight most nights, get into a hot tub, and start working. Everything had to be memorized. I believe this was a result of her Broadway training. Gene had appeared in only two plays, *Mrs. O'Brien Entertains* and *The Male Animal*, before coming to Hollywood, but she'd received rave reviews in both. She often said she missed the stage, the exhilaration of interacting with a live audience; she liked the atmosphere and pace of the theater. The performances were mostly at night. Her days were free, and she could enjoy the sunlight, the change of seasons in her beloved Fairfield County. She often spoke wistfully of missing autumn, of never seeing the daylight. In Hollywood, she lived in caves; her days were spent on the large, dark soundstages. I think all this darkness took its toll on her over time.

Still, Gene was very serious about acting in films. She was of the old school in this. She didn't interpret the role or try different readings. She learned her lines and left the rest up to the director. *I* was the one who experimented. Reading scripts with her five, ten, fifteen times each night was so boring that I would try different accents (French, English, Italian, Russian) and humorous (I thought) inflections. She would grow furious with me. "Stop it! You're ruining my concentration. . . ."

Yes, but she was ruining my evenings. We would read scripts through her bath, through dinner, and then on into the bedroom, Gene in bed and me sitting in a chair next to her. There was a compulsiveness to her behavior; she *had* to know her lines. And I was willing to indulge her: indeed, this was my great Svengali secret, my great hold over her—total devotion.

Our days usually began at five. Invariably, it would still be dark when we awoke. We'd have a quick cup of coffee and then I would drive Gene to the studio, down the canyon in the foggy half-light, across Beverly Hills to Twentieth Century-Fox. She had a very elaborate dressing room and a staff of retainers: the hairdresser and makeup man, and wardrobe, and so on. She doted on the people and insisted that I do, too; she needed to believe that their devotion to her was personal rather than professional (I thought all the "Good morning, dahling" effusiveness was a bit much). We would arrive at 6:30 A.M. and continue working on the script together, as these people worked on Gene, until nine, when she would go to the set. Often there would be last-minute script changes—the writers worked all night at times—and these changes would throw her into a panic.

I frequently spent my afternoons at the West Side Tennis Club, communing with fellow members of that unique Hollywood purgatory, those who were "between projects." Eventually, several of my closest tennis associates would have great successes. Buddy Adler would go on to become the head of Twentieth Century-Fox and the husband of Anita Louise; Kurt Frings would become an important agent; I would have my success as well, in time. In those days, though, we were ignored by the Hollywood community, which had a curious ability to ignore people completely when they were down, and then embrace them completely and immediately, as an old friend, when the wheel of fortune turned, as it almost always did. There seemed no middle ground.

I knew that I was performing an important service for Gene, that I was, in a quiet way, crucial to her peace of mind and thus her career. At times, I would act on her behalf in business matters. This was especially true when her agent, Leland Hayward, sold his business, including her contract, to Jules Stein, of MCA. "Oleg," Gene asked, "can I just be bought and sold like that?"

I read through the contract, and thought it murky enough to raise this point with Stein and Lew Wasserman, who was then his assistant. They took a hard line at first, but I was adamant, and rather than face a protracted legal battle, they agreed to give Gene a considerable sum in order to continue representing her.

Still, I hated the idea of being in such an inferior position. It drove me crazy. Gene was very understanding, but my pride was hurt. I thought about going back to New York or Washington to find work, yet I couldn't bear the thought of leaving her. Finally, out of a total, *physical* frustration, I took a $5-a-day job on the Mexican construction crew that was renovating the main house on our property. I spent eight hours a day carrying stones up the hill, rebuilding the house. It was exhausting work, but at least I was involved in productive labor. It certainly was more productive than the endless hours I spent in the antechambers of various studio executives' offices, looking for work as a designer even though the blackball was still in effect and my cause was quite hopeless.

I felt a real attachment to that house when it was finished. It was a charming place, removed from the cares of the world. It had two levels. A very large living room and the master bedroom (and a spacious closet—Gene was a maniac about closets) were on the lower level; above, there were two bedrooms and a library. The most notorious room in the house, celebrated in the press by Sidney Skolsky, was the "Mad Room," an idea we came upon jointly. Every time we had a fight, we would immediately go to the Mad Room and not leave until it was resolved.

Gene truly loved me, I believe. We shared an all-devouring, protective kind of love, very fierce and physical in those early years. Still, I think Gene considered me an anachronism, like my father in a way, too polite and naive and European ever to be a success in business. I think she resigned herself to this early on and decided to love me despite it.

Once, years later, I was having dinner with Ben Hecht and he said, "You know, I know why you're unhappy."

I was surprised. "Unhappy?" I said. "I'm not unhappy."

But Hecht was convinced. "You're unhappy because Gene loved you in a way that no one else did, or ever will again."

Perhaps. There is a certain sweetness to rebellious love, and we were shunned by much of Hollywood in the first months of our marriage. We weren't complete outcasts, though; there were my tennis-playing friends, and Fran and Ray Stark, and a small circle of people who really *knew* us.

We sometimes spent an evening playing cards with Fran and Ray, David and Hope Hearst, Eddie Judson, who was married to Rita Hayworth, and Palmer Beaudette and his wife, Cobina Wright, Jr., the society girl. The game we played was penny-ante poker, silly poker, just an excuse to get together and have some fun. Often we played strip poker, a game in which the women somehow always excelled. Never was a breast revealed, but I have seen Ray Stark down to his shorts more times than you can imagine.

Gene often accompanied me to these games, but sometimes she was too busy memorizing or too tired. I remember one evening in particular during this time, when Gene came along and then wanted to leave early. I'd had a couple of drinks and didn't really want to go; everyone was having a great time. But Gene was angry with me on the way home. She said poker was only an excuse for me to get close to Hope Hearst (who was indeed a very attractive girl). She said she'd had it with me. She said I was always flirting.

Well, I wasn't feeling very charitable about her, either. A lot of frustrations were building in me; I was sick of merely being Mr. Tierney, of not having a career of my own. "If that's the way you feel, I'm leaving," I said, quite pompously drunk. "Here's the keys. It's your car. It's your house. Everything's yours . . . except the dog. You won't mind if I take Butch. I know where I'm not wanted."

"That's right," she said, equally angry. "Get out. Go find someplace to stay."

And I began to walk down the canyon to Beverly Hills with sodden dignity, Butch in tow. It was perhaps four miles from our house back to the Starks', and I walked it in a rage, but a curious thing happened along the way. Butch and I were joined by other dogs, strays perhaps, a whole pack of them. By the time I reached the Starks' apartment on Fountain Drive, I had ten, maybe fifteen dogs following me. I rang the bell and Ray came out. "You came back!" he said. "We're just finishing the evening."

"I came back," I said, "and I want you to see who my real friends are."

Well, everyone came out and saw all these dogs sniffing around and they all had a good laugh about it. Ray even invited Butch in for a drink (he lifted the lid of the toilet seat in the bathroom and Butch was happy). Then he called Gene and had her come down and pick me up. Eventually, as always, we found our way to the Mad Room. But the issues raised that night—my frustration over work, her frustrations with her family and me—would plague our marriage. I could understand Gene's misgivings, but my flirtatiousness was innocent. It was a form of behavior that was not only accepted but considered *bon ton* in Europe. In America, the only acceptable form of marital behavior was high fidelity, or the appearance of such. In America, husbands and wives had to prove their devotion in public, incredible as this might seem, by doing such things as holding hands and staring moon-eyed at each other, as if they'd just met. In Europe, that sort of behavior would be considered not only unsophisticated but also a bit naive. It was *assumed* that one held one's own wife in high esteem, and so it was considered *gallant* to pay the compliment of harmless romantic attention to the other ladies in the room. I suppose this sort of behavior lost something in the translation; certainly Gene never understood it.

Despite the boycott, I did get some free-lance design jobs during this time. The first was for one of Gene's films, *The Shanghai Gesture*, directed by Josef von Sternberg, the man who had made Marlene Dietrich a star in *The Blue Angel*. Both Gene and I were hopeful. A prestigious director, a good cast (including my friend Victor Mature as "Omar the Arab")—perhaps this would lead to other opportunities. But the film was an overwrought turkey destroyed by the critics, who gave Gene her first bad reviews. My costumes were not even mentioned in passing.

As a souvenir of this experience, Gene had brought home carved figurines of each character in the film—they had been used in a particularly absurd dinner scene near the end. When the picture opened and bombed, I took the figurines out to the backyard, lined them up along the top of our fence, and executed them with a hunting rifle. "How could you do it?" Gene screamed when she learned about the firing squad. "You know I wanted to keep them!"

"Those characters deserved to die," I told her. "Now, at least, we won't be constantly reminded of that dreadful movie."

Soon after, I was asked by Sam Spiegel to do some work for his first Hollywood extravaganza, a movie called *Tales of Manhattan*. Spiegel—he went by the name of S. P. Eagle at the time—was a wonderful guy, a Middle European with a mysterious past who came to Hollywood by way of Canada. He was extremely intelligent, a great talker and convincer. He had convinced half of Hollywood to be part of this picture, which was a series of vignettes featuring a great many stars in cameo roles.

I had a cameo role as well. I was to design one dress . . . for Rita Hayworth, who was at the peak of her popularity.

The picture was being made at Twentieth Century-Fox, and I hoped that a good showing on my part might end the cold war between the studio and me—a vain hope, since Charles LeMaire, the head of the wardrobe department, was very much opposed to interlopers on his turf. "The studio has enough designing talent. We don't need a free-lancer to do this," he told me. "Rita is very important to this picture."

"Very well," I said, "but Mr. Eagle disagrees."

I designed a white dress, a classic dress—it would still be *right* today —sculpted in silk jersey, with bands of light blue and purple crossing on her chest. When the dress was finished, Hayworth fell in love with it. She kissed me and said, "You really understand me."

But LeMaire was fuming. "We have to test it," he said, and barred me from the test. I had no rank: I was an outsider. And, of course, it was found wanting: the purple absorbed too much light, it was said. Well, that could be handled easily enough. All you had to do was lighten the shade a bit. But LeMaire wanted me to fail, and conspired against me. He went to Hayworth; he went to Charles Boyer, who was to play the scene with Rita (he would be dressed in tails, and the wily wardrobe man argued that the white dress would dominate the frame and make him disappear). He even went to Darryl Zanuck. I learned about all these machinations from Spiegel, when he called. "We're having problems. . . ."

"If it's only the purple," I said, "that can be changed easily enough."

"But Rita's been turned against you," he replied, "and I'm afraid that's it." Such were the politics in the big studios.

I felt more unhappy than ever. The news would no doubt spread: I could only imagine what Hedda and Louella would write. The gossip may not have been as bad as all that; perhaps I was just being oversensitive. But I was feeling vulnerable, and defensive, and jealous. I flirted with other women constantly, obviously, whenever I could: it was something I did naturally, but also I wanted to send a message to Gene—that I shouldn't be taken for granted. But what were my harmless flirts when compared with her grand screen passions?

There was always pressure from the studio for romantic gossip. Hints were dropped about Gene and her co-stars, including Tyrone Power and Henry Fonda. I knew it was nonsense, but it irked me nonetheless. I had very mixed feelings about these leading men. Some I liked, some I didn't . . . but I was wary of all of them.

I liked Tyrone Power quite a bit. He was handsome as a god and enormously charming, in a naive way. Everything came easily for him, and he assumed it was the same for the rest of the world. He might be thoughtless, but there wasn't any malice to it. He, Errol Flynn, and Cary Grant were similar in that way. Each had an overwhelming charm that enabled him to live by his own rules, blithely disregarding society's, but doing it so smoothly that no one seemed to mind.

Henry Fonda, however, made himself difficult for me to like. In late 1941, he and Gene were working together on a picture called *Rings on Her Fingers*, and he struck me as a rather arrogant, disdainful sort. He had that wonderful voice and easy manner, and seemed to exude confidence that he could seduce Gene anytime he wanted. He made it very clear that he considered me just a hair in the soup, a distasteful encumbrance on the set (they were shooting on Catalina Island). There was real tension between us, but never a confrontation, a lot of double entendre barbs flying back and forth. Later on in life, we became quite friendly.

I remember that on December 7, 1941, we were returning from Catalina on a studio yacht—Gene, Fonda, and I, and several others—when the radio erupted with the news of the attack on Pearl Harbor. There were all sorts of rumors at that moment about Japanese subs off the California coast, and we raced back to Los Angeles, worried that we might be intercepted. Both Gene and I were preoccupied on this trip home; we knew that life was going to be very different now. I would soon be eligible for citizenship and, therefore, military service.

I had mixed feelings about this. My atavistic Russian and Italian blood raced—the opportunity for great heroism and sacrifice loomed; at the same time, I was concerned about going off to war and leaving Gene. It seemed that most of the leading men of Hollywood were managing to get themselves appointed Major This, Colonel That, and even Brigadier General; they served gallantly in the defense of Sunset Boulevard. There were notable exceptions, like Tyrone Power, Clark Gable, and Jimmy Stewart, who *really* went to war, but the film community was filled with stories about people like Turhan Bey, who pleaded incontinence to his draft board to escape the service ("Does this problem affect you when you are dancing at Ciro's with Lana Turner?" he was asked); John Payne was an antiaircraft gunner on Santa Monica Beach, and Rosalind Russell's husband, the agent Freddie Brisson, was an aide to a colonel in Hollywood's Ninth Service Command. It was said that he fought bravely and well throughout the grueling Beverly Drive.

* * *

There were delays in processing my citizenship papers. Finally, the papers were cleared. I became an American citizen on July 22, 1942, in another event orchestrated by the studio: "Cassini becomes citizen; renounces title."

I didn't mind shedding my title; it had only caused me trouble in recent years (and I still knew who I was). The studio loved it, though. For the first time I became *persona grata* at Twentieth Century-Fox. It was a touch of patriotism at just the right moment—Hollywood Goes to War —and with my military obligation, there was the additional benefit of having me out of the picture for a while, no longer the meddling husband, perhaps even *hors de combat*. Gene Tierney, grieving widow, would have been a gold mine at the box office. . . .

I volunteered for military intelligence, figuring I would be a natural, given my language abilities, but I didn't receive a reply until several years later.

After I became a citizen, Ray Stark suggested, "Why don't you join the coast guard?"

"Why don't we join the coast guard together?" Victor Mature proposed to me one day in the commissary at Twentieth Century-Fox.

In those first, frightened months after Pearl Harbor, private yachts actually were being solicited to patrol the coast, in search of Japanese submarines. Mature had a yacht, a sixty-four footer called *The Bar Bill*. "Listen," he said, "we'll be able to do our bit and stay close to home. I don't think this war is going to last very long, anyway."

Victor Mature, for those who have somehow forgotten, was a great slab of a man from Kentucky. His parents were Swiss, but most people thought he was Italian, with his dark, curly hair, Roman nose, and thick lips. As an actor, he had essentially two moves: the raised eyebrow, which expressed a rudimentary skepticism; and the curled lip, which had to suffice for every other emotion. These two moves carried him to the stardom he craved, but I liked him all the same, even after he told me how he'd ruined my flirt with Betty Grable. He was, at once, very vain, entirely self-involved, and yet very funny about it, always making jokes at his own expense. He proposed that we proceed immediately to the coast guard recruiting center and volunteer the yacht—in which I offered to buy a half-interest.

Much to our surprise, the coast guard accepted all three, and we were soon patrolling the waters off Catalina, with a crew of eight and an allotment of depth charges—which, no doubt, would have blown us to pieces if we'd ever fired one off (since the yacht hardly had the power to clear the area quickly enough). I was designated fireman first class, but was immediately elected cook because I had an Italian name. Each man had $8 per diem for food, which wasn't bad. When pooled, it produced enough money for us to eat fabulously. No doubt we ate better than any other unit in the armed forces. I spent all my time preparing the most elegant continental cuisine. The men were very appreciative, except for Mature, who was always hungry. My portions were never sufficient, and he would invade the galley between meals, focusing on the mayonnaise, which he ate *au naturel* from the jar with a tablespoon.

Victor volunteered for more perilous duty on deck. He was the lookout, which enabled him to spend all day, every day, working on his tan, so he could be presentable when accompanying Rita Hayworth to premieres on our nights off.

Perhaps the best part of this service, aside from sitting on the deck with a good cigar after dinner while the others washed dishes, was the amount of time I spent at home. We patrolled for forty-eight hours, then returned to port for forty-eight. I was able to be with Gene, play tennis, and enjoy Hollywood life.

Indeed, I enjoyed Hollywood society somewhat more than Gene, since she was working. I spent my shore leaves as did many another sailor, and this led to perhaps the most embarrassing moment of my life.

Arthur Rubinstein, the great pianist, and a good friend of ours, was living in Los Angeles at the time and held a large party at his home one evening. Gene chose not to attend. I was left to my own devices and got drunk, never very difficult for me—two martinis and I was lost. I found myself involved with the very attractive wife of a very popular European actor of the time. The lady also was tipsy, I think, and we found our way to my car and then to a quiet side street in Bel Air.

I returned home; Gene was asleep. With the counterfeit lucidity that often accompanies the end of a drunken evening, I was determined to cover my tracks. I laid out my uniform *very* neatly; I took fresh underwear and laid it out on top of the uniform, also *very* neatly. I balled up the underwear I'd been wearing and hid it somewhere.

I was awakened by Gene the next morning. She was dressed and ready to go to work. "I want to see you later," she said.

"Yes, I'll come to the studio."

"No, not there. I want to meet you at six . . . at my lawyer's."

"Your lawyer's?"

"Yes, we're getting a divorce." And before I could say "But why?" she had produced my balled-up underwear, which had a rather unmistakable smear of lipstick in an entirely compromising location. The neatness of the carefully folded underwear and uniform had aroused her suspicion, of course; she had already, by that tender hour of the morning, found out the identity of my partner (a simple call to the Rubinsteins': "Oh, so sorry I couldn't come. Oleg had a wonderful time. Who was that he took home?"), and had called the aggrieved European actor and told him about it. He was very much the gentleman, and said, "You must be mistaken." But Gene wasn't easily placated; she insisted that I apologize to him, which I did, to everyone's discomfort. It was, in fact, an excruciating price to pay for a harmless peccadillo. But, of course, it was a situation I should never have gotten myself into. It was a huge *faux pas*, both humiliating and stupid.

Gene was rather displeased with me at that point, nevertheless. She thought my military career insufficiently distinguished—at the very least, I should become an officer (everyone else in Hollywood seemed to be). But there was an unwritten law in the navy and the coast guard that officers had to be native-born Americans, and so Mother went into action on my behalf in Washington.

She couldn't arrange a commission in the coast guard, but she did manage to engineer something even more rare: an act of Congress enabling me to transfer to the U.S. Army Cavalry, which allowed foreign-born officers. There was no guarantee of a commission. I'd have to go through basic training at Fort Riley, Kansas, like everyone else, and then be accepted into Officer Candidate School on my own merits. It wouldn't be a picnic like the Hollywood Signal Corps, but it *was* the cavalry, a branch of the service that triggered all sorts of rumblings in my Italo-Russian soul. Now, perhaps, I would finally fulfill my destiny as an officer and a gentleman.

I suppose I was rather pleased with myself in those last few days before I went off to the army. I remember one dreadful scene I caused during a birthday party for Joan Fontaine at Romanoff's restaurant. Otto Preminger was there, blowing very hard about the need for opening a second front to relieve the Russians. This was the left-wing line of the moment: the Communists were our noble allies, bearing the full brunt of the Nazi invasion and deserving of support. I was having none of it. I told

Preminger, in no uncertain terms, that I thought Churchill was right: we should ignore the Russians, consider them potential enemies, and occupy the Balkans instead.

Preminger had a great bald head, pellucid blue eyes, and an imperious manner. He scared the hell out of most people with his screaming, but not me. He said, "What do you know about this? You're just a soldier!"

"What do *you* know about it, Otto?" I replied. "You're just a director."

We almost came to blows right there, and had to be separated. Later, he would direct Gene in several movies, most notably *Laura*, and we became good friends. For some reason, perhaps because I stood up to him that day, he never exploded at me again, not even when I was designing costumes for his films, which made me almost unique among his associates. He liked to talk about women and appreciated my taste; eventually, in the late 1950s, he married one of my favorite models, a striking girl named Hope Bryce.

I seemed to enjoy fighting over lunch at Romanoff's; soon after my confrontation with Preminger, I got into it with Orson Welles, who had been rather conspicuously (and, many thought, suspiciously) declared 4F. Despite that, he was being touted by Elsa Maxwell and others for governor of California. I found myself at lunch one day with Welles and several others, discussing this absurd idea. Welles, as was his habit, was doing most of the discussing. I made a remark that clearly wasn't intended to be flattering, and he came back at me. At which point I calmly told him, "I think you're just a *bocca grande* and I'm not going to waste my time listening to you." Then I stood up and walked out. Gene was terribly embarrassed.

The business with Welles was not quite finished, however; months later, it was Father who carried on the struggle while I was serving at Fort Riley. I had asked him to go to Los Angeles and stay with Gene while I was away—I didn't want her off alone in that isolated house on Mulholland Drive. Father actually served as an elegant extra in several of her films; he might have gone far in this line of work but for an uncontrollable urge to stare at the camera. Father was there one night when Welles accompanied Gene to a party and brought her home. He stopped in for a drink, and the two of them were talking amiably, Welles obviously angling for something more, when Father burst in, shouting, "It's terrible! Terrible! Disgraceful! Your husband is off defending his country and you're here *entertaining* people!" He was quite marvelous in my defense. Welles was routed. He stood and bowed to Father magnificently, said "I beg your pardon" in that great voice of his, and departed.

I transferred to the U.S. Army on November 17, 1942, and left immediately for Fort Riley, Kansas, a post that had great traditions and facilities but the least amenable climate I've ever encountered, including Russia. It was always extreme: blizzards and tornados, freezing in winter, sweltering in summer. Still, this *had* been Custer's headquarters; General Patton and a great many other legendary figures had served here. It was the home of the First Cavalry Division, which would soon distinguish itself in the South Pacific. The expression "spit and polish" had originated at Ford Riley; it was the unit's motto.

I arrived with a certain amount of hope, half expecting to be welcomed to the cavalry as I might have been to the Imperial Guards, as a gentleman. I hoped that appearance, good manners, horsemanship, and leadership ability would be the qualities that counted. In the beginning, though, I was confronted with the egalitarian humiliations of basic training. I was just another GI at first, a most unlikely one at that, and a perfect target for ridicule.

Because of the strange manner of my transfer from the coast guard to the army, I arrived at Fort Riley unexpectedly, between basic training classes. There was no uniform for me. The army could not allow me to merely sit and wait, though: I was made to drill in the clothes I had, which were a gabardine suit and a camel's-hair coat. My distinctive garb made the peculiarities of my background even more apparent. The army does not encourage peculiarity; it arranged an initial program of nonstop KP duty to eliminate any ideas I might have had about special treatment. But even after my basic-training class was assembled and uniforms distributed (mine was five sizes too large, standard U.S. military couture), I was made to pay for my distinctions: for my former title (I was called "Count Off"—very clever of them), for my movie-star wife, for my manner of speaking, for simply being different.

When Gene came to visit after several weeks, I was allowed to meet her at the Junction City train station. "My God," she said, when she saw me—GI haircut, no mustache, perhaps fifteen pounds lighter, wearing an ill-fitting uniform. "Oleg, what have they *done* to you?"

I think she had the idea that I would immediately join the ranks of officers and gentlemen; no doubt she was disappointed. As might be expected, her arrival caused something of a stir in camp. She was invited to the officers' club one evening, and—this was considered quite a joke—I was invited to do KP duty at the club that same night. The word spread quickly; it was big news. "Hey, Count Off's wife is dancing with the brass while he's peeling potatoes."

Actually, I was washing dishes, and fuming. But I knew that this was standard operating procedure; indeed, I wanted no special favors. I wanted to prove myself to the others and, gradually, I did just that. Even though I was years older than most of my fellow recruits—I would turn thirty at Fort Riley that spring—I was in peak physical condition and always performed quite well in running, the obstacle course, and calisthenics. I was a good shot, though inept when assembling and disassembling a rifle. Most important, though, was my horsemanship. We were the last group being trained on horses by the U.S. Army. The cavalry was becoming mechanized, a tank corps—an inevitable development, but something of a mistake, I believe, since horses might have proved quite valuable in certain circumstances, such as reconnaissance in mountainous areas (in the Italian campaign that would soon begin, for example).

Our basic-training class was composed primarily of New Yorkers who'd only seen horses pulling carriages in Central Park, and also a few cowboys. To my surprise, the cowboys had almost as many problems as the novices. They rode Western style, slouched back in their saddles.

The army had its own equestrian style, which, happily, coincided with what I'd learned in Italy: the weight was kept forward to ease pressure on the horse (it was called the "forward" or Chamberlain seat), using the cumbersome wood and leather McClellan saddle. Naturally, this was much to my advantage. I was promoted to corporal and named an instructor in horsemanship when basic training ended—quite an honor, I thought, and certainly one of the best jobs attainable for a noncommissioned officer at Fort Riley.

Officer Candidate School was still my goal, but I was pleased with my progress. In fact, I had managed to achieve a measure of notoriety among my colleagues in the barracks. They considered me a tough guy, a status to which I'd always aspired. My reputation was the result of a single incident. There was a terrible bully in the horsemanship department, a raw-boned, long-nosed, rough-and-ready fellow who had been a prizefighter at county fairs. He terrorized the barracks each night, coming in drunk from the PX (quite a feat, since they only served 3.2 beer) and shouting, "Piss call, piss call," then roughing up those he knew wouldn't challenge him, which meant just about everyone. One night he brutalized a rather flaccid corporal, and no one did anything about it. There seemed no way to challenge him. Even the tough guys were scared.

I knew he'd come after me eventually—I was slim and foreign, a natural target—and I began to sleep with my cavalry boots under my pillow. Sure enough, he came at me in the dark one night. I had an upper bunk, which was an advantage. He had to reach up, and I had a good deal of leverage when I swung the steel-reinforced heel of my boot down on his head, and followed that down on top of him, yelling and stomping and hitting him with everything I had. It seemed as if ten minutes had passed before the lights went on and they pulled me off him. He was out cold, and I was a hero.

The funniest part of it was that no one had seen the boot—it was still up in my bunk—and they assumed I'd done the damage with my fists. I was very modest, of course, very Gary Cooper about it all. But the word spread: "That Cassini fellow hits like a mule!"

I also managed to win commendations for my actions during two emergencies at Fort Riley that spring. One was a stampede. About five hundred horses from the corral had escaped and were cascading down the frozen rimrock—a mesa that ran parallel to the Republican River—rolling and tumbling like a waterfall. I was out for a ride at the time with Colonel Holman and several others when we heard the thunder and saw them coming at us. We did some very fancy riding that day, leaping the gullies that veined the plain to get away from the stampede, then doubling back to divert and quiet the herd, limiting the damage to a minimal loss of horseflesh.

The other emergency was even more serious. One day I spotted a tornado heading straight for the camp. It was perhaps five hundred yards from the stable and one hundred and fifty yards from the officers' mess. I ran first for the stable and released as many horses as I could, then to the mess, yelling, "Tornado, tornado!" We'd been taught to get outside when a tornado came, to find a ditch, a low place of some sort, and I jumped into a gully just as the storm hit. It hit with full force, disastrously; two men were killed, and several horses. I saw one of the dead men; he'd been run through by a flying two-by-four.

Gene joined me after basic training was over, determined to be an army wife like any other. She didn't like the scripts she was getting and wanted to take a vacation from Hollywood. We bought a little house near the area reserved for officers, and Gene began to decorate it, beautifully, from nothing. She bought some barrels, for example, which she painted red and used for bar stools. She had chintz sent from Los Angeles, which she made into curtains. Soon our little cottage, nothing more than a prefab standard-issue place, was looking something like a Norman inn.

She also learned to cook, for the first time. She did this as she did everything, methodically, expending great effort over cookbooks, learning the recipes as she learned her lines. And, I must say, her roast beef was always done just right. "You've become a chef," I would tell her, "but you were a born *rôtisseur*."

It was one of the happiest times of our marriage. Even the prospect of a script like *Laura*, which arrived in the mail, could not bestir her; indeed, her first reaction to that most important role was negative—she'd be playing a character who'd be "dead" through much of the movie; neither of us could foresee the magic that Preminger would weave.

And then, what could Hollywood offer compared with the glamor and bright lights of Junction City, Kansas? Junction City's normal population was a few hundred people; at that time, though, it was swollen to five thousand. Neither Gene nor I had experienced such a place before. It had one hotel, the Bartell (also known as the Cockroach Inn), one movie theater (the Popcorn Inn—the floor was squeaky with stale popcorn), and a restaurant actually called the Greasy Spoon, whose chef endeavored mightily to live up to the name; one of the specialties was deep-fried steak. This was a far cry from Florence, or even Connecticut. It was indescribably bad.

On the other hand, after I became an officer, Gene and I felt quite at home in Fort Riley society—a term that I do not use lightly, since the very best horsemen and polo players from all over the country had congregated at the cavalry school (and it had some of the best horses—Darryl Zanuck, Jock Whitney, and others had donated their strings of polo ponies to the cause for the duration). Our neighbors were the Bostwicks, the Van Stades, and others of the horsey set. Paul Mellon was there, and Cappy Smith, who was one of the finest equestrians in the country. Nor was Gene the only celebrity wife in camp. Gloria Vanderbilt was there, married then to my friend and fellow man-about-town Pat De Cicco. They had met over dinner at our Cherokee Lane home a year earlier. Gloria was then only seventeen and very shy, but also very pretty and already quite famous, of course. She was the subject of fierce competitive wooing that evening by De Cicco and Bruce Cabot. It was great fun to watch from the sidelines, for once, and I wasn't at all surprised when De Cicco eventually carried the day, sweeping Gloria off her feet with an outdoor spaghetti dinner that he and his cousin, the producer Cubby Broccoli, had prepared. "I won her," he'd later say, "with my pasta."

He was quite a character and a good pal, a man of enormous appetites —for food, for women, for fun. He was about six foot one, 275 pounds, but gave the impression of being even larger, with gigantic shoulders and dark, curly, slicked-down hair. He made his living as an agent for Howard Hughes, when Hughes owned RKO. Pat assembled and managed a stable of thirty-six girls under contract to Hughes, none of whom ever appeared in a movie. They were on call like stewardesses, standing by the phone until midnight each night in case Hughes summoned. It was perhaps the first great American harem.

De Cicco was one of the polo players at Fort Riley, but despite this, he didn't endear himself to the others. You see, he had concocted a lower back condition that enabled him to be driven around much of the time, and the men thought he was taking advantage of his status as a celebrity husband (Gloria, by the way, never asked for special consideration; she was always a sweet, charming girl, very attractive, very kind).

I joined the polo set after I graduated from Officer Candidate School. We would play indoors during the winter at 5:00 P.M. daily. Officers had a choice of playing polo or jumping; one or the other was required. I enjoyed the polo, even if I wasn't quite as good as some of the others. We played three-man teams, by invitation only (from our commanding officer, Colonel Holman). I was on a regimental team with Pete Bostwick and Charlie Van Stade, both of whom were among the finest players in the country and the social elite. Bostwick was a little fellow with startling blue eyes and bandy legs; he was the perfect build for a gentleman jockey, and had ridden in the Grand National. Van Stade was tall, blond, blue-eyed; he had everything in life, which made his death several months later in Europe, when his jeep tripped a land mine, so hard to accept. There were more than a few officers I served with, and troopers I trained, at Fort Riley who would die in the war. I remember their names and their faces. They haunt me to this day, as do the memories of my Italian friends who were lost fighting on the other side.

I enjoyed polo for its danger; it enabled me to compete aggressively against superior officers, charging at them on horseback, swinging a mallet, sometimes aiming a ball right at them. A favorite target was a lanky, insufferable reverend major nicknamed "the Gestapo," whom I'd always find ways to attack with my mallet in the chukkers we played against each other.

This was a fantasy life. There was a war going on and we were playing polo—and fox hunting, too! We had a hunt every Sunday, with the wives participating (Gene didn't ride); it was a drag hunt, and I was often selected by Colonel Holman to drag a sack scented with fox urine through the roughest terrain I could find, making the ride as challenging as possible for the fox hunters and their dogs. At the time, I was also training all the colonel's eight horses on a daily basis.

All of this was quite appealing to Gene; it was almost like living in Connecticut. There was none of the pressure of Hollywood, none of the constant memorizing or the anxiety involved in choosing a new script. She was a happy housewife, spending her days chitchatting with Laura Bostwick and the others, playing house . . . although we did more than just play at it: Gene became pregnant that spring.

Graduating training school and becoming an officer of the U.S. Army Cavalry was very important to me, perhaps even a turning point in my life. Thirty-year-old, formerly titled foreigners did not routinely succeed in Officer Candidate School. It was a real achievement. Gene was proud of me, and so was Hollywood. People like Darryl Zanuck began to understand and respect me more; from then on, we would be welcome in his home—and in David O. Selznick's, Jack Warner's, and Sam Goldwyn's.

Hollywood's attitude was best stated by none other than Ronald Reagan, who had been at Fort Riley. I bumped into him on leave one night. Gene and I were at a party at Claudette Colbert's. I was in uniform, and Reagan, also in uniform, wearing the insignia of the Signal Corps, noticed the crossed sabres on my lapels. "Oleg, those sabres really do something to me . . ." We talked for a while about the cavalry tradition, and I could tell that he knew I'd paid my dues.

Still, Lieutenant Cassini was not quite the typical U.S. Army officer. I remained who I was, never really becoming a can-do, technocratic American field officer who could perform math equations and blow up bridges. It is interesting that when a cooperative experiment with the British took place at Fort Riley, with each of us rated by officers from both countries, the British officers, commanded by Brigadier General Briscoe, ranked me first in the regiment, certainly much higher than my own American officers did. (A stray image from this time: I remember battalions of German prisoners of war, remnants of the elite Afrika Korps, marching off to construction work in perfect order with their shovels; when they passed me, they would present the shovels, and I would salute in return, until General Marshall ordered this military courtesy discontinued.)

I was more European in style. The British, especially, were more concerned with how an officer looked and talked, and with intangibles like leadership quality, than the Americans were. My uniforms were carefully tailored, the shirts made to order. I had high leather boots with spurs, made by Peel (only cavalry officers were permitted these, since leather was scarce), which caused quite a stir when Gene and I visited New York during my two-week leave after graduating OCS. It was a wonderful time; there was the triumphant return to the Stork Club and a visit to Washington, where both our mothers were now living. Cissy Patterson celebrated our arrival with a gala party for one hundred guests at her home on Dupont Circle. Many of my old Washington acquaintances from the embassies were there, including Count Potocki and Senator Reynolds; there was an orchestra, a black-tie, sit-down dinner. It was the first time Gene (or her mother, who also attended—with gritted teeth, it seemed) had really seen me in my element; of course, Mrs. Patterson also was quite pleased to introduce so glamorous a star as Gene Tierney to Washington.

I felt very proud, very dashing walking the streets of New York and Washington during that leave, and was often mistaken for an officer from a foreign country because of my high boots.

This style caused problems back at Fort Riley, where there were more than a few officers who were career army men—former sergeants and such, who had been promoted only because of the war. These were not always educated or sophisticated men. They scorned the draftees, ROTC men and "ninety-day wonders" who had invaded their preserve. By and large, they had no use at all for me, a ninety-day wonder who was also a "furriner." One, in particular, was rather appropriately named Peeveridge Null. He was tall, thin, sharp-featured, bowlegged, a seventeen-year army veteran and a real hillbilly. He spoke an obscure military dialect that was incomprehensible to anyone who wasn't a career army man. No doubt I was incomprehensible to him as well. He certainly had difficulty understanding my desire to wear pajamas at night when we were out on bivouac. In response, I quoted the British general Jumbo Wilson: "Any fool can be uncomfortable in war." But Null was not amused. He also was furious that my dog, Butch, whom Gene had brought from Los Angeles, would follow me out on maneuvers. One day, during an inspection, he found dog biscuits in my tent and tried to have me busted for "unmilitary" behavior, but he didn't succeed.

I was nearly court-martialed, though, for another incident. It happened during a birthday party that a group of us had at the officers' club that summer for Major Schliesher, who was a good friend. All our wives were there; we were dancing and drinking and having a good time. It was terribly hot, and we kept the doors open, and I suppose we were making quite a bit of noise proposing toasts, blowing party whistles and all. We were pretty far gone when the birthday cake was brought in—a huge cake topped with individual cream puffs. I think it was Captain Bobby Nairn, the colonel's personal aide, who threw the first cream puff. No matter. Soon we were all into it, the cream puffs flying thick and fast, the women, Gene included, screaming and dodging. All of which ended abruptly when a cream puff I'd aimed at Nairn went sailing out the door and hit a chaplain who happened to be walking past. Unfortunately, the chaplain lacked a sense of humor.

For a time, it seemed charges would be preferred against several of us. Eventually, I was merely denied officers' club privileges, which was inconvenient but not a tragedy—and didn't last long in any case, for I was soon transferred from Fort Riley and was en route overseas on a secret mission.

Military intelligence had contacted me in the last weeks of OCS. A captain named Emil Bonnet, whom I'd known in Los Angeles, approached me. He said that my ability to speak French and Italian fluently might prove useful. He promised a promotion to Captain if I agreed to take part in a secret operation, which he described as very dangerous. I was reluctant to go overseas because of Gene's pregnancy, but I did have the proper qualifications for the work and felt it was my duty. Gene and I decided that if I should be called away before the baby came, she would have the child in Washington, since both our mothers now lived there. We visited a local obstetrician, and made all the necessary arrangements.

In early October, I received orders to report to Newport News, Virginia, for assignment overseas.

At the port of embarkation, I was given a special code number and intelligence gear, including a pistol and knife. I was quarantined then, unable to receive messages or send them. (I remember seeing the actor Sterling Hayden there, also headed overseas on a similar assignment; I'd known his wife, Madeleine Carroll, and we passed some time talking about Hollywood.)

And so there was no way for Gene, or my mother, or her mother to get word through, to let me know. . . . I had to read it in the post newspaper: that the actress Gene Tierney had given birth to a premature baby after an emergency operation at Columbia Hospital in Washington. The baby was a girl, weighing two and a half pounds.

Immediately I ran to the post commander and requested an emergency leave. I showed him the newspaper. He said he'd have to clear it with military intelligence, and I sat there for several hours, biting my fingernails, before permission was granted.

Gene was sedated, in fragile condition after giving birth, but delighted. She was so happy that the baby—whom we named Daria—was going to survive despite a difficult delivery and the premature birth. I sat with her in the room, kissing her. We had a moment together.

The doctor appeared then and asked me to come with him. He took me to his office; I didn't like the look on his face. "You realize that your wife has had a very difficult childbirth. I can assure you that she will be fine," he said, in a way that led me to believe that this was not the whole story. He repeated several times that she would be fine.

"But what is the matter?" I asked, and even in asking, I felt the anguish flooding me.

"Your daughter," he said. "She's not in good shape. First, she's premature . . . and then"—he was struggling with this—"there's an opacity. I don't think she'll ever see. I think she's blind. There are cataracts in both eyes."

I rushed to the baby, and it was true. It was also just the beginning of our agony.

I went to Gene. I had to tell her, of course. I said, "Gene, there's a problem, a *serious* problem, and you have to be strong." Like the doctor, I was having trouble getting it out, but there was no choice. "My heart is broken, but there's something wrong with the eyesight of the baby."

And she seemed to shatter then. She fell apart and, I believe, never really managed to put the pieces back together again until many years later. She became hysterical. She cried and cried. It was so terribly sad. I didn't have the strength to soothe her, or even to say anything. She cried and I sat there. She continued to cry; she would not stop. I began to suspect that perhaps her health was as delicate as the baby's.

I rushed to military intelligence headquarters, to the major I'd been dealing with there. I explained the situation. I told him I couldn't possibly go overseas now. He understood, but told me I was on orders. "There's nothing I can do," he said. "You have your assignment . . . but I'll try." And several days later, I learned that I had been reassigned to the cavalry pool at Fort Riley.

Then I hurried back to the hospital. Mother was there, and I told her the terrible thing. We went to see the baby together; nothing had changed

—although there was always the hope, the foolish hope, that it was just a bad dream, that it would go away.

Mrs. Tierney was there as well. We had a momentary peace with her, although I remember her saying over and over, "We've never had trouble like this in *our* family." And something about how you could never tell with old European families what might be passed on. . . .

I could barely comprehend what she was saying. I was overwhelmed by this tragedy, the sight of that little baby so helpless in the nursery. I ran from the hospital. I ran and ran; I couldn't stop. I ran for miles. I ran uncontrollably, the same way Gene had cried. Finally, I stopped at a bar somewhere. I ordered a drink, then another and another. I drank till I was senseless, but even then the pain persisted in the ever-conscious recesses of my soul. The pain was constant, inescapable. It exists to this day. It will not give me peace.

Several days later, the doctor called me in again. He told me about recent studies that had been done in Australia about the disastrous effects of German measles on pregnancies. Gene had contracted German measles during her first trimester, when she was in Hollywood filming *Heaven Can Wait*. I was off at Fort Riley then; neither of us had thought it very significant at the time. How could we have known?

And now I had to go back to Gene in the hospital with news that was far more horrible than anything we could have imagined: our daughter was not only blind but also most likely retarded because of the German measles. Helplessly retarded. There was nothing that could be done for her.

Gene received the news very calmly. In a way, this reaction was more shocking than her earlier crying. There was nothing in her eyes; the light-blue color that was so alluring when we'd met seemed eerily vacant now. She was almost catatonic; certainly I could not reach her. I would see that expression again and again over the next few years; I would see it every time there was bad news about Daria . . . and the news was always bad.

In New York, a decade later, I met an attractive redhead and went out with her. Later in the evening, she told me: "I was a great fan of your wife's. In fact, during the war I was a sergeant in the marines, stationed near Los Angeles, and I heard she was going to appear at the Hollywood Canteen. I had to go. I had to go even though there had been an outbreak of German measles in our camp and I was being quarantined. I went and shook her hand."

I was struck dumb by this. Was it possible that this woman had caused such agony so cavalierly? I was overwhelmed by the knowledge; I didn't know what to do with it. I considered calling Gene, but her health was quite precarious by then and I decided to spare her the pain.

As it happened, I later learned that Gene had—incredibly, unbelievably—already met this woman herself. She had met her at a tennis party in Los Angeles; she had been told the same story. And she had reacted the same way as I: with numb disbelief—without ever telling this woman the consequences of her incredibly careless action. Why should she know? What might it have accomplished? Still, the vile, corrosive randomness of these chance meetings suggested an almost biblical curse upon us. What had we done to deserve such suffering?

Later, the story of Daria inspired Agatha Christie to write a mystery called *The Mirror Crack'd from Side to Side*, in which a famous actress murders the woman who infected her with German measles during her pregnancy, causing her baby to be born retarded. If only life were so simple, if only satisfaction could be gained from a murder . . . but there was no satisfaction for us, no answer, only a sea of pain with no horizon, no solution, no hope.

CHAPTER
6

My memory is not too good here. The world, our lives, proceeded in a blur for a time. I guess I was trying to forget. It proceeded logically, but in a spiritless forced march from day to day. Gene and I were good soldiers; we did as we were told. We were heartbroken, bereft, unable to think for ourselves, and so we did as we were told.

Gene was advised to get back to work. Immediately. It was the best cure, they said—and, in the short term, it was. She returned to Los Angeles with Daria and began a sequence of films that would prove to be the best of her career: *Laura*, *Leave Her to Heaven* (for which she won an Academy Award nomination, but lost the Oscar to Joan Crawford), *The Razor's Edge*. Was it just coincidence that she was doing her finest work now? I think not. It was as if the birth of Daria had emptied her, and she filled herself up with these roles.

Her greatest performance, without doubt, was as Ellen Berent in *Leave Her to Heaven*. She played a madwoman, an insanely jealous wife who would destroy any rival for her husband's attention, even his younger brother. It was, obviously, a rather melodramatic film and demanded a great deal of restraint to be at all credible. Gene's performance was remarkable in its passion and intensity. It was the only time I ever saw that less accessible but very real and tempestuous side of her personality on screen. The insanity in the film—aggressive, venal—was of a different sort than Gene's own developing illness, however. Hers was more of an

157

implosion, a crumbling from within that proceeded subtly, with only inter-mittent moments of rage and drama, over time.

In fact, when I think of Gene's illness, I think more of Laura, which was her most famous role. It is ironic that through much of the film she played a girl presumed dead who was actually alive; in some ways, Gene was quite the opposite. After Daria's birth, she seemed to die inside. There was a ghostly quality, an evanescence, to both Laura and Gene. Even after Laura is found to be alive, she has a certain mystery, an aura, that permeates the film and gives it much of its magic. And Gene? After Daria, there was a distance I never seemed able to bridge. I don't think she was ever truly happy again. She played at happiness, pretending to laugh when the occasion called for it; but it was a role she performed so as not to disappoint or alarm others. This distance was a wound that crippled our marriage.

Most disturbing to me, in a way, was her ceaseless, entirely unreal-istic optimism about Daria. She searched continually for specialists to examine her. She was certain a solution would be found. She was con-vinced that Daria would improve, or that a "cure" would be discovered, or . . .

Gene was like the Ancient Mariner on our horizonless sea of pain, always hoping for some sort of redemption: this couldn't be happening to her, to us. There had to be an answer. Gene had been raised an optimist; the idea that there *wasn't* an answer, and never would be, was impossible for her to contemplate. But the reality of our situation was this: the child could not even recognize us. She had no real life, and her lifelessness was killing us, especially Gene, draining vitality and energy each day she ex-isted.

As this desperate truth became apparent, I considered killing the baby. I thought about this very seriously. I would take her to the ocean. We would drown together. I would die with her because I could not live with the thought of what I had done or the shame of having to hide it. But I couldn't kill myself—my sense of self-preservation was too strong—and so I couldn't kill Daria.

I didn't have the heart to contradict Gene when she went on about the baby, full of hope for a cure. This was one thing we didn't argue about. But the strain of silence obviously affected our marriage; we fought, fu-riously, about other things. For the first year after Daria was born, we saw each other only intermittently, as I was in the army. After the war, we had our troubles. We had good times, good days, good weeks; but other times were not so good. There were nights when I was banished, and found shelter with friends like Roger Valmy; at one point, Freddy Heineken and I shared a beach house in Santa Barbara for several weeks. He asked me if I wanted to sell his beer in America. What an idea! Who would ever buy Dutch beer in America?

I needed to live in order not to die—and Gene no longer seemed to know how. I would like to believe that this frustration was a silent cause of some of my less admirable behavior during that time, the many public fights I waged, the occasional private indiscretions. In retrospect, it seems we reacted in entirely different ways to the afflictions of Daria: my pessimism and her optimism, my effusions and her anguish. This was not so apparent at the time, just the escalating conflicts, the telltale signs of a marriage gone bad. Our love must have been strong, though, because we held on to each other, and remained married for more than a decade, through scores of separations, short and long.

I returned to Fort Riley, but the war was over for me. I had lost my taste for it. I was numb. There was no longer any desire to go overseas on a secret mission; I wanted to go home. I wanted to do what I'd once scorned: defend Sunset Boulevard against kamikaze attacks. It is interesting—but perhaps not inexplicable—that my health began to fall apart at this point. I became accident-prone, and nearly lost an eye when I careened into an icy branch one freezing night on mounted patrol; the impact knocked me off my horse, and I might have frozen to death there if not for my faithful Butch, who had accompanied me as always. I fell off my horse another time, too, dizzy with viral pneumonia. I was given last rites then. I know this because my mother was there; she'd come to see if she could talk me out of dying. It was a strange, wonderful feeling, skating along the edge of consciousness. I was in a state of elation. I had never felt better in my life. I was the only patient in a large ward at Wichita General Hospital, delirious, running a high fever, exhilarated. Mother sat with me every day, talking to me. "You're not going to die," she said, over and over. "You've always had weak lungs, but you're strong enough, and you will get well."

"Of course," I said. "Of course."

I was given leave afterward to recuperate. I took a cargo plane heading to Los Angeles from Kansas City. The plane crashed in a field outside Oklahoma City. I walked away from the wreck, numb, and got on a train. The train was filled, as trains were in those times, with soldiers and sailors. It took me to Wichita, where I waited for another train, also jammed with soldiers, hot and uncomfortable. I stood the whole trip, and did not sleep for days. I arrived home semiconscious and Gene put me to bed. I would spend a good deal of time in military hospitals over the next two years, treated for pneumonia, the eye injury, and asthma.

I went through my paces at Fort Riley. I behaved at times without thinking or caring. There were weekends in Kansas City with my fellow officers. We would rent a room at the Hotel Muehlbach, empty it of everything but mattresses and pillows, and have parties. The bars were clotted with women who worked in the nearby defense plants; the ratio was something like seventeen to one. They stood on line to get into the bars, as if they were waiting for a movie. We would simply introduce ourselves to the girls we wanted to meet, and invite them upstairs. They were there to have a good time and to forget, and so were we.

There was an interesting episode with the actress Donna Reed during this period. She came to Fort Riley on a USO tour with another young actress, a friend of hers. I was assigned to escort her around the post. We spent the day greeting the troops, a boring, dusty exercise, and that night we found ourselves back in the special barracks room to which she'd been assigned. She invited me to stay because we had a meeting early the next morning and my quarters were quite some distance away. I offered to sleep on the floor, but she said no, that wouldn't be necessary, and so the three of us spent the night on the bed—a situation complicated somewhat by the fact that my legs had swelled during the course of all that walking and greeting the troops and I couldn't get my boots off. Normally, under such circumstances, I had a bootjack that I could use to pry them off; in this case, Donna and her friend both tried to help, to no avail. Eventually, our struggles were transformed into maneuvers of a different sort. Donna fell asleep, but her friend and I continued an exploration of the intricacies of the cavalry uniform. Naturally, with my britches tucked into my boots, I wasn't able to remove them, either. It was an evening that was at once frustrating and creative.

I do not know if I was bold, but opportunities presented themselves and I took advantage—in Kansas and back home in Los Angeles. Gene was invited everywhere then, to all the best parties—large garden parties held almost every Saturday night—by someone or other—in a big tent, with dinner and dancing for several hundred. I remember one such party at Cobina Wright's house. Gene and I were talking with Gary Cooper and his wife, Rocky. Of all the actors in Hollywood, Cooper was the man I

My father, Count Alexander Loiewski

My mother, Marguerite Cassini. The daughter of the czar's ambassador to the United States, she was the trendsetting toast of Washington at the turn of the century.

Recorded for posterity: my first date

At El Morocco in its heyday, with Emilio Pucci and Pier Angeli

Out on the town with Merry Fahrney, my first wife. The gossip columns assumed we were discussing a court's invalidation of her divorce from her previous husband, but Merry would have never been caught having a conversation about anything of substance.

Gene Tierney

Our studios and the Tierney family were strongly opposed to Gene and me getting married. But as soon as they learned we had stolen away to commit the deed, they set the publicity machine rolling, which included releasing this quaint staged photograph to the press.

Because we eloped, Gene didn't have the chance to wear the gown I had designed for our wedding. She finally had the opportunity four years later in her film *The Razor's Edge*.

"New Citizen Rewarded with Kiss" was the headline that accompanied this photograph of Gene and me taken on the happy day I became a U.S. citizen. During those patriotic war years, my renunciation of my title and my eagerness to join the armed services was excellent copy for Hollywood.

I admit that I was proud to show off my hard-earned U.S. Cavalry uniform when we went out.

A designer couldn't ask for a more exquisite woman to dress—Gene modeling a gown I designed for her film *Shanghai Gesture*.

Attending another Hollywood affair: Gene is dressed as a Southern belle for this costume party, and I as a riverboat gambler.

Hollywood stories always have to have happy endings, which is why this photograph was released exclaiming that our baby girl Daria was "healthy and thriving" and "intently watching a rattle" in Gene's hands. The terrible truth that could never have been released to the public was that our poor darling daughter had been born blind, deaf, and severely retarded due to an unthinkable act by an overzealous Gene Tierney fan.

AP/WIDE WORLD PHOTOS

At the Academy Awards ceremony, 1946, the night Gene lost the Oscar to Joan Crawford. I often felt that the Oscar might have been a much-needed boost to Gene's spirits in those dark years after Daria's birth.

AP/WIDE WORLD PHOTOS

Breakfast with my daughter Christina

Sketching in my office, early 1950s, making sure every dress for my line was perfect

With Grace in Cannes, during the filming of *To Catch a Thief*. I think Grace was at her most charming a magical on these delightful days o

I had been seeing Grace Kelly platonically in Los Angeles and New York. Events took a turn after she wrote me from location in France: "Those who love me shall follow me."

With Hitchcock and Grace. Grace is wearing a dress I designed for her, with a variation on the famous white Peter Pan collar, which exemplified the Grace Kelly Look. It is obviously *not* the dress that is capturing the eye of Hitchcock, whose crush on Grace was a well-known secret.

At Joan Whitney
Payson's *bal masqué*,
dressed as Paris and
Helen of Troy

I will not participate in fashionable innuendo and false gossip
about Grace. We were in love. We were engaged to be married—
no more, no less.

In Palm Beach, with my look-alike, Stash Radziwill. Yes, I suppose there is some resemblance, but I still cannot understand how my longtime friend Franklin Roosevelt, Jr., could have kept getting us confused.

With two of my models. I've always wanted the women who model my lines to be not merely beautiful, but also full of vigor and enthusiasm.

Left: The sketch that helped
convince Jacqueline Kennedy to
name me her official couturier. I
envisioned for her a look of
exquisitely simple elegance,
using the finest materials. *Below:*
Jackie wearing the actual gown
at the Inaugural Gala. For some
time, she tried in vain to have
it—rather than her Bergdorf-
designed ball gown—featured on
her official Smithsonian
mannequin.

Showing sketches to the leading fashion editors. The interest in Jackie's wardrobe was unbelievable and certainly unprecedented for a First Lady.

Left: Dancing with Jackie. *Right:* With the President and Mrs. Kennedy. I do think that my social position as a close friend of the Kennedys helped to raise the status and image of American designers throughout the world.

Joan Kennedy appearing in a fashion show she had asked me to host in Boston for a charity event sponsored by Cardinal Cushing

A playful reaction to the inevitable talk concerning Jackie's wardrobe

Informal merrymaking with the President

With old friends in Megève, the French winter resort. Left to right: Benno Graziani, me, Fiat Motorworks owner Gianni Agnelli, my brother, Igor.

The spirited Loiewski-Cassinis—we survived and prospered. Left to right: Igor, Mother, me, Father.

With Johnny Carson and Leslie Caron. I've enjoyed making television appearances since the early 1950s; it occurred to me early on that television would be a very effective medium for a designer.

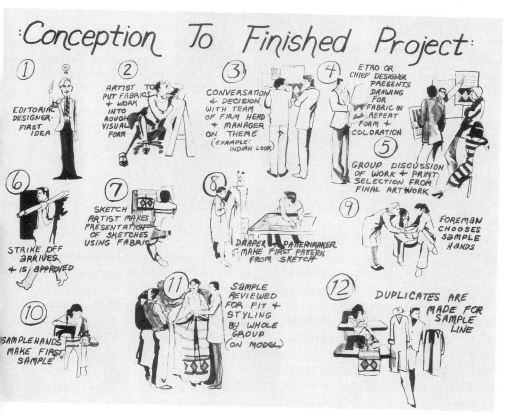

Conception To Finished Project:

1. EDITORIAL DESIGNER - FIRST IDEA

2. ARTIST TO PUT FABRICS & WORK INTO ROUGH VISUAL FORM

3. CONVERSATION & DECISION WITH TEAM OF FIRM HEAD & MANAGER ON THEME (EXAMPLE: INDIAN LOOK)

4. ETRO OR CHIEF DESIGNER PRESENTS DRAWING FOR FABRIC IN REPEAT FORM & COLORATION

5. GROUP DISCUSSION OF WORK & PRINT SELECTION FROM FINAL ARTWORK

6. STRIKE OFF ARRIVES & IS APPROVED

7. SKETCH ARTIST MAKES PRESENTATION OF SKETCHES USING FABRIC

8. DRAPER & PATTERNMAKER MAKE FIRST PATTERN FROM SKETCH

9. FOREMAN CHOOSES SAMPLE HANDS

10. SAMPLE HANDS MAKE FIRST SAMPLE

11. SAMPLE REVIEWED FOR FIT & STYLING BY WHOLE GROUP (ON MODEL)

12. DUPLICATES ARE MADE FOR SAMPLE LINE

"How to Make a Dress"

At Bernie Cornfeld's unimaginable Swiss villa, with Victoria Principal and Cornfeld

I think fashion shows, above all, should be fun and entertaining, and there's no reason why they can't have an occasional spontaneous moment of silliness.

Continuing my lifelong tennis efforts: At the 1976 Robert F. Kennedy Tennis Tournament, receiving victory cup from Howard Cosell and Jackie.

A new passion—harness racing. With my equine comrade at the Pompano Beach racetrack.

admired most; the least affected, the least "starlike," a solid American man (the archetypal American man, perhaps). We were standing in the garden talking when a cinematographer, fairly well known, came up and started pawing at Gene, drunkenly perhaps, but pawing, kissing her neck.

I decked him. It was a surgical strike, a quick left and he was flat on his back in the flowers. Cooper nodded, as if to say, "Nicely done." His wife laughed and said to him, "You only do that in the movies . . . why don't you ever do that for me in real life?"

Real life. Gene and I floated along, the marriage slowly losing air, punctured by Daria, by our frequent separations, by our respective moods and tempers. Gene was understandably upset by my behavior at those grand parties. It was so easy to lose oneself in conversation with the fascinating creatures who populated them. It was so easy to disappear in such a crowd. There were certain telltale signs of availability. My favorite was the husband and wife who couldn't keep their hands off each other, lots of little kisses and hand-holding. It was guaranteed that one or the other was having an affair.

I met Barbara Hutton at one of these garden parties, and a rather bizarre adventure ensued. Barbara was the talk of Hollywood that year. It was, literally, "Barbara says this" and "Barbara did that" and "Barbara *bought* that." Everywhere she went, every time she made an appearance, people surrounded her, vying for her attention, and there was a steady buzzing in the room: "Barbara, Barbara, Barbara . . ." It was clear that the stars of Hollywood could be as sycophantic as anyone. Their money had come from stardust and tinsel; hers had come from Woolworth's and in abundance, although what distinguished Barbara was not the size of her fortune but her willingness to spend it. Her parties were considered a *must*.

She was very much in her prime then, thirty-one years old and married to Cary Grant, her third husband; they were the ultimate couple, a dream couple (a fantasy couple, if the truth be told). They lived on the old Douglas Fairbanks estate in Bel-Air, an immense Spanish Colonial, with a slew of servants and Barbara's usual retinue of jesters and spongers, whom Grant didn't care for at all.

I thought she was quite beautiful, in a vulnerable sort of way. She was born to be plump, but had starved herself thin. She was about five foot seven and blonde, with a full, pretty mouth, a delicate neck, slim shoulders. Her face was dominated, though, by her eyes, which were marvelous—enormous and blue, with long lashes.

When we met that night at the party, she immediately admired my garb. "You look jolly well in your uniform," she said. "It's very well cut. Your boots are excellent."

I nodded, or perhaps bowed. I knew of her weakness for European nobility, as did anyone who read a newspaper. Barbara's first husband had been Prince Alexis Mdivani, a Georgian polo player and playboy (he and his brother, Serge, were called "the marrying Mdivanis"); the second had been Count Kurt Haugwitz-Reventlow, an imperious Danish nobleman. Both had emerged millionaires from their interludes with Barbara (as would each of her seven husbands except Grant, who didn't need the money). Indeed, the lady seemed intent on refurbishing a sizable portion of the noble houses of Europe. She was what Merry Fahrney had pretended to be. Her interest in me interested me; I was flattered.

"The world is going to be so different now," she sighed. "The Germans will keep all of Europe. There will be no place to go. No Lido, no Paris . . . Can you imagine life without the Excelsior [in Venice]? I suppose we'll just have to live in California and make the best of it."

I knew all of these places and could discuss them with her. She decided to invite Gene and me to dinner the following Saturday night.

It was a small dinner, but sumptuous, served by liveried butlers. Barbara appeared, as she often did for formal occasions, dressed as a Hindu princess (she had a wonderful collection of saris), weighed down with the most impressive jewels. There were expensive gifts for each of her guests; I was given a beautiful gold watch.

Cary Grant wasn't there that night, perhaps because Barbara's cousin Jimmy Donahue was. They didn't get along very well. Jimmy had a strong, bizarre hold on her (he would later exhibit similar powers with the duchess of Windsor); he was defiantly, hilariously gay—a style that would not become popular for many years ("I'm just an old queen," he would say)— and he set the tone for many of Barbara's entertainments, which featured the oddest assortment of people. There were movie people there that night (the director Delmer Daves and his beautiful wife, Mary Lou, among others); flagrant friends of Jimmy Donahue's; and a military contingent, including a certain General Cousins, one of Sunset Boulevard's most fervent guardians.

"General," Barbara said, introducing me with her usual light touch of a British accent, "this is *Leff*tenant *Count* Oleg Cassini."

"Oh," he said, "I didn't know there were any officers with aristocratic titles in the U.S. military."

"Just Lieutenant Cassini, sir," I said, with a laugh. "just plain Lieutenant," and I made a little joke to paper it over, and we laughed together
and chatted awhile.

After dinner, Barbara and I had another chance to talk. She was quite
sensitive and sophisticated, very well versed in art. We talked about
travel and horses and painting. Then she made an evaluation: "Oleg, you
are a cultured man. You're not as handsome as some of the other men in
my life, but you do have that certain quality and I could even fall in love
with you."

I figured this was hypothetical flattery. She was married to the most
charming man in Hollywood (although there were rumors of difficulties).
I figured she was indulging in idle, romantic chatter, until some days later,
when Jimmy Donahue approached me and said, "You know, Barbara
is very impressed with you. She likes you very much, and things aren't
going too well with Grant. You might do well here for yourself, and for
Barbara."

Much to my surprise, he then gave me an address in Hollywood and
a time for a meeting. "Barbara would like to see you privately," he said.

I met her there. It was a cozy, candle-lit *pied-à-terre* with fabrics
draped and covering furniture and walls, glittering and dark. There was
music playing and the scent of sandalwood incense in the air. We talked
for a while. She read poems that she had written. I wasn't much for this
sort of thing—Gene had exposed me to samples of her own work early on
—but I played along, waiting. At one point, I remember, I held her hand,
but there were none of the signals in response that might lead me to press
onward. I began to suspect that *this* was what Barbara Hutton considered
"romance."

Eventually, she said, "I'm so lonely. Cary is causing me all sorts of
problems. I'm going to divorce him. I'm so tired of this place. I must get
away. You must come with me . . . you and Gene must come with me to
San Francisco this weekend. You must come as my guests."

Gene had her doubts about this. She was annoyed, but also—and this
would have been a common reaction among any of the big stars—flattered.
We went to San Francisco, where Barbara kept a grand suite of rooms at
the Mark Hopkins Hotel. We stayed with her that weekend, part of her
traveling road show; we went shopping at Gump's, the famous specialty
store where she bought many of her Oriental *objets*; she showered Gene
with gifts, as was her wont.

At one point, the phone rang and it was Cary Grant calling *me*. "I'd heard you were up there this weekend," he said. "Barbara speaks so well of you. I would very much like to meet you, to get together and talk. Can you lunch with me this week?"

All of this was happening in a very compressed period of time, a matter of several weeks. Barbara Hutton had swooped into our lives and seemed to have taken over for a while—especially mine.

I met with Cary Grant for lunch. He was wearing a blue suit, white shirt, and regimental tie; he was impeccable, as always. I will say that I have met many charming people in my life, people who used their charm in powerful ways (like President Kennedy), people who have been cleverly, diabolically, sensually charming (like Errol Flynn and Tyrone Power). But none was more charming than Cary Grant. He seemed almost a force of nature; it was dazzling. He said, "Oleg, I understand Barbara thinks the world of you. You know, we are having problems. I hope you don't have any interest in her personally, because frankly that would be a terrible blow to me. Now, if I can trust you, if I am sure there is no romantic interest there, if I'm convinced you are a friend, I will ask you to do me a favor—intercede on my behalf. Be a peacemaker. Please tell her to be reasonable."

Without quite knowing how or why, I was nodding my head, agreeing to act as a go-between in their marriage. As I said, the man was quite charming.

Barbara and I met for tea at her home a day or so later. I told her about my lunch with Cary. "He's an extraordinary man," I said. "You should give him another chance."

"No," she said. "My mind is made up. It will not work. It's true he's the handsomest creature imaginable and a charming fellow, at times, but he also has a terrible temper and we have basic differences . . . and anyway, Oleg, it would be much better if you and I married."

I suppose my jaw dropped. She proceeded to weave a fantasy life for us; I believe such fantasies were the closest she came to courtship. "We're destined to be together because we speak the same language. We are used to the same things. . . ." And then she wooed me in much the same manner as Merry Fahrney, with promises of polo ponies (always polo ponies!) and a life of leisure. Only I knew, in this case, that she wasn't fooling around. It was Barbara Hutton's custom to give a million dollars to each of her husbands as a wedding present.

"I don't want to do you any harm," she continued, "but if you decided to divorce Gene, I would be very generous. I don't think she understands you as well as I do, and this might be the best solution for everyone. I will give her a million dollars, and then you and I will be married."

"What can I say to that?" I said, flummoxed. "I think this is fantastic, what you are telling me . . . and *you* are fantastic, but I don't know how I could bring this up with Gene."

"Don't be so egotistical," she said. "Gene might well like the idea."

"*Touché*. You are absolutely right."

And yes, I did bring it up with Gene. I tried to make it into a joke, but I was curious nonetheless. "You know, you might not think I'm worth much, but there are others who do. Would you ever give me up?"

"Gladly, anytime." She laughed.

"Would you give me up for a million dollars?"

"I told you I'd do it for free."

Then I told her about the conversation with Barbara, and she continued to laugh. "Do *you* think you're worth that much?"

But I persisted: "Be serious. Think about it. Think about the reservations you have about me, about my character. You have the opportunity now to do something about it. You would have financial security. You might be well rid of me, and able to meet someone else, someone in a better position. Be serious with me now, for a moment, because I don't want to ever again hear about all you've given up for me, or what I should have been, or the man you might have gotten. I can clear the slate with one stroke here."

She said, seriously now, that she wasn't interested and asked, "How do you feel about it?"

"I love *you*," I said.

And it was true: I would never have left Gene then, for any amount of money.

Barbara Hutton and I remained friends, but only friends; I never for a moment regretted the decision not to pursue her, especially in view of the sad downward spiral that ensued. I don't believe any man could have saved her from her fate. Looking back now, I can see what the headlines might have been if I'd tried: "Naughty Count Rides Again—Leaves Tierney for Poor Little Rich Girl." I would have forfeited any claim to being taken seriously in my life. Besides, I'd had enough of polo ponies at Fort Riley; what I wanted now, more than anything else, was to go home.

I had Gene contact General Cousins, whom we'd met at Barbara Hutton's party, to see what he could do about getting me a transfer to Los Angeles. The general, a handsome, gray-haired man, vainly assumed this was an invitation to waltz with a glamorous movie star; it wasn't. The general told Gene he could do nothing for me.

One day, I heard a group of officers talking about a notorious character named Colonel Kimberly—once a very promising officer but done in by wine, women, and song, especially wine, and passed over for promotion to General several times. He was said to be the army's oldest active colonel, holding the fort at the Ninth Service Command, the military police headquarters in downtown Hollywood.

Once again, I sent Gene into action. She visited the colonel, and this time, miracle of miracles, a transfer to the Ninth Service Command was forthcoming in a matter of weeks. I arrived home in early 1945. The war was not yet over, but the outcome was clear.

Colonel Kimberly was as advertised: a distinguished-looking man, a West Point graduate, a delightful conversationalist, with a red nose that announced his proclivities. He was very interested in women, especially movie stars, and it quickly became apparent that my duties as a member of his staff would include finding him dates.

"Well, Oleg," he'd say each morning, "who do we have tonight?"

We'd have dinner at our headquarters, which was the old Doheny mansion, and then go out. I could usually find him a starlet or two, but that wasn't enough. He wanted the real thing, and there was a joking menace to his demands. "If you don't come through, I'm sure there'll be work for a man with your talents when we invade Japan."

And so I approached the actress Virginia Bruce, a very beautiful girl with whom I'd had a serious flirt before my marriage, and said to her, "You have to help me out. He's a very charming fellow. You'll enjoy it, and have the satisfaction of knowing that you saved my life."

It was true that Colonel Kimberly was quite a charming fellow—I'd brought him along to several Hollywood parties and he'd done well—but there was one thing I wasn't telling Virginia: Kimberly was from the Deep South, and quite intractable on matters of race. Virginia, on the other hand, was somewhat to the left, which meant she was *very* sympathetic to our noble Soviet allies and the oppressed of the South, and indeed, the oppressed everywhere—except those oppressed by having to listen to polemics on these subjects. I would have a difficult tightrope to walk that night.

I don't remember exactly what started it—perhaps the colonel said something like, "You Northern folks just don't know how to handle your colored," as he often did—but it started almost immediately. Within minutes she had called him an America-Firster, a reactionary, racist, Fascist, and he called her a Commie dupe, fellow traveler, and parlor pink. Colonel Kimberly got so red in the face that I began to wonder if I was indeed on my way to Japan, and he continued the next morning, shouting at me, "That's what's ruining our country! People like her . . . dupes!"

The colonel never sent me to Japan, but then he never got the chance. He was retired from the service a week later.

Kimberly's replacement was a Lieutenant Colonel Hunt, who was the spitting image of Hitler—the resemblance was remarkable, really—and no friend of mine. He had been jealous of my closeness to Kimberly and, immediately, sought to get rid of me. In the heat of the summer of 1945, I was transferred to duty along the Gila River in Arizona, guarding the border from attack, I suppose, and also keeping watch on a Japanese relocation camp nearby.

I did not last long on the Gila River. The midsummer heat was simply unbelievable. You could not go outside during the day; even at midnight, driving along in an open car, it was hard to breathe. I was in charge of six enlisted men. We spent most of our time in the barracks, tossing ice cubes at the electric fans to keep cool. My eyes began to act up again, becoming red, swollen, and painfully itchy. I could hardly see.

And so, back to Los Angeles. One night in the officers' club at Pasadena Hospital, I had a massive asthma attack. I was gasping for air; I couldn't breathe—it must have seemed as if I were choking on a piece of food. A doctor rushed to my aid, and when the attack passed, he said that it was ridiculous to keep me in the army. I went to his office the next day and, after assuring him that I did not hold the army responsible for my asthma, was honorably discharged from the service.

I sometimes wonder what caused the psychological chaos that led to my infirmity during that time. Was it the threat of remaining in the army interminably, of being sent on occupation duty in Japan? Or perhaps the knowledge that I'd soon be *leaving* the army and would have to deal with the question of what to do when the war was over?

I know I was very concerned about my future; Gene was, too. She was confused about what she wanted for me. On the one hand, she wanted success, especially in traditional East Coast terms. She wanted me to be an executive somewhere, going to work each day, wearing a gray suit and carrying an attaché case. She wanted me to be as her father had seemed. At the same time, though, I think she wanted me to take care of her as I had before the war, to subordinate my career once more.

This was unacceptable. I wasn't sure what the future held, but I knew that I had to do something soon or life would pass me by. I certainly had no intention of merely being Mr. Gene Tierney. Sometimes, when I was out and about in Hollywood, I would hear people saying, "Look, there goes Gene Tierney's husband."

I hated it and was frustrated by Gene's conflicting demands on me. I needed to prove myself, and this led to a great many unfortunate scenes, public arguments, and fistfights. The years after the war were perhaps my most bellicose. I was deceptively fit, "deceptively" because I appeared to be very slight. I weighed about 160 pounds and had a 29-inch waist, but my back was broad and strong and I was in excellent shape after the army. Most important, I knew how to fight.

One memorable, and as it turned out, rather productive, fight occurred on an afternoon when Gene and I had attended the races at Del Mar. We were leaving the track with Roger Valmy and Laura Bostwick, one of Gene's old friends from Fort Riley. There was terrible traffic, bumper to bumper, made worse by the jeep to the rear, which kept tapping us. I was annoyed, but figured it was accidental; when it persisted, I turned to get a closer look. Two fellows having a hell of a time. One had a bottle in his hand.

"Watch what you're doing!" I yelled at them, along with some other things.

"Don't pick a fight," Gene said. "You have your best suit on. Let them pass."

I waved them past. We continued on around a bend and there was the jeep, stopped in the middle of the road. I pulled up behind them, and they *backed up*, bumping us again, then drove off. I was seething. "If I find those guys, I'm going to beat the hell out of them!"

I found them soon enough: several miles down the road, at the Del Mar Hotel. The jeep was in the parking lot. "Here we go," I said to Valmy, pulling in. "We're going to teach those guys a lesson."

"Well, you know," said Roger, who was about six foot one, with a magnificent build, "I've got a bum shoulder. I don't want to get into any trouble."

I went into the bar, which was crowded. Valmy followed at a discreet distance, the women behind him. The bar was on the right; there were tables on the left. And directly in front of me were the two jokers from the jeep, just arrived, ordering drinks. They were big and red-faced; they sounded like Texans. I had no real plan of action, just a lot of adrenaline and a completely berserk calm.

I tapped one of them on the shoulder. "Are you the fellow who was driving that jeep?"

"Yes."

And then I hit him with a simply gorgeous left, placed just perfectly, at the point of his chin. His friend looked down in amazement, and as he was doing that, I hit *him* with the biggest uppercut I have ever thrown in my life.

This had all transpired in silence, or so it seemed; silence and slow motion. Now the bar seemed to erupt. There was an enormous commotion, people rushing at me. I was still in my rage, ready to take the next one on. Someone grappled my shoulder and I whirled, ready to go at it, but the fellow was reaching to shake my hand. "Fabulous, fabulous," he was saying. "That was just terrific. Come sit down with me. Let's talk."

It was Jack Warner.

"I've never seen anything like that!" he said. "Not even in the movies. From now on, you're going to be known as 'One-Punch' Cassini."

The police had arrived and were restoring order. Gene came and sat with us. "This is some fellow you've got here," Warner said. "He's better than Errol Flynn."

He laughed, and we began to talk about other things. He'd heard I was a tennis player, and invited me for doubles at his private court. "Call me, call me," he said, as Gene and I left.

"You know," Gene said, "I hate it when you fight . . . but if you're going to do it, you couldn't have had a better audience. A friendship with Jack Warner could prove very useful to you, and I think he liked you a lot."

I suspect it was Warner who gave the story to Louella Parsons, because I was front-page news in the *Examiner* the next day. And Gene was right: Jack Warner did become a good and valuable friend of mine in the years to come. We played tennis at his house almost every weekend. We talked about girls and horses. I thought he was a genuinely funny man —although I'm sure there are hundreds of former employees at Warner Bros. who could tell you what a tyrant he was—and I was happy to laugh at his jokes.

Jack would love to hold forth after dinner, lavishly served, always; Warner's table—his estate, in fact—was one of the few in the United States that could compare with Europe's finest. He would stand up and deliver something very much like a borscht-belt routine—lots of jokes and laughter, both sycophantic and natural. I remember one evening, however, when Laurence Olivier was the guest of honor and Jack went into his routine. Everyone was laughing, as usual, except Olivier. Jack told joke after joke, gradually directing his attention more and more toward Olivier, straining harder. The rest of us were laughing less now, and Olivier wouldn't even grant him a polite smile. It was as if he were saying, "You might be a bigshot in Hollywood, but *I* don't laugh if I don't feel like it."

I was rooting for Jack, hoping that he'd come up with a real zinger, something that would cause Olivier to laugh despite himself. But he didn't, and eventually just gave up, mumbling. It was the only time I ever saw him embarrassed.

Gene was right about his being "useful," too. Eventually, Jack asked me to be head of wardrobe at Warner Bros.—at a time when I had other plans and chose not to accept. That wasn't the only business dealing we had, though. There were others, the first of which was quite curious. It involved a brief stint I had as a Hollywood agent.

In the months before I left the army, I'd been surveying my options. One day, when I was still in uniform, I had lunch with Charlie Feldman, the president of Famous Artists, a debonair playboy type. "What's so good about making clothes?" he said. "It might mean something in Paris, but in this town you're just another technician, like makeup or lighting or the hairdresser. Listen, Oleg, you could make some real money. Use your talent. You know horseflesh. Find me some talent, sign 'em up. You'd be a natural agent."

Feldman had a secret agenda, I suspect. He wanted Gene to sign with Famous Artists. But he offered me a large salary, Gene or not, and a title: Executive Vice-President in Charge of New Talent.

I took this very seriously. Before I accepted the job, I figured I'd see what it would be like, and spent some time scouting for talent. A friend of mine, a producer named Robert Haggiag, said that he'd just met the most astonishing Swedish girl. She lived with several friends who were almost as beautiful. "I guarantee you, Oleg," he said, "you have never seen anything like her."

I immediately called Jack Warner. I knew he appreciated a good-looking girl. "Jack," I said, "I have something very special for you, a girl who will drive you crazy, a natural star. Let's have lunch, but not in the studio—away from the commissary. I guarantee you, Jack, you've never seen anything like her."

I suppose this was brazen, not having seen her myself yet, but the gamble paid off. I went to the apartment early to make sure that she was dressed well and knew how to present herself . . . and an absolutely stunning creature opened the door.

"Hello," she said, in that clear-eyed, no-nonsense way that Swedes have. "I am Anita Ekberg."

She was quite young, late teens. She wasn't expecting me till later, and was wearing only a loosely tied robe. We began to talk. I wanted to coach her for lunch. I asked her, "Anita, how would you go about seducing a man? What would you say?"

"I would say nothing," she said, standing. "I would just do this."

With that, she opened her robe. And she was right. I have never seen a body like that. I couldn't resist; nor, apparently, could Jack Warner. He was entranced with her at lunch, which I'd arranged at a small, out-of-the-way place. I selected a peasant-style blouse for Anita to wear, off one shoulder, and no bra. After a while, I pleaded another engagement and left them to their own devices. Soon after, Anita was given a part in a Warner Bros. film.

Well, I figured that I had a big future as an agent . . . but Gene wanted no part of it. She was adamant. "You won't get anywhere," she said. "You'll never be part of the inner circle. And anyway, all Charlie Feldman is interested in is signing me."

She had other plans for me. She wanted me to design clothes for pictures again, now that the blackball against me had been lifted.

Gene arranged a meeting with Darryl Zanuck. He was an interesting fellow; short, very energetic, with protruding teeth and a big mustache. He knew the business as well as anyone, having worked his way up from screenwriter to head of production at Warner Bros.; he and Joe Schenck had created Twentieth Century-Fox in the mid-1930s, and built it into a major studio in just a few short years. But the Old Guard, like Mayer, the Selznicks, and the Warners, who'd created Hollywood, considered him something of an outsider. They didn't think his motion pictures had "class." Zanuck responded by striking a very macho pose. He played polo, and never let anyone forget it. He would strut around the studio brandishing a little polo mallet; he was very interested in horses, and was one of a group (which included Will Rogers and John Huston) who played polo and had steeplechase races at the Riviera Club in Santa Monica. He knew that I'd been a cavalry officer; he also knew that Gene and I had been married long enough for me to be considered a permanent part of the Hollywood scenery, although I don't think he knew my work very well at that point.

He offered me a trial assignment on a cowboy picture called *Green Grass of Wyoming.*

"Darryl, this is a joke," I said. "This is no picture for me."

"Why not? You've spent the last five years with horses."

"Gene thinks I'd be right for *The Razor's Edge*," I suggested. It was going to be a very important movie, from the book by Somerset Maugham, starring Gene and Tyrone Power, directed by Edmund Goulding. It was set in the 1920s and would require a knowledge of period clothes, but they would be glamorous, high-fashion clothes—especially the gowns Gene would wear—and I knew I could handle it easily.

"No, I don't think so," he said. "Get your feel back, man. Do well with this one and we'll work out something."

I was very disappointed. I went home to Gene and said, "See, this isn't going to work for me. I'm going to become an agent, or maybe sell Freddie Heineken's beer."

"No. You're going to do *The Razor's Edge*," she said, and stormed down the mountain to Twentieth Century-Fox.

"I want Oleg to do the clothes for *The Razor's Edge*," she told Zanuck.

"No," he replied. "Costumes are going to be very important to this picture. They have to be right. Your husband has been out of touch for too many years. I can't take the chance."

"Very well," Gene said, "then I won't do the picture."

"Very well," Zanuck replied, "then I'll put you on suspension."

Gene then came back up the mountain and told me what had happened. "You're crazy," I said. "I wish you wouldn't do that for me." When word got out that Tierney had been suspended because she insisted that her husband design her clothes, and Zanuck wouldn't let him, it would not seem very good for me.

Gene was suspended for two weeks, and then Zanuck relented. He said I could design the clothes for the two leading women, Gene and Anne Baxter. The regular wardrobe staff would do the others. I was given a cottage at the studio to work in, and a nice salary . . . and I think I did some of my best work for that picture. There was one dress in particular, a slim black one with fringes, suggesting the flapper style of the 1920s but appropriate for any era. It was very décolleté, with spaghetti straps and a matching cape. I later included something like it in my early collections and did quite well with it.

In the end, Zanuck came around. When *The Razor's Edge* was done, he sent me a note saying that he'd been wrong about me, that I'd done a superb job. He suggested that I continue designing Gene's clothes, and promised to give me other special projects.

Actually, the year or so after I was released from the army was my most successful period in Hollywood, professionally. I not only worked at Twentieth Century-Fox; I had two other jobs as well.

One was a partnership with a fellow named Paul Portanova. (He was divorced from one of the Texas Cullens, and his son, Baron Ricky de Portanova, is one of the richest men in the world.) Paul was a rogue and an entrepreneur who sold all sorts of things—umbrellas, furniture, garden equipment—from a showroom on La Cienega Boulevard. He wanted to get into clothes: high-priced, tailored, gabardine ladies' suits, which were very popular in California then. This sounded like a good idea; I especially liked the name of our company, Casanova, for CASsini and PortANOVA. I had always been a great admirer of the corporation's namesake, who was one of the great literary figures of the eighteenth century, in addition to the talents for which he was best known. Casanova was a superb writer, whose memoirs I've read and reread; they have always lightened my spirits.

The only problem with Casanova (the corporation) was the scarcity of piece goods in the months after the war ended. Fabric of any sort was hard to come by, but gabardine, especially quality gabardine, was virtually nonexistent. Making money in fashion was no secret at that point. If you had the cloth, you had a gold mine. But why should a manufacturer consign any of his precious assets to a couple of nobodies on the West Coast when he had regular customers to keep happy?

Because we had a secret weapon: Gene. She was more than happy to go to Forstmann's in New York, manufacturer of *The Best* gabardine on the planet, and see if she could charm them. Apparently, they were delighted by her visit. She called, very excited, from New York: "I've got you a quota!" It wasn't large enough for us to make a fortune, but we sold what we produced.

My third job during this time was a lot of fun. I was head of wardrobe for Eagle Lion Studios, a well-financed British operation run by one of the most colorful characters in Hollywood, Bryan Foy. He had been one of the Seven Little Foys, the famous vaudeville act, and liked to think of himself as the king of the "B" pictures. After many years in production at Warner Bros., he had found backers to start his own studio (it was located on Melrose Avenue), an operation devoted to the virtues of time and budget. Nothing else mattered; not script, not actors, certainly not clothes. The producer was the *auteur*, not the director; production was art. I once attended a meeting where a producer complained that he couldn't bring in a picture on time; Foy took the script, ripped twenty pages out of the middle, and said, "Now it should work." Another producer was having trouble with a temperamental actor. "Kill him in the first fifteen minutes and improvise," Foy said.

Foy's advice to me was similarly succinct: "Don't worry about anything. Just have fun. We're gonna have some great-looking girls here, you want a couple? We'll put 'em on contract. They'll be your slaves."

The girls weren't bad, but the pictures were. I don't remember a single title, a willful act of amnesia, but I did have fun working for Foy, whom I'd known since my days in the Wolf Pack (his regular crowd was rather continental: the writer Barney Glaeser, the director Jean Negulesco, and Peter Lorre, among others). And he paid me a very generous salary. In fact, taking all three jobs together, I was making a small fortune: $2,000 a week.

Gene was making a large fortune, however: $5,000 a week. She was at her peak now, and wanted to live that way. She decided it was time for us to come down from the mountain and join Hollywood society in earnest. She sold our property on Mulholland Drive, much to my regret, and bought a fairly traditional movie star's mansion in the Holmby Hills section of Bel-Air. It had the requisite manicured grounds and gardens and swimming pool.

We were now as "in" as we'd once been "out." We were regulars at Jack Warner's house and David Selznick's; "in" with Zanuck's horsey set and with the English group—David Niven, Rex Harrison (with whom Gene starred in *The Ghost and Mrs. Muir*), Alfred Hitchcock, Charles Laughton, Douglas Fairbanks, Jr., and Elsie de Wolf, Lady Mendl.

Cole Porter was especially fond of Gene, and we'd often be invited to dinners at his home. It was one of the most coveted invitations in Hollywood: invariably dinner for twelve to sixteen carefully selected people, who were expected to be clever and literate (no silly industry babble allowed).

One evening we were invited there for dinner and Gene said, "Cole wants to put you next to Katharine Hepburn."

I knew Hepburn only by reputation, and hoped to make a good impression. She was one of the few people in the business with a real sense of style, an obvious cut above the rest in talent and sensibility.

Unfortunately, though, I'd made a late-afternoon appointment with the actor Forrest Tucker, whom I'd known at Fort Riley, and several other old cavalry mates who happened to be in town. We went out for drinks and reminisced, the nostalgia extending to our choice of beverage, boilermakers, which we'd drunk with abandon at the Hotel Muehlbach in Kansas City. I drank with somewhat more restraint now, but not enough. It was a hot day; the beer was going down easily. I felt okay.

I felt okay in the car, driving to Cole Porter's house, but not great . . . a little strange, nothing to worry about. I felt okay during the cocktail hour, making small talk. I was introduced to Hepburn, who, in that direct, ebullient manner she had, said, "I'm not going to talk to you now. We're seated together at dinner, and I've got lots of things I want to know about you, so prepare yourself."

I was complimented by her interest, and was very happy as we sat down . . . and then, about ten minutes into the dinner, the boilermakers struck. I excused myself and, in my suave, continental manner, lunged for the nearest door. It was a smallish house, surrounded by greenery, with a bit of a pond, hidden by trees; I made for the trees, and lost what seemed to be ten pounds. I stayed there for perhaps fifteen minutes and then returned, wan and exhausted, excusing myself by saying that I'd made an important long-distance call to Europe.

Hepburn resumed conversation as if nothing had happened, but I was so devitalized that I could do little more than nod my head. I'm sure she was convinced that I was a perfect bore. I found *her* fascinating, though. She had created an elaborate façade for herself, a more developed and sophisticated image than most of her competitors, but she wasn't afraid to make light of it all, even to parody herself—as if to say, "Isn't it odd that this contraption, this personality I've created for public consumption, actually works?" It was quite winning, but remote, too. There was no getting past the façade; it was smooth.

This, I found, was often the case with stars. Their "personalities" were little more than a carefully selected assemblage of mannerisms, easily identifiable, easily marketed. Often it was just a *look*, like Veronica Lake's peekaboo bangs and pout and voice, that conveyed an image—in Veronica's case, of sultriness—that wasn't necessarily there. Beneath these glorious images and carefully rigged personalities, most were very much the same: workaholics, frantically concerned with their weight, their hair, their lines, and the silent enemy: age. These concerns were obsessive. *So much* was at stake. They didn't leave much room for fun, or compassion, or anything *complicated* that did not pertain to their careers.

On the other hand, the atmosphere was highly charged sexually, and there were constant romances. These were the results of the concentration of the select group of people who had looks, money, fame, and leisure, living in a small area. It could be James Dean and Ursula Andress or Jimmy and Pier Angeli; or Tyrone Power and Anita Ekberg or Tyrone and Lana Turner; Greg Bautzer and Joan Crawford or Greg and Ginger Rogers; or Victor Mature and Betty Grable or Victor and Rita Hayworth; or Gary Cooper and Dorothy di Frasso or Gary and Patricia Neal.

Friendship among stars also was a curious phenomenon. Gene had no friends who might be considered competitors, and this was quite typical. She could be friendly with older women—like Lenore (Mrs. Joseph) Cotten—and with men—like Clifton Webb and Tyrone Power—but no one her age, really. This was true among male stars as well. The big ones expected to be treated as royalty; each was as a sun, with various dimmer satellites swirling about him. For a time, I sought to become friendly with Errol Flynn—we played tennis together; his natural dash and flamboyance appealed to me—but it wasn't possible. Like most big stars, Flynn expected deference from his friends. His circle included lesser stars like Bruce Cabot and David Niven, and adventurous characters like Freddie McEvoy, none of whom questioned his suzerainty.

The stars were people who might dazzle or charm you; they didn't *converse* much. There wasn't a great deal of elegant repartee to be found in the film colony; the delicate arts of flirtation and seduction were largely unknown . . . an oddity, since the ability to seduce—seduce the public, that is—was the coin of the realm. I remember one night at a tent party at Joan Fontaine's. Gene and I were seated at separate tables, and afterward, on the way home, she complained, "You didn't pay any attention to me all night. We didn't dance at all. I was so bored."

"Why? Who were you sitting with?"

"Clark Gable and Jimmy Stewart."

"Don't you realize," I said, "that almost every woman in America would swoon at such an opportunity?"

The problem was that everyone was in the same line of work, a very insular business. They worked very hard, all the successful ones, and there wasn't time to *know* much beyond industry gossip. And so, when conversation waned, we often engaged in party games, especially at smaller dinners: charades, hide-and-seek, anything to pass the time.

There was a night at Jack Warner's when Elsa Maxwell came up with the notion of a design contest. Each man would pick the name of a woman from a hat, and then have to select some materials from a box of rags and odds and ends you might find in a hardware store, and create a glamorous costume for his partner. I was lucky enough to select Lana Turner, and as we ascended Warner's magnificent staircase to do our work in private, she was giggling, "I don't know if I'm lucky, but you're the only designer playing this game. What do you have in mind?"

"I want you to take your clothes off," I said.

"Why do we have to do that?"

"I must," I said, "create from the skin up."

Well, she was laughing and I was laughing—we'd had some champagne—and we began to hunt and peck a little. She played the coquette: "What can we do here? We have no time."

"There is always time," I said.

"Well, perhaps we do have a little time. . . ."

We re-emerged to oohs and ahhs. I had made a hoop skirt from a lamp shade and draped her in muslin with various baubles and pieces of equipment: she was a junkyard Scarlett O'Hara. There was applause, and cries of "Unfair! Unfair!" We received marvelous Cartier watches for winning first prize (and I was presented, privately, with another reward for my efforts: Lana's phone number).

The most memorable game I ever played at a Hollywood dinner party was also the most tragic. It was at Tyrone Power's house in Bel-Air, an intimate gathering but formal, as most every Saturday evening was, the men in black tie, the women in evening gowns. Tyrone was married at that time to the French actress Annabella. It was a decidedly English crowd: Rex Harrison and Lilli Palmer, Richard Greene and Patricia Medina, and David Niven with his beautiful young wife, Primula Rollo Niven.

After dinner, and after the conversation began to wane, someone suggested we play sardines, a form of hide-and-seek played in the dark. It was just something to do to be silly, and perhaps do some creative groping. I was selected to be "it" and began counting to one hundred while the others hid. It was during this process that I heard a thud, but didn't think anything of it . . . until I began my search for the others and heard moaning. Perhaps someone was leading me on? I found a door, opened it, and almost lost my balance. It led to a lower level, a garage-like area with a cement floor, but the first step was very tricky, greater than expected. The moaning was distinct now, and sounded serious. I couldn't find the lights and called for Tyrone. He came immediately, and there, fallen in a heap at the foot of the cement staircase, was Primula Niven. She appeared to be semiconscious; there was some blood on her temple.

David and Tyrone carried her to the living room and placed her on a sofa. A doctor was called; he came quickly. He took her pulse, looked into her eyes—you must imagine the rest of us gathered around in our evening clothes quietly watching, stunned, Niven perhaps the calmest of us all, in his classic British manner. "She'll be all right," David kept saying, as if to reassure us. "Don't worry, she'll be all right."

He was saying this even as they put Primula into the ambulance. The diagnosis was a concussion; the doctor wasn't sure how serious it was, and thought it best that she be taken to the hospital for observation. She died there the next night.

There was a memorial service organized, I believe, by Barbara Hutton. Niven was remarkably composed throughout; consoling the rest of us, it seemed. His composure set the tone for the occasion; if not for that, Gene might have really fallen apart. She was in tears, very emotional, but quietly so.

Daria was nearly three now and not all that different in appearance from other girls her age. In fact, she was beautiful: blonde, with her mother's features—an angelic little child—and this made the tragedy of her fate so much harder to accept. Gene still searched for a solution; we went from doctor to doctor, from hope to denial to despair.

And that is how Howard Hughes entered our lives. He became an integral part of our search for an optimistic, or at least conclusive, prognosis. He was very solicitous of Gene (he had made an unsuccessful play for her before we'd married), always calling to find out how she was, leaving messages with the harsh Prussian caricature who served as Gene's secretary in those days: "Mr. Hughes called. Urgent. Please call back."

"What's this about?" I asked. "What's so urgent?"

"He wants to help with the baby," Gene said. "He's a saint."

Indeed, Hughes had volunteered to bring the best brain surgeon in the country to California, in one of his planes, at his own expense, to examine the baby. I was very grateful, of course . . . and terribly disappointed when the doctor pronounced Daria incurable. But now, finally, Gene began to see that there was no hope; she agreed that it was time to look for a humane private institution where our daughter might live in peace. (Daria lives to this day, mostly blind, deaf, severely retarded. It is not known whether she can distinguish one human being from another.)

The decision to send our daughter away was terribly difficult; it seemed to increase the distance between Gene and me. The situation was made worse by Hughes's continuing presence in our lives. I soon noticed that his phone messages hadn't stopped with the doctor's prognosis. He was indeed a very persistent fellow: "Mr. Hughes called. Urgent. Please call back." I assumed the worst.

Hughes was a formidable rival. He was tall and slim, black hair slicked down in Argentine gigolo style; he conveyed a sense of strength, of rigid power and studied nonchalance. He was a careless dresser, usually in a dark suit and tennis sneakers (he was the first man I ever saw who affected that look—because of bad feet, he claimed). He had an exaggerated Texas accent, which he seemed to think was very charming. It was all rather obvious, larger than life, too self-conscious to be very convincing, I thought, and yet it worked for him.

He had a terrible reputation for using and discarding women. One day, in the heat of one of our battles, Gene told me that he'd said to her, "I want to marry you. Divorce your husband. I love you." He had brought a large box of jewelry with him. "I'll give you everything on earth," he said, opening the box. "Please take what you want."

Gene had, of course, refused, just as I had refused Barbara Hutton (the offers were oddly analogous). But I was concerned.

Several weeks later, we were invited to Jack Benny's house for a party—the usual Hollywood thing, a tent, an orchestra, dinner. Hughes was already there when we walked in, and, absolutely indifferent to my presence, he approached Gene, took her hand, and said, "I want to talk to you."

He sat down with her and began to talk animatedly, for quite some time.

It was usually my policy in such situations to affect indifference. I might engage the most beautiful woman I could find in conversation, or display my abilities on the dance floor, or go wandering about, but never, under any circumstances, would I show weakness or concern by going over and joining the conversation or interrupting it. My policy was: let Gene find me.

And yet . . .

This *was* Hollywood and he was making a rather obvious show of it, I thought, and I didn't want every gossip column in the Western world to be speculating the next day, so I went over and said, "Howard, you and I must talk." Then to Gene: "You must leave us alone for a few minutes. This has gone far enough and Howard and I have to decide where things stand."

Hughes agreed. Gene departed, and I said, "You are really bad news.

I'd hoped there would be some decency in you and you wouldn't compromise a woman's reputation, particularly a woman who is vulnerable because of the condition of her child. But I'll tell you: I think you're a bullshit artist. I don't believe your good intentions. So I propose this to you. If Gene wants you, I will step aside, on one condition: you must announce publicly that you are going to marry Gene. I don't want you to do to her what you've done to so many others—skip and run. You must announce it publicly and then I'll believe you."

"I'm a Texan," he said, "and a man of my word."

"Your word means nothing to me," I said, still insisting on what seems now a downright ludicrous point of pride. "Either you make the announcement or you stop calling her and offering these insulting baubles, and making a nuisance of yourself. If you don't announce your intention to marry Gene, if you continue your attempts to see her anyway, I promise you this: I will beat the shit out of you. I don't care where I find you—on the street, in a restaurant, at a party like this. But I will teach you a lesson."

"This is embarrassing," Hughes said.

"You have only seen the tip of the iceberg," I concluded. "You have no idea how embarrassing I can make this situation if you insist on behaving like a cad." Then I calmly walked away.

It was my custom in those days to go to the boxing matches in Santa Monica every Monday evening with Roger Valmy. Several weeks later, Roger and I went as usual, but I wasn't enjoying myself; I had a sixth sense that something was up. I asked Valmy to take me home.

As soon as I saw the German secretary, I *knew* something was up. She was white as a sheet. "Where's Mrs. Cassini?" I asked.

"I don't know. I don't know . . ."

"You know," I said, "and if you don't tell me, you're fired."

"She's with Mr. Hughes," she said, agitated, trembling. "I don't know where they went."

I was beyond fury. I went out to the garage. I rummaged about for something to hit Hughes with—I was going to kill the man—and finally came up with a piece of wood, a two-by-four. I hid there, in the garage, waiting for them. Time passed, two hours perhaps; I did not grow calmer over time, but more furious with every passing moment. My mind was in an uproar—I was really out of control—when the car pulled up (Hughes drove a Pontiac, as I did, rather than something fancy; it was another affectation, like his sneakers). I heard him imploring Gene, "I must see you again."

"No, it's not possible," she said. "It's not right."

She went up the stairs to the door then, leaving him alone . . . and at my mercy.

I did show mercy. Something, I don't know what, prevented me from hitting him over the head as I came up from the rear; if I had, this might have been a jail-house memoir. I truly could have killed the bastard. But I did show sense: I whacked him a good one in the behind. He leaped up with a yelp and raced for his car.

It must have been a humiliating moment for him, but I wasn't satisfied. I wanted blood. I jumped in our car—Gene was screaming "No! No!" —and took off after him.

He headed south, turning onto Wilshire. I stayed on his tail. When he noticed me following him, he sped up and began running red lights. I ran them right behind him, the two of us breezing down Wilshire Boulevard in the middle of the night. He turned into the Town House Hotel, where he had his suite. I was still just behind him, but not fast enough. He was in an elevator, doors closing, as I entered the lobby. Completely crazed, I went to the front desk. *"Where's Hughes?"* I demanded. "I have an appointment with him."

I went over to the elevators. I was going to look for him, but the next one down was filled with his bodyguards. They muscled me toward the door. "Get outta here," they said.

"I want Hughes!"

They kept me moving toward the door. I realized the situation was hopeless. I advised the bodyguards, "Well, give that bastard a message. Tell him what I said before still stands. Tell him to never walk alone in this town."

It was a good line, and restored some of my pride—for the moment. I sauntered out of there, and back to Gene. "How could you do this to me?" I demanded.

"Howard's an old friend," she insisted. "He's been trying to help."

"Where did you go."

"To Las Vegas."

"Las Vegas?"

"He said he could only concentrate in his plane, and when we got up in the air, he tried to corner me again. He told me that he loved me."

I didn't want to hear any more.

Then, several weeks later, we went to a party at Connie Moore and Johnny Maschio's, and there, standing in the middle of the floor, was Hughes. As soon as he saw me, he knew what was coming—I must have looked like a madman—and he raced up the staircase, with me in hot pursuit, and locked himself in the bedroom. I stood there pounding on the door, yelling, "Coward! Coward!"

I could hear him talking on the telephone and soon, sure enough, four of his men arrived again, and escorted him out of the bedroom, down the stairs, and out the door, with me taunting and threatening him all the way. It was a dreadful scene and Gene was horrified . . . but it didn't stop Hughes, and it wouldn't have stopped me had I ever seen him again. He continued to call. He told her, I later learned, "You are married to a madman."

No doubt, to the American sensibility, I did seem strange. I had a complicated, Old World view of marriage that was incomprehensible even to Gene; although, I must say, the purposeful naiveté of American marriages seemed equally crazy to me. For Americans, marriage was an all-or-nothing proposition. If the urge for sex, or desire, or companionship faltered for even a day, for even a moment, that was it, *pffft!*, the marriage was over. It seemed a rather harsh way of doing business.

To my mind, Americans confused sex with romance, and romance with love, and all of the above with marriage. Europeans, on the other hand, were perhaps a little more hypocritical about the institution of marriage, but more true to themselves and human nature.

I thought of marriage as a lifetime partnership. I was in it for the long pull. One might be temporarily swayed, but that did not mean the marriage, the companionship and all the rest, had to collapse. I fully expected to remain married to Gene for the rest of my life. I might engage in peccadillos, especially when the marriage was under strain (and during our mini-separations), but discreetly always, without embarrassing her. At the same time, though, I demanded both the appearance and the reality of fidelity from Gene. Was this unfair? Perhaps. Was it silly of me to go berserk over the not very credible studio "romance" between Gene and Tyrone Power during the filming of *The Razor's Edge*? Undoubtedly.

Actually, Tyrone Power was a good friend throughout our marriage, but there was a period after the war when he angered me greatly. He and Gene were co-starring in *The Razor's Edge*, and the studio (for reasons of its own, to get some publicity) decided to foment a love affair between them in the gossip columns. Now, I knew this was laughably untrue, but our marriage was in a difficult stage and I felt humiliated.

I played Errol Flynn for the West Side Tennis Club championship that year, a match I should have won easily. But Flynn kept delaying. He'd call the club and say, "So sorry, old chap, but could we put it off another hour? I'm stuck on my boat in San Pedro." I was quite out of sorts by the time he arrived . . . and then Gene and Tyrone showed up, *together*, and I became so furious that I lost my cool and allowed Errol to beat me, the only time that ever happened.

That was nothing, though, compared with the Olaf affair. Gene and I had a wonderful white German shepherd named Olaf, a very rare dog with a grand personality, one of the best dogs I've ever had. Tyrone came by one day, admired the dog, and Gene said, "Take him!" Just like that. Now, an event so poignant, so touching, so outrageous couldn't pass unnoticed by the studio publicity department. It was in all the papers: "Tierney Gives Power Beautiful German Shepherd!" Needless to say, I wasn't mentioned in any of these stories; nor did I care to be. I just wanted Olaf back, a sentiment the dog shared, apparently, for he escaped Tyrone's house near Malibu and somehow found his way back to ours, a distance of twenty miles. And Gene gave him back to Tyrone *again*. This was one of the most serious battles she and I ever had; it was actually, I believe, one of the things that contributed to our first separation, especially when I learned several months later that Power had gone off on location somewhere and put the dog in a kennel, where it was mistreated and malnourished. I went to retrieve the dog, and was furious about its poor condition. I was going to tell Tyrone Power a thing or two, until I got him on the phone, and he disarmed me totally. "How awful!" he said, agreeing immediately. "I didn't know. I wasn't aware. I'm *so* sorry."

And I think he really was. Even after all that—the dog meant a great deal to me—I couldn't remain angry with Power for long. Eventually, he returned the dog.

There was another evening during this time when I went to pick up Gene on the set and couldn't find her. I went over to Tyrone's dressing room and found three guys playing cards there; one of them was Power's longtime secretary, Bill Gallagher. I should mention that the dressing rooms at Twentieth were quite elaborate. Tyrone's had oak paneling, leather chairs, and hunting prints. I asked the poker players, "Do you know where Gene is?"

And one of them, with a mocking look, said, "Probably in the shower with Tyrone."

This was right after the Olaf affair, and I was feeling pretty touchy. I moved on him with everything I had. I slammed him up against a wall, then picked up a chair and started swinging it around, wrecking all the furniture in the room. Nothing could stop me; I was out of my mind.

I suppose I might have acted differently later, when I became more successful, but I felt terribly vulnerable, always needing to defend myself; my pride was at stake.

This was another of those periods when more events than seem possible in retrospect were packed into every day. I was working my three jobs. Often, I was sneaking off to Santa Anita with Valmy in the afternoons; and it was during this time, too, that I met Marilyn Monroe.

She was a starlet then, one of the parade of girls who tried to make themselves conspicuous during lunch at the commissary—but even then, you—I—could tell she had something unique. It was in the way she walked, the way she moved. The fact that she very obviously did not wear underwear during these noontime perambulations also served to distinguish her. Our friendship began when she came to my cottage at the studio one afternoon. It was a large, not very private bungalow, where I did my designing. (When I wanted to sneak out to Santa Anita, I would pull down a scrimlike shade and place a bust of a man's head in the position where my head would've been; this always worked, although I'm not certain that the powers at the studio were all that concerned about catching me, so long as my work was good and done on time, as it was.)

In any case, Marilyn came to tell me that she'd just been given a bit part and was going to wear a dress I'd designed for one of Gene's earlier films (often, dresses would be assigned to central wardrobe rather than discarded when a film was over). She just loved the dress. She wanted me to know how much she liked it, and also to get some advice on how to improve her appearance in general; I was known as a dispenser of such advice. I began to work on the dress, adapting it for her, and one thing led to another . . . indeed, the denouement had been inevitable from the moment she entered the room; she was quite wonderful.

Well, I found this girl very interesting. I saw clearly the qualities that would later make her so successful: the sweetness, the vulnerability, the curious triple-edged naiveté; at once innocent, encouraging, and gently mocking of male desire. This was not just another body walking around; there was a brain attached. And even though she was a much different type of girl from my usual cool, sophisticated preference, I was certain she had a future and I wanted others to know that I'd spotted her first (I also had a little bit of a crush on her). I invited her to a big party

Gene and I were having . . . invited her *alone*, and a bit too conspicuously for Gene's taste. (The invitation itself, by the way, was a subtle boost to Marilyn's career, separating her, in the minds of the powerful men who were there that night, from the herd of starlets sadly parading the commissary each day.)

This party was an important moment in our marriage. We had never given a tent party before. We were known as the "hundred-to-one" Cassinis: we'd receive one hundred invitations for every one we sent. But the Holmby Hills house was in shape now; Gene had decorated it brilliantly, with some rooms done in Early American style and others in Victorian. And so, we prepared a classic Hollywood do—a sit-down dinner for three hundred; two orchestras, Latin and jazz; champagne, the works. Everything was done precisely, as was Gene's habit, including the seating arrangement. But somehow the invitation to Monroe had slipped her notice and, unfortunately, Marilyn was one of the first to arrive, creating waves of sexual turbulence in her immediate vicinity, leaving quivering eddies of desire in her wake.

"I believe you know each other," I said.

"Yes, I know Miss Monroe," Gene said, coldly. Then she said to me, "By the way, when you have a moment and are not *too* busy, I'd like a word with you. I'm going up to my room *now*, in fact; I have to pick up something."

I followed her dutifully, and she said, "How *could* you! How could you invite that little . . . that blonde tramp!"

"But Gene, you can't have a party without pretty girls," I said, trying to make light of it. "You can't be the *only* beauty."

"But she's a *nothing!*"

I was beginning to get a little angry. "So what? This is Hollywood. She may be a big star tomorrow—bigger than you. Stranger things have happened. Don't always think about what exists today. Try to—"

"Oh, you're impossible," she said. "You and your girls."

"She's not one of my girls," I said, lamely. "She's just a friend."

A party like that is an exercise in crisis control. The guests—and each of these tent parties seemed to have the same, identical three hundred guests—arrive in a stream of limousines (parking was a horrendous problem, always), each intent on making a grand entrance in furs and jewels, wafting in on a cloud of perfume. Cocktails are served, trays of champagne; then a five-course meal: caviar, soup, fish, meat, dessert. Something propitious, portentous, or calamitous is always happening;

marriages dissolve, affairs begin, friendships end, trays of hors d'oeuvres are spilled on silk evening gowns. The host rushes about in a daze. That evening, for example, I was summoned to the gate, where Huntington Hartford had arrived in a gray suit (it was a black-tie affair, of course) with ten uninvited guests.

"What is this, Hunt?" I asked. We'd played tennis together and were on good terms. "You know we have a very precise number of seats."

"Well, Oleg," he said, "these people were just over for cocktails, and I thought—"

"Perhaps you should go to a restaurant and entertain them," I interrupted.

"I may do just that," he said, "and then I may come back here, or I may not."

I didn't have time to worry about whether this was the end of our friendship with Huntington Hartford, as I was summoned to another crisis: Ginger Rogers, married to a young fellow named Jack Briggs, was trying to overturn our seating arrangement. The idea had been to separate husbands and wives, to have a more sophisticated seating plan. Ginger insisted, though, that she sit next to Jack. She raised so much of a fuss that we were forced to make the adjustment, and they sat there holding hands all night, staring into each other's eyes, holding each other close and passionately on the dance floor. Two weeks later, their separation was announced.

I wonder how passionately devoted to each other Gene and I appeared that night.

Our marriage was at a sensitive juncture. Gene was increasingly testy with me, and behaving less than rationally at times. My first year out of the army had been a particularly difficult one for her. There had been the final, conclusive diagnosis of Daria, and then, at just about the same time, she had lost the Academy Award to Joan Crawford. It was an expected loss, but painful nonetheless. The Oscar might have changed Gene's life, boosting her spirits at a time when she so much needed a lift. It might have helped financially, too, and she was growing rather concerned about such things, as I was. We were now faced with the lifetime prospect of maintaining Daria in an expensive school. The loss of popularity was a thought that plagued every star, always. (In retrospect the pressures of stardom took their toll on many actresses of this generation in one way or another: Gene, Rita Hayworth, Lana Turner, Ava Gardner . . . and, of course, Marilyn Monroe—all would suffer in the years to come.)

We seemed to fight over everything and nothing. We had a terrible argument over the movie *Forever Amber*. Zanuck wanted Gene for the lead, and I thought she should take it. He was offering her a lot of money; it was a prestigious role, an important movie. The trouble was, Gene was his second choice and she knew it. His first choice had been an English girl named Peggy Cummins, but she hadn't worked out. Zanuck was in a spot; if Gene played her cards right, she could have negotiated anything out of him at that point. But she was too proud. She refused to take the part, even though Zanuck eventually offered annuities worth several million dollars if she'd accept. I thought she was crazy. I thought it was an Oscar-winning role. I also suspected that her refusal had something to do with my insistence that it was the right move.

As it happened, the film, starring Linda Darnell, was not the second coming of *Gone with the Wind*. But Gene's disrespect for my opinion—not just on scripts, but also in matters like real estate, investments, anything of consequence (except clothes)—was beginning to irk me enormously.

For example: I proposed that she buy the Beverly Hills Hotel for $75,000. The Barclay Hotel in Manhattan and a fifteen-floor building on Madison Avenue could have been had for very little. In short, she could have been extremely wealthy, but she disregarded my advice in everything.

Her testiness and impatience with me; her disappointment that I had somehow been unable to become a corporate executive like her father while also pursuing my career as a successful designer *and*, simultaneously, remaining the fellow who had devoted himself entirely to her in the first years of our marriage—all these conflicting, confused feelings seemed to intensify in the autumn of 1946. Gene was going to New York to visit family—or so she said; I soon learned the purpose of the trip was far less innocent. It was clear now that her attitude toward me had changed; we were heading for a break.

When Gene returned from New York, she asked for a formal separation.

CHAPTER

7

T his is how Gene and I welcomed the New Year of 1947, according to the New York *Daily News* and, no doubt, other newspapers across the country: "Gene Tierney's Oleg and Tycoon Start Year Right—to the Nose."

Hollywood, Jan. 1—The orchestra began playing Irving Berlin's "Let's Start the New Year Right."

It was one minute to midnight. One minute to go. Inside swanky Ciro's, they were dimming the lights to kiss the old year out, the new year in.

Then wham! In the parking lot outside Ciro's, Jimmy Costello bounced one off the beak of Oleg Cassini, estranged husband of actress Gene Tierney.

Oleg, the ex-Russian count turned dress designer, battled back. His arms churning, he tore into the paint tycoon from Newark, New Jersey, and blood began to flow.

It was more than Hollywood's usual one-punch brawl. Nearly a hundred bobby-soxers waiting at the front entrance to the screenland restaurant dashed for the ringside.

They got there in time to hear Gene scream and to see her, with her sister Pat, try to stop the brawl.

Gene had wanted to start the New Year right. Oleg had persuaded her to forget their separation for an evening. . . . Pat, who is sultry and cute like Gene, and Jimmy came along. Pat's heart is wrapped up in romance with Jimmy, who flew here a few days ago with a big diamond ring.

The four of them had a few drinks. Ciro's was filling up. Betty Grable and Harry James had a party going over at one end. Gene and Oleg nodded to Carmen Miranda and her crowd.

They danced a bit. Then Costello and Cassini began arguing. "It was just one of those silly New Year's arguments," Gene related today. She couldn't quite remember just how it started.

Suddenly, Gene and Pat decided to go home. They got their wraps and left down the back stairs to avoid the bobby-soxers out front.

"Give me the keys to Pat's car," Oleg demanded of Costello.

"Nuts, brother," Jimmy answered. His fist shot out and caught Oleg above his little black mustache.

Before a parking-lot attendant could pull them apart, witnesses said the First Hollywood Brawlers of 1947 had landed at least a dozen good punches each.

Jimmy's black tie peeked around the side of his neck. Blood spattered the white shirtfronts of Oleg and Costello.

With the help of an attendant, Gene got Oleg into the car and then sat beside him.

From inside Ciro's came the strains of "One Minute to Midnight." (Costello approached the car window and said to Cassini, "This isn't over yet.")

Oleg then threw a punch out the window, catching Costello squarely on his already bloody nose. Jimmy sprawled over backward. . . .

Infuriated by Oleg's punch, Gene began slapping and scratching him.

Then she jumped out of the car, ran around the other side, opened the door, and jerked Oleg out.

Screaming and punching him, she shouted at the man she eloped with five years ago when she was only 20:

"I hate this. I hate this and you know it!" . . .

Oleg and Jimmy, nursing what friends say are black eyes today, weren't talking.

The above is reproduced not because it is accurate (I gave the fellow a hell of a boxing lesson, in fact; he never landed a punch) but in order to convey some of the flavor of our initial estrangement, and also because the events in my life are often so extreme that they require independent confirmation. I have to say that I had similar confrontations with the bandleader Xavier Cugat and also with an Arthur Murray dance instructor who rather peremptorily eliminated Gene and me from a dance contest during a charity ball in New York, where we were attempting another reconciliation (the dance instructor had been a Golden Gloves boxer and packed a wallop, by the way).

The evening at Ciro's was my idea. I wanted to re-create our first, magical New Year's Eve together, the night we almost eloped; obviously, it didn't work out as I'd planned. As it happened, our separation proved to be every bit as tangled and *emphatic* as the rest of our marriage. It had begun rather dramatically. Gene had returned from her trip East, glowing, and promptly asked me to leave.

"Fine," I said. "I think you're crazy . . . but why?"

"Because," she said, measuring her words, "I think that I could not stay married and act the way I am going to act, because I'm in love with someone else."

"Who is it?" I asked. "Hughes?"

"No, not Hughes. But I can't tell you who it is," she said, laughing. Then she got serious: "Look, I want this handled as quickly as possible, and I want you out of the house."

"But this is terrible," I said. "Why not take your time? Why pay for lawyers when you're not completely certain?"

"I *am* completely certain," she said.

But she wasn't completely certain. At least, she didn't *act* as forcefully as she spoke. I continued to design her clothes; we continued to see each other—on New Year's Eve, for example. She *was* spending more time back East with her mystery man, though, leaving me at loose ends in California. I was quite depressed, and confused; I lived on nothing but Bloody Marys for weeks.

I bumbled along in a haze, unwilling to face my future without Gene. I did crazy things. One night at David Selznick's, John Huston mentioned he had a horse that was supposed to run a steeplechase the next day at the Riviera Country Club, but the jockey was ill. "It's a damn shame," he said. "The horse is in great shape. He was ready to win."

"I'll ride him," I said. Huston raised an eyebrow. I told him of my war experience in the cavalry and assured him that I, too, was fit: 160 pounds, standard gentleman-jockey weight.

"Come and get the colors from me in the morning," Huston said. I liked him, although we weren't close. He was a rather macho fellow, and something of a left-winger politically. One night, at another Selznick party, I saw him battle Errol Flynn over some political issue—a fight every bit as good as my more publicized bout with Costello. There was a challenge, then the two of them calmly walked out the door and began throwing punches. They fought across the front lawn, all the way down the street, and out of sight. They simply disappeared into the night.

I arrived at the Riviera Club the next morning fortified by half a bottle of bourbon and feeling no fear. The trainer said, "This horse should go. Just don't take the lead. Stay behind the leader till near the end, then let's see what happens."

It was a 1⅟16-mile race, with about ten jumps from a free start. There were six horses in the field.

I started well enough, and was holding third position halfway through, but I was weakening and so was the horse. It wasn't fit to run, and I wasn't helping it very much, either; we were losing ground at every jump. Finally, at the last one, just before the finish, I fell off the horse rather dramatically; no serious damage was done, but the fall was spectacular and entertained the crowd. Huston was stoic. "Good try, old boy," he said.

Among the crowd that day were the actor Franchot Tone and his wife, a beautiful blonde starlet named Jean Wallace. Tone was a good fellow, very well respected, an officer in the Screen Actors Guild . . . and it is a measure of my unhappiness over the loss of Gene that, despite our friendship, I began an affair with his wife. It might have been after the steeplechase that she said to me, "Why don't you come over for dinner," and she named the night. "Franchot has to go to a Guild meeting."

The three of us had dinner together very amiably; then Tone left for his meeting and Jean and I repaired to the couch, where, fifteen minutes later, I was caught in the act (or, more precisely, in the preliminaries) yet again. Tone had returned unexpectedly. He saw me kissing his wife and went out of his mind. He pulled us apart, then began to slap her. I separated them and told her, "Get out of here." Then I pinned him to the ground. I was much stronger than he was, and holding him there, I apologized profusely: "I cannot tell you how sorry I am. I violated your hospitality. It was all my fault—your wife didn't do anything. I just tried to kiss her. . . ."

I felt terrible. I prided myself on my discretion and loyalty to friends, and this had been horribly embarrassing. Word of the episode reached Gene eventually, and the next time I saw her, she literally tried to scratch my eyes out.

"What is this?" I said, grabbing her arms. "Are you kidding me? *You're* the one who left. I was indiscreet, yes, it was embarrassing, but what business is it of yours?"

"But she's not right for you!"

Gene's signals were, as always, confusing. Several weeks later, she finally filed for the divorce. It was March 1947; it would be a year, by California law, before the decree could become final.

"Look," I said to her, "if you're so serious about this fellow, don't you think you should tell me who it is? Or would you rather that I learned it from the gossip columns? It's Hughes, isn't it?"

"No," she laughed. "You know who it is. You met him. It's Jack Kennedy."

I *had* met him once. It was at a party in a restaurant, given by Betsy Bloomingdale. I saw Gene having a long conversation with this handsome young naval officer; as was my custom, I didn't interrupt. Later, on the way home, I asked her who the fellow was. And she said, "Didn't you recognize him? That was Jack Kennedy."

It was a familiar name. His father, Joseph P. Kennedy, was well known in Hollywood. I also knew of the son's exploits on PT-109, which had already received a great deal of attention in the press. But he didn't make a big impression on me, except that Gene obviously was interested in him.

As I look back, the attraction was understandable. Jack Kennedy represented everything I didn't, all the "safe" things that Gene had willfully discarded when she took up with me: New England, Ivy League, Irish Catholic aristocracy. (He was, I would later learn firsthand, a wonderfully entertaining fellow.) He was extremely thin—wraithlike, almost, in those days—but certainly quite handsome in his navy uniform. In the months since their first meeting, Gene had dated him on the East Coast, seeing him in New York and later, after he was elected to Congress, in Washington. She was quite infatuated. She said, "I think I've finally found someone who is the solution to my problems, emotionally."

And they might have made a wonderful couple, the ultimate lace-curtain Irish-American couple, but for the fact that Gene was already married and Jack Kennedy would never jeopardize his Catholicism, or his political career, by marrying a divorced woman. Gene seemed not to understand this.

"Are you out of your mind?" I said. "He's from the most Catholic family in America. You think he'd marry a divorced woman?"

"Oh, he'll marry me," she said, glowing. "He'll marry me."

Whether or not Jack Kennedy would marry Gene was moot, as far as I was concerned. She certainly didn't seem to be in love with me anymore, despite the mixed signals and her attempt to scratch my face. And I wasn't about to remain in Hollywood as the former husband of Gene Tierney. I latched on to something Zanuck had said to me: "We're in the twilight here. The studio system isn't going to last forever. I'd look to New York or Europe, to the world of fashion, if I were you."

Well, the studio system seemed solid as a rock at that point, but I was looking for straws to grasp and I convinced myself that Zanuck was right. I sold my interest in Casanova. I told Briny Foy I wanted out of my contract at Eagle Lion.

"Why the devil do you want to leave?" he said. "You got it made here. The sun is good. You're getting well paid. You want a girl? Pick one. We'll put her on the payroll."

"No, it's not that," I said, and he reluctantly agreed to turn me loose.

In retrospect, leaving California was one of the smartest moves I made in my life. Perhaps it was the pain that gave me clairvoyance. Eagle Lion folded soon after; fashion waned in California; and I would, in a matter of years, succeed beyond my wildest expectations in New York. For the moment, though, I was fleeing a bad scene. I knew only that I had to get out of there.

I called my brother: "Look, I'm in bad shape. I want to get out of this atmosphere."

"How's your tennis?" Igor asked.

"My *tennis?*"

"There's a tournament in Palm Beach. I'm headed there. Why don't you join me? It'll be great for us to be together again. We'll play a few tournaments. You'll see some people you haven't seen in a while. Everything will be all right."

That was Igor: always, everything would be all right. His optimism was quite understandable at that point, though. He had returned from the war to become Cholly Knickerbocker, the Hearst society columnist, and was now a real power in New York, Newport, Palm Beach, wherever the rich gathered to divert themselves. He and Bootsie had an intriguing divorce (she would soon become Mrs. William Randolph Hearst, Jr.); he had married a second time—a beautiful young girl named Darrah Waters —and was about to meet wife number three, Charlene Wrightsman, the daughter of oil baron Charles Wrightsman, one of the pillars of Palm Beach society. Igor's equanimity was most apparent, by the way, in his relations with former wives, all of whom remained friends. I once saw him having lunch with three of them, a remarkable achievement, as anyone who's ever been divorced must know.

In any case, he was right. Palm Beach did wonders for me. We were the winning doubles team at the Bath and Tennis Club Tournament, much to the dismay of the locals, who seemed to consider us undesirable aliens (their attitude toward Igor, who chronicled their most embarrassing moments—scathingly, at times—was always cool); their rage made our victory that much sweeter. I did begin to move in East Coast society once more, becoming friendly with Nicky and Bunny Dupont, who also had suffered the tragedy of a baby affected by German measles. And I reestablished my friendship with Prince Alexander Hohenlohe and his beautiful wife, Peggy Biddle Schultz.

Alek Hohenlohe was a Wagnerian fantasy: tall, blond, blue eyes, enormously handsome, and very full of himself—full of old pre-World War I notions of aristocracy. I was a count (at least, I had been) and therefore worthy of his consideration; everyone else was a peasant. He was not very popular in society then. He was scorned as a sponger, taking advantage of Peggy Schultz; that he had been a millionaire many times over before the war wiped out his holdings in Poland was conveniently forgotten.

Peggy's attitude toward Alek was similar to Gene's toward me: she thought he was a gentleman, a mannered person who would never amount to anything. She felt that I, at least, was willing to make an effort. "You'll succeed," she assured me. "The trouble with you is that you attached yourself to a secondary position with Gene and haven't thought enough about your own life."

One evening at dinner, I said to Peggy, "Why don't you make Alek work? You want him to work, to become an American. Why don't you have him start a company with me?" She thought this was a fine idea, and so did I. Indeed, I was expecting a healthy infusion of Biddle money to get us going, but it was not forthcoming. The company was underfinanced from the start. We had a fine office in a building across from Bergdorf Goodman on Fifth Avenue, and an excellent production man named Jules Dardick, who had come from Hattie Carnegie. Still, I knew that without more money we were a long shot at best. I tried to raise as much as I could to get us launched; I even managed to borrow $14,000 from Gene.

Oh, yes, Gene. We were "dating" again. Her affair with Kennedy had dissolved over the question of marriage, as expected. Hardly a month had passed before she began calling again. She came to New York to see me, and stayed at the Plaza, just around the corner from my office. We renewed acquaintance, and, as such things often happen, were on much better terms than we'd been in years.

I considered myself completely free at this point. She was the one who'd left; if Gene wanted me back, she was going to have to court the hell out of me. I was not above exacting a sweet revenge. One evening in New York, we had dinner with a spirited Argentine fellow accompanied by a very, very pretty girl from Connecticut to whom he was engaged. During the course of the evening, the girl and I danced and she told me that she was going to Washington the next day. This was one of my favorite situations. "What a coincidence!" I said to her, "I'm going there, too."

"We'll have dinner together," she said.

It turned out to be dinner and dessert, and Gene somehow—she always had an uncanny knack for such things—found out. She told our friend of her suspicions, which were soon confirmed by the girl. He proceeded in the best Argentine manner, to announce his intention to kill me. I confronted him directly and, I must say, deftly. "I've done you a service," I told him. "If I can come in so quickly and so successfully, there's something wrong with your situation here. You should reconsider marrying the girl." He didn't, and later paid the price.

Gene was not so easily placated. Several days later, I showed up at the Plaza for a date we'd scheduled, and she had one of those typical Gene looks on her face, which told me something drastic was about to happen. As soon as I got in the door, she slapped me across the face. Twice.

"What are you doing?" I said.

She said, "How dare you do this to me! How could you do this to your fiancée?"

"*Fiancée?*" I said, trying to stop myself from laughing. "We're *divorced*. What are you talking about, *fiancée?*"

My heart went out to her a little at this—it was so sad, in its way. She was always searching for some plain old American normality, and I was always the least likely fellow to provide it. But I did love her, and I allowed her this fantasy: we were going steady.

Alexander Hohenlohe also had a fantasy: he thought he was working. Alek would arrive at the studio at 11:00 A.M. most days; at 12:15 he would announce, "I am very hungry." We would discuss this for fifteen minutes and then, most often, go to a restaurant called Armando's on Fifty-sixth Street, sometimes with dates. He would have five martinis. Then he would go home and sleep off his martinis, while I'd go back and work with Dardick, who was outraged by Hohenlohe's princely schedule. At five, Alek would awake from his nap and phone me: "What's up, Oleg? What are we doing tonight? Where should we go?"

Despite this, I could see the vague outlines of success if he could just keep going. I knew the ropes now; my designs were good, too. *Life* magazine did a two-page photo spread of Jean Murray Vanderbilt wearing Cassini originals. If we could only raise more money, we might have a chance.

But Peggy Schultz saw what Alek wasn't doing, and wasn't about to indulge him any further. After less than a year, this latest incarnation of Oleg, Inc., followed its predecessors into oblivion. It was one of the last straws, too, for the Hohenlohe-Schultz marriage. Peggy left Alek eventually, and he responded with a rather pathetic suicide attempt. He tried to shoot himself in the heart and missed by an inch. "He couldn't even do that right," Peggy's mother, Mrs. Biddle, observed. Alek later married the dynamic, outrageous, and quite wonderful Southern belle Honeychile Wilder ("Honeychile Hohenlohe" was agreeably alliterative) and meandered his way through several more courtly, imperious decades of life.

Gene and I continued to "go steady," a ritual that worked best when she was in California and I in New York. I would travel to California every other weekend, a journey that was not only time-consuming—the flight took ten hours in those days, with a stop in Kansas City—but also rather expensive. I was drawing only $150 per week with Hohenlohe and spending most of it on airline tickets. On one of these trips, I was just broke. After taking Gene to dinner, I had no money left and so I said, "Gene, I hate to ask you this, but I need a few dollars for the trip back."

This was very difficult, since the prevailing delusion of the moment was that I was really making it, and Gene made it even harder. She gave me $15. "That's enough for the cab and a hamburger in Kansas City."

"What about the cab home in New York?" I asked.

And so, the old differences—over money, over the future—were still there, beneath all the sweetness of our reunion. They were as much a part of the marriage as the very real love we felt. For the moment, though, love had the upper hand and we plodded toward a formal reconciliation. There was no dramatic decision. Gene simply didn't complete the divorce proceedings when our year of legal separation elapsed on March 10, 1948. A month later, the studio issued an announcement of our reconciliation, complete with a picture of Gene kissing me on the cheek.

I spent part of the spring with Gene in Sun Valley, Idaho, where she was shooting *That Wonderful Urge* with Tyrone Power. Despite the recent business failure, I was feeling pretty good. I had prospects. Mike Todd was planning another of his Broadway spectaculars and he'd asked me to design the costumes. Soon I'd return to New York and begin work. Gene was going to join me there, and we'd have another spell of the quiet domesticity she so enjoyed—a mandatory respite from Hollywood in this case, because Gene was once again pregnant.

Our second daughter, Christina, was born in New York on November 18, 1948. She was a perfect child physically, and would only suffer the handicap of having a father who often was too busy to be much of a father, and a loving but precarious mother who would be quite ill through most of her childhood. I was so wrapped up with Mike Todd at the time of her birth that it was difficult to remember much about it except relief, an exhilarating relief that she was healthy.

"Oleg," Mike Todd said, "I'm going to do something for you that has never been done for a costume designer before: I'm going to put your name in lights, right up there with the stars. Your name has a lot of marquee value, a lot of panache . . . and the costumes will be as important as any star in this show."

What a charmer he was, one of the great bullshit artists of all time. Mike Todd was a short, thickset man with unlikely, chiseled features and beautiful eyes. He was constantly chomping on a cigar, fulminating, selling, flying by the seat of his pants. He was married to Joan Blondell at that point and lived like a king, in a Tarrytown mansion, which Gene and I visited.

The show was called *As the Girls Go*. It had lots of girls, lots of glitz, and lots of costumes, a hot-air balloon of a show. I remember thinking, years later, when I saw his crowning achievement, *Around the World in Eighty Days*, that perhaps the hot-air balloon was Mike Todd's vehicle of choice. I doubt if anyone else on earth could have kept *As the Girls Go* aloft, but Mike kept puffing, subscribing backers. "It might be better if we fail," he told me with a wink in Boston during our pre-Broadway trial. "I'm oversubscribed."

But he also said, "If I don't make it with this show, I'll blow my brains out."

I never learned the precise financial arrangements, but it was clear that he was mounting this extravaganza with blue smoke and mirrors. It was a large amount of work for me, the equivalent of half a dozen films. I might have to do thirteen changes in a film like *The Razor's Edge;* I had more costumes than that *per scene* in *As the Girls Go*. It involved hundreds of sketches and, again, different technical principles from film work. These costumes would be used over and over again, night after night; they had to be built to last. Happily, Mike hired the best—Madame Karinska, an elderly Russian woman with decades of experience—to make them. *Unhappily,* Mike stiffed her, and halfway through she refused to do any more work.

We arrived in Boston with costumes for the opening and closing numbers and a few in the middle. But there were whole scenes that were undressed. "You've got to come up with more money," I told him. "Karinska won't give you any more credit. We can't go forward."

"Always money! Stop bothering me with money," he said. "Find some solution."

"What do you want me to do?"

"Be creative."

I did do something rather creative for one number. I sent an assistant out and bought fleece, the material that is used for sweat suits, and made warm-up outfits dyed in different colors, thus predicting the athletic look of the 1980s (it seemed rather strange in 1948, though, especially in the opulent context of that show; one critic said it was "incomprehensible").

It took some time to put these suits together. They weren't ready for dress rehearsal in Boston, and Todd started bellowing, "Where's the designer? I'll kill him! I'll kill him!"

And then, in front of one hundred people, this man who could be so charming read me the riot act: "Cassini, you son of a bitch, you don't know your work! You're going to ruin me! Where are the costumes?"

"The costumes will be ready as soon as you pay for them, you son of a bitch," I said. "And if you don't like my work, I can leave here right now."

I took off, but, sure enough, Todd was right behind me. "Listen, Oleg, I'm sorry, but I had to say something. I had to have some excuse—"

"Look, Mike," I said, "you're a great guy, but don't use me as your excuse. Find money or we won't have a show."

He found money. We had a show, although I was never able to complete all the costumes as originally planned.

And Mike Todd managed to survive *As the Girls Go.* It was even a financial success. My work was well received by the critics, but I was disappointed. I had expected that with my name up in lights, more Broadway costume jobs would follow; they didn't immediately and I went back to the old standby, designing clothes for pictures, including a few with Gene. She made several with Otto Preminger in the late 1940s, trying to recapture the magic of *Laura,* but never quite succeeding.

Preminger was irascible, always bullying, bellowing (later there would be rumors—not true—that *he* drove Gene crazy). He was one of the most energetic people I've ever met. "Americans have a terrible habit," he once told me. "They work and work and only after they achieve power and money do they begin to enjoy their lives—if then! I believe in living every day. For instance, last night I went out with this actress. I took her to dinner and then we made love all night. All night! And now I have worked all day!"

And he stood there, roosterly, as if he expected me to congratulate him. "Well, Otto," I said, "*now* it all makes sense. No wonder you're always in such a lousy mood. You're so goddamn tired you can't control your temper."

But we had a pretty good relationship. In fact, he gave me a role—as a designer, Oleg Mayer—in the film *Where the Sidewalk Ends*. I would say my performance was worthy of the film's overall quality . . . although I did design a dress that was voted "most *risqué*" of the year by a fan magazine, and that Preminger called "dangerous." It was of red velvet, a very tight mermaid silhouette—Gene said she couldn't walk more than six steps in it—very décolleté; the bosom was quite exposed and sustained by a clever manipulation of red velvet spaghetti straps. Marilyn Monroe would later be photographed in it.

When Gene went to London to film *Night and the City* with Richard Widmark, we had the chance to spend some time together in Europe. We visited Paris, and had a holiday in Deauville. Europe at that time was a very exciting place to be; just recovering from the war, it was like the reopening of a beautiful flower. The optimism, the mood of the people, was infectious. Deauville was the same as in the days of Colette's novel *Gigi*—glamour, wealth, gambling, and rain—just as it is today.

Gene and I were treated to many parties and country weekends. It was all very pleasant to be sure, but at the same time I was restless. I was thirty-six years old and wondering if my ship would ever come in. I was confident I had the talent, the contacts, and the will to succeed.

Joe Kennedy, whom I'd met in Palm Beach, had encouraged me to get going: "If you don't do it soon you're not going to do it at all. And do it yourself. You don't want to spend your life as someone's employee. You'll never be free then. Be selfish; stick to your work and think about yourself for the next five years. It is not enough in life to say, 'I will try again,' and to beat your head against the wall."

I had trained myself to think of Gene first; at the very least, I had bought the assumption that her *career* came first. I felt tied to her by a thousand gossamer threads, but the nature of our entanglement was changing. Gene was having trouble keeping her mind on her work. Her mood swings were more pronounced, less predictable. It seemed that her career was slipping, too; she was still getting scripts, but not the quality of *Laura* or *The Razor's Edge*. She'd always had difficulty choosing her roles, and now it appeared she was constantly choosing the wrong ones. She was frightened by this, and I was concerned as well; she needed me more than ever, as did Tina and Daria.

There was one time during this period that her need saved my life. She was finishing *Night and the City* in Europe; I was heading back to New York, booked on Air France. Gene tried to dissuade me. She wanted me to stay with her, stay for another week; if not a week, then a few days. I told her I had to go. She became more adamant on the way to the airport. "Please don't take that flight," she said. "I have a very bad feeling about it."

"Don't be silly," I said. "Everybody flies."

She became quite agitated. "Please," she said, "if you have any feeling for me . . ."

Finally, I agreed to stay. The next morning, I saw in the paper that the plane had crashed sixty miles off course in the Azores. Everyone on board had been killed, including the famous French boxer Marcel Cerdan. Gene was terribly upset when I told her; she began to cry. I asked her, "How did you know?"

"I don't know," she said. "It was like a tremendous weight on my chest. I couldn't breathe . . . it was an overpowering feeling. I knew I had to force you not to go."

There is a portentous quality to such events. Near misses may be mere coincidence, but they tend to concentrate the mind. I felt that I was at a crossroads; my life was about to change dramatically, although I wasn't sure how or where or when this would happen. There was a feeling of *opportunities* floating about in the ether.

I had options. They ranged from the most conservative—I could continue on, designing costumes for movies—to the outlandish. Freddy Heineken often would pop into town, and he still wanted me to become a beer baron. But the most likely option, the very best path, seemed to be the offer Jack Warner made at that time, to become head of the wardrobe department at his studio Warner Brothers. It was a very important job. So why was I reluctant?

I wasn't too keen on returning to California . . . and there was still the sense, implanted in me by Darryl Zanuck, that Hollywood was over, and Joe Kennedy's admonition that I'd never be happy as somebody's employee. But there was no *logical* reason to refuse.

And so I booked a flight to Los Angeles. It was the autumn of 1949. On the evening before my departure, I went out to bid adieu to New York with a martini or two in the bar at Gogie's, a midtown restaurant owned by a friend of mine. I sat there dreamily, relieved and yet resigned, knowing that a corner was being turned.

I remember that moment very clearly, almost as well as the next one: the moment that my ship—unexpectedly, unbelievably—came in.

CHAPTER

8

I t was a most casual introduction, the sort of thing that's happened ten
thousand times in my life: a beautiful model—this time it was Barbara
Dunne—sees me in a restaurant or at a social gathering and intro-
duces me to her date. . . .

"Oleg, this is Bill Hunt. Bill, this is Oleg Cassini. I did some work for
him."

"What sort of work do you do?" Hunt asked, with a raffish smile. He
was a middle-aged man, a handsome, stylish man; the sort who didn't feel
overmatched dating a top model, as Barbara Dunne was.

"I'm a designer."

"And a good one," Barbara said. She had worked for me during the
Hohenlohe experiment.

"Do you live in New York?" Hunt asked.

"I did," I said, "but it seems I'm moving to Los Angeles tomorrow."

"You don't sound very excited about it."

"Not really," I said. I liked Hunt immediately. He had a direct, busi-
nesslike manner.

"So why don't you stay here?"

"Because I don't have the money to start my own company, and I've
been offered a job in Los Angeles."

"How much would it take to get you started?"

He made it sound as if he might put up the money himself. I figured
he was just toying with me, trying to impress the girl. But on the wild

chance that his leading question was leading somewhere, I figured what the hell and gave my best estimate: "One hundred thousand," I said (the equivalent of one million dollars today).

"That sounds reasonable," he said, coolly.

We had a drink together, and another. Hunt asked me to stay for dinner with them. He was just back from China, where his career in the diplomatic service had been cut short by the Chinese Revolution. He had made his money earlier, as a businessman. He ran a company called International Banknote, which did a lot of business in the Far East. Now he was looking to make investments back home, in the United States.

We talked some more about my work. I told him why the attempt with Hohenlohe had failed despite some positive signs. Barbara was very helpful here: "Oleg is so talented. He knows everyone. All he needs is a chance."

Then Hunt said, "You know, I like you. Why don't you come to the Metropolitan Club tomorrow morning at nine and we'll see what we can do about setting you up?"

I figured, *This guy must be joking. He's just trying to win over Barbara. Tomorrow he won't even remember my name. This is impossible, it's like something out of a movie. Things like this don't happen in real life.*

And yet . . .

What was the harm in staying an extra day to find out?

I called Gene and told her I had to stay over in New York for a business appointment.

"A business appointment?" She laughed. "What sort of business could you possibly have?"

"I'm chasing an idea," I said.

I arrived at the Metropolitan Club—awesome in its hushed grandeur, the sort of place where a peace treaty might be signed—at the appointed hour. My own business there seemed inconsequential by comparison and, suddenly, *plausible*. Was it possible that this fellow Hunt meant it? I was ushered into an elegant conference room. Hunt was seated there with three others. "Tell them what you propose," he said to me.

I told them. I'd actually been doing a lot of thinking about how to succeed on Seventh Avenue. I had spent my life designing dresses for individuals—first in Rome, then in New York, then in Hollywood. It was no way to earn a living. In America, no one got rich making one dress at a time.

I told them a story about Prince Matchabelli, who created a large fragrance empire. The prince had once said, "When the customer comes to you in a Rolls-Royce, you go home in the subway; but when the customer comes to you in the subway, you go home in the Rolls-Royce." The interpretation I gave them was that selling ready-made couture, as I proposed to do, was far more profitable than made-to-order couture for one customer at a time. They liked the analogy.

That led to my key point: American fashion, with the exception of sportswear, was traditionally a pale imitation of what had been shown in Paris a season earlier. This was literally true. American designers would slavishly attend the Paris shows, make notes, and then adapt the designs for American use. But what was the magic of Paris? Why should Americans (or Italians or Japanese) be so entirely derivative? This was an American era. The United States had supplanted Europe in countless ways: in military strength, in industry; it was taking the lead in many of the arts. Why not fashion? I thought it was time for a young, fresh, defiantly *American* look in ready-to-wear clothes that owed nothing to Paris. This would be American couture.

I told these men—whom I'd never met before and would never see again as a group—how the $100,000 would be spent. I would need a production man, a sales manager, a *première*, sample hands, piece goods, a design room, and a showroom. "This money I am requesting is not for one year but for one collection only," I told them. "If my ideas are no good, then it will be apparent immediately. If I succeed, you will receive double your money in return."

Hunt looked around the table at the others. They were businessmen he'd known in the Orient. After they conferred a moment, Hunt said to me, "Okay, you've got the money."

Just like that.

He started talking about banks and arrangements and so forth. I was very excited. He said to me that in business it was important to make the deal first, and only then to call in attorneys to put the deal into a legal format. . . . Then he was saying, "Get to it, don't waste a moment," and I was nodding and thanking them, shaking hands all around. It was just too incredible.

To this day, I have no logical explanation for why Bill Hunt would support me. It could not have been only that he was trying to impress a beautiful model (whom he later married, by the way.) My ideas were sound; history would prove me right. But no matter how convincing my proposal, why would a man who didn't know me at all, and had no experience on Seventh Avenue, take such a risk? Well, perhaps only someone who wasn't familiar with the conventional wisdom about Paris could have done so.

Gene certainly didn't believe it and, indeed, she almost scuttled the whole deal. Naturally, she wasn't very happy that I wouldn't be joining her on the West Coast, and was rather dubious about Hunt as well. Within days she came East, and I introduced the two of them over dinner—at the same restaurant, for good luck, of course. We had champagne, and Hunt said, "You've got quite a husband. It's clear he's very talented and I think he's really going to make a go of it in New York."

"Yes," she said, "he's talented, but he'll never make it in New York."

"Why do you say that?" Hunt asked, somewhat nonplussed. I was taken aback as well. What was happening here? Perhaps she was joking? But no:

"Because it's too tough."

And then suddenly she lost control of herself completely. She stood up, tossed her glass of champagne in my face, and walked out of the room.

"Well," said Hunt, "either she's crazy or I am. I can stop the deal if you wish."

"I hope you won't, despite this unfortunate scene," I said, trying to gather myself, be calm, salvage the deal. I continued to talk, drying my face with my handkerchief, not giving it any importance. "I don't know what's the matter with her."

Clearly, something was. There were times when Gene was as she'd always been, times when we were as happy together as we'd been at Fort Riley . . . but there were also emotional explosions, horrible rages, scenes that I tried to ignore. Perhaps if we'd spent more time together in those years, I might have seen the pattern more clearly, but she was in California, and I in New York . . . especially during the first few months of the new enterprise, when I worked harder, with more concentration and purpose, than ever before in my life.

My life changed then. I had been living from day to day, seeking only the pleasures of the moment. Now, for the first time really, I lived for the future. I was pointed toward a goal—the fall collection, which would be shown in May 1950—and I trained for that moment like an athlete. It was a one-shot deal. I *had* to make a success of this collection.

There was so much to be done: I needed a staff, a design studio, and a showroom on Seventh Avenue; factories had to be contracted to make the garments once the orders came in. But most of all, I needed to be inspired. I needed to design a hot, hot line that buyers would *immediately* see was different. I had one chance to distinguish myself from the pack. I had to give it my very best.

Had Roger Valmy been handicapping my chances, I doubt that he would have had me at less than 50–1. New companies simply do not burst upon the scene in fashion; most build slowly. Actually, that's not true. Most fail. The ones that succeed usually build their sales over time, convincing buyers one by one. Buyers are a skeptical breed and stubborn; most are unwilling to take a chance on an untested line. They always hope some *other* buyer will go first, so they can wait, see the results, and then join the bandwagon. Or say, "I told you so." I didn't have the time to convince these people one by one; I needed a stampede of buyers.

I realized I would need more than inspiration; I would need luck— and luck seemed to be with me from the very start, luck and coincidence.

The first coincidence occurred during my search for a loft on Seventh Avenue. This wasn't an easy process. There were only a few buildings, along Seventh Avenue and Broadway in the garment district, where showrooms were desirable. Why? Because buyers did their shopping during a concentrated period of madness called Market Week (which lasted two weeks, usually). During that time, they rushed from show to show, seeing one line after another, spending no more than an hour with the work of any designer. And so the garment center was organized for *their* convenience. You had to be in one of the buildings where other companies were located, one of the traditional showroom buildings, or the buyers wouldn't come to see your line.

I heard there was a company going out of business at 498 Seventh Avenue, and immediately went to see if the loft was available. The coincidence was that the company was run by Miss Sadofsky, the same Miss Sadofsky who had been Jo Copeland's partner and had hired and fired me twelve years earlier. Now the tables were turned, and I was embarrassed by her misfortune . . . but I did manage to negotiate successfully for her space, paying $24,000 for the key.

It took me only a week to secure the loft, and my luck was just beginning. Within a month I found an excellent production man, also named Sadofsky (another coincidence), and an equally fine salesman, named Moe Popell. The three of us were the triumvirate that made the company go—if any of our work on the first collection had been less than excellent, we would have gone under. That is no exaggeration; our margin was that thin. There was a fourth person, too, who was instrumental in our success: I found an Austrian woman named Marie, who served as *première* and who had a superb ability to understand the nuances of my sketches and transform them into realities.

Still, despite this very fine staff, I was alone. The company would stand or fall on my ideas. I needed someone to talk to, a partner . . . and so I invented one: a skeptical manufacturer whom I, the designer, was constantly trying to convince of the merit of my work. Our dialogue was continuous. I went around talking to myself all the time. "Well, what is going to be your message?" the manufacturer would ask. "Are you going to be a California designer? Who are you designing for? Who is your customer? Where will she wear these clothes? Who will you hang with? Who is your competition."

"I am going to do something new," I would argue back. "It will reflect the things I've always believed in fashion."

I have always felt that women make their fashion selections based on the following, in this order: *color*—the first thing to catch her eye; *fabric* —she will want to feel the texture; *style/silhouette/label*—she will look to see who the creator is and if she likes the concept; *fit*—if she likes all the preceding so far, she will then try it; and *price*—if she is convinced on all other points.

"Where would it fit in the market?" the manufacturer would ask me.

"I want to be at the upper end of the spectrum, but not out of sight."

"To whom are you going to sell?"

"I want to reach a woman who could be a teen, or fifty. But she must be the sort of woman who is proud of the way she looks and has kept herself in shape."

The imaginary manager (and my very real staff) suggested that I price the dresses in the $55-to-$69 wholesale range, which would mean $150 in the stores (the equivalent of about $1,000 today). There were also several top-of-the-line dresses that were priced between $200 and $250 wholesale. To buy a Cassini original, then, would be a significant financial statement, but well within the range of the new, expanding executive and professional class in the United States, a group of people whose ability to spend was positively exploding in the years after World War II.

In the beginning, we would go to stores together, the phantom manufacturer and I, debating all the way. It was just as I thought: there were some good clothes around, but most were obvious copies of Paris couture;

there was an almost palpable sense of staleness. "You see," I would tell the phantom, "I am proposing something that doesn't exist."

"Well, perhaps," he'd reply, "but you will have to work hard. You will have to live like a monk."

"Like a monk?"

And so I did. I was living at the time in the town house on East Sixty-first Street that I had purchased a year earlier. I would be up at 7:00 A.M., have a cup of coffee, and then run—*run*—down to the studio (usually I had a change of clothes waiting for me there). I spent the morning sketching. I did hundreds of sketches. I immersed myself in books—art, history, folklore—looking at military, classical, and period costumes for inspiration. I did not copy *Vogue* or *Harper's Bazaar;* I would have none of that. I worked with a color chart in front of me. I tried different color combinations. Indeed, I experimented with separates, different pieces that I coordinated together, which no one else was doing at the time. I also enjoyed mixing fabrics and textures: wool and satin (a light, elegant gray flannel dress with a satin collar), leather and knits, linen and velvet.

I realized that I must do something like what Chanel had done, and have a true personal inspiration. She had been influenced by the military uniforms of France, a fact that I had noted on my visits to the Musée de la Grande Armée.

I put all the ideas I had accumulated during the course of a lifetime into that first collection, from the modified military look I'd first experimented with on Nadia Berlingieri in Rome, a cross-pollination of some men's-wear looks into women's wear, for example, using the Eton uniform as a tailored idea; to many of the things I'd learned in the movies—little white collars that framed the face, for instance. I used versions of several dresses I had designed for the movies, employing the concepts I'd mastered in Hollywood, to great advantage, but, above all, my basic philosophy about clothes informed it all. My goal was an elegantly sexy collection; I wanted clothes that would enhance women, that men would appreciate also. I have always felt that the body is more important than the clothes —a dress or costume is born out of the movement of the body—clothing is an envelope. I liked simplicity—I used the sheath a lot—and fine fabrics.

After a quick bite at noon, I would be back, working on my sketches until five or so, when the parade of piece goods began. I spent all my evenings with fabrics, a steady stream of representatives from the textile mills from five to seven. I reinvigorated taffeta that season; most cocktail dresses had been of crepe. I shirred the taffeta. I liked the idea of black taffeta with little white Peter Pan collars—a boyish look: innocent sexiness, uncynical without being unsophisticated, fresh rather than calculating, American rather than European. The idea of America as one big, enthusiastic college campus was floating somewhere in the back of my mind as well.

And on I would work. A cup of soup after the piece-goods parade was over, then back to the studio and concentrated work until midnight. I did not drink liquor. I did not smoke. I had no dates. I was abstemious in every department and, as I remember my state of mind from that period, it was not unlike the feelings I'd have before an important tennis match or a downhill ski race or, later, a golf tournament. It was a mixture of fear and eagerness.

The fear, of course, was that I would not be as good as I thought I was. I knew that talent was necessary . . . and courage. The eagerness was a product of my confidence. I felt, I was *convinced*, that I was creating something worthy. I was going to give it my best shot. There would be nothing halfhearted about it. There would be no excuses if I failed, and if I succeeded, I wanted nothing less than a triumph. I had had successes in my life. But I was anxious, finally, for an unqualified triumph.

Throughout the late winter and early spring of 1950, I worked. My discipline never varied. As the day of our opening approached, Moe Popell went into action, using his contacts from a lifetime on Seventh Avenue to convince buyers to come see my collection. There was, I suppose, a certain curiosity about me as well. My name had been in the papers. People knew that I was the husband of Gene Tierney and that I'd been a successful designer in Hollywood. There was glamor attached to the name Cassini.

While Popell worked on the crowd, I selected the models. This was very important. I was doing something different and I wanted my models to reflect that. I didn't want wraithlike, opaque-faced human clotheshangers. I wanted them to seem fresh and happy and, above all, alluring in a subtle way. (In those days, it was not desirable for models to have much of a bustline, especially for photography. In the '50s, waist cinchers, girdles, and flat chests were de rigueur. There was even something called a "model's girdle," made of rubber, that could reduce the hips from a size ten to an eight. Top models who were well-endowed, like Dorian Leigh, would strap the extra bosom down, under the armpits. The garments of the '50s were structured, many having built-in bones, crinolines, and the like.)

We sent out invitations to the opening and had very good responses, considering that we were competing against all the established firms . . . but people were curious. They were also hungry, I believe, for something other than the same old routine. "We have to discuss the presentation," Moe said. "What happens in that first hour will determine the future of this company.

Until then, there had been a rather dour, formal, almost religious quality to the presentation of a new line of clothing. The designer was nowhere to be seen; the models paraded down the runway to suitable music; an unseen voice called out a number: *43 . . . 67 . . . 13.* I thought, *Why not make it more interesting? Why not give the dresses* names *instead of numbers? And then, why not amusing names? If I am going to be the American upstart, why not act like one?*

Actually, the real breakthrough idea came from my staff. "Mr. Cassini," I was told during the preparations for our first show, "we believe you should be present and launch the line yourself. It's not generally done, but you are known as a personage, an interesting fellow outside the world of fashion, and these people will be curious to meet you, to see what you look like. So you should make an appearance, present your collection, explain to them what you are trying to do and why they should buy it."

Well, this was a terrifying thought. I had never appeared before a crowd of people before. I was by nature very shy. I might think my line was worthy, but to have to get up and *sell* it was a different story entirely. I became more and more nervous as the day of the show approached. I was in a jittery state.

And then it was the morning of the show. I was extremely tense, and must have looked it, for an assistant suggested, "Mr. Cassini, perhaps you should have a drink."

I had two martinis, straight up, and I felt better, but still not exactly confident.

Suddenly the room was crowded. I could hear people sitting down, murmuring. I had a small loft, and there were perhaps three hundred people in my showroom, including Mother and Father, squeezed together like sardines, and then I could hear the voice of Moe Popell saying, "We are very pleased to introduce to you what we believe will be an excellent collection, by a masterful young designer."

And there I was.

The curtains parted. All these faces were looking at me. I felt almost dizzy. I couldn't focus my eyes, or my mind. I began to blubber something.

215

There was laughter—totally unexpected. This gave me courage. I began to explain who I was and what the collection was about. I could see that they were listening attentively. This gave me still more courage, and my message became clearer. I told them I adored women and that my career was dedicated to their enhancement; that I was an international designer with experience in Europe, Hollywood, and Seventh Avenue . . . and that the marketplace needed a new approach, that of a connoisseur, someone who appreciated the way women looked. And then I told them about Paris. "I don't think Paris has all the answers, because French designers do not know how American women live. I think there's room for something fresh, daring . . . and American."

There was applause—sustained, heartfelt applause; apparently I'd touched a chord. I was beginning to feel pretty good; the martinis were taking hold. The show began, and I continued talking, telling them about each of the dresses, cracking jokes, *silly* jokes. One of the things I'd brought back that year—they were absolutely dead—was knits. Traditionally, knits will be successful for five or six years and then disappear. I had made a very cute group of knits, and introduced myself as New York's "number-one knitwit." They liked that. I named each dress as it came out. Some were fairly outrageous: one, very décolleté, I called "Missionary's Downfall"; another, worn by a model who looked like Vivien Leigh, was "Harlot O'Scara."

This was a different sort of show from any the buyers had ever seen before . . . and somewhat different from what I'd been expecting, as well. I began to feel comfortable in front of that audience; I found that I enjoyed making them laugh, and had no qualms about being silly. "Man-oh-Manischewitz, what a line!" I'd say, that sort of thing. And, amazingly, it worked. I could *feel* it working.

In those days, most firms were presenting 125 or so pieces, trying to squeeze as many into an hour as possible, thereby forcing the buyers to rush frantically from one show to the next. I made mine a more leisurely affair: 65 pieces, 45 minutes. Everyone had time to relax, to think about what they'd just seen . . . and time to come up and congratulate me, which a great many of them did. I was surrounded by representatives of stores I'd never heard of. They were shaking my hand, telling me how refreshing the line was. Moe Popell was right next to me, saying as each one came and left—a receiving line it became, just about—"You got him! You got him! Do you realize who that is?"

I had no idea, and it was difficult to tell just how successful I'd been. But over the next few hours we began to get an idea. First, there were the elevator boys whom I'd befriended. They were the ones who ferried the buyers from floor to floor, from show to show. I had paid them a little money to listen for reactions. "You've got a hit, Mr. Cassini, a real smash," they said. "We only heard the best things."

A more tangible sign was Moe Popell's calendar, which was rapidly filling with appointments to "write" orders. On the second or third day, Moe came to me and said, "A most extraordinary thing has happened. Mrs. Shaver has heard about your collection and she wants to come see it herself. This is very unusual, O.C., and very important."

Mrs. Shaver was Dorothy Shaver, the president of Lord & Taylor. She was a very tasteful and creative woman who had single-handedly made Lord & Taylor the most important store in terms of fashion at the time. I arranged a special show for her alone, without the hoopla of the other presentations. Just the clothes.

"Your collection is brilliant," she said, and kissed me. "I am going to give you all the front windows in the store."

This was, of course, a tremendous first step. All too often in business, though, it is the *second* step that tells the tale. Too much initial success can be as dangerous as too little. We still had to produce the clothes. They had to be well made, and then, naturally, they had to sell. But first there was production, and I had no money left. I had spent Hunt's entire $100,000.

I went to see Leon Rosenbaum, a banker and a gentleman, a friend of mine to this day, at Irving Trust. He was an expert in the garment business; he looked at my orders and knew what I had. "Normally," he said, "I couldn't give you a penny. You're just too new. You have exhausted your capital, and though you have orders, you have not delivered a single dress yet. But I believe you will. I may be taking a risk, but I believe in this idea and I believe in you."

He gave me a $100,000 loan for production, and later, another loan to pay off my backers. I doubled their money in a year, as promised, and became the sole stockholder of Oleg Cassini, Inc. I still am.

And the clothes sold. They practically flew out of the stores. There was a point when we were averaging 150 reorders a day, in a business and at a time when reorders were very rare. It was known as the "horseshoe" line among many of the buyers because it sold so well. We did about $750,000 in sales in 1950, a figure that would increase each of the next five years. By 1955, our sales had reached $5,000,000 (in today's money, about $50,000,000).

At one point, about six firms that specialized in copying designer originals were producing my designs and living off my creativity. In France, stealing designs is punishable by law, but not in America. But as Chanel once said, "Imitation is the sincerest form of flattery."

A corner had been turned in my life, quite clearly. I had proven to Gene that I was tough enough. I had proven to Mother (who'd also been skeptical) that better ready-to-wear made more commercial sense than *haute couture* (in the sense of one dress specifically made-to-order for a customer). I had proven that success was possible for a designer who ignored Paris; indeed, who made a point of never going to the Paris shows.

Perhaps I made too strong a point of it. I remember Jacques Fath, who was a friend of Mother's, telling me, "My dear boy, now you must come back and open a *maison de couture* in Paris. The true artist must also have his expression in Europe."

"I disagree," I said. "I am an American designer. I will have my studio on Seventh Avenue. I don't need a palace on the Avenue Montaigne."

I was wrong—but for commercial, not artistic, reasons. At least fifty percent of the "mystique" of Paris was the city itself. What buyer could resist spending a week at the Ritz, eating in the best restaurants, and being treated like a queen by the regal-looking design establishments? Such extravagance could make even the flimsiest excuses for garments seem significant. Also, fashion was treated as a major industry in France. The government encouraged export and supported it. All the top models would arrive in Paris and do the collections. The different American magazines would send photographers, writers, and editors.

I made another mistake. Eleanor Lambert, the most influential publicist in fashion at the time, offered to represent me, but I didn't take the opportunity. I had hired a fellow named Al Davidson to do publicity, and felt a certain loyalty to him. It was a costly error, because Eleanor never forgave me.

My sales and reviews were such that I could not be dismissed. But I wasn't mythologized, either, in that breathless, fawning way that a small coterie of self-proclaimed experts in the field celebrate . . . genius! I thought, and still think, most of that was so much hype, and not entirely reflective of the real world. They spoke a bizarre language—fashionese— and most often valued their own words over the actual look of the dresses. They tried to sell fashion as art is sold, by the judgments of a few insiders. Balenciaga for many years would not allow the press to see his collections, and yet he was universally accepted as the greatest designer. By what criteria, I've always wondered, did the fashion press decide that (which may very well have been the truth) without seeing his work?

I always found it peculiar that the female body would be rediscovered each season by various couturiers. Dispatches would leave Paris: Dior has discovered the bosom, or the next year, the fanny or legs. Had they been overlooked somehow?

Perhaps they thought my style of presentation—the jokes, the dress names—was disrespectful, too. In any case, I was trying to sell "America" twenty years before "America" and "Milan" and "Tokyo" and all the other creative venues of a civilized world became acceptable.

The attitude that the experts had toward American design became very clear one day when I went to lunch with Nancy White, who was then editor of *Harper's Bazaar*. I asked her, "Miss White, how can you build Norman Norell to the sky after his collection when he admits that every single dress is a copy of Chanel?"

"Yes," she replied, "but he did it better."

I will tell one final story about fashion myths and then let it be:

In the early 1950s, there was a famous American couturier named Mainbocher, who had succeeded in Paris and then opened a branch of his business in the United States. Among his clients were two ladies who were friends of mine—Irene Wrightsman and Joanne Connelly, the wife of the famous golfer Bobby Sweeney (who also was known for having received one of Barbara Hutton's million-dollar gifts). The two of them came to see one of my shows and suggested, "Why don't you copy some of these little dresses Mainbocher makes and put them in your collection? You'll have a tremendous success."

"Let me see them," I said.

They showed me the dresses they'd just bought. The average price was $1,500, ten times more than mine. I looked at them and said, "They are not as well made as mine." The fabric was similar, a peau de soie that cost $5 to $8 per yard, but where did the rest of that fabulous cost per dress come from? "But maybe you are right and I am wrong. Let me show them to my salespeople, and just as an experiment, we'll include them in the line and see how they do."

Moe Popell didn't like the idea. "Mr. Cassini, you are a better designer," he said. "Don't put them in."

I insisted, though. They were in the next show. Often, in my presentations, I would make editorial comments such as, "I like this dress immensely," when I thought it would be a really big seller, or, "Frankly, if I were you, I wouldn't buy this one, because I don't like it"—and there would be laughter—"but I put it in because my salesmen told me it would sell." I described the two Mainbocher dresses, using fashionese: "This is a new look here . . . a pure look, rather clinical, unobtrusive, it puts the body at its best . . ."

After two weeks of shows, I hadn't booked three dresses of that type and I asked Popell why. "The buyers say they're all right," he said, "but they don't show the value." It was remarkable. These $1,500 dresses didn't show the value at one-tenth the price. That little trick cleared my mind forever about Paris fashions and Paris prices.

I called myself an American designer, but the truth was I didn't know very much about America or Americans—at least, those Americans who lived between New York and Los Angeles. If I were to have a sustained success, I was going to have to learn who these people were and what they wanted, so I volunteered to do something unheard of at the time. I told several of the top stores that I would be willing to go out and do fashion shows to promote my line for them in various cities. When word of this got out, my competitors laughed at me.

Larry Aldridge, a competitor who was an excellent businessman (and later became a good friend), said, "You're out of your mind. This is ridiculous."

"Larry, you're established," I told him. "You know everything and I know nothing. I am going to go out there and talk to the people."

The first store that accepted my offer was Saks Fifth Avenue. They asked me to do essentially the same sort of show I'd done on Seventh Avenue—the jokes, the models, the music—at each of their branch stores, twice a day, for their best customers. "We'll promote you and give you all the windows when you arrive," the merchandising manager told me, "if you agree to give us an exclusive distribution among department stores in the cities where we are—except for the New York stores with branches—and you can also have two specialty stores." I was the number-one resource in the "French Room" (couture) at Saks and Neiman-Marcus.

And so, I became a road show. It was exhausting, but it helped business enormously. Entertainment was, after all, different in those days. Television was just coming in, and people didn't have as much exposure to visual stimulation; my shows were a major event everywhere I went. The two shows a day usually turned out to be more like five. There would be the two shows scheduled for Saks's best customers, but also an early-morning show for the store's personnel, a luncheon show for the local press or the local TV, and often an evening show at a charity ball. Most people assumed I had a team of writers working on my scripts and assistants helping to prepare the shows. But there were no scripts—I improvised everything, helped by drinks—and no assistants.

I ran an incredible schedule, sometimes traveling by train, but most often driving myself from city to city in a station wagon accompanied by several models and trunks full of dresses. I drove at night on icy roads, often arriving in some godforsaken place at 3:00 A.M. with a show scheduled for eight the next morning . . . and all sorts of logistics to work out beforehand. I'd always need local models to supplement the two regulars, and it was difficult to find the right sort to fit the clothes. Today, people are paid to do such things; they are called "fashion coordinators." In those days, I was the coordinator, host, raconteur, chauffeur, designer (at times, in the midst of a tour, I'd have to fly back to New York for a day or two for fittings or to put new sketches into work) and, all too often, nursemaid to the models, who could be as skittish as thoroughbreds and unruly as hell.

I had one model, whom we'll call "Z," who was very beautiful but drunk all the time—a total alcoholic. Once, in Detroit, I returned to the hotel after midnight, having spent hours in a meeting with Saks executives, getting reorders and planning future shows, and there was a knock on my door. It was Z, totally naked and drunk out of her mind. She had been walking the corridors like that. I had a horrible premonition of what would happen if word got out. I was building a reputation as a designer of elegant clothes, worn by only the most fashionable women; I was afraid that it might all be destroyed if rumors spread that I had naked models running about.

I said to Z, "What do you think you're doing?"

She ran off, down the hall. I got my raincoat and ran after her; we played a nerve-wracking game of hide-and-seek until she ran out of steam and decided to engage in a perverse attempt at Gandhian passive resistance, lying flat in front of the elevators. We had a bit of a struggle—I was trying to put the raincoat on her, but not having much luck—until the elevator came and I decided to get out of there. I didn't want to be seen grappling with a naked model engaging in an apparent act of civil disobedience in the hallway. I went back to my room, and realized that I'd closed the door behind me on the way out. It was locked. I was locked out in my pajamas.

I took the back stairs down to the lobby and located the hotel detective. "I have a terrible problem," I told him. "One of my models is drunk and running naked through the halls of this hotel. I'll give you one hundred dollars if you can catch her."

So we stalked Z through the halls and finally, working together, managed to subdue her and get her back to her room, which she had completely destroyed in a fit of rage. The detective was very helpful in keeping the episode quiet, but I had to let the model go.

Actually, I made something of a fashion breakthrough in my use of models during that time. In this case, it was an unwitting innovation and long overdue.

It happened the year I broke my rule against attending Paris shows, and went to see Pierre Cardin's latest. I have always appreciated Cardin's work, but the highlight of the show was a most spectacular, devastating Eurasian model named China Machado. She moved the way only the most talented models can: as if she were floating on air. She made every dress live. It is an intangible quality, one you cannot explain or teach: she made all the clothes she wore winners.

China was like a cat, with slanted eyes and dark, beautiful skin. She had white teeth and full lips and long, raven-black hair. She was stunning. (She would later become one of the favorite models of Richard Avedon, and the fashion editor of *Harper's Bazaar*.) I saw her and was overwhelmed. I gave her a look, and she returned it. After the show, we went out for coffee.

"How would you like to come to America and work for me?" I asked. "I'd love to have you do my collections."

China was agreeable, and I said, "I'll tell you what I will do: I'll get you an apartment and plenty of work. But, please understand, I am only interested in you as a model."

"I know." She smiled.

She agreed to come . . . and was quite a hit. I could see it very clearly from the order books: every dress she wore was a commercial success. There was one very serious problem, however: my Southern accounts protested. "Mr. Cassini," one buyer said, putting it right on the line, "we cannot buy your line if you have a black girl modeling it."

How odd. I could not imagine this. I considered those who made distinctions among the races hairsplitters of an odious sort. These buyers were particularly ridiculous. First of all, she was not "black." Second, even if she *were*, what difference would it make? My response to them was simple: "If you don't like it, don't order."

They didn't. My business in the South suffered that year . . . and I began to *seek out* black models. Eventually, they would have a major impact on fashion, but, much to my surprise, I was the first to use them. It was, as I said, an innovation that was exceedingly late in coming.

One of the most magnificent models I used during this time was an American girl of Scandinavian descent named Lois Balchen (she was related to the famous Arctic explorer of the same name), whom I'd met briefly at the bar of the Hôtel Georges V in Paris. Several months later, I spotted her walking down Madison Avenue. She was difficult to miss: about five foot eight, with short blonde hair and an imposing physical presence. She looked something like Mia Farrow.

Lois was along for one of my more memorable excursions to the heart of America. I'd been asked by Famous-Barr, the store in St. Louis, to present several shows. It came at a time when I was exhausted and ill—double pneumonia yet again. My mother, who had moved to New York with Father to be near Igor and me, suggested a doctor who worked miracles. His name was Jacobson. Later, he would be better known as "Dr. Feelgood," the man who treated an array of celebrity patients, including President Kennedy, with amphetamine shots. I remember him as a dark-haired, very muscular man with thick glasses and an intriguing diagnostic manner. He asked me only one question about my health: "You feel sick?"

"Yes," I said. "Very."

"This will make you feel better."

And he produced the biggest syringe I'd ever seen, filled with red liquid, and gave me a shot. "Come for another one tomorrow morning," he said.

I began to feel the effects within ten minutes: first, a strange metallic feeling in my mouth, then hot flashes—I was boiling hot—and then, maybe ten minutes later, I felt like the king of Spain. I was strong as an ox. The pneumonia was a distant memory. My mind was working at a fantastic pace. The next morning, I went back for a second shot and then boarded a plane for St. Louis, with Lois Balchen and Alek Hohenlohe, who was along for the ride. We hit a terrible blizzard. We had to land in Kansas City, and found a late-night train to St. Louis. We were up all night, and arrived in snowed-in St. Louis the next morning. I still felt great, despite the lack of sleep, despite the pneumonia. I gave one of my best shows, and we did quite well in St. Louis.

I suppose I should be thankful to my regular physician, who advised me that amphetamines were dangerous and told me never to return to the gentle care of Dr. Feelgood, but there were times, driving bleary-eyed through the American night in my station wagon filled with clothes and sullen models, when I could have benefited from his services. I didn't let up on the hectic pace for five years. I pushed every advantage. As long as I was successful, I was going to make the most of it. I'd spent more than enough of my life at the economic mercy of others and had no intention of ever being in that position again.

I was still married to Gene, officially. She was in Los Angeles or on location; I was in New York or on tour. The arcs of our careers had crossed. I was on the way up now; Gene was still a major star, but the studio system was changing in ways that she didn't quite understand. I encouraged her to be more selective about her roles. I thought she should make no more than one carefully chosen, prestigious film a year. To do more didn't even make financial sense: the difference between one movie and two was only $17,000, if one considered fiscal realities. She responded by making four films in 1951, including *On the Riviera*, with Danny Kaye, hardly the sort of role that would enhance her career as a dramatic actress. In short, she continued to accept most of the scripts the studio sent her and she suffered—physically, mentally, maritally—as a result.

Gene did not begrudge my success; she was thrilled that I'd finally proven my worth, but, I think, in her heart of hearts, she missed the Cassini who'd provided moral support and paid so much attention in the early years. It was no longer conceivable that I would spend hours reviewing her script lines; it was becoming less plausible that I would sit at home by the phone on those few evenings when I wasn't working, and wait for her call instead of going out and enjoying myself. I made it clear to Gene that if she insisted upon spending her time away from me, I should not be expected to curtail my social life.

I was no longer of a mood to waste my weekends commuting back and forth to Los Angeles; too much was happening in New York. Igor was at the peak of his power as Cholly Knickerbocker, the ultimate arbiter of who was "in" and who was not. Mother helped. This was a renaissance for her, a wonderful time. Both her boys were doing well, but I think she especially enjoyed her role as Igor's unofficial assistant (he had a quite competent official staff as well, including the excellent Liz Smith). Mother had her own little coterie, people who flattered her and whispered in her ear, using her as a back door into the column. She would lobby for her friends. She and Igor would often have lunch together at the Colony, the restaurant that he popularized and made his unofficial midday headquarters, across the street from our adjoining town houses. He could make or break restaurants, nightclubs, shows, performances, anything.

Igor was also the first newspaper personality to have his own television show. He was soon followed, more successfully, by his rival columnist, Ed Sullivan. Igor tried a different tack, something more like *The Tonight Show*, interviewing celebrity guests, and with regular appearances by his older brother. I was expected to be entertaining on an impromptu basis, which was my specialty at dinner parties (and, of course, fashion shows). It was all rather haphazard; we were at sea in the new medium and the results were sometimes hilarious, most often unintentionally so. On his very first show, Igor was allowed by the producer, who seemed to know as much about television as we did, to interview Huntington Hartford interminably while Bing Crosby, Bob Hope, and several other celebrities were kept waiting in the wings. They never did get on that day.

The show began on NBC, then moved to the DuMont television network, then was canceled. It might have been resuscitated but for a serious faux pas by me. I was in California on one of my increasingly rare visits with Gene when Igor called: "Look, we may have a real opportunity here. Despite our lack of success, we might have a new sponsor—a very powerful Austrian fellow with a big cosmetics company. He wants to meet with us. When will you be back?"

We made an appointment for the following Wednesday. I flew in Tuesday night and, as was my custom, repaired immediately to El Morocco. I had a date waiting for me, and my usual good banquette. Seated next to us were an attractive redhead and a little man with a monocle and a pointy head. Midway through the evening, I returned from the dance floor and inadvertently sat on the redhead's fur wrap. The fellow pulled at it and said, "Can't you see you're seated on my wife's fur?"

"Oh, I'm so sorry."

"You *should* be sorry," he said, combatively. "I can't think of anything more thoughtless."

"Listen, sir, I apologized and that's it. So don't give me any bullshit or I'll wipe the floor with you."

Of course, he turned out to be our prospective sponsor, Evyan Perfumes. His interest in the project diminished markedly when he set eyes on me at our meeting the next morning. I attempted humor; he found my humor lacking. Igor considered fratricide for a time, but got over it.

* * *

New York social life in the early 1950s was not all that different from what it had been in the 1930s. There were still El Morocco and the Stork, the debutantes and postdebs. The same cast of characters—Billingsley, Perona, Winchell—were still holding forth. *I* had changed somewhat. My social predicament was quite the opposite of what it had been in the 1930s. I now had the money to divert myself, but not the time. I was considered a member in good standing, not only of café society, but also among the fading remnants of real society, filled with the descendants of the *Mayflower* and the nineteenth-century industrialists with estates in Connecticut and on the North Shore of Long Island, many of whom were my old polo-playing colleagues from Fort Riley.

This was an aspect of life in New York that Gene quite enjoyed. When she was in town, we often spent weekends with our old friends, the Bostwicks and the Rutherfords, on Long Island. The Bostwicks had a marvelous two-hundred-acre estate in Westbury. These were the last days, really, of serious fox hunting in America; certainly there wasn't much open country left to gallop through on Long Island. There were no foxes left, either, so most of the time we had drag hunts. The greatest problem, though, was the expense. In addition to the need for a great deal of land, fox hunting required the maintenance of a pack of hounds and a stable of horses. For a time, in the mid-fifties, I, too, had a stable of hunters, as well as three Thoroughbreds who raced at Aqueduct and Belmont; they were trained by Betty Bosley, but failed to distinguish themselves (I was so busy in those days I never got to see them run). The most beautiful horse I owned, a scion of the great War Admiral, didn't do well in the races, but turned out to be an excellent hunter.

Gene didn't ride; she didn't want to risk her career on a serious fall. But she and Laura Bostwick loved gardening and spent a good deal of time discussing that. Hunt-club society was rather odd. These were people who lived on the most elegant estates, who would spend $100,000 for a horse—the equivalent of $1,000,000 today—and then serve cold cuts for dinner. They were very big on drinking, on appearances, on Saturday-night parties with the Lester Lanin orchestra, but food was a blind spot.

In general, I found the hunting women more pleasant than many of the men, who were drunk most of the time. They lurched through the social occasions in a semistupor—it was considered manly to go hunting hung over. Those who weren't members of the cavalry during the war had been marines, and fistfights were a common pastime. I was, as always, suspect because of my profession and was frequently called upon to prove my mettle.

Still, I quite enjoyed the scene. Fox hunting was a sport in keeping with my atavistic fantasies; it was pleasing, on a visceral level, to be able to divert myself as my ancestors had. I rode in hunts throughout the Northeast; for a time, I kept horses stabled with a farmer on the Pennsylvania-Delaware border. I was an enthusiastic member of the Smithtown hunt, serving as a "whipper in"—a position of some honor, reserved for only the better riders, who could keep up with and control the movement of the hounds. The master of the hunt was a striking fellow named Tim Durant—tall, thin, white-haired, with hawklike features—who became a good friend of mine. Durant was another of those people (like the boxer Jimmy McLarnen) who were obsessed with diet long before it became popular. His particular, and decidedly peculiar, habit was to chew meat very thoroughly, sucking it dry of its juice, and then spit the rest out. This was not the sort of thing I'd recommend for a quiet dinner for two, but it seemed to work for Tim, who always was in the finest physical condition. He was a devoted rider and hunter, so much so that after he lost his foot in a fox-hunting accident, he decided that life was no longer worth living. He became morose and withdrawn, and actually willed his own death.

I was not as obsessed by the sport as Durant, but I did ride most weekends during the 1950s, often riding with friends like José Ferrer and Fern Tailer. It was strenuous activity and, at times, dangerous. Often we'd be out chasing across the countryside from eight in the morning till dark, sometimes in freezing conditions in late autumn and early winter. We'd race down narrow avenues between fields; both horse and rider would become fatigued—two mounts were necessary for a day of hunting —and there would be serious accidents, including one that just about ended my hunting career.

This was a week when I was serving as master of the hunt in Tim Durant's absence. I had borrowed one of his mounts, a good hunter but skittish with a new rider and an unfamiliar snaffle bit. I was having some trouble controlling him as we raced along a narrow, tree-lined corridor. It was a real riding challenge, marked by occasional obstructions, jumps and ditches to be vaulted. Somehow my mount did not spot a chest-high wall in our path. He slammed into the wall and we somersaulted in the air, the horse falling on top of me and rolling over. I am not sure how I landed; it must have been head first, because my riding helmet was split in two like a melon. The impact of the crash also had somehow twisted one of my thick metal stirrups out of shape. I was somewhat twisted as well: two broken fingers, two broken ankles, and a broken nose. José Ferrer, riding immediately behind me, heard me scream as we hit the wall and then saw me on the ground, unable to move. He thought I had broken my back. The hunt was stopped; I was carried in, still in a state of shock, but gradually regaining feeling in my extremities—all of which seemed in terrible pain. Still, I felt lucky to have gotten off so easily.

Despite such mishaps, I loved the ritual of the hunt, the cavalcade. There was one lady, a Mrs. Hannum, who would allow you to ride in her hunt only if you had at least two mounts and were perfectly appointed. I had enjoyed looking well ever since Florence and, once again, had the money to indulge myself. My riding habit came from Wetherell in London, my boots from Peel. Indeed, almost all my clothes were made-to-order in England or Italy; in those days, the idea of a ready-made suit was entirely foreign to me. I studied dress; I was fascinated by the detail and philosophy of it. What made one fellow seem just right, while another, equally fastidious, didn't quite make it?

The best-dressed man I ever saw was the duke of Windsor, with whom I later played golf on several occasions in Palm Beach. He was rather generous with his scoring during these games. If he muffed a shot, he'd say, "That didn't count, someone walked by and spoiled my concentration," or he might casually, elegantly, move a ball to a better lie. This was a form of *droit du seigneur* and, of course, everyone let him get away with it. In terms of dress, though, he took no shortcuts, although his trick was to make it seem so. His intention was to give the appearance of nonchalance. Indeed, this—I have always believed—was the essence, the definition of style: feeling that no effort at all had been expended in selecting the paisley tie and checked jacket that just happened to go together perfectly. The duke of Windsor cared tremendously about appearances, of course, but affected an attitude of *je ne sais quoi*, of casual abandon, of effortless grace.

I don't know how many hours a day he spent selecting those paisleys and checks that went together so naturally, but some of the other well-dressed men I've known thought about, and worried over, their clothes to the exclusion of almost all else. During the early 1950s, I met a fellow named Maurice Bosdari, who was one of the three or four best-dressed men I've ever known, and certainly the most obsessed. He was tall, very distinguished-looking, and quite meticulous, a former Italian cavalry officer who had married an American heiress. He had one topic of conversation: appearances. He thought of nothing else. We would sit and talk about clothes by the hour, not just where the best stuff might be purchased, but also—invariably, eternally—how it should be worn; indeed, how it should be *prepared* to be worn. Maurice could happily pass any social occasion in critical contemplation of everyone he saw: "The upper button on that fellow's suit over there . . . just a smidgen off." That sort of thing. A trouser pleat had to fall just so; there had to be a quarter-of-an-inch give at the cuff. His shoes were burnished—not too obviously shined—a particular shade of brown, and he would keep his feet balled up (it must have been painful) in order that the shoes remain uncreased. "Lapels must be tortured," he said, and he would manipulate them, crush them with his hands until they rolled just right. "Clothing must never seem new; it must look old, but not too old." He was the type of man who would take a new pair of riding pants and jump into a tub of water with them so that they would take his shape. He would then emerge—relieved!—and say, "Ah, now they're right. The natural crease."

His obsession with clothes—he had a certain critical intelligence about women's dress as well—led me to do a rather odd and self-destructive thing: I hired him as an adviser and publicist. It wasn't my idea. Nino LoSavio, a very popular figure in New York society whom I'd known since the 1930s, suggested it. "Maurice needs something to do. He needs to earn a living now that he's divorced."

Bosdari had worked for me for about a year—well, "worked" isn't quite the word; he was an intelligent presence in the office—when I asked him to actually do something. "Maurice," I said, "Mrs. Vreeland is a friend of yours. Why haven't you had her here to see the collection?"

He made excuses. He was very shy. It was bad form to drag one's friends. *"Merde!"* I exclaimed. "You're *working* here. This is Seventh Avenue, not the court of Louis the Sixteenth!"

He produced Mrs. Vreeland. We had a special showing for her, just the three of us and six models. At the end, she made some comments: "Maurice, it is a good collection, isn't it? What do you think?"

Bosdari was silent a moment, then bestirred himself. "Ah, there was a belt—green and mauve—on that red dress that I thought rather nice."

Exit Mrs. Vreeland. *Tête-à-tête*, Bosdari and I. "Maurice," I said, "your enthusiasm for this collection overwhelms me. We show ninety pieces and you manage to find one belt interesting. I find that I now have a similar level of enthusiasm for your continued employment."

Mrs. Vreeland eventually asked me to redo some of the dresses in green, and used them for her magazine. Bosdari returned to Italy and lived the rest of his life in semiseclusion, a visitor to the twentieth century from an earlier era.

Gene and I had now been married ten years, after a fashion; the last five had been a series of separations and reconciliations, some of which were rather unlikely. There was the period, in 1951, when Gene decided that our only hope was to pretend we were a happy suburban couple. We settled in Fairfield County, Connecticut, near her sister, Pat, and her brother, Butch, and allowed ourselves to stultify for a time. Gene was able to play a favorite role: contented wife of a successful businessman. The pretense did not work for long: I was hardly the commuting type. I suffered the New Haven Railroad daily, my brain feeling as if it had been twisted into a pretzel by the time I reached Grand Central Station each morning. I couldn't stand the regimen; it was death on creativity. In truth, Gene was bored as well, despite her best intentions. She was a movie star who happened to enjoy housework; the reality of a lifetime of recipes and furniture repair wasn't very exhilarating. She was searching for peace of mind, an increasingly elusive goal; I allowed myself to go along for the ride.

But then, a day came when I refused to go along for the ride: Gene was leaving for Argentina to do a picture called *Way of a Gaucho* with Rory Calhoun. She would be gone for three months, starting in December 1951. She insisted I come along, even though I was busy with my spring collection.

"I am not going," I told her, "and you shouldn't, either. It's a silly picture and will do nothing for you as an actress."

"If you don't come, I'm going to divorce you."

"That will be your decision, not mine," I said. "I'm not going."

I didn't, and we did divorce. I received desperate calls from Gene while she was in Argentina, and letters—lengthy, rambling, frightening letters. Everyone was against her: the director, her co-star, even the hairdresser was a conspirator. I knew something was happening to her. For a time, I thought about giving in, going there, joining her. But I knew, on some level, that if I went I would ultimately be giving up my business as well, that the priorities in our marriage would have been set in concrete, forever. I have never been a very good writer of letters, but I wrote her then: I begged her forgiveness, but I had to stay in New York, working.

She returned to California in February of 1952, and proceeded with the divorce. It was said in court that I threw a hot spoon at her. I do not know where or when that happened, or how the spoon was heated; I did not attend the divorce, nor did I contest it (Gene was there with Fran Stark, both wearing Cassinis). When the gossip columnists called for "my side" of the story, I told them, "I have no side. This is a very unfortunate circumstance. I have nothing ill to say of Gene. I hope we will always remain close, even though we may not be married." I also told them that the spoon hadn't been very hot.

In truth, I could have stopped it. Several days before the case went to court, Ray Stark called me. I was in Detroit, doing one of my shows for Saks. "Look," he said, "Fran and I have talked with Gene. She doesn't really want this. She said that if you drop everything and come right out here, she will stop the divorce proceedings."

"But Ray, that is exactly the point. I am no longer in a position where I can drop everything."

"Gene wants a sign that you are willing to sacrifice for her," he said.

"It's not a question of sacrifice. It's a question of responsibility. She has to understand that."

"Very well," Stark said, realizing all was lost and not wanting to end on a heavy note. "I'll introduce her to Kirk Douglas. He wants to meet her anyway."

"You wonderful guy."

And so, Gene and I were finally divorced. We did remain friends. We talked frequently and she often asked my advice, especially during her brief, much-publicized romance with Aly Khan. This came as something of a surprise to me: she had written from Argentina that she had met this fellow with baggy pants and dirty fingernails who was pursuing her relentlessly, but she did not find him attractive. She said he looked like a thinner version of Orson Welles. Aly was immune to rejection, though, and he continued to pursue her relentlessly, as was his fashion, and eventually succeeded. Mrs. Tierney, still about, had the bizarre idea that they could make a Connecticut Yankee out of Aly, that they could convince him to settle down. I knew the fellow; I knew how silly this was. "Gene," I told her, "he is, in his heart, a Moslem prince. He has certain attitudes toward women. He will never marry another actress. The Aga Khan forbids it. You should read *The Seven Pillars of Wisdom* and pay close attention to the Moslem philosophy of marriage, and you will see, this fellow is not going to make you happy."

She did not take my advice, and was terribly shaken when they split. Her mental condition continued to deteriorate; she was given electroshock therapy at a clinic in New York and a hospital in Connecticut, and received treatment at the Menninger Clinic in Kansas. She would call me from there, quite distressed. The doctors wanted her to find a new "identity," and so she was working as a salesgirl at a boutique in Wichita. This was terribly demeaning, I thought. Did they think she would find redemption through humiliation? I thought this course of "therapy" was foolish. My feeling at the time was that her problem was a chemical imbalance, and this later proved to be true; Gene's health improved significantly when new drugs were developed that could address this imbalance. Still, her downward spiral was quite unbelievable, and painful for me. I took full financial responsibility for our daughters, and tried to be as much of a father as I could for Christina, who was raised with her Tierney cousins in Connecticut, and with me in New York. Eventually, Gene recovered and married a businessman named Howard Lee from Houston, Texas. They lived quite happily together until Mr. Lee's unfortunate death.

Gene and I still remain close. We speak frequently by phone. I will, on occasion, send her some clothes or a gift to brighten her day. Sometimes, though, she will slip a little. She once called and asked me to meet her at the house in Green's Farms, the house we shared briefly in 1951 when I pretended to be a Fairfield County commuter. She told me that the key was on the ledge above the door, that she would meet me there. It was so sad. Our few months there were a fleeting moment of calm in her life, an oasis from the pressures of Hollywood and the debilitating trauma of Daria; it is a place she still visits, it seems, when she needs to find peace. I do not disabuse her of this solace. We shared great joy and terrible heartbreak in our lives; there is a bond between us that will never be broken. We will always love each other in our fashion.

In 1952, though, the distance Gene and I had drifted apart was illustrated by the fact that my life didn't seem all that different after the divorce. I was sad, I knew that it would be difficult to ever find someone of Gene's quality again, but day-to-day life continued on. I managed to be in the company of beautiful women with soothing regularity. I had several serious episodes, but nothing that impinged on the real love of my life at that moment: my business.

I would often wake up during the night and grab a pad to sketch or put down ideas. Inspiration is the most elusive thing; one has to force it to emerge and flow by constant prodding and concentration. To create a good collection is a complete catharsis of one's creativity, leaving the creator drained and exhausted—a feeling that I am sure is shared by other designers. There were four new collections a year, each one like an opening on Broadway.

This is not to say I couldn't indulge in a little levity with my collections. When the chemise—also known as the sack—was becoming a look in the '50s, I included in my show a dress that was an actual sack, a potato sack. I introduced it by saying, "Here comes the new silhouette," and people were starting to laugh and applaud (it was a very well-made dress, but out of sack cloth). Then I said, "It has a marvelous hood," and when the model raised the hood, some Idaho potatoes fell out. I also came out with my own version—a combination of sack and sheath—the Shack.

For five years, my business came first . . . but gradually I realized that the business was now on firm footing. We had established a good relationship with the finest stores in the country, and sales were booming. On the other hand, there was something missing from my life—the sense of danger, of excitement, I'd had in the past, when I wasn't so successful. I needed an adventure. I needed to take a chance, and have some fun.

This was made quite apparent to me by the beautiful English actress and comedienne Kay Kendall, who was then married to Rex Harrison. He had come to New York to perform the role of his life, Professor Henry Higgins in *My Fair Lady*.

I'd been happy to learn that Rex was in town. He'd always seemed to me a cut above the others in Hollywood, more sophisticated, with a sense of irony about his role. I remember him telling me, "This is the luckiest period in history for actors. We are the aristocrats of the era; this odd meritocracy has placed us at the top. In the Middle Ages, throughout most of history, in fact, we were nothing—jugglers, itinerant clowns, fed scraps from the master's table."

The trouble with Rex was: that was what he was—an actor. He could talk for hours with Olivier about the theater, but was not much interested in social life. I arranged a dinner for him when he first arrived in town, a New York (as opposed to Los Angeles) dinner, with a wide variety of sophisticated people from society and different professions. He was surrounded by lovely girls—the Murray sisters (one of whom later became Mrs. Alfred Vanderbilt) were there—but he seemed at a loss, even bored, and then left early.

Rex and Kay Kendall eventually settled into a fine house in Westbury, and I stopped there for dinner one evening on my way home from the Hamptons (I had a house in Quogue in those days). We had a pleasant dinner; it was the first time I'd met Kay Kendall and I thought she was a superb woman, witty, with a distinguished beauty, tall, with dark, flashing eyes and that sharp, distinctive nose. After dinner, she offered to show me the house; Rex was busy on the telephone. At one point, we stopped in the bedroom and began to talk about this and that—nothing very serious—but Rex found us seated there, on the bed, and he simply exploded.

"You arranged this," he accused her. "I can't trust you."

"Now look, Rex, we were just talking," I said.

"Don't say a word, I know what *you're* all about," he said to me, not far wrong.

"I'll not stay here a moment longer," I said.

"As you wish," he said, and I left.

The next morning, about nine or so, there was a ring at my door in the city. It was Kay Kendall. "Look, I'm leaving him," she said. "I'm going to London. I've had it. You want to come with me? Get packed. Let's go."

"Where can I call you? I have to get in touch with my office and all that."

She gave me a number. I called her there and said I had business, but would be ready to join her in two days. "Too bad," she said. "Forget it. You lost your chance. You don't have the dash I thought you did."

And, I realized she was right. She and Rex managed to patch things up—it was, no doubt, one of the temporary rough spots that every marriage endures—and I was stunned when she died several years later of leukemia.

I had learned a lesson from her, though. I vowed that the next chance I had to do something romantic and crazy, I was going to do it. I would forget the damn office, drop everything, live a little. What was money for, anyway, except to be enjoyed?

As it happened, the next "chance" turned out to be Grace Kelly, and the result was one of the most memorable romances of my life.

I n early 1954 I had, as usual, begun to take a sort of mental inventory —an activity that generally followed a negative or unsatisfactory period in my life. I was at loose ends. Despite all the problems we'd had, I was missing Gene. I did not think that in my lifetime I could ever replace her. The material things that I had aspired to gain were present; what I wanted was to reach a higher plateau of emotions, of feelings.

It was in that state of mind that I went, one afternoon early in 1954, to the movies with my good friend Bobby Friedman.

I am glad, in retrospect, that Bobby was there, because he is the sort who never would have believed what happened later that evening if he hadn't seen it himself. Bobby was an owlish-looking fellow, heir to a large scrap-iron business, and the kind of friend every busy man should have. He was an arranger, always planning social activities for me: weekends, evenings, tennis matches (we were frequent doubles partners). He was willing to play Sancho Panza to my Quixote because he was fascinated by beautiful women, anxious not only to meet them but also to learn the secrets of how to behave with them. Bobby was not a handsome man, but neither was Cyrano de Bergerac—and history is filled with toads who managed to convince women that they were princes; fantasy and cleverness are almost always more potent than a fortuitous configuration of physical features. For most men, romance is conquest; for certain women, though, the more interesting ones, it is a form of entertainment. Bobby wanted to learn how to be entertaining.

The movie we went to see was *Mogambo*. It was set in Africa, and featured Clark Gable, Ava Gardner, and a young actress I'd never seen before, Grace Kelly.

Grace was soon to become such a sensation, and later a veritable institution, that it is hard for many people to remember that she was not an overnight hit. She had appeared in only one film before *Mogambo*, the Western *High Noon*, with Gary Cooper, but it was a small role, a performance not nearly so memorable as Coop's. In *Mogambo*, she played the icy, aloof wife of a weak Englishman. There was a rather unlikely love scene with Gable at Victoria Falls—complete with roseate glow, à la *Gone with the Wind*—but *Mogambo* was Ava Gardner's picture: she was beautiful, sexy, and funny. She dominated Grace in their scenes together and, ultimately, won the competition for Gable in the movie.

I was smitten, though. Grace Kelly's coolness was magical, the delicate perfection of her face, her voice—everything. She seemed ethereal, an apparition.

"Well, the search is over," I whispered to Friedman, after a half-hour of the film.

"What do you mean?"

"She is going to be my next romance."

Later, leaving the theater, I repeated it: "I'm going to meet that girl."

"You're serious!" he realized. "You're out of your mind. What makes you think she'd be interested in you? What makes you think she's not already in love?"

Such prosaic questions.

"Bobby," I said, "you must understand: I don't care. That girl is going to be *mine*."

We had a reservation for dinner at Le Veau d'Or, the little French restaurant on East Sixtieth Street. We sat down, Bobby and I still talking about the movie and, naturally, surveying the crowded room for familiar faces . . . and there, not three feet to my right, was a French actor I'd known from Hollywood, Jean-Pierre Aumont, with his date for the evening, Miss Grace Kelly.

I saw her only in profile at first. I saw the utter perfection of her nose . . . the long, elegant neck . . . the silky, diaphanous blonde hair. She wore a black velvet two-piece, very demure, with a full skirt and a little white Peter Pan collar. Later, when she stood, I noticed that she had a pleasing figure: tall, about five foot eight, good broad shoulders, subtle curves, and long legs—a very aristocratic-looking girl.

She was gorgeous, but not striking, as Gene had been. She did not stand out in a room; her beauty was subtle, the sort that required a second look. She often wore glasses, dressed quite conservatively, and was very reserved; later, she would say to me, "If I'd been a little less good-looking, I might have been just a typical schoolteacher." She did not have the classic movie-star glow or presence. In Hollywood, there was always a buzz, almost a physical sensation, when a star entered a room. Grace seemed to disdain such pyrotechnics.

Meanwhile, I was making my move. I was more than happy to make it on Aumont, who had called Gene frequently when I was in the army, asking for dates. Now the shoe was on the other foot. The challenge, however, was to horn in on his date without seeming to do so.

Immediately, I said hello to Jean-Pierre, in the most friendly possible manner, and engaged him in conversation, pretending not to recognize his table partner, half glancing her way from time to time so as not to exclude her, but also to make an introduction necessary. Sooner or later, Jean-Pierre would have to say, "Grace, this is Oleg Cassini," and I would have my opening. He knew this. Finally, with a sickly smile, Aumont mumbled a hasty introduction, which I acknowledged politely, with a small bow, but nothing more. To Bobby Friedman's amazement—and I could see the glazed shock behind his thick, owlish glasses—I didn't tell her that we'd just seen her in *Mogambo*, or acknowledge her profession in any way. I treated her casually, as someone who was as sophisticated as we were and —naturally—familiar with wine, or travel, or Paris, or whatever it was Jean-Pierre and I were pretending to talk about as we angled for position. I sensed the direct, frontal approach would not work. I wanted only to establish a beachhead, to create an agreeable presence in her mind. I did nothing more that night.

I could afford to be patient. I had all the time in the world. I was now quite convinced that Grace Kelly and I were destined to be together. Fate does not provide such a coincidence in life without reason.

Later, there would be ceaseless articles in the movie press about how unapproachable, forbidding, mysterious, and challenging Grace Kelly was; she would be compared to all manner of icy things, especially glaciers and mountains. A University of Chicago sociologist would interview men about why they were daunted by her. The secret of Grace Kelly—who she *really* was—would become a national obsession.

I will not say that I could foresee the full, Himalayan dimensions of the myth that was about to be created around her; I did sense, however, that this was not the sort of girl you simply called for a date. A program of action was needed, a plan—something outrageous, romantic, even silly —to pierce her reserve. It might take weeks, even months. It would have to be cerebral, and titillating in the best sense of the word.

The first step was to find out everything I could about her, and I set my secretary on it. Within hours, I knew her address in New York (430 East Sixty-fifth Street), her phone number, her agent, her schedule (weekdays in the city and weekends with her family in Philadelphia for the next few weeks, then back to Hollywood for another film).

My belief was that if I could spend an hour alone with her, just talking, the worst part of the battle would be over. The question was how to get her to agree to that first hour.

I did it in the most rudimentary fashion, but with a twist. I sent a dozen red roses to her apartment the next morning, and a card. The card said only this: "The Friendly Florist."

The morning after, I did the same. And the next, and the next. I did this for a week, perhaps ten days. Then, one day I was walking past the Plaza Hotel and there, in one of the boutiques, was a stuffed animal, a copy of the wolf in Walt Disney's version of *The Three Little Pigs*, a predatory beast with its tongue hanging out, a wonderful caricature. I sent it to her with a note: "The Friendly Florist is approaching."

The next morning I called her, trying to disguise my accent a little because I didn't want her to recognize me immediately. "This," I said to her, "is the friendly florist calling."

There was a pause, and then that charming little laugh of hers, and I knew I had won. As Napoleon said, "A woman who laughs is a woman conquered."

"But who," she asked, "*is* the Friendly Florist?"

"An excellent question," I said. "But should I reveal my identity to you? You wouldn't be so bold as to accept a date with me for lunch or dinner without knowing who I was."

"No, I think that would be going too far," she said. "Reveal your identity and I'll consider your offer."

I told her. Another pause. I don't know if she was surprised or disappointed or had already guessed, but I couldn't afford the luxury of any more dead air. "Look, let's have lunch," I said, figuring it would seem less dangerous than dinner—I was aware that I'd acquired something of a reputation by then—and she agreed. She did agree.

We met at the Colony. She arrived punctually, dressed exactly as I imagined she would be: in a tailored suit, wearing glasses (she was nearsighted), a great beauty trying to pass as a maiden schoolteacher. A very strong message was conveyed by this—a remoteness, defensiveness, and depth. But then again, she *had* been lured to lunch by the Friendly Florist. This was a woman asking to be romanced, but it could only be done stylishly, without a false step. She sat there coolly, appraising me, as if to say, "Okay, show me what you've got. Entertain me. What's your game?"

Meanwhile, I was thinking to myself, *Okay, one thing you cannot do: you cannot get discouraged. She is going to test you by setting up road-block after roadblock. You must surmount them all, cleverly. Do not lose your patience, or all is lost.*

My opening gambit was dramatic, a continuation of the tone set by the Friendly Florist. "Do not say a word," I told her, pulling a paper and envelope from my jacket pocket. "Before we say anything to each other, I am going to write something and put it in this envelope. A year from now we will come here, much closer than we are now, I hope, and you can open the letter and see what it says."

She laughed at this. "Well, if you wish, go ahead."

I summoned Gene Cavallero, the owner of the Colony, and with great ceremony introduced him to Grace, saying, "Gene, could you please put this in the safe with your most precious properties and keep it there for me for a year?"

I put the date on the envelope and "For Miss Grace Kelly, to be opened on . . ." The proprietor, who loved intrigues of this sort, played his part beautifully, bowing slightly as he received the precious envelope. "Of course," he said. "One year."

It was, I must say, a hell of a start. She was defrosted then. Apparently, I'd caught her off guard; she had prepared no defense for romantic silliness. The ice—which seemed almost an actual property with her, along with the glasses—was broken, and we could proceed with the most pleasant conversation about Hollywood, and her co-stars (she'd had a flirtation with Gable, she told me), directors, and all. Later, she would say that she knew from the first that, if nothing else, I would not bore her. For my pains, for this enormous effort and creativity, she agreed to have dinner with me two nights later.

But then, just as I was shining myself up for our rendezvous on the appointed evening, preparing myself physically and psychologically for round two, the phone rang and it was Grace. "I'm terribly sorry," she said, "but my sister is in town and I haven't seen her in a long time, so I'm afraid I won't be able to make it tonight."

I knew that this would have to be overcome. It was the first little test she'd prepared for me. I kept her on the phone, one way or another, for a half-hour, working on her gradually but persuasively. The three of us went to dinner that night, and it progressed quite to my advantage. Her sister Peggy seemed a good deal less constrained than Grace, with a wonderful sense of humor. We got along famously. I paid the sister just a bit more attention than I did Grace, and I could see that I'd traversed another hurdle. "And so now, perhaps we can reschedule tonight's original dinner for tomorrow?" I pressed.

"But you must realize, Oleg," Grace said, "that I have other friends. You can't monopolize all my time."

"Very well, then, we will invite your friends."

And I did. I arranged a small party for the private room at El Morocco and invited several of her close friends.

We danced for the first time that night, creating a mild stir at El Morocco. For once, Grace had not attempted to hide her beauty; she was wearing a black dress, and people were watching us. I was struck by her subtle perfection. Her skin, her hair . . . Later, the makeup man on *To Catch a Thief* would say that he had less work to do on Grace than on any other woman in films. She was not voluptuous; the attraction was more cerebral than physical, but she could be as sexy as hell when she wanted to be. She was, I realized, the ultimate, idealized version of the casually aristocratic American college girls I had pursued in Florence. The time had come, I thought, to make a move, but Grace had a pre-emptive strike prepared. "I have two little surprises for you, Oleg," she said, as we were dancing, "or perhaps three."

I could hardly wait.

"One," she said, "I happen to be in love. Two, I am leaving for California tomorrow. And three, you have known me before. . . . Not only have you known me before, but you tried to ask me out, and I said that I didn't go out with married men. . . . Do you remember the Four Feathers ad? I was the model."

The Four Feathers ad—I remembered it vaguely. I had designed a special dress (with four feathers, I think) for a full-color print advertisement for the liquor of that name. I remembered the ad, but not the model.

"I was the skinny girl," she said. "I was the one you said was too skinny, but you made a brief pass at me anyway, until I told you that I did not date married men."

Ah yes, the skinny girl.

"I haven't gained any weight since then," she said. "Do you still think I'm too skinny?"

But my head was swimming from the first two surprises. I wasn't too concerned about her being "in love." If she were really in love, I wouldn't have gotten this far with her. I was not too happy, though, about her imminent departure. My plan was to attack on all fronts, to keep up the pressure: *"L'audace, l'audace, toujours l'audace."* This would be difficult from three thousand miles away.

"Well," I said, "I assume that someone as beautiful as you would always have people in love with her, and sometimes imagine herself to be in love as well. My concern is to find out why you are in love with this man, and whether it is good for you."

"Don't presume too much," she said, but not angrily, still playing with me, perhaps a bit amused. "I don't need you to help me decide if someone is right or wrong for me."

I think my gall did amuse her. Shock was the only treatment possible with Grace, because it was so difficult to get through to her. In the course of our relationship, I would see man after man freeze in her presence. She could destroy a fellow's confidence easier than anyone I'd ever met. But I would not be put off that way. I might lose altitude for a time, but I was determined to keep fighting back.

"I think you *should* discuss it with me," I insisted. "After all, I am not a disinterested observer . . . and anyway, you don't even know what I wrote in that letter at the Colony."

She pressed me then to tell her, and I capitulated: "I wrote that when you opened it a year from now, you and I would be engaged."

"Mr. Cassini," she said, "you are out of your mind."

"Perhaps, Miss Kelly," I said, "but I will stand by my prediction."

"In any case, my departure would seem to put a damper on your plans," she said.

"Quite the contrary. When something is worthwhile, distance is the smallest of obstacles."

All this was happening while we were dancing . . . and I made sure to keep my distance. I was pursuing her, yes, but I did not want her to feel that I was hanging on for dear life. I did not even kiss her when I brought her home. I did ask her who my competition was, however. "I'd like to know how difficult a task I face," I said. "You owe me this, at least."

"I owe you nothing," she said.

"Yes, you owe it to me because I am the man of your destiny."

She laughed and said, "*You* may think so, but I'm not so sure. . . . However, I do feel that you are a man of discretion and so I will tell you it is an actor, an Englishman, very handsome. I have done a picture with him, and his initials are 'R.M.' "

It was, of course, Ray Milland. She had just finished shooting *Dial M for Murder* with him. He was married.

"Well, your choice is excellent," I told her. "I think it proves all over again the same good taste that led you to go out with me." She laughed, and I continued: "But you are certainly intelligent enough to know that romance on the set is often confused for the real thing. And then too, there is his wife. She is very well respected, much admired, and I don't think she would ever divorce him."

"You're not the first person to tell me this," she said. "But it doesn't matter. In any case, you have an ulterior motive."

So, she left for California. I began to write her little notes. We spoke on the phone, always briefly, lightly. I maintained an almost daily presence in her life, even though I was hearing through the grapevine that the romance with Milland was still in progress. Meanwhile, I was scheduled to go to California on business and had to make a decision: should I approach her or not? I did not want to seem too eager. I decided to hold back. Instead, I called the prettiest girl I could find, an actress named Faith Dawn, and we went to Mocambo, a nightclub that had become as popular in Hollywood as Ciro's.

And, of course, sitting no more than thirty inches from me at Mocambo was Grace Kelly.

She was with a young fellow, who, I later learned, was a college boy, the brother of a friend and no threat. She reacted to my presence there with a certain amount of surprise, but not displeasure: "Why don't you join us?"

In no time, we were dancing—the college boy was dancing with Faith —and Grace asked, "Why didn't you call?"

"Well," I said, "I'm a very strong competitor, but frankly, from what I've been hearing, I didn't want to bother you. I didn't think there was much sense to calling."

"Perhaps," she said, "you were foolish not to."

"Perhaps," I agreed. The next day I called her, and I picked her up at Paramount, where she was making *The Country Girl* with Bing Crosby and William Holden. She was as conscientious as Gene when it came to work, though, and would never go out the night before shooting. I'd be able to see her only on weekends. This left me to make an important choice: should I take her meager encouragement on the dance floor as a sign of progress and stay in Los Angeles, conducting my New York business by telephone?

I decided to give it three weeks.

During that time, I did manage to visit Grace on the set several times. An image lingers, Grace in her dressing room, lying back, eyes closed, having her hair rinsed. . . . I leaned over and surprised her, kissing her on the lips; she began to giggle (I remember that little laugh of hers so well), and pulled me toward her as her co-stars and crew cracked up. Her natural coolness appeared so formidable that her spontaneous moments—and she had a wonderful, coy sense of humor—always seemed fresh and delightful.

For the most part, though, our meetings were dictated by her shooting schedule. This left me with quite a bit of time on my hands, and I spent some evenings dancing very obviously at Ciro's with Anita Ekberg and Pier Angeli, a very beautiful Italian star of the period. These dates were quite enjoyable, but something of a ploy on my part. I was not disappointed when they were duly noted in the *Hollywood Reporter*, articles that apparently did not escape Grace Kelly's notice.

"I don't understand you," she said to me one weekend.

"It's very simple," I said. "You are busy. It seems I'm not very important to you. I like to dance, I enjoy pleasant company . . . and also I have a reputation to maintain."

It seemed to me, though, that she wasn't dismissing this very lightly. Something was happening.

It seems difficult to believe now, but at that moment Grace was quite concerned that MGM wouldn't renew her contract. She'd only made one picture for the studio, *Mogambo*, and Dore Schary, MGM's chief of production, seemed all too willing to lend her out to Warner's (for the Hitchcock films) and Paramount (for *The Country Girl*). I had more than a few connections in town, of course, and decided to see what I could do to ease Grace's mind. First, I arranged a lunch for her with Ray Stark, who was one of the most powerful agents in Hollywood by then. I was sure he would leap at the chance to represent her. But when I called Ray afterward, he said, "Sorry, Oleg. No sex appeal."

"Rabbit, you're out of your mind," I said. "You think I'd ever go out with a girl who had no sex appeal?"

In retrospect, I think my friend was reacting to a stellar performance by a fine actress: Grace was playing her role of the moment, the quiet, dour, mousy Georgie Elgin of *The Country Girl;* she was, in fact, suffused with this role, living it on screen and off. Her dedication would win her the Academy Award, but her insistence on an unglamorous appearance during this time was a matter of concern.

I raised this problem over dinner one night. "Can I suggest something, Grace?" I asked. She nodded. "When you arrive at the studio each morning, don't come as Georgie Elgin. Be glamorous, be *perfect*—and then become your character. It will create a mystique about you. It will enhance your reputation."

"But I want to be taken seriously," she said. "Producers won't if they think I'm just some glamor girl."

"On the contrary," I said. "If you want to be considered a serious actress, show your range. Show them you are more than just the role you are playing at this moment; show them you can be glamorous and sexy, too. You don't have to dress like a schoolteacher or please the headmaster at Bryn Mawr. You are becoming a major star, and should be a leader in fashion also."

Grace seemed to see the wisdom of this and we began to discuss and work together on ways she could look more glamorous. I selected a wardrobe for her from my collection, and even designed a few dresses with her specifically in mind. Then I asked Milton Green, the famous fashion photographer, "Milton, what do you think of her?"

"She's exquisite."

"Of course," I said, "you and I know that, but they don't seem to understand it in Hollywood. Can you do anything for her?"

"You must help," he said. "You must design a dress that conveys your sense of her, how you feel about her."

I thought of her as a pale, delicate English rose: the gown had a simple top and a complicated, petal-like skirt; it was made of heavy taffeta, an almost antique, soft pink, carefully selected to complement her skin tones.

Milton Green photographed her in the dress, and also took some other, informal photos of her in an oversized sweater (one of my own; I'd given her several) at her home, which was Grace's favorite look, and one that would come into fashion thirty years later. He presented these photos to *Look* magazine, which put her on the cover in the oversized sweater (the photo of Grace in my pink dress was used inside).

Within a matter of months, *Dial M for Murder* would be released, and she would no longer have to worry about her contract being renewed.

She would also make the Best Dressed list for the first time that year, thanks to her new wardrobe. I created the "Grace Kelly look" for her; I put her in subdued, elegant dresses that set off her patrician good looks. I told her that her beauty should be set off like a great diamond, in very simple settings. The focus was always to be on her.

For the moment, though, in that spring of 1954, Grace was concerned enough about her status that she agreed, to her everlasting dismay, to do a film for MGM with Stewart Granger called *Green Fire*. It would be shot in the jungles of Colombia.

"I'll come with you," I volunteered. "No one will know. The jungles of Colombia are a terrible bore. Let me come as a protector against the boa constrictor."

She thought this an amusing concept, but equivocated. It should be noted that the fashion assistance I'd given her had no effect at all on our personal relationship; this was one of Grace's firmest rules. "My work is one thing," she often said. "My personal life is another. They have nothing to do with each other."

She was grateful for my help, of course, but the status of our romance remained what it had been: we were still fencing. I decided to return to New York, partly to find out how my business was getting on without me, but also to make clear that I could do quite nicely without her. If she wanted to hedge, I would find other diversions. With Pier Angeli, for example. She was now in New York, and I held a birthday party for her with four hundred guests at my home on Sixty-first Street. The gossip columns noted this and, indeed, there were marriage rumors (started, I suspect, by her mother, who always traveled with her). "I see you are keeping yourself busy," Grace said, by phone, before leaving for Colombia. "You're not wasting any time."

We continued to correspond, back and forth, while she was in Colombia, and it was during this time, in her absence, that *Dial M for Murder* was released. Things were truly beginning to happen for her. In addition to *Look*, she was on the cover of *Life* magazine: "A Year of Grace" was the title. There were stories everywhere . . . and now the mythmaking began in earnest. People were hungry for news about her, for insights into the mystery of Grace Kelly's appeal. Her name had never been "linked romantically" with anyone, as the columnists invariably put it—except Milland (and those rumors were vehemently denied by all concerned). Now, though, it was recalled that she and I had been seen together frequently during the shooting of *The Country Girl*, and while Hedda and

Louella might dust off their old "Cassini the Svengali" stories, most everyone else in Hollywood seemed to regard this as another example of my ability to judge star quality. I was no longer a mystery man in the film community; I didn't have to prove myself in Jack Warner's or David Selznick's eyes, but the idea that I might be on the verge of replacing Gene Tierney with Grace Kelly certainly did nothing to harm my reputation.

The reality was, however, that our relationship was still distressingly platonic. We remained in contact, but no discernible progress was being made. She returned to California to finish the shooting of *Green Fire*. We were still exchanging notes and phone calls. A breakthrough was needed, and it came in the form of a postcard from Grace, which said only this:

"Those who love me shall follow me."

She was going to France, to the Riviera, to shoot *To Catch a Thief*, with Cary Grant and Hitchcock. The South of France was not the jungles of Colombia. I had all sorts of excuses for a trip to Europe: Emilio Pucci and I had been discussing a merger, plus there were other possibilities. My business was doing very well, and I remembered the vow I'd made after the Kay Kendall episode. I would not fail this time for lack of daring.

In any case, Grace stopped in New York on her way to France and we had a date. The photographers were swarming all about her now. We were photographed together, cementing my position in the columns as the "number-one guy" in her life. Now all I had to do was accomplish the same in reality.

"You know," I said to her that night, "I think I'll go over there with you tomorrow."

"Oh, you do?" she said. "I'm going to be very busy."

"Of course," I agreed. "But I'll just come for the weekend."

Now, these were still the early days of jet travel, and the idea of going to Europe for the weekend was something of a novelty (in any event, I had no intention of staying merely for a weekend; this was it—I was going over for the duration, until my mission was accomplished).

She was quite taken by the gesture. "You would follow me to Cannes for one weekend?"

"Why not?" I said, still keeping it light, wanting her to believe it was the sort of thing I did all the time.

But, horror of horrors, I arrived at the airport the next day to find that I had taken care of every detail but one: my passport. It was no longer valid. The romantic moment was lost; there seemed no end to the roadblocks. I left Grace to the care of my friend Barney Strauss, who happened to be taking the same flight. Later, she told me he spent the whole flight trying to make a date with her.

I did manage to get my passport renewed and arrive in Paris the following week. I called Grace from there and told her I was on my way.

"So you *have* come for the weekend," she said.

"As promised, and only a week late."

"We can have dinner tonight," she said.

I arrived in early evening at the Carlton in Cannes, in time for a bath and to put myself in what I considered to be the right uniform for the climate: an open silk shirt, slacks, and a jacket. I rang her; she said she'd meet me in the lobby.

I waited for her there, and when she emerged from the elevator, she rushed toward me, then stopped.

"Where is your tie?" she asked.

I had left my business, traversed the Atlantic Ocean, raced from Paris by train, and *that* was her greeting.

"A tie?" I said, believing perhaps I had not heard her correctly. "You don't have to wear a tie in Cannes."

"But I wish you'd put one on."

"Very well," I said, "if you insist."

We had dinner. I was the only man in the room wearing a tie. She noticed this, but didn't say anything. Then she said, "I have good news. We won't be shooting for another two days. You can stay a little longer."

I thought, *This girl actually believes I've come just for a weekend!* (I stayed for two months, until the end of filming.)

I was very disappointed. I wondered, "Perhaps she *is* made of ice. She is acting as if I'd only traveled from New York to Philadelphia to see her. This is crazy. I must have been mad to come here."

We went to the casino that evening and danced. She gambled a little and won, her Irish luck holding sway. We dined superbly: Kir Royals, to start; then *mousse de trois poissons, turbot poché,* followed by *steak au poivre,* which she loved. Grace was *"une bonne fourchette,"* a good trencherman. For dessert, a *soufflé framboise* and *petits fours;* and, of course, Dom Perignon—two bottles, I remember. We were feeling no pain. She was not, however, giving me any romantic openings. I made a decision: I would give it another chance tomorrow, but that was all.

I planned a picnic. I packed cold duck and a bottle of Montrachet '49. We would go to a secluded cove on the Mediterranean. There was a raft in the cove, surrounded by dramatic rocks and clear, clear water. It was very romantic, a good place for a picnic.

But just as I was about to leave that morning, there was a phone call —a gentleman to see me. Barney Strauss. His girlfriend had stood him up and he needed consolation, or so he said. Then Grace was there, and he was chatting with her, inviting himself along with us for this picnic. I was beginning to feel more like Sisyphus than Casanova.

I did manage to get rid of him eventually . . . and then Grace and I were on that raft alone in the Mediterranean sun, and I was attempting my last gambit, which was no gambit at all. I told her I cared for her very deeply. I told her about my life, my past, very seriously—for the first time, really. I spoke simply, honestly. I said, "Grace, this has been a long and strange relationship. We have danced about very cleverly, from continent to continent—New York, California, the Riviera; almost South America, too. You have been very elusive, and stubborn; I think you have resisted just for resistance's sake . . . but we must come to some decision now. My persistence and devotion should give you some indication of the depth of my feelings. I am tired of chasing about. Enough is enough. We are totally alone here, on a raft in the Mediterranean. The sun is warm; the waves are lapping gently against the wood. There is no need for artifice any longer."

Grace looked very closely at me with her blue eyes. "Who are you, Mr. Cassini?" she asked. "I know that you are very wild, very pleasant, very extravagant, and very dangerous . . . but who *are* you?"

I thought for a moment. "Well, I am an aesthetic man, and I enjoy things of great beauty. I have committed a lot of mistakes. I have been immature, anachronistic. I am, most of all, a romantic."

I kept talking, not sure of what I was saying, returning her gaze.

She said, "Believe me, dear Oleg, a man can no longer succeed by being only romantic."

"If I have exaggerated my sentiments," I told her, "I am at least indebted to my romantic nature for a hatred of treacherous and dishonorable conduct towards women. You know that I care for you very deeply. Our relationship is now yours to decide."

She said nothing, but she was looking at me in such a way that I knew I had won.

We returned to the hotel. We seemed to float there, glowing, mesmerized by the intensity of our feelings. She smelled of gardenias, at once exotic and very pure. There was a translucent, pearl-like quality to her;

everything about her was clear and fresh and fine—her skin, her scent, her hair. I was enraptured, aware only of the transcendence of the moment, the perfection that she was.

My victory was brief.

On our second evening together, there was a terrible fight. I accompanied Grace to her suite, but when I walked in, she turned on me: "You cannot stay, Oleg. Everything has its place: romance, work, friendship. The work week is going to start tomorrow. I must study my script tonight and get my sleep. I have no more time for you now."

"What do you mean, you have no time?" I said, reacting very badly, angrily, stunned by this. "That's ridiculous! You're behaving like a child!"

"I'll tell you what," she said. "I will call the unit manager and tell him you are making me lose sleep and have him ask you to leave the hotel."

"You would do that?" I asked. "You must really be made of stone, as they say."

"No," she said. "But I cannot have my work disturbed. Even the man I marry will have to respect that."

I was very annoyed. I left and began to pack. I must have packed and unpacked five times that night. At one point, I wrote a note that rather melodramatically announced my departure from her life. I slipped it under her door . . . and then reconsidered. I went back then and retrieved it. I was on all fours in the hallway, trying to maneuver my fingers through the crack under her door, nipping a corner of the note, finally achieving a tentative grasp, when I had this thought: *This lady is making a monkey out of you.* The intended victim of the conquest was turning out to be the conquerer. I said to myself, *You're acting out of character. Don't be a fool. Be yourself, be casual.*

It rained that day. She couldn't shoot, so we had lunch. "Do you think you'll resume the schedule soon?" I asked "I'm thinking of leaving town for a while."

"How nice," she said.

"Oh, by the way, I was rather silly last night, losing my temper, thinking you were actually serious about not wanting to spend the evening together," I said lightly. "I must get used to your wonderful sense of humor."

She didn't say anything to that (I thought, at least she isn't contradicting me) and it continued to rain, and so I had more of an opportunity to re-establish myself in her eyes. I felt that once she knew the real me, everything would be all right. We explored the Riviera, an area I knew well from my childhood and from more recent summer trips. We drove all over. Grace hated to drive, so I took the wheel on the narrow, dangerous roads. The Riviera can be wonderfully seductive: soft breezes, twisting mountain roads, and the sun glistening on the sea. I knew perfect little inns in the mountains. I talked to her about wines, and history, and the Mediterranean temperament. I told her stories of my childhood at Forte dei Marmi. We went shopping, and visited small country markets. We spoke French together, which she did quite well.

We went to church together every Sunday, and Grace went to confession regularly. We talked about religion; we discussed how our two churches had once been one, and how the eventual schism had occurred for political and not religious reasons. We were essentially of the same faith. I would try to draw her out with questions about herself and her roles. I asked her about the character she played in *To Catch a Thief*, an heiress who falls in love with a cat burglar (Cary Grant). "Why does she fall for him?" I asked.

"Well, to me, the man is so powerfully attractive," she said, "that *who* he is doesn't really matter. Anyway, a strong woman always believes she can change a man."

"Do you think you could change me?" I asked.

"Of course," she laughed. "But I wouldn't want to change your adventurous quality. You're kind of a pirate, you know."

"A pirate?" I smiled. "Like Bluebeard, perhaps?"

"Well, I know this," she said. "I used to live a very strict life in New York, at the Barbizon Hotel for women. My curfew was midnight . . . and, of course, no visitors. My family demanded these regulations, and sometimes they conflicted with my life as an actress. It was difficult to reconcile my career with my background at times. And now, I've broken all my regulations with you."

"Well, perhaps that's because I can understand you in a way that most men can't," I said. "I know what your profession is like. I know that you are a great many women. You are all your roles and more: the roles you've not yet played."

The days passed, wonderfully. I forgot about my meeting with Pucci. I forgot about New York. I became part of the company, with Cary Grant and his wife, Betsy Drake, and, of course, Hitchcock—who, I later learned, was at the height of his own (vicarious) romantic obsession with Grace. He didn't seem to resent my presence, however, and we would often have dinner together—the Grants, the Hitchcocks, Grace, and I—a grand occasion always, very carefully orchestrated by the director himself. He had one of the most curious eating habits; his diet consisted of one spectacular meal each day. He would fast until evening, drinking only water during the filming. Then he would take a bath and we would gather for dinner at the restaurant of his choice, for the precise meal of his choice. We always ate in restaurants rated three stars or better. Still, Hitchcock would review everything in advance: the wines, the soup, the fish, the meat, the sorbet between courses, the dessert, the fruit and cheese. He would preside over it all, like an emperor, savoring each morsel. I've never seen anyone enjoy a meal more. He would grow expansive then; we would discuss philosophy. He was, of course, a complete autocrat. He believed anyone on a film (except him) could be replaced. I argued the opposite, the importance of individuals, especially the unique "chemistry" generated by stars like Cary Grant and Grace Kelly. They could not be replaced. Hitchcock believed, though, that he could make anyone a star. He was wrong, and would spend the rest of his career proving it, as he searched—unsuccessfully, of course—for an actress who could replace Grace Kelly.

Hitchcock had a very cute English girl who served as his secretary, and one evening she committed the most embarrassing verbal slip I've ever heard. It was at a birthday party for Hitchcock, held in a suite at the Ritz Carlton. Quite a few people were there, and, as often is the case at a cocktail party, everyone happened to squeeze into one of the rooms, leaving the other quite empty. The secretary, attempting to distribute the traffic more evenly, clapped her hands and said, "Could I have your attention for a moment? Would you all come into the other room, please, and have a piece of Mr. Hitchcake's cock."

It was quite hilarious.

Our time in Cannes was coming to an end, and I was beginning to wonder what would happen. I realized that I was committed to Grace, but I wasn't sure what *she* wanted. I was plagued by feelings of doubt and unworthiness. It was odd. Finally I had a success in every area of my life, more success than I'd ever imagined possible. I had been bold throughout this courtship. I had attained my goal. She loved me, but now I grew cautious and passive. I waited for events to take their course.

One night in Cannes, we went to a little restaurant on a pier—not very fancy, but one of the two or three best places to eat fish on the

Riviera. I ordered a bottle of wine, and we began to talk. The mood was serious, bittersweet. She looked down at the boats in the port, the beautiful yachts, and said, "Ohhh, if only there was a man who could take me away from all this—take me to Tahiti, on a boat like one of these, away from the drudgery of this routine."

"Well, I was in the coast guard," I said, "I might be such a man. I might happily leave civilization behind, if you were to come with me."

We daydreamed in this manner through dinner. Finally Grace got down to cases. "Well, here we are, Mr. Cassini," she said, with a little laugh. "You've been following me all over the world. What do you have to say for yourself? Isn't there anything you want to say?"

Well, actually no. I was perfectly happy the way things were, but there was a Roman Catholic soul lurking inside Grace Kelly that obviously was expecting some sort of proposal from me. "The depth of my feelings should be clear," I said. "I think I would be happy to continue as we are right now, or to take this in any direction you want, including marriage. What do you wish?"

"I want to make my life with you," she said quietly. "I want to be your wife."

"You've got it," I said.

"This calls for a celebration," she said. "Let's go to the casino."

I was tremendously happy at that moment and flattered that she wanted to marry me. I was filled with pride and love, and was entirely enraptured by her. We ordered champagne to celebrate our engagement. It was an altogether magical evening. We danced and gambled a bit—and Grace won, as she always did. She never gambled much, or out of control, but she always won. She was one of the lucky ones, one of those people to whom everything is given; all too often, in my experience, these are the people from whom the gods also take everything, in a single blow.

In the midst of our celebration that night, and somewhat to my surprise, Grace began to talk about preparations for our marriage with the flushed enthusiasm of a typical American Junior Leaguer: where we would be married, what church, what she wanted to wear . . . "I want to write home immediately and let them know," she said. "Mother will be on my side in this, I'm sure of it. . . . There may be some difficulties with Father. You're not exactly his type."

Her parents. I had been so involved in my efforts to win her that I hadn't given very much thought to Mr. and Mrs. John B. Kelly of Philadelphia. But now that I thought of it, I assumed their reaction would be rather similar to the Tierneys'. They were, after all, yet another member of the Irish-American aristocracy, a prototypical family of the breed. Tierneys, Kellys—it made no difference. The father was, invariably, a self-made man and a *paterfamilias* in the classical sense, free to engage in peccadillos, but fiercely protective of his wife and children; the mother, angered by her husband's roving eye, was constantly on guard lest her daughter fall for a similar rogue. There was also, shades of Butch Tierney, the requisite handsome, manly brother—John B. ("Kel") Kelly, Jr.—an Olympic oarsman, as his father had been. Grace thought the world of him, and called him "Kel-Bel." He was the exemplar, the Olympic ideal —the sort of boy the Kellys wanted her to marry. I was another sort entirely.

Why was I putting myself in the path of these people? They were always so intent on achieving a bizarre, straightlaced vision of "propriety." It was a fantasy, of course; true sophisticates tended to be more careless and carefree, less serious about themselves. There was never the slightest possibility that these stubborn Celts would allow an Italian cossack like me to make off with one of their daughters. They wanted one of those neatly folded, unmenacing brand of Ivy Leaguer. I was too good a dancer to be trustworthy. But why were the daughters always so dazzling?

To be fair to the Kellys, they were a solid family. Jack Kelly had started as a brick mason, and built a very successful construction company. He had run for mayor of Philadelphia once, and lost. He was a rather parochial fellow as a result. Philadelphia was his world. Grace's success in Hollywood didn't mean all that much to him; he probably would have been more impressed at her penetrating Philadelphia Main Line society (the stories that identified Grace as a "society girl" reflected the aspirations of the Kelly family—and the studio—rather than the reality; the Kellys had made their money too recently to be accepted by the Protestant arbiters of acceptance in Philadelphia). John B. Kelly's wife, the former Margaret Majer, came from similarly prosaic stock. She was the first woman ever to teach physical education at the University of Pennsylvania. She had been a lively, attractive woman in her youth, then turned strict and formidable in middle age. She had been born a Lutheran, but converted to Roman Catholicism.

If there was any hope for me in this, it was that the family had, on occasion, accepted non-Irish outsiders like "Ma" Kelly, as she was called; it also had included some rather wild cards, like Grace's uncle George

Kelly, a very successful Broadway playwright of the 1920s and '30s. Uncle George had always been Grace's favorite; she had tended toward rebellion against the family's strictness and provincialism. The question was how far she would be willing to carry this tendency.

There were signs from the start that she was going to be cautious, however.

I left for Paris several nights after we decided to be married. Grace had only a few days of shooting remaining, and I had business to attend to. I suspect, too, that I needed to gather myself and take stock. Marriage to Grace Kelly was not something I'd truly anticipated. I had strong feelings for the girl, but, to this day, I am not sure that marriage was what I really wanted. It is interesting that I had several opportunities over the next year to close the deal, as it were, and each time I acted indecisively. I felt enormous pride that she wanted to marry me, I certainly didn't want anyone else to marry her, but still: as soon as the question of her parents was raised, I would grow remote. If this was going to be a struggle even remotely similar to my travails with the Tierneys, I had no heart for it. I was an accomplished, successful, well-known, respectable American now; there was no need to endure another such nightmare, to have my good intentions—and my good name—questioned.

Grace and I spoke by phone each night while I was in Paris, and planned the future. We talked about having children (some, but not too many). We decided that my business would be our primary means of support; she would make one carefully selected film each year, the proceeds of which would be hers, to spend as she wished. There was cause for optimism. We were in agreement on almost all the basic issues that subvert marriages between successful people.

But there was always the specter of her family haunting us, preventing me from getting *too* serious about all our plans. And then, in one of these conversations she told me that it would be best, in view of the fact that so many newspapers had linked us together (*Paris-Match* had photographed us on the Riviera, and Louella Parsons had written entire columns about the possibility of a marriage), to travel separately back to the States. We would have a better chance with her parents, she said, if the appearance of propriety were preserved.

I agreed to this, and the strange, indecisive mating dance began that would continue, on both our parts, for the next year. She would take the boat back to New York with the Grants and the Hitchcocks; I would take a plane. Once again, boldness was indicated and I was passive. Maybe I should have found a priest and married her right then and there. But I sensed that I could not force myself upon her, that if marriage was what she wanted, it would have to proceed at her pace. Certainly it would have been bad form for me to *insist* that I accompany her home. I might have maneuvered my way on board—in a light, clever way, of course—and continued the chess game of our courtship; but we were engaged now, and my audacity, mysteriously, had disappeared.

I accompanied her to the boat, said bon voyage, then flew home . . . and found the world had turned in my absence. Grace Kelly was now the biggest star in America. The mad fascination, the references to mountains and glaciers, the mythology had finally caught hold. Half the men in America had fallen in love after her dazzling and decidedly sexy performance in *Rear Window* with Jimmy Stewart; even Ray Stark now acknowledged her appeal.

And everyone seemed to know what had happened to us on the Riviera. New York was buzzing with it. The gossip columns were full of it. Our romance was a *cause célèbre* in the tabloids. Neither Hedda nor Louella considered me worthy of the golden girl. This was curious; I could no longer be confused with the mysterious "nonentity" who'd made off with the teenaged Gene Tierney.

And yet, Hedda and Louella, Louella and Hedda. Especially Hedda. I was once again—literally—a Mephistophelean character. In one column, she called me too "devilish" for the "ethereal Miss Kelly." In another, she wondered about the nature of my appeal. Why, with all the good-looking men around, had Grace Kelly chosen me? "It must be his mustache," she concluded.

I'd had enough of this, and sent her a telegram. "Okay, Hedda, I give up. I'll shave mine if you shave yours."

I was nervous, though; I wasn't happy. My friends called me, absolutely thrilled. "You did it!" they said. But *had* I done it? I am, by nature, a terrible pessimist. We had been apart for too long. I sensed, too, that the Grace Kelly boom would have ramifications for us. I knew Grace well enough to understand that her immediate reaction to all the attention would be to pull back into her shell. I hoped the intense emotional and physical chemistry we had found on the Riviera would not disappear in the explosion of flashbulbs that was sure to greet her.

I was there waiting when the boat arrived. Her sister Peggy was also there—still favorably disposed toward me, I thought—and her younger sister Lizanne, with her beau, Donald LeVine. LeVine, who was Jewish, and I had an understanding from the start. We were both outsiders seeking acceptance from the Kelly family. I began to feel better. I had some allies here. But when we went to Grace's cabin, the poor girl appeared to be in shock: the room had already been overwhelmed by agents and retainers and hangers-on, fawning and flattering and nagging at her. The crowd simply refused to disperse. Indeed, these gnats and mosquitos would be a constant source of irritation in the months to come. They were, almost all of them, inclined to have a negative view of me, of course; I was a threat to their meal ticket. One, Gant Gaither, was particularly vitriolic in his opposition. "How low in the sewer can you go?" he said to her. "How can you associate with this type of man?"

Our meeting at the boat, then, was very public, very "correct," and entirely unsatisfactory. Grace greeted me with a kiss, but not a very passionate one. I didn't have much of a chance to convey my disappointment, however, because she was whisked off to her family's summer retreat at Margate, near Atlantic City. I had hoped she would come with me to the country estate in Westbury that I'd rented for the summer; I had hoped that our life now wouldn't be all that different from what it had been on the Riviera. This was a dream, of course. Even under the best of circumstances—even without the gnats and mosquitos conspiring against us—it would have been difficult to have much time together by ourselves. I began to realize that she was going to have to love me very much to withstand all this.

We spoke by phone almost every night. She continued to express the hope that her parents could be won over. It would have to be done in stages. Lunch with her mother first, then a visit with the family and an introduction to the toughest nut to crack: her father. Meanwhile, I had been invited by Payney Payson to a *bal masqué* her parents, Charles Shipman and Joan Whitney Payson, gave each year to celebrate their anniversary. This was always one of the major events of the New York social season, held at Greentree, the Paysons' fabulous estate in Manhasset, Long Island. Each year, a thousand guests would be invited, an eclectic group chosen from the theater, literary life, politics, and society. A typical party would include everyone from the Averell Harrimans to the Sid Caesars, from Robert Benchley to Gary Cooper, from Diana Vreeland to Gene Tunney. The huge drawing room would become a ballroom. A great carpet would be rolled out to the pool—an enormous pool, by the way, filled with ice-cold water—where a late dinner would be served under a marquee flying the Greentree stable colors, black and watermelon pink. Quite often, the evening would end with a great many of the guests splashing about in the frigid pool.

When I told Grace about the invitation, she not only agreed to join me, but said that she had convinced her mother to come to New York to meet me for lunch the day after. Immediately, I set about designing costumes for the ball: we would go as Helen of Troy and Paris. She would wear a long, togalike gown of gold and a golden laurel tiara; I would have a short Greek tunic, sandals, and a helmet.

Her appearance at the ball caused quite a stir. Red Payson whisked her off onto the dance floor—my memories of this period consist almost entirely of Grace being taken off hither and yon—and I didn't see much of her for the rest of the evening, as she was besieged by a giddy assortment of Vanderbilts, Whitneys, and Paysons. The next real memory I have is of our lunch with her mother, which was, of course, a complete disaster.

Mrs. Kelly had a firm jaw and a cold look. I tried to set her at ease; she was having none of it. I met them at Grace's apartment and then we took a cab to the Colony, where I'd made a reservation in the hope that I'd be able to lure Mrs. Kelly across the street to my town house after a friendly lunch and let her see, without bragging about it, that I had the means to support her daughter well. We never got there, though.

I was in trouble, in fact, before we left the cab. We were riding along in a thick silence. I sought to break the ice. I said, "Well, here we are—the unholy trio."

"You, Mr. Cassini, may be unholy," Mrs. Kelly responded. "I can assure you that Grace and I are not."

This set the tone for the rest of our meeting. Indeed, at lunch, Mrs. Kelly began a lengthy discourse on my unworthiness. I was a divorced man. I had a checkered past. I was a playboy. "We do not consider you good marriage material, Mr. Cassini," she said. "I can see why Grace might have been swayed by you. You are charming and literate. You have had a great deal of experience with women. But we believe Grace owes it to herself, to her family, and to her parish to reconsider."

I was stung by this. I shouldn't have been, but I was. I tried to make a logical response, but only seemed to make things worse: "There is no attractive man, including your husband, who has not been popular with the opposite sex. Why do you penalize me for success?"

Where was Grace? Why wasn't she saying anything?

Mrs. Kelly was on the attack again: "We propose a six-month moratorium on this. We don't think you should see each other for that time, and then Grace will be able to see if it was just Europe, or your charm, or this pursuit you put on her . . . "

"That's absolutely unacceptable," I said. Grace didn't say anything. She hadn't said a word throughout. It was almost as if she were merely a bystander, willing to go along with whatever her mother and I decided. She left me to my own devices. I was furious with her.

Later, on the phone, I said to her, "You'll have to make the decision. I don't think it's up to me to sell myself to your mother. I think you have to explain to your family why I am exceptional enough in your eyes, and why they should not stand in the way of our marriage."

Grace did not respond directly, but several days later sent me a warm note, encouraging me to remain optimistic—she was certain we could win them over—and inviting me to the family's summer home at the beach in New Jersey. It was the weekend of the Miss America Pageant in nearby Atlantic City, to which I would accompany Grace—a very public acknowledgment of our relationship, on her part. She wrote:

> It has been a year since I have been at home, and there are a million relatives and friends that I haven't seen for a much longer time—so I am exhausted and all the kids in the neighborhood are driving me insane —Meg and Mary Lee conduct the tours—
>
> Can you come down Friday for the weekend? Adelaide is leaving the apt. upstairs so Mother's guests will stay there—Bring a dinner jacket since Sat. night we will have to pop in to the ball following the pageant for a few minutes—that and a bathing suit is all you need—
>
> Tomorrow most of the people should go home so maybe we will be able to relax—We have been going into the water every morning before breakfast and it's heaven! I miss you terribly.
>
> Love,
> Grace

As it turned out, it was an unforgettably unpleasant weekend. In retrospect, it would seem the invitation had been extended because the Kellys didn't want to seem unfair. Clearly, though, they didn't want to seem very hospitable, either.

The house was a big, ramshackle wooden structure, a classic but not very distinguished turn-of-the-century beach house. I was imprisoned in a cubicle down the hall from Mr. and Mrs. Kelly. I was trapped there at night; my movements were easily monitored. There was no possibility of a private moment with Grace.

Mr. Kelly and Grace's brother made their feelings toward me quite apparent. Indeed, her brother already had made his feelings public, in *Time* magazine: "I generally don't approve of these oddballs she goes out with. I wish she would go out with the more athletic type. But she doesn't listen to me anymore."

If Junior had expressed these sentiments directly to me, I would have been happy to provide a demonstration of my athletic ability, but no matter: neither John B. Kelly Junior nor Senior would acknowledge my existence in their home. They actually refused to say a word to me, even in response to questions. At one point, Grace and I were swimming and she said, "Try and talk with my father." But whenever I attempted a conversation with him, he looked right past me. He would not say a word. It was infuriating, humiliating . . . and I waited for Grace to do something. In similar circumstances, fifteen years earlier, Gene Tierney had come to my defense. When her family had treated me badly, she'd screamed at them, "You can't treat him this way!"

Nothing from Grace, though. Not a word. Once again, I felt as if she were standing back, watching the show, punishing both sides with her silence. It was almost eerie.

One of her biographers would later see this as a pattern. She would rebel against her family by bringing various candidates home, allow her parents to make fools of themselves, and then quietly capitulate. I'm not sure; I don't think I was being used as a pawn in some obscure Kelly family game, but I have no adequate explanation for Grace's tolerance of their rude behavior, either. In any case, I left Atlantic City with *mort dans l'âme* (death in my soul), convinced my cause was lost. The Kellys would never approve, and Grace would make no effort to convince them.

Apparently, Grace had decided to abide by her parents' silly moratorium . . . or, at least, give the appearance of compliance. The embargo was never actually in effect. We continued to see each other constantly, if somewhat surreptitiously, in New York. We often dined at her apartment, with either her or me doing the cooking. Once, the phone kept ringing intermittently during the evening. I asked her, "Aren't you going to answer that phone?" She replied, "No! If it's personal, then I don't want to hear from anyone, because I am with the one person who I care about the most. There is no one else I'd rather be speaking to. On the other hand, if this is business . . . they will call again." She smiled sweetly, slyly. I remember one night during this time when we not only appeared publicly but also had perhaps our only public disagreement.

It was at a banquet for Town and Tennis, Don Budge's very exclusive midtown tennis club, to which both my old friend Bobby Friedman and I belonged. Grace was at the height of her popularity. Heads turned, there were gasps and sometimes applause when she entered a room—and this evening was no exception. Bobby Friedman was in a state of rapture, seated not only at the same table as Grace but next to her. He made rather clumsy efforts to let everyone know that this was not mere chance. He knew Grace Kelly, they were friends, close friends; and in the course of leaning in her direction, he nervously began to eat from her plate, sticking his fork in her fettucine, twirling the noodles suggestively.

Now, Grace had a very strong sense of gastronomic territoriality (as do I). She found nothing charming, or forgivable, about Bobby's incursions. She had her hair pulled back into a French twist, and was looking rather severe in any case that night; as Bobby continued to lean her way, she grew positively glacial. I could see that she was furious. Finally, she got up and stormed out. I followed her, casually, pretending nothing was wrong. I finally caught up with her and said, "Grace, darling—"

She turned on me and spluttered, "You must stop that uncouth friend of yours from playing with my noodles!"

As soon as that came out we both laughed . . . and, only somewhat placated, she returned to her seat.

We spent many weekends at Sherman Fairchild's beautiful estate, a medieval castle in Huntington, Long Island. Often, on the way back to New York, we would stop at Rothman's in East Norwich for dinner, perhaps with Peggy and Alek Hohenlohe, Ron Holmberg, or Nancy and Billy Talbert. Grace particularly liked Billy. We saw each other in Los Angeles as well. Grace came to watch me play at the Los Angeles tennis club. I teamed with agent Bunty Lawrence and we narrowly lost to the number-one Davis team from Australia, Worthington and Rose.

There were other times, though, when I didn't see her for weeks on end. She spent several months in North Carolina shooting a dull costume epic called *The Swan*. I was in Westbury with Mother and my daughter Tina, and I hadn't seen Grace for several weeks, when one day she called from Los Angeles.

"The hell with this silly moratorium," she said. "I don't care what my parents think. I miss you. Let's get married anyway."

I was so excited by her declaration of independence that I ran out of the house and jumped off the diving board into the swimming pool with all my clothes on.

It was in midair, I think, that I remembered the pool had been drained. I landed face first.

In the next few days, I was sent a barrage of letters from Grace, who was staying at the Bel-Air Hotel. The first I received said, in part:

Darling—
I . . . can't wait to see you, now that I know I want to marry you. We have so much to learn about each other—there are so many things I want you to know about me. We must be patient with each other and go slowly without wanting results too quickly. But we need each other and we must be completely honest, at all times—
I feel for the first time ready to approach love and marriage in an adult way.
Last November, I hit rock bottom and never thought I could be capable of thinking and feeling this way. Thank God I had my work to help me through that period and thank God for you. But in this last year, six pictures have taken so much from me physically and emotionally that it will take a while to recover. Please, darling, try to understand and to help me—I love you more every day and I hope you feel that way too. One time you said to me that you couldn't love me any more than you did then. That upset me terribly, because I so hope that we shall never stop growing and developing our minds and souls and love for God and each other, and that each day will bring us closer—
I love you and want to be your wife—
Grace

I arrived at her hotel several days later with a badly swollen, bandaged, broken nose and two black eyes from my swimming-pool disaster. Grace opened the door, looked at me, then closed it in horror—a nice touch. She always did have a sly sense of humor. "Mosquito bite," I told her, after she let me in.

It was a sweet reunion, but brief. I found a priest who was willing to overlook my divorce and marry us in Virginia. Arrangements were made for a small wedding . . . but it never happened. Why not? I don't know. We both hesitated and the moment was lost. There were other moments.

There was a memorable lunch that Grace and I had at La Côte Basque with Joseph P. Kennedy, the patriarch of that other illustrious Irish-American clan. Joe and I played golf together and had a regular weekly dinner on Tuesday at La Caravelle, which was his favorite haunt in New

York. I'd often asked his advice on business matters. By this time, I had
become friendly with the entire Kennedy clan, designing clothes for Rose,
Pat, Eunice, and Joan.

In any case, I solicited his aid. I wanted him to tell Grace that the
religious issue was of no consequence; I hoped that he would be so enthusiastic in my support that he might even volunteer to intercede personally
with the Kellys. "Joe," I said, "I'm having trouble with this family, and
the one guy who can fix it is you."

"Don't worry, Oleg, you big donkey," he said. This was a term of
affection. "Introduce me to the lucky girl and I'll settle everything. I
guarantee it."

I arranged lunch at La Côte Basque. We sat at a corner table: Grace,
demure and elegant as always; Joe Kennedy, with his brilliant blue eyes,
an incredibly vibrant man even then; and me. I was feeling pretty confident.

Immediately Joe took Grace's hand. "Grace dear," he said, "the Kellys, the Kennedys, people like us, we have to stick together."

He paused. I expected something like, "But the Cassinis are okay
too." But no. He just stared at her with those blue eyes. Then he looked
at me and said, "You know, Grace, I know this donkey. He's a pretty
good boy, but you'd be making a terrible mistake to marry him. He's
a good, honest guy, but is that what you really want to do with your
life?"

"Joe," I said, "cut it out . . . Grace, he's kidding."

He wouldn't cut it out. He might have been kidding, but he wouldn't
cut it out. "Come on, Joe," I said, laughing, keeping it light. "What's
wrong with me?"

"Nothing," he said. "You're just a big donkey."

"Well, then—"

"But Grace," he said, "you know what sort of fellow this Cassini is.
We Irish have to stick together."

"Joe, that's not fair," I said. "You let your own daughter marry Peter
Lawford, who is not only an actor but an *English* actor—and you once
told me they were the worst kind."

I was beginning to wonder if Joe Kennedy wasn't attempting a move
of his own on Grace. He was stroking her hand. He was trying to make a
date with her.

"We have to discuss this thing, you and I," he said. "You can count
on me. I am at your total disposal."

What a funny fellow old Joe Kennedy was! How humorous! Smiling, always smiling, I interrupted with a light treatise on the famous instances of treachery in history.

Actually, I'd probably have tried a similar maneuver had the situation been reversed. And I'm certain that Joe Kennedy would have been happy, and favorably impressed, had I emerged victorious in the Kelly affair. On the other hand, he did tell me later, "Oleg, I probably did you a favor. Those Kellys would have been on you like octopuses. They would've driven you crazy."

The story of La Côte Basque never failed to amuse his son, either. It was one of Jack Kennedy's favorites. More than once, sitting with a group of close friends, the President would say to me, "Oleg, tell them how Dad screwed you up with Grace Kelly."

But Joe Kennedy didn't screw me up with Grace Kelly; I did that all by myself. She and I screwed ourselves up. With all our games and hesitations, fits and starts, we didn't have much of a chance. One time Grace said to me, "Oleg, one of the problems we have when you and I try to communicate is that you are so fast—you analyze and decide about things right away, and it takes *me* quite a bit of time to digest my thoughts and feelings, to plan my course of action." There was also the matter of my terrible and often silly temper. We had some awful fights, most of which were my fault. At one point, Grace was going to have dinner with the Bing Crosbys and I exploded. There had been rumors (untrue) that she'd had a romance with Bing, and I didn't want people reminded of that. I behaved badly, and Grace sent me the following, from which I quote:

Darling—

You have upset me so that I could die . . .

It is incredible to me that having dinner with Lizanne and the Crosbys can make you behave like a schoolboy—If I went out with Bing alone you would be absolutely right—and I would never do that to begin with—because I have no interest in anyone but you—but this I shouldn't have to explain—

Bing is a wonderful person and a very dear friend. I have great respect for him and hope he will be our friend for many years—

I told you he said that he was in love with me—but there are many people he feels that way about and after the emotional strain of playing Country Girl, this was only natural. But Bing would never try to do anything about it. Unless he thought I wanted it that way.

I have very few friends here—please don't ask me to give up their friendships.

Another time, Grace asked my permission to go out to dinner with her agent and Frank Sinatra, who wanted, supposedly, to discuss a film. I made a bad scene about it. I said to her, "Don't you know this agent trick is the oldest in the world? Let's face it: Frank just wants to meet you. I will not be a part of this charade. . . ."

As I raged, I was already regretting it. Grace was looking at me coldly; and when I was through with my outburst, she began to speak:

"I must explain something to you right now—with no interruptions. The extravagance of your jealousy did not displease me at first. But isn't it about time that you stopped this silly behavior? It shows nothing but a lack of confidence. I love you, but your anger isn't very endearing. Indeed, it is slowly destroying the warmth I've felt for you. If it is so important to you, I won't go out with Sinatra. But please, stop this behavior right now!"

I was terribly embarrassed, of course. I'd always found it difficult to control myself when I was angry. Grace's reaction in a fight was quite the opposite: she would become deathly still. Eventually, the silence became overwhelming. Yet, there was never a final break; there was always the hope of another reconciliation, until the very end.

Finally, Grace called and said she had something very important for us to discuss. We met on the Staten Island Ferry, of all places.

"I know this is going to be a difficult conversation," she said, "but you must hear me out."

"We have had many difficult conversations in the past," I said. "I can't think of anything that you could come up with now that would surprise me."

Then she came up with something that surprised me quite a bit. "I want you to know first of all," she said, "that within my capacity for caring, I have cared more for you than anyone I have ever known and will probably continue to do so. However, for various reasons that should be apparent, I have decided to marry Prince Rainier of Monaco."

I was stunned, and perplexed. "Why?" I asked. "How and when did *this* develop?"

It had, in fact, materialized out of thin air. She had met the fellow once, when they were photographed together—briefly—during the Cannes Film Festival. Later, Rainier's personal priest, Father John Tucker, had contacted friends of the Kelly family and arranged a meeting in Philadelphia over Christmas of 1955. Rainier proposed two days later, and Grace accepted. It was called a fairy-tale romance.

"Are you going to marry someone because he has a title and a few acres of real estate?" I asked her on the ferry. "Central Park is as large!"

"I will learn how to love him," she said.

"Very well, then," I said, numbly. I might have had mixed feelings about our getting married, but the prospect of life without Grace left me in unmitigated pain. But I was not about to argue with her; she was determined. "I wish you all the best. I'm sure you are making the right decision."

Actually, I wasn't at all sure, but her choice was not incomprehensible to me. It was a very "continental" sort of arrangement, a conjunction of title and beauty, a marriage of state. Prince Rainier was an attractive, cultured man, the reigning monarch of a small, idyllic principality. He brought with him the highest social, financial, and also religious prestige, as the princes of Monaco are Catholic princes, closely associated with the Vatican. And I do not agree with those who have argued that Grace agreed to this *mariage de raison* simply because Rainier offered her a better part, with greater long-term security, than MGM could. I think it was more complicated than that.

I believe Grace had been attracted to me for many of the same reasons as Gene. I represented a liberation from the straightlaced, self-righteous background she came from. I had a sense of irony, and this was something of a relief. It loosened the armor that was always threatening to suffocate her. It allowed her room to maneuver, to breathe, to be funny. There was also a very intense emotional chemistry between us . . . and I think all this freedom, in the end, proved a bit too threatening to her solid, controlled, conventional core. She was intrigued by the chemistry, but never entirely comfortable with it.

In retrospect, her retreat to a medieval fantasy seems almost inevitable. The world saw it as a grand romantic gesture, but I thought it had tragic aspects. I saw it as a capitulation, a decision to avoid the wondrous turmoil of life. But I truly did wish her well, and it is my opinion now, as it was then, that Grace made the right decision. The marriage seems to have been a good one. It certainly was a boon to Monaco, which had been suffering hard financial times before Aristotle Onassis assumed the management of the casino (in 1953). Grace made it glamorous again, the jewel of the Riviera. This was a marvelous role for her, the ultimate international hostess. She played the princess for the rest of her life, at every ball, at every dinner. The world was her stage. It was a smashing run. Grace would enter the pantheon of gods and be loved worldwide.

Years later, I met Grace's mother at a Philadelphia charity ball. Indeed, she—of all people—was to present me with an award, the Philadelphia Cup, for my contributions to fashion. As she handed me the ceramic bowl, she whispered, "I think perhaps I made a mistake about you after all."

I saw Grace only once more. I was cruising the Mediterranean on a yacht one summer with my friend Ben Jackober, a young fellow named Philippe Junot, and several others. We put in at Monaco one day, and I was running along a beach when, suddenly, I saw her sitting on a bench with a friend, the designer Vera Maxwell. I stopped dead in my tracks and stared at her. She met my glance and nodded. "Hello, Oleg," she said. "Hello, Grace," I replied. We looked at each other for a moment, perhaps. Then I turned and left to catch my boat.

I do not remember exactly where or how I learned of her death. I remember only the emotional roller coaster that followed, the flood of memories, the bittersweet reminiscence of our time together. Almost before I knew it, the various news organizations were after me, asking about her. I felt somewhat uncomfortable cooperating with them, but I did feel a need to talk about this, to reminisce—it was a way of saying good-bye. I was struck by the almost mythic status that already seemed to be enveloping this very real girl whom I'd loved; I was surprised that some interviewers even seemed to *resent* the fact that Grace and I had nearly married. So human an impulse was an imperfection they refused to acknowledge. I have learned that the best way to respond to such attitudes is to try to rise above the insinuations and respond simply and straightforwardly. I remember one interview upon the publication of a biography about her. *The CBS Morning News* asked me to appear, and I agreed. The interviewer, Pat Collins, said, "Mr. Cassini, tell us about your *alleged love affair* with Grace Kelly."

"Well, it was not *alleged* and it was not an affair," I said, wounded terribly by the insensitive tone of this interrogation. "We were in love. We were engaged to be married. That is the truth. No more, no less."

CHAPTER
10

T here was a small Italian restaurant on the west side of Palm Beach that was very popular in the 1950s. It had a wine cellar that was a favorite hideaway of my dear friend Porfirio Rubirosa, who was perhaps the greatest playboy of our time.

Rubi would utilize the cellar in this manner: he would say to his date, "I want to see if there is a wine in this place that might be drinkable . . . my dear, why don't you come with me?"

And there, amid the musty bottles (and the potential intrusion of the wine steward), he would make his move, and almost invariably succeed.

I mention this because a decade later such artifice would not have seemed necessary: in the 1960s, all you had to do was say "Let's do it" and it was done; indeed, as time went on, the girls began to take the initiative themselves. The art of seduction was replaced by demystified, unromantic physical gluttony and, I believe, a great deal was lost in the transition.

This, of course, is not to imply that I am prudish or put off by successful women. No, I've always been more interested in those who had careers, were independent, had minds of their own (certainly Gene Tierney and Grace Kelly qualified in all those categories). But the so-called sexual revolution of the 1960s cost both men and women a great deal of fun. It eliminated the coy sideways glances, the subtleties, the small dramas and titillations of the chase.

The 1950s were, I believe, the Golden Age of Romance, because they were a time when grand gestures were still possible; it was the age when high-speed, transoceanic wooing became viable for the first time. The airplane had opened enormous romantic vistas. One could say, "I will meet you in Cannes for the weekend," or, "Here's a plane ticket. Why don't you meet me in Gstaad?" And then, in Cannes or Gstaad or Cap d'Antibes or a hundred other romantic venues, the game of seduction would still be played subtly, cleverly, with a fillip of uncertainty. Such artful maneuverings were almost always ceremonial in nature, like Rubirosa taking his girls down to the wine cellar (his reputation was such that any woman who accepted his invitation to dine not only expected to be made love to but anxiously anticipated it; the question was only when and how). But the need for creativity, the requirement that a lover be entertaining, subtly surprising in a pleasurable way—as well as the possibility of making a wrong move—were all part of the ritual, which added piquancy to the game and made victory ultimately that much sweeter.

I had been a student of such activities since my youth in Florence. I had read about the great generals and statesmen, but also about those who chose pleasure over achievement. I admired Petronius, Nero's arbiter of elegance, whose job it was to create an atmosphere of luxury and sensual abandon in the court. I admired Cesare Borgia (and his father, Pope Alexander VI) more for his unbridled pursuit of pleasure than for the political qualities that caused him to be the model for Machiavelli's *Il Principe*. I studied the various myths of Don Juan (an archetypal character who occurs in a great many cultural traditions), and was tickled by the knowledge that art and reality had converged in eighteenth-century Prague when the aged Casanova, librarian to a German nobleman, was consulted by Mozart and Lorenzo da Ponte on the libretto for *Don Giovanni* (or so he later claimed). Throughout history, the great lovers had been disdained by the priests and politicians. But they were not merely satyrs; they had to be multitalented—thespians, musicians, magicians, tacticians—to succeed at their chosen art; they used these skills in pursuit of pleasure, not power, which seemed to me a saner course. It was this historical tendency which may have had its ultimate flowering at the end of the Machine Age, in the 1950s.

My brother coined a term in his column for those glamorous, frivolous souls who indulged in habitual continent-hopping in pursuit of pleasure. He called them—us—"the Jet Set." The concept has been trivialized over time; the frivolity has been made to seem fatuous, the romance forgotten. It was, however, a far more graceful era than that which followed. It had a mischievous innocence, lost now, perhaps irrevocably. It was a moment when the last of the great playboys flourished, amused, no doubt, by the exaggerated drama and notoriety accorded their exploits by the media. It was the decade when the sybaritic spirit was institutionalized in America, and raised to an ideal, by Hugh Hefner.

I met Hefner at the Latin Quarter one evening in the 1950s. We engaged in friendly competition for a showgirl and both won. I liked Hef; I admired the way he had his life organized. He was an excellent judge of beauty, but I was struck by the pristine quality of life at the Playboy Mansion, where I often stayed when I visited Chicago. It was a sumptuous place. Contrary to popular belief, there were no rampant orgies (although discreet liaisons were possible); his ideal was "the girl next door," and the mansion was populated with them. Milkshakes were as popular there as champagne. Hef was, in fact, a deceptively traditional fellow, a one-woman (at a time) man. I remember him sitting there in his pajamas, smoking his pipe, holding hands with Janet Pilgrim, his girlfriend of the moment; he seemed essentially monogamous. Certainly, he was not the sort to go from room to room in the mansion, taking random samplings of his harem. His devotion to the libertine spirit appeared to be more an intellectual commitment than a sensual reality.

When I think of the man who truly embodied the spirit of those times, Porfirio Rubirosa is the one who comes to mind. He was an apotheosis, the ultimate playboy, a strange combination—one of the few Don Juans I've ever met who was a man's man *and* a ladies' man. Rubi was an athlete —he played polo and boxed—but he also had the gift of knowing how to talk to women. He was of medium height, well muscled but trim, with rugged good looks . . . and, of course, he had the most remarkable piece of equipment; he was known for it. A common joke when dining out in those days was to refer to the sixteen-inch pepper mill as "the Rubirosa." His nickname was *Toujours Prêt* ("always ready"). It would be a mistake, though, to attribute his great success with women solely to the beneficence of nature. Rubi was one of the most charming men I've ever met, a man who knew quality and devoted himself to enjoying the best things in life.

I know there are those who scorn the unbridled pursuit of pleasure. But I will not indulge in the middle-class morality of shopkeepers when judging Rubi. I will say only this: everyone pursues pleasure in his own way. Whether it is through intellectual stimulation, mystical rapture (I would include religion in this category), or the more tangible excitements of the senses.

I knew Rubi for many years, in Palm Beach and Deauville and New York, but I will always associate him with Paris in my mind. I often visited with him and his last, stunning wife, Odile Rodin, at their *petite maison* just outside the city, called Marnes la Coquette. It was surrounded by trees, and brilliantly furnished.

Rubi lived like a pasha and had the most incredible schedule. He had transformed one of the rooms of this house into a boxing ring, and first thing in the morning, he would go there and spar several rounds with a professional boxer. After a shower and breakfast, he might play some polo —he was a low-ranked player but well mounted—or go shopping with Odile. In the afternoon, his coterie would begin to gather; invariably, there were younger men who surrounded Rubi, seeking to learn his secrets or just enjoy his lifestyle. They would arrange the evening's entertainment for his amusement. Eventually, Rubi would ask, "So, what do we do tonight? Let's do something interesting."

Often we would go to the Tour d'Argent for dinner. The proprietor of that sumptuous place, Claude Terrail, was a fellow polo player who enjoyed the elegant life as much as we did. "Perhaps," Rubi would say, "Claude will bring out some of his good ducks for us, for a change." The Tour d'Argent was, of course, known for its duck. After that we would go to L'Eléfant Blanc, which was my favorite nightclub of all time—an exciting place, with two orchestras. Latin rhythms were very popular then, as was jazz. In later years, we would go to Regine's or Castel's. We would stay out most of the night. There were always beautiful girls, certainly, and competition in that area. There was always the goal of appearing with the most beautiful, or most wealthy, or most famous, or most fun. Toward dawn we would go to Calvados, a café on the Avenue Montaigne, where they served excellent sausage and potatoes. We would eat, and have another drink, and talk. Rubi could appear to be entirely saturated with alcohol and still perform socially and, more important to him, sexually. More than one night I said to myself, *He's gone. He's had enough.*

And Rubi would be saying, "No, let's have one more glass of champagne. The night is young, eh, Oleg? Are you kidding? *Que personne ne bouge.*" ("I don't want anyone to move.")

He wouldn't return home until dawn, and then he would sleep the entire next day. That was how he lived: one day off and one day on. It was one of his secrets, a regimen strictly maintained. You could not call Rubi on the day of rest. Everything was dark. No sound; nothing. He relaxed himself totally, preparing for the next performance. And it seemed to work. I never saw the man look tired or haggard.

There was another, rather exceptional secret about Rubi that directly involved his reputation as a lover, and as a man. He suffered from a rare sexual malaise: priapism. He was in an almost constant state of arousal but unable to be satisfied. He achieved orgasm very rarely, and then only after hours of struggle. It must have been very painful, and frustrating, although it may well have been a product of Rubi's obsession. He knew that thing of his was a potential meal ticket, and he actually trained to keep it in peak condition. He did exercises. He would drink each day a potion called *pago-palo*, which he said came from the bark of a certain tree in the Dominican Republic; he believed that it guaranteed performance. He claimed to be able to think himself from semitumescence to full sail, and I believe he could. He was very proud of his abilities and endowments and would, at times, perform parlor tricks. He could balance a chair with a telephone book on it atop his erection. "It's a muscle like any other," he would say. "It can be strengthened."

I was friendly with Rubi during the last decade or so of his remarkable career. He had already been married to both Doris Duke and Barbara Hutton, the latter for a mere 53 days, during which time she showered an estimated $1 million in gifts and $2.5 million in cash upon him, which must be some sort of record.

Rubi was born in the Dominican Republic, but he did not, as myth has it, come from a lower-class family. His father was a general in the army who later became the Dominican *chargé d'affaires* in Paris. Rubi went to the best schools, and moved in the best circles of French society. He returned to the Dominican Republic to study law in 1926, at the age of seventeen, but soon left the university for a military career. He was already a captain, at the age of twenty, when he was noticed by the dictator Rafael Leónidas Trujillo, who had recently staged his coup. Trujillo rather pointedly sent Rubirosa to the airport one day to retrieve his plain daughter, Flor d'Oro. Rubi took the hint and married the girl. Trujillo rewarded him with the same diplomatic post his father had held in Paris; remarkably, Rubi remained in the dictator's good graces even after he divorced the daughter in 1940. He kept his diplomatic post, but, given his fabulous lifestyle, was in constant need of money; and so, he used women to finance him.

He believed his services were fair exchange for the fabulous sums that were visited upon him, and apparently his conquests did not disagree (at least, until it became clear that they would not have exclusive rights to those services). In her diary, Barbara Hutton would note: "He is the ultimate sorcerer, capable of transforming the most ordinary evening into a night of magic." And also: "[He is] priapic, indefatigable, grotesquely proportioned."

During the 1940s, Rubi was married to the French film star Danielle Darrieux, and then, in 1947, to Doris Duke, the tobacco heiress. The latter ceremony was marked by a rather bizarre scene. Just before the marriage was about to transpire, a battery of Duke's attorneys arrived with a prenuptial agreement for Rubi to sign. He was so infuriated by this that he smoked a cigarette throughout the ceremony. His wounded pride was mitigated somewhat by his wedding presents, which included a check for $500,000, several sports cars, a converted B-25 airplane (Rubi was a pilot), and the inevitable string of polo ponies. The marriage lasted thirteen months.

The marriage to Barbara Hutton was a complete fiasco. Rubi was having a much-publicized romance then with Zsa Zsa Gabor (while she was married to George Sanders, who named Rubirosa as corespondent in his divorce petition); Barbara was well on her way to oblivion—she had deteriorated physically and mentally—and was furiously squandering her fortune. I could not imagine marrying her in that state, but Rubi was desperate.

You see, he was a true playboy. He was unable to work; the very thought of it made him ill. Indeed, he was quoted by *Newsweek* as saying, "Work? I have no time for work." (At one point, Rubi sent a young Dominican named Oscar Renta to me, to work as a design assistant. I didn't have anything for him, but Mother made some introductions; later he became the famous designer Oscar de la Renta.) I remember once, years later, Rubi had lunch with me at a Chinese restaurant in New York. I knew he needed money and I had a plan. He and I would open a ski resort in Europe. It would be very exclusive, membership only (like the Ski Club Ten at Sugarbush, Vermont, which I opened). I had a specific mountain in mind, not forty-five minutes from Nice and virgin territory. "This could be very big," I told him. "Everybody knows you, and likes you. People would be dying to become members."

He listened, dully, as I went on for about twenty minutes. Finally, he pleaded with me: "Stop, Oleg, stop. I have a headache. This business talk is killing me."

I was amazed. He considered my relatively vague fantasizing business. He couldn't continue. He had to go to bed. Rubi's mind was attuned to *la dolce vita* and a few sports; the very idea of earning a living exhausted him. And yet, it was something that he had to think about often in the last years of his life, since he had done something that was, for him, rather odd: he had married for love.

Odile was a teenager when he met her, an aspiring actress who came from a middle-class family. She was about five foot seven, with blondish hair, blue eyes, freckles—she had *joie de vivre* and was altogether lovely. He was madly in love with her, though. There was a chemistry, a remarkable thing. Odile had the key that unlocked him. She had cured his priapism . . . and she drove him crazy. Odile had the power over him that he had, all his life, wielded over others. She exhausted him, and made him jealous. She liked to have fun. She even liked the scene, the crowd that followed Rubi about. She could stay out all night just as he could. "I don't understand it," he said to me. "All my life I have controlled women—every woman I've ever met, except this one. She is under my skin."

I was with Rubi the night he died. He was worried about money. He was worried about Odile, with whom he'd quarreled. She'd gone out with someone else. There was a celebration that night: a victory by the Brazilian polo team. Normally, he would have gained a great deal of satisfaction from such an occasion. Champagne was being poured into the championship cup; everyone was laughing, drinking. I remember looking at his face. He was trying to smile, but the fun had gone out of him. His eyes were dead. He said to me, *"Eh bien,* Oleg, let's go out. We've had enough of this. Let's go to Calvados and have a drink or two."

Rubi unburdened himself as we drank: "Oh, I am not happy. It is always the same thing. I don't have any money. I don't know if I should sell my house. I don't know what's going to happen . . . Odile, she is impossible."

It was getting late and I had business the next morning. I was staying at the Hôtel George V, just down the block from the café, and wanted to excuse myself. Rubi was not yet ready to call it an evening, of course. He said, "Hey, *mon vieux,* come and stay with me at the house. We can have another glass of champagne and talk."

"At another time—any other time, my friend—I will come for breakfast, or lunch. We can talk all night some other night, but I have an appointment early in the morning. I must go," I told him. "Go home, go to bed."

I remember thinking I should go with him.

But then, I'd seen him in that condition so many times. Rubi could hold his liquor better than anyone I knew. He never would have allowed me to drive his Ferrari racer, in any case. And I *did* have business the next morning. I thought about it and then shrugged it off.

The next morning I learned that Rubi had driven his car full speed into a tree, not more than a mile from the café, and killed himself. I am not certain if the true cause of death was alcohol or depression, but perhaps it was for the best. It was 1965, and Rubi's time was passing. He would not have been happy with the sexual revolution.

A final irony: Rubi died in the same manner and in almost the same spot as his fellow playboy, Aly Khan, who'd been killed in a freak auto accident—his car was hit from the rear—five years earlier.

I never considered myself a playboy, although others put me in that category. There were periods when I behaved as one, devoting my entire life to an amorous project. But I was plagued by this American idea: I wanted to succeed in business. I wanted a personal, artistic success; that was what made me feel good. I suppose I could be "moral" about the virtue of this course, especially when compared with Rubi's—but how boring! It was simply that, one way or another, I was constantly faced with the decision I had to make that last night with Rubirosa: work or friendship, work or romance, work or fun.

And all too often, especially in the early 1950s, when I was building my business, I chose work. Indeed, I was so busy during those years that for a time I routinized my romantic life, creating my own harem of seven girls, for each night of the week. They were models, exquisite-looking creatures, and quite happy to be compartmentalized in that manner. It allowed them to be seen at the best places in my very finest dresses and, I might add modestly, in good company. This arrangement eliminated some of the drama and excitement from my life—at least, for those months when I was busy in New York working on the next collection— but it was, obviously, an improvement on the monkish existence I had maintained while preparing for my debut. I enjoyed the variety, and the fact that each of the seven was, by definition, more a fling than a romance. If I felt that any of the girls was growing too attached to me, I would advise her, "I think you are losing time here, and time is very important to you," or simply, "I am not good enough for you." My personal belief was that all is *not* fair in love and war; on the contrary, to make false promises to a girl is like stealing—stealing the lady's valuable time, the best time.

I suppose that by Aly Khan's dictum—the most important quality of a great lover is time—I was only an intermittent success. I had my moments, but to play in Aly's or Rubi's romantic league, one needed the obsession and concentration of a great athlete. I was never as friendly with Aly as I was with Rubirosa—his relationship with Gene precluded that. Also, he was one of those who are more ladies' than men's men. But I respected his prowess and was intrigued by his methods. Aly didn't have to worry about making a living at this line of work, as Rubirosa did. He was a Moslem religious leader, a prince, and a millionaire many times over, and so he could concentrate his attentions on movie stars (only the biggest names, like Rita Hayworth and Gene Tierney, of course), not heiresses. For him, the exposure of the conquest, the international publicity, was as important as the triumph itself. It was better, as the *bourgeois gentilhomme* might say, to have people think you were having an affair with a woman of stature, even if it was never consummated, than to actually have the affair without anyone knowing. And I will be honest: I shared that feeling at times.

Even though there was no financial pressure, Aly Khan pursued his prey with the avidity of a desperate man. He was not a hydraulic marvel like Rubirosa and, thus, was forced to be more creative. I have heard from several reliable sources that Aly's great secret was his fluency as a cunnilinguist (I have searched for a more elegant way to convey this curious fact, and failed). He made it a practice to keep his conquests off balance, enthralled—and, no doubt, exhausted—by performing his devotions thrice daily. It was also his habit to place buckets of ice on either side of his bed and, just before the moment of climax, thrust his arms into them up to the wrist in order to prolong his performance. This was mere technique, though.

The real ability that great playboys like Aly Khan and Rubirosa shared—and that I too could manifest when I had the time—was only this: they truly appreciated women. They enjoyed nothing more in life than talking to them, entertaining them, listening to them, looking at them. Their greatest pleasure was to please them, whatever that entailed, and almost always they had an uncanny knack of sensing what it might be.

Another, less important, but curious trait playboys shared was that they actually liked to play. There was an odd strain of madcap humor, of practical jokes, of downright silliness to those times.

I remember a gala evening in New York, the premiere of Ray Stark's film *The World of Suzie Wong*. Ray was friendly with Aly Khan and constantly trying to get the two of us together, and sure enough, Aly was there with Gene that night (Gene was wearing the exact same dress of mine, by the way, as my date, China Machado). I decided to be friendly that evening—I didn't want to ruin Ray's party—and we got along fine. Indeed, we were getting along so well that when we arrived after the film at the restaurant in Chinatown where the celebration was to be held, we decided to do something funny. We were among the first to arrive, and someone spotted the remains of a recently completed Chinese banquet in one of the rooms. We set upon it, rearranging the food, sculpting it into piles on platters. Aly added several overflowing ashtrays and leftover drinks to the mix; we covered the platters with rice and sauce and served them to Ray Stark's guests at the party. They never noticed what they were eating.

Yes, well, perhaps you had to be there.

I was the victim of several practical jokes in Paris during those years. One was arranged by my friend Ben Jackober, who held an elegant dinner party in my honor at his fabulous home one evening. It was the most extraordinary house, exquisitely appointed; he later sold it to the shah of Iran. The company that night fit the surroundings: charming men, all of whom I knew; beautiful girls, all of whom were new to me. I had just arrived in town and was rather groggy after a long flight. We sat down to dinner—excellent food, of course—and then, unfortunately, I was called to the phone, a transatlantic call. I sat there waiting for it to be put through, five, ten minutes before receiving word that the call had been lost, and, somewhat miffed and embarrassed (it had been rude of me, I realized, to disappear like that), I went downstairs to rejoin the party, which continued as before, except for one detail: all the girls were completely naked. Jackober had hired them from Madame Claude, who specialized in only the highest-quality girls, including models, actresses, and society women. There was laughter and applause when they saw my shocked double-take. Ben had arranged it all—the phone call, everything —just for that moment. Actually, it was the beginning of a very thrilling evening.

I was always eager to do something, anything, my first night in Paris, which is one of my favorite cities, but also can be very sad when you are alone. My habits in Paris were well known to my friends. I stayed frequently at L'Hôtel Napoléon, a smallish place near L'Étoile that was owned by a Russian who knew me and treated me well. (Errol Flynn also stayed there.) Everyone always knew when I was coming, because I would call in advance to try to arrange a party, a dinner, anything to keep myself entertained when I arrived. One of the few times I failed in these efforts, I happened to receive a call at the hotel from a friend, Baron Renzino d'Avanzo, who'd been a recent guest in my home. He said that he knew a place where interesting girls congregated—*demi-mondaines*, he said.

It was a nightclub, very dark, very Paris—the music was pure Piaf —and we met there. I immediately spotted an extremely pretty girl, and we began to dance. Her face was vaguely familiar; she reminded me of someone I knew but couldn't quite recall. I kept suggesting that she come back to the hotel with me, and she said, "Of course, I would like to very much, but I don't want people to think that we just met here on the dance floor and you are taking me away. Appearances, you know. I will leave separately and join you there later." I was overjoyed. She was beautiful, and full of charm. I returned to the hotel, ordered a bottle of Taittinger Blanc de Blanc . . . but no one came. I went to sleep disappointed, and feeling rather foolish. The next morning, there was a message with the concierge:

> Dear Oleg,
> So terribly sorry I couldn't come as planned. Hope to see you some other time.
>
> > Best wishes,
> > Jeanne Moreau

How stupid of me. I had been set up perfectly by this fellow, who had arranged the joke with his friend Moreau. But what a clever joke.

I had, I suppose, an eighteenth-century sense of romance. I loved jokes and plots and games, *bals masqués*, mix-ups and mistaken identities. I enjoyed weaving my plots in pursuit of beauty, but I didn't mind being the quarry, either, when a clever young lady decided to engage in similar maneuverings, as long as the results were pleasurable.

I was invited once to spend a weekend at the castle of the duke of Caraman, near Paris. He was married to an exquisite English girl named Mita Macklin, with whom I had a certain immediate rapport. We passed dinner in a subtle minuet of nods and fluttering eyelashes; I sensed a situation developing. We seduced each other with furtive glances. Afterward, I whispered to her, "Would it be possible?"

"Yes," she said.

My room was in the tower, very picturesque and accessible only by a stone spiral staircase, just the sort of staircase one might imagine, and desire, in such circumstances. I lay in wait that night, so excited I was scarcely able to breathe. Then a soft rustling, a shimmer of silken petticoats up the stairs . . . and then I was joined by a warm, soft, fantastic-smelling creature. We had a most intoxicating evening, the pleasure heightened by the secret quality of it. I fell asleep, and when I awoke, she was gone.

I saw her at breakfast and attempted to resume our furtive communication; she merely smiled at me. What was this? Even the best actress would have been unable to completely hide her emotions after such a night. I was perplexed, and finally managed a moment alone with her. "Did you sleep well?" I asked.

"Oh, dear Oleg," she laughed, "that wasn't me. It was my sister-in-law. She liked you, too."

I'd had no flirtatious contact with the other girl, but now that I noticed her (smiling, blushing), I saw that she did look like her sister-in-law.

My friend Frank Shields, one of the great tennis players of that time, told me that he had a similar experience once. We were in Las Vegas and he developed a crush on Zsa Zsa Gabor. He pursued her in the grand fashion, but seemed to be getting nowhere. Finally, she agreed to meet him in her room at the hotel after her last cabaret performance. He arrived at the appointed hour and was immediately, passionately engulfed in the darkness. He experienced, he said, a remarkable night of lovemaking that lasted till dawn, when he noticed, in the first glimmerings of daylight, that his partner in romance had not been Zsa Zsa at all but her mother, Jolie Gabor.

I appreciated such things. Humor, practical jokes, a light romantic touch—that was my *modus operandi* in those days. As the years passed and my business became more successful, I had more time to enjoy myself. And though I would rarely concentrate all my energies into this area, I developed a reputation as something more than an amateur when it came to the pursuit of women.

My romantic life was governed by two adages. One was from Napoleon: "The greatest victory in love is flight."

The other was an old Jamaican saying: "Softly, softly, catchee monkey."

Softly, softly, I sought to envelop my quarry, to engage her intellect, to capture her imagination—my approach was, I believe, somewhat more cerebral than some of the others'—and, ultimately, to pamper and titillate her to the point where success was inevitable. This might require an extended campaign, or nothing more complicated than a glance. The primary weapon I used was charm, which is a quality you develop when you are not sure you have others.

I never grew tired of the challenge and mystery of the process; I never quite understood it, either. Recently, I met someone with whom I'd once shared a flirtation and she mentioned how odd our time together had been: "You manage, somehow, to capture the mind of a woman so that she thinks there is no other man in the world. You were very fair, but very tricky. You never put any pressure on me. You created an atmosphere that was unthreatening. Sex never seemed the goal, though it clearly was part of it—and slowly, little by little, everything fell into place."

She reminded me of the strategy I had used on her. "You are very attractive to me," I had said. "Physically, I think you are perfect. I don't have any sense of your character, though; nor do you know me. But in order to concentrate and see what sort of possibilities the two of us may have, let's not chop up our time with other people. We will go steady for ten days. At the end of that time, we will have some idea whether we have the prospect of another ten days, or of a great friendship."

As it happened, we knew all that had to be known in half that time. We are friends to this day.

Love, I believe, is a virus, the greatest virus. When the virus is there, and the immune system breaks down, then love "overpowers"—and it can run its course in five minutes, an evening, a weekend, or remain a chronic affliction for a lifetime.

I felt confident enough of my abilities and reputation in those days to call anyone—anyone!—and ask for a date. At one point, Jayne Mansfield was appearing in a show on Broadway. I called her and said, "This is Oleg Cassini. Would you like to go out with me?"

"Meet me at the theater after the show," she replied.

We went to a nightclub. I thought she was very funny and charming —playing at that blonde, buxom image, rather than taking it seriously— and I made the next move: "Can you come to my place for a drink?"

"Why don't you come to my hotel?" she suggested. "I'm staying downtown. I have some animals with me and the hotels uptown wouldn't accept them."

"I understand," I said. "I love animals."

She took me to a decidedly third-rate hotel, with ratty furniture in the lobby, overwhelmed by the smell of stale cigars. We went immediately to her room, and it was incredible what she had there: a Great Dane, a Chihuahua, four cats, and a little girl running around. The cat box in the bathroom was full, and reeking. Any romantic notions I had disappeared instantaneously. She thought it was all very charming and entertaining, this menagerie. But the smell and the animals . . . the whole business made it impossible for me. Such incidents caused me to reach this conclusion: if love is a virus, antidotes abound.

(A girl named Bea Ammidown once told me a similar story about how fleeting the romantic urge can be. She had been swept off her feet by Errol Flynn. He had taken her—spur of the moment, in the best playboy fashion—to Havana, leaving behind her husband. They were having a most intimate, lovely dinner overlooking a moonlit ocean . . . when he lost one of the caps on his teeth. It just fell into his plate. Her feelings changed immediately; the mood was lost. All the effort that poor Errol had put into the project was wasted.)

For many years, I had a series of beautiful girls serve as my personal secretary. The position did not involve typing or steno; the secretary traveled with me and handled the logistics of my life. Anne Marie d'Escot was the most memorable of these, a stunning French girl of nineteen who was the top debutante of the season. She was tall, dark-haired, magnificent. She came from a fine, conservative family, and I had to do a lot of talking to convince them that my intention was only to give their daughter a career. I did not take advantage of my position, but was happy to note the gasps and chuckles among my friends when my "secretary" accompanied me on business. Occasionally, I even was able to find a wife for a friend. Howard Oxenberg was someone I knew from Seventh Avenue. He had a successful dress company and was a good-looking, athletic fellow with a lot of style; we both liked to ski. One year, I invited him to come with me to St. Anton, my favorite ski resort in Austria. I always stayed at the Hôtel de la Poste. We had a regular group each February, and I would give a party to celebrate our annual reunion. It was customary for Jacqueline de Ribes to arrange the party for me, select the menu and wines and so forth, for about one hundred people. One of the guests that year was Princess Elizabeth of Yugoslavia, a beautiful brunette, of medium height, well educated, and very witty.

She was the sort of girl I might have been interested in myself, but I knew that one did not tread lightly here—and I also was restrained by my innate sense of the system. I assumed she would be looking for someone of royal background. Howard Oxenberg had no such restraints, however, and he made an immediate move, to which she responded quite favorably. There was a chemistry between them. The princess used me as a confidant: should she go ahead and marry him? I told her yes: "Although you are worlds apart. While the passion is there, it will go . . . it might end well." She took my advice, and it did go—and the charming actress Catherine Oxenberg was one happy result of this unique coupling.

I often found myself acting as an intermediary between two worlds. Both my American and European friends would ask me for emotional translations, romantic analyses, of Old and New World behavior. I found myself suspended on the cusp between the two.

The differences were readily apparent, even on the slopes. My European friends might make three or four runs in a morning, stop and reflect for a moment on how wonderful the skiing had been, then rest and have lunch. The Americans would make their four runs, immediately think, "If I hustle, I'll have time for another before lunch." Then they'd rush to the lift, career down the mountain, and, no doubt, risk injury to squeeze more unappreciated "enjoyment" into their day.

I was an American . . . and a European. I was an American designer. I had the American disease: the need to be a "success" in business. I was proud of my accomplishments, but my European self, still lurking within me, maintained a careful eye on Cassini the workaholic lest he start spending more time on the phone with his stockbroker than with friends. I kept my priorities in order. My goal in life was not to be rich as Croesus, or to pretend that I was some calcified pillar of rectitude now that I was established; it was to pursue the good life.

In truth, this was not a difficult struggle. I might have an American passport and some aspects of the New World sensibility, but a good part of my soul resided on the Continent, and now, for the first time, I was able to return to that older home in triumph, as I'd hoped when I left Rome in 1936. I was able to spend several months each year in Europe, to return to old haunts and habits and friends. I hadn't skied in years, really, and now I would spend weeks each winter in St. Moritz, Gstaad, and St. Anton. I spent many summers on the Riviera; most of the others were passed in more exclusive lodgings than the Hotel Carlton—in the villas and on the yachts of friends.

St. Tropez was a favorite watering hole for me in the '60s and '70s. There were always a lot of Italian playboys, international types, and fashion people from Paris about, in addition to the number-one citizen, Brigitte Bardot. It all made for an interesting mélange.

All too many of my old friends had been lost in the war, but Pucci was still about, and also the little boy I'd played with in the sand at Forte dei Marmi, Gianni Agnelli—he was now the maharajah of Fiat. I thought of him that way, as an Oriental nobleman, although he liked to be called simply "*Avvocato*" (lawyer). But he lived like a maharajah, and looked like one: enigmatic, handsome, with heavy-lidded eyes. He was slim, with slightly wavy hair and an elegance that was difficult to describe, because every movement, every gesture was distinctive. It might seem studied, yet was quite natural to him. He was immensely well dressed, a dangerous man, literally. He lived dangerously, roaring along the *haute corniche* from his villa—La Leopolda, formerly the summer home of King Leopold of Belgium—to Cannes at one hundred miles per hour. He had nearly lost his leg in an auto accident, but that didn't deter him. I made the drive with Gianni at the wheel on several occasions, scared out of my wits as he roared around curves and through dark tunnels, shifting gears without putting his foot on the clutch. He was the only driver I've ever known who understood his car and its motor well enough to do that.

Gianni enjoyed scaring people with speed, on land and on water. He had the most remarkable powerboat, a yacht with a motor that could propel it at 120 miles per hour. He would take groups of people, twenty at a time, on this boat and roar from Leopolda to St. Tropez, speeding straight for the dock, terrifying his passengers, each of whom was holding on to a safety bar for dear life, and then stop . . . just at the last moment, maybe fifty yards from the dock.

I would spend weeks at a time at Leopolda with Gianni and Marella, who was tall, regal, beautiful . . . and tolerant of her husband's mercurial nature. Later, the Agnellis would sell Leopolda. But it was a most luxurious scene while it was still going strong in the 1950s. There were often twenty houseguests, some of whom stayed for weeks, as I did on occasion. There might be as many as one hundred guests for a gala dinner party, a mix of the most glamorous people from international society, politics, and entertainment.

When I stayed at Leopolda, I would have my own little guest pavilion, set off from the main house, with a separate swimming pool and liveried servants in attendance. If you desired champagne or something to eat in the middle of the night, all you had to do was ring a bell and a butler wearing a striped jacket, black pants, and white gloves would appear.

There were always fresh flowers in the pavilion. The bed was turned down each night, pajamas neatly folded on top. It was a little like Versailles. Later, I would spend time with President Kennedy in Newport and there would be the appearance of a grand lifestyle—helicopters, yachts, a Secret Service brigade in attendance—but never the numbers of servants, the sheer luxury of Leopolda.

The style was somewhat different in Cabasson, where Paul Louis Weiller kept court in the summer, but no less impressive. La Reine Jeanne was an enormous medieval villa, like a castle on a promontory overlooking the Mediterranean, about fifteen miles south of St. Tropez. The style was somewhat more austere than at Leopolda; the younger guests were given stark stone rooms with only a bed and a washstand next to it. The luxury was the place itself, the quality of the food, the entertainment, and the company.

Captain Paul-Louis Weiller was about twenty years older than I. He had made a fortune in munitions during the First World War and lived well ever since. He was—and is—a remarkably vibrant man, still water-skiing each day at the age of ninety. Once I attended a most incredible party he gave in another of his homes, on the Île Saint-Louis in Paris. He spent more than $150,000 on caviar for this party—this was in the 1950s; the figure might well be $1,000,000 today—and the guests served themselves heaping, spaghetti-sized portions from large crystal bowls with tablespoons.

At La Reine Jeanne, Weiller kept a permanent collection of kings, queens, and assorted minor royalty as guests, like Jean Paul Getty II and his exotically beautiful wife, Tahlita. The queen of Italy seemed always to be there. The most memorable guests during the weeks I stayed at the villa during the 1960s, however, were the Chaplins: Charlie, Oona, and their seventeen-year-old daughter, Geraldine, with whom I had a flirt.

I had known Chaplin in Hollywood. We were both bachelors then, and tennis players. I played often at his house; sometimes Bill Tilden—the great tennis player, but a sad fellow, persecuted for his homosexuality—would be there. Chaplin and I got on well. He was tickled by my ability to do a quick-step imitation of his famous walk. "How do you do that?" he asked. "I have to speed up my cameras to get that effect."

Chaplin was a passable tennis player, but he had great physical dexterity . . . and, unlike some stars, who were deadly dull offscreen, he was a marvelous conversationalist and a nonstop entertainer. He was perhaps the ultimate dinner-party guest; he could—and invariably would—keep any audience enthralled for hours, utilizing his entire arsenal of abilities: musical, physical, and mimetic. I remember one evening he kept a group of us captivated by showing how he'd once flirted with Somerset Maugham. Chaplin was heterosexual, of course—quite a ladies' man, in fact—and Maugham was openly bisexual, but Charlie found himself playing the piano one night at a Hollywood dinner party, and Maugham staring at him languidly. Without quite realizing what he was doing, Chaplin returned Maugham's gaze, flirting with him a little—and then more so—acting (you can picture Chaplin doing this) as if he were a shy fifteen-year-old girl surprised and flattered by the famous author's attention. He was so much into this role that he quite lost track of the fact that, in reality, he was leading the poor fellow on; when Maugham approached the piano, with obvious amorous intent, Chaplin skittered off, still in character, a young girl now frightened and somewhat guilty to have aroused the older man. He was able to re-create this scene for us perfectly; it was quite amusing.

In the great medieval dining room at La Reine Jeanne, Chaplin once held an entire dinner party in thrall with another, somewhat scatological story. He was sailing on a yacht through the Greek islands. There were two beautiful English girls on the trip, one of whom he was courting, and they wanted to visit a small, picturesque fishing village nearby. The three of them got into a dinghy and began to sail toward land, when Chaplin had a sudden, overpowering attack of diarrhea. It was a moment of pure terror and embarrassment. He held on, to the boat and to himself, trying to be charming with the girls, all the while searching desperately for the coast. He was wearing only a white silk shirt and white pants, by the way, and so any accident would have been painfully apparent. He was able to control himself somehow until the boat reached shore, and there he hopped out gingerly—and found himself in the midst of a group of locals who, not so remarkably perhaps, recognized him immediately. "Charlot! Charlot!" they cried.

"*Cabinet? Cabinet?*" he responded.

Several children took him by the hand, and, dancing through the street, with the crowd growing as they went on, and chanting, "Charlot! Charlot," the children led him to a classic outhouse—wooden slats, a foul-smelling hole in the ground. He rushed in, unbuttoned his pants, and let go, sweat pouring—and all the while he could hear the crowd outside, shouting, "Charlot! Charlot!"

Then he was done. And realized there was no paper. He did not know what to do. He had no handkerchief, only the white silk shirt and the pants. He had no choice: He took off the shirt, ripped it to shreds, and used it. Now he had to make an exit, after all the noises and such. He dramatically opened the door, made Charlie-like motions to indicate that he wished to go swimming, then rushed down the street to the beach and jumped into the water—waving good-bye, to the cheers of the crowd!

When not entertaining, Chaplin was a rather complex fellow, especially regarding politics. He was the great leftist; he was for the poor, the workers. All his pictures were about that. In the meantime, he accumulated vast sums of money and kept it in Swiss banks. He also was quite adamant when people assumed he was Jewish. There is a story that Mrs. Sam Goldwyn once made such an assumption at dinner and Chaplin bluntly responded, "I am not even circumcised. Would you like to see the proof of it?"

There were other interesting contradictions about him. He was a great ladies' man and yet an overbearing and protective father. His daughter complained to me about this, and I saw evidence of it once at La Reine Jeanne. There was a *bal masqué*. He came as Napoleon, I as Don Juan, and Geraldine as a Gypsy or some such thing. That night, by a prearranged series of signals, Geraldine left the party and met me down by the beach. Nothing really happened. We just sat on the dock there, looking at the sea and the stars. We had a long conversation—about what it was like to live with her father, and what her dreams were. She even told me about this mania she had to lose weight. She said she was taking pills to do it. I was advising her against this when we heard her father calling her name, and then saw him running around the beach dressed as Napoleon, trying to find his daughter. This struck both of us as very funny, but also had a dampening effect on any plans for the rest of the evening.

The next morning at breakfast, Chaplin confronted me: "Where were you last night?"

"I always walk in the woods after dinner," I said.

"Don't you dare now! Don't you dare now!" he said. "I know men like you."

"You sure do," I said, "because you're one of them."

He tried to keep a stern countenance, but couldn't help laughing at that. "All right," he said, "but I don't permit any license with my children."

* * *

289

The winters in Europe during those years were every bit as entertaining as the summers. I hadn't skied in years—the techniques, the equipment, the clothing had all changed dramatically. The social life at places like St. Moritz and Gstaad had become so institutionalized that more adventurous souls were looking for options.

St. Anton was less social than St. Moritz—more serious skiing, rugged and dangerous. Nobody would go there who did not enjoy active skiing under very difficult conditions—except, perhaps, for a few of the penniless Austrian aristocrats who found it a more convenient, less expensive winter rendezvous than the Swiss and French resorts.

I was introduced to it by my friend Jacqueline de Ribes, whom I'd met in Paris. She was married to the vicomte de Ribes and already, though quite young, a social power. She had the kind of aristocratic face that would have fit perfectly in ancient Egypt or a royal court in the seventeenth century; she was very tall and broad-shouldered, elegant to the point of distraction, and full of life. I was in Paris at the end of the 1950s, about to return to New York, when she said, spur of the moment, "Oleg, don't be foolish. Don't go back. Come to St. Anton—we're all going there. Paul de Ganay is going."

Paul de Ganay was a good friend of mine, and one of the handsomest men in France. She mentioned other names, people I knew. It was clear that it had been decided, in the ineluctable way things often are, that this was going to be *the* thing to do that winter. I couldn't resist, and Jacqueline took me shopping that day: skis, boots, jacket, ten pairs of the new, elasticized ski pants that I thought were quite innovative.

Our headquarters in St. Anton was the Hôtel de la Poste, where we would gather in the evenings at a long, narrow table for dinner. My style in those days was still rather high-energy. Perhaps I was not yet sure of my success, but I'd often take it on myself to entertain the group with jokes, dares, silly games. It was *épater le bourgeois*, be as outrageous as possible. Anything to entertain. I once bet that I could walk up to the top of the Valluga mountain with my skis on my back (and I did). Usually, though, I would find less strenuous ways to keep the group diverted.

St. Anton became a regular part of my schedule. Every year, I spent February there. And as time went on, I introduced some of my American friends to the group there—Howard Oxenberg, as I mentioned, Bobby Friedman, and Armando Orsini, the restaurateur.

St. Anton also was the spawning ground for an episode that had Casanovan echoes. This concerned a most unlikely woman from the Iberian Peninsula who was blonde, freckled, a daring skier, and—unfortunately, I thought (at first)—married. It began at dinner, at the Hôtel de la Poste. There were perhaps thirty of us that night; the Iberian woman was seated next to me. We immediately grew interested in each other. Gianni Agnelli was planning an enormous celebration to mark the opening of his own ski resort, Sestrieres, just north of Turin on the French border. He had invited 120 of his most interesting friends to get the new place started right; he wanted Sestrieres to be known as the most elegant new resort on the Continent. I called him and managed to secure, at the last moment, an invitation for the lovely Iberian and her husband.

It was a truly exceptional time. For three days, no one slept. Among other things, the skiing was fantastic. Agnelli had arranged, in his incomparable way, for helicopters to take us up each morning; we were ferried to the top of a glacier, higher than the regular lifts went, and when we'd get there, we would be greeted by champagne and caviar—a brief repast before the trip down. In the evenings, there would be gala dinners at the Principe Piemonte, the hotel where we all were guests. It was a classic, old-style European hotel, very elegant, and each of us would be given an assigned seat for dinner. There was frantic bartering of these assignments; I was especially active, arranging to place myself near the Iberian (and to put her husband at tables where he might be sufficiently diverted not to notice my maneuverings). I was successful in my efforts; it was a memorable time.

A decade later, in 1963, I would enjoy a similar spree when Edmond de Rothschild opened the Hôtel au Mont d'Arbois in the ski resort Megève. It was a gala party, 100 guests for 100 hours. This was *le tout monde* reunited again.

There was a seamless, effortless quality to my social calendar in those years. The summers were spent in Europe and on Long Island; autumn and early winter were given to fox hunting; the deep winter was spent skiing, most often in Europe; late winter and spring were the traditional season for formal balls and debuts—and these were still going strong in the New York of the 1950s and 1960s. (And during all this, my work was hardly forgotten. My collections were always foremost on my mind wherever I was.) It seemed there was an occasion most every weekend to put on tuxedos and dance to Lester Lanin in the grand ballroom of the Waldorf or the Plaza or the St. Regis. Each year, there was the Bachelors' Ball (ten bachelors, of whom I was one, would each invite twenty of their friends), the White Russian Ball, the April in Paris Ball . . . and the Knickerbocker Ball, held every year at the Waldorf, each year with a different theme.

There was one truly memorable Knickerbocker Ball. It was a benefit that I arranged for the American Indians, who had remained, through all the years, a keen interest of mine. There was Indian decor, traditional and Indian food (venison, corn, and so forth), and representatives from various tribes. Senator Kennedy and Jackie attended, along with many other prominent people. I had by then acquired a considerable library of books about Indians and a large collection of artifacts, some of which were quite rare. A friend, the French consul in Phoenix, was also quite interested in Native Americans, and he and I traveled extensively through the Southwest, visiting reservations. For a brief time, I lived on the Navajo reservation, where I learned about the daily life of the people and had long conversations with their leaders.

It was difficult to maintain the romantic images of childhood after seeing the stark reality of Indian life, the poverty and, especially, the despair of many Indians. On the other hand, I still felt a visceral and intellectual attachment to the tribes who had resisted the white man; perhaps it was that their ancestors and mine had similar roots on the steppes of Asia. I admired especially the fighting spirit of the buffalo hunters, the great horsemen of the plains, perhaps the greatest light cavalry in the history of the world—the Sioux, the Cheyenne, the Arapahoe, the Crow.

At one point, I put my knowledge to frivolous use as a guest on *The $64,000 Challenge*, which was then at the height of its popularity, the number-one television show in America. My appearance was considered quite amusing and unlikely: the Russo-Italian dress designer who was an expert on American Indians. I studied hard for the show, not wanting to make a fool of myself, and survived four weeks in the isolation booth. One would go into this sealed glass capsule to think of an answer while silly "music-to-think-by" was being played; I played along. Of course, I'd been instructed to appear to be thinking furiously, searching my mind for the answers. When I reached the $32,000 plateau, they caught me on a trick question. I was shown a piece of leather and asked what it was. I said it was a belt, which was true; but it was also used as earrings. So much for that. Later, when the quiz-show scandals broke, I was questioned by the FBI and informed them that, sadly, I had failed without any covert help from the producers. They also found out that my winnings had all been donated to the Indians.

The Knickerbocker Ball may not have seemed like much, but we did raise $250,000—not an inconsiderable sum in those days. Afterward, I had a meeting with the Eisenhower administration's Commissioner Emmons of Indian Affairs (which had been, historically, one of the most corrupt government agencies). He said, "It was very nice of you to do this, Mr. Cassini. Give us the money and we will put it to good use."

We were sitting at a long, formal conference table—Emmons, perhaps half a dozen bureaucrats, and I. I suspect they thought I was a fool.

"What will you do with the money?" I asked.

"We will establish a commission to study what can be done for American Indians."

"There have been commissions and more commissions," I said. "The Indians never see a cent of that money, and I'll not have that happen now. I'll figure out some way to spend the money myself."

Eventually, a scholarship fund was established with the money—a small thing, perhaps, but of lasting use.

My desire to do something positive for the Indians was, in retrospect, part of a sense of guilt with the way my life was proceeding. I was not conscious of it at the time, but perhaps things were going too well. There are those for whom the good life isn't always so good. I could only survive as an intermittent Epicurean. I needed stimulation and struggle; a life of unmixed frolic seemed little more than a slow death. I couldn't live without intellectual challenges. I needed to believe that my best efforts, my greatest triumphs were still to come . . . as, indeed, they were.

CHAPTER
11

December 8, 1960

Diana Vreeland
Harper's Bazaar Magazine

Please contact Oleg Cassini for dress for Avedon picture. Have just chosen all my evening clothes from him and they are heaven. He could do whatever you have in mind as he knows what I like.

Much love,
Jackie

I was off on one of my frolics—in Nassau, visiting my old friend Pat De Cicco, with a date, the beautiful and witty actress Jill St. John—when my future beckoned.

There was a call from the secretary to President-elect Kennedy. It was an invitation. "Mrs. Kennedy would like to see some of your ideas for spring. Can you visit her in the hospital at Georgetown [she had just given birth to her son, John-John] with some sketches in the next few days?"

My immediate reaction was a swirl of intense emotions, mainly excitement. I was excited for obvious reasons. This was a chance to do something unprecedented. To design clothing for the First Lady of the United States was a great honor, of course . . . but I knew that this particular First Lady was going to be unlike any of her predecessors. Mamie Eisenhower, Bess Truman, and Eleanor Roosevelt were all fine women, but one could hardly imagine them having an impact on the world of fashion. It seemed, from the efficacious, unobtrusive frocks they favored, they were not even aware that such a world existed. Certainly the idea of couture was something foreign and frivolous.

Jacqueline Kennedy would be different, though. She had been raised among the elite. She was very young and very beautiful. She had a subtle, sophisticated sense of style in all things—in food, in furniture, in the arts. In clothes, she was a follower of the conventional wisdom: Paris was fashion, she believed. Of course, no one knew then just how large an impact Mrs. Kennedy would have on the world of fashion, least of all Jackie herself. She would have found it hard to believe that an American president's wife, dressed almost exclusively by an American designer, would soon become the most emulated fashion figure in the world. It had never happened before; it has not happened since. Edith Head said Jackie Kennedy's was "the greatest single influence in history."

I know we are all older and wiser now; but do you remember how exciting it all seemed them? Do you remember how young they were, how *fresh* they looked, and how proud we were of them?

The American Era reached its apogee in the Kennedy moment. There was, after so many years of doldrums, an unprecedented commingling of charm and idealism and beauty. The most handsome couple in the world suddenly was the most powerful as well. It seemed a fairy tale, even then. How perfect it was! Such fortuitous convergences of beauty and power are rare in history. I could not think of another such instance since Caesar and Cleopatra, or Napoleon and Josephine.

Before the election, I had sent Mrs. Kennedy a note. I'd never been any good at selling myself, and it was very modestly worded. I suggested that a great many talented people would no doubt be interested in designing her wardrobe after the election—which I was sure would be a victorious one—and I hoped that in view of my reputation and ability, she would include me in her considerations.

In fact, although I didn't say so, I sensed that it was nothing less than the greatest design opportunity of my lifetime. It was a chance to create a look that would be remembered for years, photographed, copied, memorialized in museums and history books.

But there had been no response to my note, and I made no further moves. Only a fool would have campaigned for the job. I hoped that my long friendship with the family, especially with Joe Kennedy, would have an impact on the decision, but I assumed Jackie knew her own mind. So I went to Nassau, and did not think about it . . . until the phone call from the President-elect's secretary.

I had two days. I was not prepared. I had no paper, no pencils, no ideas. I bought some paper in a store and sat, staring at the water. Nothing. Why did this always happen to me? Why did I always have to pull rabbits from my hat, under fire, under the most extreme pressure? It had been like that from the start, from the time I'd stayed up all night doing the sketches for Paramount in 1940. Actually, the memory of Paramount, and of designing clothes for the movies, proved to be something of an inspiration for me.

I thought: *Oleg, you have to do this as if you were designing for a star. You have to forget about the market, and what might sell, and the costs of production. You must forget all the things you've been dealing with for the past ten years and go back to the source. Think about the woman, and her role. Forget every other detail; think of Jackie. You know her taste better than any of your competitors. You know the people she sees and what she likes to wear. Think of Jackie and what she'd want for tea with the prime minister of India, or for a state dinner . . . or for the Inauguration itself.* And, in the process, I realized that it was time to be bold. Why not go all out? If I truly believed I could do the job better than anyone else, why not convince her to let me do it all?

This was, I assured myself, part of the grand design of my life. I had spent years preparing for this very opportunity. All the pieces fit, even the symbolic ones. I had been born to be of service to a royal court; it had been in the Cassini and Loiewski family genes for centuries. The Kennedy administration, with its gathering of artists, intellectuals, entertainers, and social samurai, was the closest America would come—in style, at least —to a royal court in my lifetime. I would present myself, not as some designer with pins in his mouth, but in the same manner as Arthur Cassini had—as a member of the court, a courtier who performed a valuable service. Certainly I had the social credentials for the role. I had been a designer-pugilist and a designer-adventurer. Why not a designer-courtier?

All I had to do now was convince Jackie Kennedy.

I had some good thoughts on the flight from Nassau—somehow I'm always more creative when I travel. And as I thought of Jackie, I reviewed my relationship with the Kennedy family over the years.

It had begun with an argument. Just after the war, when Igor was in his first days as Cholly Knickerbocker, he had written something nasty about Joe Kennedy, who immediately called William Randolph Hearst and demanded that the upstart be fired. "I'm not firing any columnist," Hearst reportedly said, "especially when he's doing precisely what I'm paying him to do. Look, this fellow is young and he's going to be around for a long time. You might as well get used to him. Why don't you invite him out for a drink?" Joe Kennedy did, and they became good friends. They were fellow golfers (indeed, they convinced me to take up the game, which I did at age forty-six) and neighbors at Palm Beach. Igor's in-laws, the Wrightsmans, lived several houses down from the Kennedys.

I admired Joe Kennedy. He was known as a pretty rough customer and certainly made his share of enemies, but there was a compelling charm to the man as well. He had mischievous, owlish eyes behind his horn-rimmed glasses and a knowing smile, a puckish sensibility that mocked his very direct manner. He conveyed a very strong sense of power and confidence; there was a real vitality to the man that lasted well past the age of seventy (it was there, in fact, until his crippling stroke in 1961). He pulled no punches, and divided the world into people he liked and those he didn't. But he was too intelligent to do this on a wholesale basis; he was no bigot. I enjoyed listening to him hold forth—on politics, on business, on anything—and he certainly liked having the audience. We had become friendly at a time when he decided to step away from the spotlight in order to make sure the attention was focused on his son Jack. But Joe was a strong enough personality to require his own circle of admirers, almost a salon, which he created for himself in New York at his favorite restaurant, La Caravelle.

Another reason Joe Kennedy and I became such good friends was that we shared an intense appreciation of beautiful women. He used to love to talk about them, about this one and that. We compared notes about Hollywood and New York; we knew many of the same people.

We did more than talk, too: we socialized with groups of people, especially in New York. There was a routine to this. We met every Tuesday night at 8:00 at La Caravelle. I would usually bring some lady friends—top models or society girls—although, on several occasions, Joe did the honors (and, believe me, he knew some real beauties). Despite his marriage, he felt no restrictions about being seen in the company of beautiful women. He always wanted to know in advance who was coming, and within a matter of hours he would check them out. Then he'd surprise them at dinner, knowing where they came from and how long they'd been in town; he could make this seem quite flattering, but it actually was a matter of security.

His manner was always very direct, very forceful, an outpouring of career advice and mild flirtation that was at once rather blunt and totally disarming. Staring intently, he might say, "You know, you're not going to be a model all your life. You need to plan for your future, start a career. You're going to need friends in the right places, people who can help you along the way."

Then he'd mention that he'd gotten this girl or that started at the Chicago Merchandise Mart, which he owned, and finally offer this advice: "There are two types of men, the givers and the takers. The givers may not be angels, but you'll wind up better off for having known them. Watch out for the takers, though. They're not much fun to be with, they'll leave you in the lurch, and they never really make it in life."

His intentions in all this were rather innocent. He wanted the beautiful company, the mild flirtation, and the sense that he was at center stage. I would take the girls home at the end of an evening.

There was a good deal more to our friendship than these dinners, though. I think Joe and I were bonded by our differences. He had a fantastic mind—not very cultured, but clear, analytical, a get-to-the-point sort of mind. I was just the opposite, of course. I lived in the realm of fantasy and romance, and wasn't very clever at getting to the nitty-gritty, especially when it came to business. I would pose what would seem a difficult business problem to him and he'd say, "Donkey! You're such a donkey, don't you see?"

He loved giving advice, talking strategy. He liked listening to my ideas and proposals and analyzing them; we discussed several business propositions. At one point, we considered obtaining a license to distribute some of the better European designers in the United States (this was well before licensing became the business it is today). We also talked about starting a super modeling agency. I loved listening to him talk about deals, about buying the Chicago Merchandise Mart and his maneuvers on Wall Street. He thought in tens of millions, routinely tossing off sums of money that were astounding to me. He told some great stories about wheeling and dealing. For example, he said he escaped the Stock Market Crash of 1929 while getting his shoes shined. "The shoe-shine boy told me he had just bought some RCA Radio and asked me what I thought," he said. "I figured if shine boys were in the market, the whole thing was just too damn risky, so I pulled out."

There was another time when everyone on Wall Street thought he was about to go under. "So I bought myself a new Rolls-Royce and had my chauffeur drive me around the financial district at all hours. People judge you by things of that kind. They would say, 'The word on Joe mustn't be true.' So, listen to me, donkey: when you're on the spot, spend. Be bold. It's the only way to win."

He also loved to talk about his children, all of whom were winners in his mind. "Bobby is the one who is most like me," he said. "Jack is different, though. He will always conquer his enemies with charm." Sometimes, he would grow wistful for the oldest son, his namesake, Joe, who died in the war. "He was the best of the lot," he would say. "He could have been president."

I once had a few dates with his daughter Eunice, which he did not like. "She is not your type," he said.

Rose Kennedy and I were also pals. Sometimes I would make clothes for her, and I found her fascinating because of her *joie de vivre*. Rose loved to go to parties and made no bones about it. I once had her invited to the Bachelors' Ball in New York. She came alone, and danced all night long, and had a hell of a time.

It is rather ironic, I think, that this proud old man was kept very much in the background after his son was elected president. Joe understood that his presence might underscore the rumors that he was really running the show. He also understood that his past—which the commentators always called "controversial"—might be bad politically for his son.

So, my initial and closest friendship was with the parents, not the son. Joe Kennedy spoke up for me, though. He told Jack, "Don't worry about Oleg. He's a good guy. You can trust him."

But Jack Kennedy was not the sort of man to forget. He knew that I'd been with him all the way. Our friendship had grown. I watched him develop from an uncertain young man whose health was precarious into an assured world leader; and I watched him, as president, move from caution to confidence. Jack was a handsome man, tall (about six foot one), with a golden aura about him. He had a sly, modest sort of charm; very clever, but careful too—never a false step. He was curious about everything; he was a great listener. (a very important quality in a president). Jack dominated a conversation through his questions and brief, incisive editorial comments. He enjoyed talking to me, I think, because my background was so different from anything he'd experienced before; he appreciated my classical education. We often discussed history, which was a common interest, as well as more mundane things. Like his father, Jack enjoyed talking about women. He always wanted to know what made one woman a champion, a star, while another—equally attractive, and equally talented, perhaps—never made it. "I would hate to have to compete against you for a woman," he once told me. "You'd be the toughest."

I might say here that I was later astounded when I heard all the stories about John Kennedy and women. I know that the Kennedys had a rather continental approach to marriage. Jack appreciated women . . . but I never actually saw any evidence of his acting on his predilections, certainly not during the White House years, when I was around most weekends. I am no innocent, but I suspect that a mountain has been made from a molehill here.

In any case, over time, Jack Kennedy came to know that I was in his corner. There was one thing in particular he never forgot: during the West Virginia primary campaign against Hubert Humphrey, I contributed $1,500. I never knew that Jack would even be aware of it. But after the election, he was very flattering, saying, "You and Fifi Fell were my only friends who came through for me then."

I had a sense—a very strong sense, early on—that he was going to be president. I remember having lunch with him at the Colony sometime in the mid-1950s and telling him, "Senator, you're going to do it. You'll get the women's vote." I was always very formal in addressing him, despite our friendship; later, it would be "Mr. President." I sensed that he liked that and wasn't too happy when people called him "Jack."

I remember, too, a lunch with Drew Pearson in Washington before the campaign began. "I think Symington has the nomination locked up," he said.

"I'm not so sure," I said. "I will go for Kennedy."

"Well, that's the difference between the people and the pros," he said. "You'll see what happens."

I saw. And it happened.

I had first met Jacqueline Bouvier at El Morocco, several weeks before she married young Senator Kennedy. She was there with Stanley Mortimer, a very handsome and social fellow who was married to Babe Cushing (who later married William Paley). They invited me to join them for a drink, and I was very curious about this girl whom young Kennedy had chosen to marry. Obviously she was *somebody*, a real presence in the room. She was quite attractive, well schooled, and charming: the classic debutante, but something more, too. All eyes seemed to gravitate toward her; she had real star quality, even then. We engaged in some light banter.

"What a shame you're getting married when there are fellows like Mortimer and me to get involved with," I said.

"And what sort of fellows are you?"

She had a great wit, combined with an intellectual intensity. She would listen carefully to what you were saying; I always felt the need to be at my cleverest in her presence. She demanded excellence from her friends and acquaintances; in return, she had the ability—well before she arrived at the White House—to make everyone around her feel part of a small, privileged circle. This quiet, private force of personality was quite in contrast with the rather shy public presence, the tiny, whispery public voice. But then, Jackie was famous for her elusiveness, her shifting moods. She was an original and difficult to decipher. She might be very warm one day and freeze you out the next; she did this to everyone, even her closest friends. She could charm the birds out of the trees at times; and then there were almost hermetic periods, when she refused to leave her room, reading, corresponding. She perplexed the Kennedys; she seemed quite a challenge to me. You never really knew where you stood with Jackie. I never quite knew on which foot to dance.

Actually, we did go dancing together on several occasions in Palm Beach after she was married. Senator Kennedy was ailing—he was about to have surgery on his back—and I escorted Jackie around town in his absence to several parties.

Palm Beach seemed an American Riviera in those days; all the social people were there. It was where the best parties were held and where the finest golfers and polo players gathered for the winter. I knew everyone: Michael Butler, who later produced the musical *Hair*, was a friend from fox hunting and skiing and had a house there; Rubirosa often came for the polo; Chris Dunphy; Raymond and Winston Guest; Bing Crosby (a frequent visitor from the West Coast); and a younger friend, the local Adonis, Mickey Van Gerbig, whose family had been among the pillars of Palm Beach society and who introduced me to the major golf tournaments. Igor was often there with his in-laws, and I sometimes stayed at Charles Wrightsman's formidable estate on the beach, which was stuffed with French eighteenth-century antiques, priceless paintings, and *objets*.

The Kennedy house was pleasantly situated, but not quite as spectacular as Wrightsman's. It had a comfortable, informal feeling—the furnishings were of a sort that could survive the marauding swarms of children who wrought havoc there. I remember sitting on the porch at sunset with Joe Kennedy one evening during the period when I was squiring Jackie about.

"Look, Oleg," he said abruptly, "I wouldn't be surprised if you have some ideas about Jackie. If the situation were different, I might have some ideas about her myself. But the question is: essence versus perception. I don't care what you do, but it must not be perceived. The worst thing, to my mind, would be to have the perception but not the reality—that would be silly, a real donkey's game. You understand?"

In any event, there was nothing between Jackie and me. I found her fascinating . . . and when I began to think about it, designing for her posed a most invigorating challenge. Her taste was so demanding, her sense of style so exquisite, that I was certain she would not settle for a wardrobe that was anything less than my very best work. It was a daunting proposition, but my excitement and confidence were growing: I began to take what I knew about her, about her taste and sense of style, and create the first outlines of a wardrobe on the flight back from Nassau to New York in early December of 1960. I thought about the times we had spent together in Palm Beach, and conjured up images of her in my mind.

Many of the images were Egyptian. There was her sphinxlike quality and her eyes, which were classically, very beautifully set. When I thought of Jackie, I saw a hieroglyphic figure: the head in profile, broad shoulders, slim torso, narrow hips, long neck, and good carriage. Never underestimate the importance of good shoulders: they and a long waist are the most necessary pieces of equipment when it comes to wearing clothes, and these she had. The rest was easy. I imagined her as an ancient Egyptian princess, dressed cleanly, architecturally, a very basic A line. I called it the "A Look." It would be simplicity plus: I would use the most sumptuous fabrics in the purest interpretations. My designs had to suit not only a lady with well-defined preferences but also a public figure whose life was governed by the strictest protocol.

I landed in New York with about twenty sketches, rushed to my office and checked the fabrics and colors available, then amplified the working sketches, enlarged them, placed them in a portfolio. Then I rushed back to the airport, got on a plane for Washington, and went directly to the hospital in Georgetown.

Immediately, though, I was surprised to see, upon entering her room, sketches all around her, by the best American designers—Norell, Sarmi, Andreas of Bergdorf Goodman, etc. I wasn't daunted by the quality of their work; indeed, it seemed to me they hadn't put enough thought into it. The sketches were the best of their collections—very pretty dresses. But I was proposing something much more elaborate: I was proposing an entire new look, my interpretation of how Jacqueline Bouvier Kennedy might want to play the role of First Lady. *None* of my designs were from my collection; I had invented them specifically for her. I was confident that she would understand my intention, but I *was* concerned that she would use *all* of these designers, which would create a confused fashion message. Jackie was at her most charming that day, and greeted me as an old friend, not a potential employee auditioning to do her bidding. This put me at ease. "How was it in Nassau?" she asked. "Did you have fun?"

We talked awhile about this and that, people we knew, anything but the matter at hand—which I was now rather reluctant to even mention. Finally, she said, "So, Oleg, what do you have for me?"

"Of course, I am flattered by this invitation," I said. "But look what you have around you here. All these people want to do something for you. They are all very fine, but I think it would be impossible for you to work that way. Your life will only be fittings, and people coming and going. My feeling is that you need to choose one designer, someone who will see the whole picture and create an entire concept for you. I don't intend to merely give you the best of my collection, as these other talented gentlemen have. What I've done is created a vision only for you, and I think it would be too confusing to be just one of many people designing for you . . . so, thanks for asking me here, I am very flattered, but I don't think this would be a good idea."

"Yes," she said, "but could you show me your sketches anyway?"

I opened the portfolio. The first sketch was of a simple white satin full-length evening dress that I thought would be right for the Inaugural Ball. I watched her carefully for a reaction and it was immediate, visceral.

"Absolutely right!" she said.

I described the dress in more detail. The most emphatic thing about it would be the fabric, an opulent Swiss double satin; the lines were unusually modest—there was a cleanliness to it—but the quantity of the fabric and the luxury of the satin made it regal, and altogether memorable. I told her how it would set a tone for the administration; I talked about history, the message her clothes could send—simple, youthful, but magisterial elegance—and how she would reinforce the message of her husband's administration through her appearance.

"You have an opportunity here," I said, "for an American Versailles."

She understood completely what I was trying to communicate; she began to talk excitedly about the need to create an entirely new atmosphere at the White House. She wanted it to become the social and intellectual capital of the nation. She would bring the great writers, artists, and musicians there. The food and wine and service would be impeccable.

The house itself would be restored. Everything would be swept aside: the styleless old furniture would go, replaced by antiques. "The White House looks like a Statler hotel," she said.

In retrospect, I believe she almost single-handedly created a revolution in good taste. Certainly she began the movement in America to restore the architectural treasures of the past, rather than knock them down and build anew. Eventually, her tour of the restored White House would be one of the most watched television programs of the early 1960s. But that was nothing compared with her impact on the world of fashion.

The clothes I had designed for her—simple, elegant, classic—fit perfectly into her program. From my knowledge of her taste, I had been able to predict her intentions. She especially loved the Inaugural dress. She wanted it . . . but there was a problem: she had already ordered a dress from Bergdorf's. It would be too embarrassing to renege. Her solution was to wear my dress to the Gala, the fabulous show that Frank Sinatra organized for the night before the Inauguration.

Later, her secretary, Mary Gallagher, would write in her memoirs:

> I can tell you that the Inaugural Ball gown was not Jackie's favorite. She much preferred the Gala gown, the utterly simple white one—unrelieved except for a geometric design, of the same material, at the waist —which had been made by Oleg Cassini. . . . In fact, Jackie wanted to have the Smithsonian Institution display her Gala gown instead of the Inaugural one, and I was still fighting that battle for a long time after the Kennedys moved into the White House.

(The Smithsonian, however, stood firmly on tradition, and it was only after a lengthy exchange of letters and ten months that the Inaugural gown was reluctantly sent.)

I proceeded to show Mrs. Kennedy the rest of my sketches, and the reaction continued very strong. The second one, I believe, was of a simple cloth coat with a pillbox hat that I proposed she wear to the Inauguration itself. "You see," I told her, "all the other women there will be wearing furs. This coat will set you apart, emphasize your youth—and the President's, too. It will set the tone for the whole administration."

I believed what I was saying, but I was still astounded when the very thing came true on January 20. The fawn beige wool coat, with a small sable collar and muff—and accompanied by a matching pillbox hat—was an immediate sensation. It was the beginning of what came to be known as the "Jackie Look." There was a run on pillbox hats in the stores; within a matter of hours, it seemed, copies of my coat had sprouted on every rack. And there was an explosion of media interest in Jacqueline Kennedy; there has been nothing like it since. The Jackie Look would sweep the world, giving worldwide recognition, for the first time, to an American designer.

But this was all difficult to foresee as I stood beside the hospital bed and Jackie appraised my sketches, saying, "Yes, yes, yes, and yes." And finally, "Well, I'm convinced. You're the one."

"But I'll only do it if I'm the only one," I said. "Otherwise it's too much of a logistical problem."

"Can you do it by yourself, though?" she asked. "I'm going to need an awful lot of clothes."

"Sure I can," I said, only then beginning to realize what a tremendous undertaking this would be. I would have to create a separate operation, devoted entirely to making the First Lady's clothes; it would be expensive, although the honor and the challenge would make it all worthwhile. This would be *haute couture* at its very highest and purest level. (I should mention here the financial arrangement we had. Joe Kennedy said to me, "Don't bother them at all about the money, just send me an accounting at the end of the year. I'll take care of it." He asked me to be discreet about the cost of the operation, as it might be used politically against the President. And I have been.)

After I left the hospital, the car took me to the Kennedy home in Georgetown, where the President-elect was in the midst of choosing a secretary of state. "Well, Oleg," he said, "how did things go with Jackie?"

"Very well, I think, Mr. President," I said. "She asked me to design all her clothes."

He smiled and said, "And you're sure that's what you want? You wouldn't rather be commissioner of Indian affairs?"

"No, Mr. President," I said. "The Indians will have to wait... although you shouldn't neglect them, either."

Several days later, Jackie sent me the following letter:

December 13, 1960

Dear Oleg,

Thank heavens all the furor is over—and done without breaking my word to you or Bergdorfs. Now I know how poor Jack feels when he has told 3 people they can be Secy. of State.

But I do think it turned out nicely for you—no?—and you were charming & gallant & a gentleman & everything you should be and are.

This letter is just a series of incoherent thoughts that I must get settled so I can spend these next weeks truly recuperating & not have to think about details, otherwise I will be a wreck & not strong enough to do everything I have to do.

1) I wired Bergdorf to send you my measurements so you can go ahead with clothes....

2) For every evening dress I order from you, will you please send a color swatch to

> a) Mario—at Eugenia of Florence to have evening shoes made—State if shoes should be satin or faille—if necessary send material to make shoes in—& tell him to hurry.
>
> b) to KORET— some man there...makes me matching evening bags simple envelopes or squares....Send him same material as dress—If you can do these 2 things you don't know the headaches it will save me.
>
> c) also to Marita—Custom Hats at Bergdorf Goodman's—send color swatch....She does my hats and gloves—tell her what color for each.

3) Diana Vreeland will call you about...dress she wants for Bazaar—If I can't have fitting before they can always pin it in with clothes pegs for marvelous Avedon picture.

4) Do send me sketches of cape or coat to wear with your white dress for Inaug Gala Jan. 19. It must be just as pure and regal as the dress.

5) Check with me before you cut orange organza dress—It is the only one I am not completely sure of—remember I thought of pink....

6) I seem to be all set for evening. Now would you put your brilliant mind to work for day—Coats—dresses for public appearances—lunch & afternoon that I would wear if Jack were President of FRANCE—très Princesse de Rethy mais jeune....

ARE YOU SURE YOU ARE UP TO IT, OLEG? Please say yes—There is so much detail about one's wardrobe once one is in the public eye. I simply cannot spend the time on it any more than I have this fall—I will never see my children or my husband or be able to do the million things I'll

have to do—I am counting on you to be a superb Wardrobe Mistress—
every glove, shoe, hat etc.—& all delivered on time. You are organized for
that—being in New York—better than I—If you need to hire another
secretary just for me do it and we'll settle the financial end together.

7) PUBLICITY—One reason I am so happy to be working with you
is that I have some control over my fashion publicity which has gotten so
vulgarly out of hand—I don't mind your saying now the dresses I have
chosen from you—as I am so happy if it has done you any good—& proud
to have you, a gentleman, doing clothes for the wife of the President. I will
never become stuffy—but there is dignity to the office which suddenly hits
one....

BUT—you realize I know that I am so much more of fashion interest
than other First Ladies—I refuse to have Jack's administration plagued
by fashion stories of a sensational nature—& to be the Marie Antoinette
or Josephine of the 1960's—So I will have to go over it with you before we
release future things—because I don't want to seem to be buying too
much—You can make the stories available—but with my approval first—
There just may be a few things we won't tell them about! But if I look
impeccable the next four years everyone will know it is you....

8) COPIES—Just make sure no one has exactly the same dress I
do—the same color or material—Imagine you will want to put some of my
dresses in your collection—but I want all mine to be original & no fat little
women hopping around in the same dress. You know better than I how to
protect yourself against other manufacturers running up cheap copies—I
really don't care what happens later as long as when I wear it first it is new
& the only one in the room....

Now poor Oleg you don't have to read any more—Just some tiny last
things to say to you.

1) Forgive me for not coming to you from the very beginning. I am so
happy now.

2) Protect me—as I seem so mercilessly exposed & don't know how to
cope with it (I read tonight I dye my hair because it is mousy gray!).

3) Be efficient—by getting everything on time & relieving me of
worry about detail.

4) Plan to stay for dinner every time you come to D.C. with
sketches—& amuse the poor President & his wife in that dreary Maison
Blanche—& be discreet about us—though I don't have to tell you that—
you have too much taste to be any other way.

310

5) I always thought if Jack & I went on an official trip to France I would secretly get Givenchy to design my clothes so I wouldn't be ashamed—but now I know I won't have to—yours will be so beautiful— That is le plus grand compliment I can give you—as a designer anyway!

XO
Jackie

I was astounded by the organization of her mind, and her awareness of all the details that might arise. It seems remarkable now how well she understood the problems we would face—and the successes that would be possible to achieve. So much in that letter predicted the next three years: the many evenings I spent in Washington, the "fashion stories of a sensational nature." I especially enjoy the reference to Givenchy, who later would make something of a fool of himself regarding the clothes I had designed....

There is one reference that is easily overlooked but shouldn't be, as it was the key to our relationship: Jackie referred to me as a "gentleman." She knew my background. She knew that even though I was an American designer, I had a continental sense of the relationship between couturier and customer; that I would pamper her in my way and yet remain an intellectual—and social—equal. Indeed, in the years to come, she would often consult me about whom to invite to White House parties. The Agnellis and others were asked as a result. Jackie knew she could feel secure with me in matters of style. We might have differences of opinion on this dress or that color, but our frame of reference—social, intellectual, fashion—was the same.

But the first, and most immediate, crisis I faced ("ARE YOU SURE YOU ARE UP TO IT, OLEG?") was organization. In a matter of days, I had to hire a *première*, an assistant to research fabrics and colors, a draper, a cutter, and sample hands (eight in all). One of my regular staff designers also assisted on the project. A room was set up specially for the work. We had three fitting mannequins in Jackie's measurements, plus a live model in Jackie's size. When a dress or outfit was finished, I would have the model put it on and walk around in it, so I could decide what accessories to suggest, and to make sure everything appeared to be in order. My assistant, Kay McGowan, would supervise the fittings in Washington and act as liaison between Mrs. Kennedy and me. I had someone working in Europe, scouring France and Italy for the finest fabrics—the operation was incredible.

I called those first two or three weeks "the frantic period." There were constant letters and phone calls: "Hurry, hurry, I don't have any clothes." There was great pressure to provide clothes quickly. In fact, I don't think we ever really caught up. We did more than one hundred dresses that first year, perhaps three hundred during the course of the administration, an amazing number. It seemed we always were rushing to get something done. Rushing to get ten dresses onto *Air Force One* for the trip to France and Vienna for the summit with Khrushchev . . . Once, during a snowstorm, due to a breakdown in communications, someone had forgotten to send a car to pick me up upon my arrival at Washington's Union Station. I had to queue up with hundreds of other passengers for a cab, along with twelve large boxes filled with the First Lady's clothes. I finally shared a taxi with three other people. I said to the driver, "The White House, please." They all looked at me. Naturally, we were stopped at the gate. I announced myself, and the guard made a hurried call: "The Oleg Cassini team and Mrs. Kennedy's wardrobe have arrived," after which we drove up to the front entrance.

The first crisis was over the cloth coat Mrs. Kennedy wore to the Inauguration: it had only a thin silk lining, and she was going to have to wear it on a brutally cold day, the day after a terrible blizzard. This oversight was discovered only when she tried on the coat for a final fitting the day before the ceremony. I had to race about Washington—there was no time to send it back to New York—for someone to install a warmer lining. At the last moment, I located a store, a client of mine, on Connecticut Avenue that could do it, working all night. I remember standing there shivering in my heavy coat and scarf as John F. Kennedy took the Oath of Office and thinking, *She must be freezing!* But she looked so fabulous and happy, so perfectly happy . . . and the reaction to the coat was so positive. It could easily have been the end for me. She might have said, "Well, if this is the best you can do, forget it!" But we went on from there, and created magic together.

Our business relationship worked in this way. She would send me a list of things she needed (for example: "Three daytime linen or shantung [dresses]—one with a jacket, one with nothing, one with a coat? or maybe two with jackets?" or, "Three dressier afternoon dresses—2 piece shantung with straw hat, white with black polka dots, another not too décolleté . . ."). We might discuss these ideas further by telephone; often, too, we would talk theoretically, about fashion concepts, the message we thought her wardrobe should convey. Jackie played a very active role in

312

the selection of her clothes. She loved brilliant colors—pistachio, hot pink, yellow, and white, among others. Her sense of style was very precise; she would make editorial comments on the sketches I sent her. She always knew exactly what she wanted; her taste was excellent. To paraphrase Oscar Wilde: it was very simple—she liked only the very best.

After her initial requests and our phone conversations, I would send her sketches, with swatches of fabric. She might order ten at a time, which would be created in my New York design room and fitted on a model; then Kay McGowan would take a group of them to Washington for a final fitting . . . and that is where we sometimes had problems. A sketch is a sketch, and a dress can turn out to look like something else entirely. A small percentage of the dresses we made were rejected outright; others were sent back for refitting and revisions because the color or the fabric was wrong. For example, there was one red wool hunting coat that I especially liked but that was rejected because the fabric was too heavy.

Our working relationship became easier over time as the team became more efficient. By March of 1962, when Jackie went to India and Pakistan with her sister, Lee Radziwill, we were doing quite well together, and I did the clothing for both Jackie and Lee. On March 26, Mrs. Kennedy sent me a congratulatory note from Pakistan that read in part:

> This is just to tell you that all your clothes were an absolute dream and I was delighted with them. The white coat is ESPECIALLY lovely and really looks outstanding. They are all now in a rather pathetic condition after 3 weeks of 1 night stands, and well worn. I only wish I'd gotten more, but next time I'll know better.
>
> It seemed that "Oleg Cassini" were the words most often heard by the Indians and Pakistanis, and they'll be expecting you out there to redesign their saris! When I get home I'll send you some sketches, ideas, etc., of what I would like, as I've decided to hell with Paris! You're much better, not to mention nicer.

There were some things on which Jacqueline Kennedy and I never agreed. Paris was one. She had a certain reverence for the French houses of couture, especially Balenciaga and Givenchy. She once asked me to go to Paris, to give myself a panoramic view of what the others were doing. "You owe it to yourself," she would say. "Besides, you have all your friends there."

"Fine," I told her, "although there is little point. The truth is, you don't have to be Michelangelo to be a good dress designer, and there are only a few of all those who are so breathlessly lionized who actually can be considered great."

To be great, I thought, you had to create a look that was distinctively yours. The Chanel suit. The Pucci print. Dior's "New Look." Certainly Balenciaga and Givenchy and the others did some great work; there were many individual dresses of theirs that I admired very much. But it was possible to see a splendid woman at a ball and not know that her exquisite dress came from Balenciaga or Givenchy or perhaps even Cassini. The very distinctive Jackie Look that I created was as much a consequence of Mrs. Kennedy's prominence as it was of my creativity. It was a joint venture. I am, in fact, equally proud of the new look in men's wear that I would create several years later when I introduced deep-colored shirts. It was easy then to see a man walking down the street and say, "Oh, he's wearing a Cassini shirt. That is a Cassini color."

In any case, I went to Paris and visited the collections. I was quite well-received there, invited without charge to all the shows (normally, guests are required to buy two dresses or pay the equivalent as a fee; this is very strictly enforced to guard against those who come merely to steal ideas); indeed, several of the great couturiers took me aside and suggested we work together.

It was part of my responsibility to select accessories for Mrs. Kennedy—but we used very little jewelry or other frills, which would detract from the monastic simplicity of her wardrobe. And, in deference to Jackie's admiration for Balenciaga's work, I bought her two dresses from his collection. I thought they were quite charming; she didn't. "You purposely picked the two worst dresses in his collection," she said.

"That is not so," I told her. "First of all, any dress Balenciaga puts in his collection is one that he thinks is good, just like any other designer. Second, I picked these because I liked them and thought you would, too."

She would not be placated, though—until her sister showed up several weeks later, having chosen one of the very same Balenciagas herself. This re-emphasized my oft-stated point to Jackie about the subjectivity of fashion.

Jackie had an idea about the image that I should project now that I had been designated her official designer. She felt that I could retire to an ivory tower, emerging only occasionally to make a "grand statement"—a fashion guru, the ultimate arbiter of taste, which was very flattering. I believe fashion is to be taken seriously, but not reverently. I believe fashion is an *applied* art meant to enhance and reflect. It augments the true creation: the woman who wears the clothes. Jackie and I agreed that fashion anticipates, and elegance is a state of mind. It is a mirror of the time in which we live, a translation of the future, and should never be static.

I was quite opposed to the course of action proposed by some of my colleagues during that time, which was to use my new status commercially. "Look," I was told, "one day he will not be president and you'll regret you didn't take advantage of your opportunity. You're too sensitive to their wishes."

My feeling was that the designation itself had been a significant honor; essentially, I continued on with my life and business as I had in the past.

The wisdom of this course was confirmed within days of the Inauguration. The Jackie Look had an immediate impact on fashion all over the world. Every girl in Paris seemed to be wearing a simple A-line dress, a pillbox hat, medium-heeled pumps, and her hair in a bouffant that year. It was the first time in history that a look had originated in America and overtaken the world. My role in creating that look was duly noted and I became the first American designer whose name was recognized internationally. In America, there was no contest. On October 25, 1961, Eugenia Sheppard reported in her influential column: "According to Tobe's most recent coast-to-coast survey, the best-known name in American fashion is Oleg Cassini."

This was apparently too much for Paris to handle. Monsieur Givenchy, in particular, had a difficult time, and in an act unworthy of a man of his talent, he leaked the spurious story that Lee Radziwill was covertly buying his dresses for her sister and I was taking the credit. When she learned of this, Jackie sent me a note, which read in part:

Before you explode with a cry that can be heard echoing all down 7th Avenue . . . (I should explode—isn't it breaking the law what Givenchy said I supposedly did!) . . . Just realize . . . it makes him look so absurd to be feeding out these petty stories about Lee & me. I thought he was too grand to show annoyance—so this is rather pleasant.

I have not gotten anything from him since last June—Versailles. If anyone asks you about the story just smile rather patronizingly and say, "Mr. Givenchy must be feeling the heat wave in Paris," or something very light & unconcerned—Also you could say, "A look at Mrs. K's clothes for India & Mexico, for example, will show you that they were not Givenchy inspired."

This writing paper was especially designed for writing heads of state—do you think it is good enough?

It was lovely to see you if only for a minute—

Until September.

Love,
Jackie

Jackie had bought one evening dress from Givenchy, which she wore as a gesture to France, and she was kind enough to send me a telegram from France to explain this to me. All the rest of her wardrobe for the state visit to France was by Oleg Cassini, and was greatly acclaimed by the press. But there always seemed to be controversies.

The famous pillbox hat is one that has continued for decades. In truth, it was a collaborative effort. The question of a hat arose after I had shown Mrs. Kennedy my new sketch design for the beige Inaugural coat, which showed a pillbox hat. She suggested that I consult with Diana Vreeland about it, which I did.

"The hat," I suggested, "should be an extension of the coat, rather than a message in itself."

"*Bien sûr,*" Mrs. Vreeland said, in her distinctive manner, and we began to discuss particulars. Because of Mrs. Kennedy's bouffant hairstyle (which she had started wearing earlier in the year), the hat would have to sit toward the back of her head. A beret was a possibility, but perhaps too informal for the occasion. Eventually we agreed that a pillbox look would work; the actual execution of the hat was done by Marita at Bergdorf Goodman, Mrs. Kennedy's preferred hatmaker. And so, it was rather surprising, many years later, to read in the *New York Times* that Halston had created the pillbox. An outright lie, and an attempted revision of fashion history.

To check the flow of misinformation and fashion gossip about Jackie, a letter was sent by Tish Baldrige, her social secretary, to the editor of *Women's Wear Daily* in early January 1961 that read in part:

Dear Sir,

I write to you at the suggestion of Mrs. John F. Kennedy, regarding several erroneous articles about her clothes, which have appeared in your publication during the past few months. . . . Mrs. Kennedy realizes that the clothes she wears are of interest to the public, but she is distressed by the implications of extravagance, of overemphasis of fashion in relation to her life, and the misuse of her name by firms from which she has not bought clothes. For the next four years, Mrs. Kennedy's clothes will be made by Oleg Cassini. They will be designed and made in America. She will buy what is necessary without extravagance. . . . Should you receive a report that Mrs. Kennedy has ordered clothes not made by Mr. Cassini, I would appreciate it if you would call me and I will give you a prompt and accurate answer.

Mr. John Fairchild of *WWD* approached me and asked if I would show him advance sketches of what Mrs. Kennedy would be wearing to various important events. I could not grant him his wish on two grounds. First, Mrs. Kennedy often left the final decision to the last moment; there might be two or three possibilities, and I could not guarantee which one she would choose. More important, of course, was the discretion I had promised her. It would have been disloyal and incorrect to leak sketches.

Ultimately, *WWD* did pay Jackie and me a tribute. On April 7, 1964, Ted James wrote the following in his *WWD* column:

The Kennedy era in Washington was one of elegance, glamour and good taste which affected the entire nation and probably the entire world. Elegance and taste surrounded every movement of the first family and America watched, learned, absorbed and copied. There is no doubt that Mrs. Jacqueline Kennedy probably did more to uplift taste levels in the United States than any woman in the history of our country. And, there is no doubt that the entire fashion industry received a major shot in the arm as a result of the constant stream of reports on what Mrs. Kennedy was wearing and where she wore it.

Among the clothes she wore, there are many which certainly can be considered important in fashion, as well as of historical interest. There was her official wardrobe by Oleg Cassini which she wore on her state visit to India and Pakistan, the Cassini gowns she wore when she met Premier Khrushchev in Vienna, Queen Elizabeth at Buckingham Palace, the long black dress she wore when she visited the Vatican, the blue straw lace dress she wore in Paris at Versailles . . . the one General de Gaulle liked so much, and the gown she wore when the Shah of Iran and other heads of state visited the White House and Mount Vernon.

There are in existence original sketches and undoubtedly the correspondence which the former First Lady had with Mr. Cassini about her wardrobe. . . . In all humility, I suggest that these designs, correspondence and gowns of historical importance be placed in either the

Kennedy Museum in Boston, the Costume Institute of the Metropolitan Museum of Art, or the Smithsonian Institution in Washington.

I have quoted liberally from Mr. James's column because I believe it reflects the judgment of history on the magic that Mrs. Kennedy and I created during that time. Unfortunately, his suggestion that all the sketches, correspondence, and gowns be collected in one place has never been realized; indeed, much of the correspondence was stolen from me.

There were efforts, both open and surreptitious, to replace me with some other designers, both foreign and American, or broaden the field to include a gaggle of others. This, I thought, was to be expected: my position was such a plum, and there were more than a few designers who, no doubt, would have done just about anything to supplant me. It was always very gratifying—the highest honor imaginable—that, despite these campaigns, Jackie Kennedy always stood by me. She never wavered in her support.

Jackie's fashion influence was tremendous. The top executive in the belt industry, for example, told me that because Jackie so noticeably wore belts, the entire industry had been rejuvenated. This was the case with all the other realms of fashion as well. Jackie's name was continuously placed at the head of the "Ten Best Dressed" List. She was acclaimed by the international press, and behind the Iron Curtain, too, as the unchallenged leader of fashion. There were even ads from the Leningrad magazine *Mody* showing the Jackie Look.

In the end, my social position paid off for all of them. When I entered the White House through the front door and not the servants' entrance, the status and image of the American designer changed, not only in America, but throughout the world. It became more glamorous. I was a friend of the family. I wore a dinner jacket, not pins in my mouth. This was noted in the press; my name became recognized, and a valuable commodity. (Years later, the polls would still show that Dior and I were the two best-known designers in America.) Thus began the celebritization of fashion, a trend that eventually assumed major proportions; but make no mistake, the notion that a designer's very name might be so recognizable as to be marketable began right then and there.

There was another, more immediate impact that my status as a friend of the Kennedys had on the world of fashion: I was, at times, able to convince the President to allow Mrs. Kennedy to break new ground. The President took a great deal of interest in his wife's appearance. He was very proud of her. Often, she would put on impromptu fashion shows for him, and he would give opinions on what he liked and didn't like. In one instance, I designed a one-shouldered evening gown that the First Lady loved but was convinced she wouldn't be able to wear. "You're going to have to talk to the President about it," she told me. "I don't think he'll allow me to be photographed showing one shoulder. It's too advanced."

So I went to see the President, and talked to him about the role of fashion throughout history. "From the dawn of antiquity, the queen or high priestess has always set the style," I said. "That is her role in the society, to be a little advanced and thus admired by her people. You know how valuable Mrs. Kennedy has been to you in that regard. . . . In this particular case, I am proposing nothing outrageous or undignified; indeed, the look is more than three thousand years old. The ancient Egyptians would have considered this dress rather conservative!"

The President laughed and shook his head. "Okay, Oleg, you win."

Eventually, the First Lady and I were able to convince him to go even further and allow her to appear with both shoulders bare: a pink-and-white straw-lace dress with a matching cape that she much admired, and wore in France at Versailles; the strapless dress with encrusted jewels for the unveiling of the Mona Lisa at the National Gallery in Washington; the strapless dress for the Venezuelan trip and dinner at the residence of President Betancourt. After this breakthrough, strapless and one-shouldered gowns became popular looks for Jackie, who had such beautiful shoulders and could wear them so well.

President Kennedy and I often had long conversations about a great many subjects. My relationship with him was relaxed. I was devoted to him, playing a role that I knew well from my reading of history: I was a courtier, like Beau Brummel or Petronius, *Arbiter Elegantiarum.* I enjoyed his company. My sense of the President was that he felt constrained in the White House. He had a hunger for news of the outside world, and a need to be relieved of the immediate concerns of his office. He had an impish side, a great sense of humor, and loved to laugh. He saw the comical side of many activities that other men treated pompously. But, underneath it all, there was a large dose of fatalism and he believed in luck.

I could draw on the experiences of my lifetime and discuss the Russian mind, the *Kama Sutra*, American Indians, the difference in appeal of Tyrone Power and Errol Flynn, or the relative merits of Gina Lollobrigida and Jayne Mansfield. I would design conversations that I sensed he would enjoy.

He would remark how easy it was to be a businessman. "Try it," I would say. We would joke and talk about what he would do after the White House. He would laugh and say, "Maybe I'll join you in business, Oleg."

I wanted to be known, as any good courtier does, for my wit. I tried to emulate my grandfather Arthur, the ambassador, who made dinner-party conversation an art. Mother had told me that Grandfather would spend the better part of a day preparing for an important dinner, studying the background of each of the guests, preparing topics of conversation and anecdotes appropriate to that particular group of people. I had little time to make that effort—usually, I had no advance knowledge where I'd be seated at a White House party—but I always hoped my dinner companions would be able to say to the President afterward, "That Cassini's a very entertaining fellow."

The Kennedys' dinner parties at the White House were always witty and charming. Each guest was made to feel special, and the President and Jackie involved them in good-natured jokes. At one private dinner for Jackie's sister, a photo of Stash Radziwill and me was enlarged and made the table's centerpiece. The idea was that Stash and I were "lookalikes." This was good-natured kidding, but Franklin Roosevelt, Jr., became legitimately confused, and kept toasting me as Stash Radziwill in spite of knowing me since 1936.

Smaller dinners and especially luncheons were demanding. You had to be on your toes. I would often be at the White House, and at the various weekend and holiday retreats, when the President would dine informally with family and close friends—old friends, like George Plimpton, Chuck Spaulding, Lem Billings—who were a different group entirely from his political circle and his governmental advisors. The President would often have sport at our expense. Once he announced, "Oleg Cassini will now show us how to do the twist," which was the new dance sensation from the Peppermint Lounge in New York; and I did. Or he might announce, "Okay. . . . Speech! Speech! Oleg?" And then you would have to stand and hold forth on a topic of his choice and try to be clever about it. The first time he made such a request of me was at a formal dinner for seventy-five, including Jawaharlal Nehru. I was sitting at the President's table, and he summoned me up: "Speech! Speech! Oleg, a comment or two, if you will, on this party!"

My presentation proved to be inadvertently amusing. I had no idea how to begin. I was frozen for a moment, struck dumb, searching for a word. Finally, I began, "Well, I am only a technocrat, but . . . " Everyone laughed, and I gained the confidence to continue.

I also was not afraid to be silly, when it came to that. One night, after a White House dinner for the Indian ambassador, a small group of us gathered and I—having arranged myself in a costume consisting of an impromptu turban (a towel), robe, and fireplace implement—did an impression of a quiet evening at home with the great Mogul Indian emperor Akbar. Jackie was there; her sister, Lee, and her husband, Stash; Nicole and Hervé Alphand (the French ambassador) and their two lovely nieces; Cecil Beaton; Moira Shearer; Jocelyn Stevens; Nicole Fronchomme; and Benno Graziani. Benno was a close friend of the Kennedys' and also a friend to many other important world figures. He was an extraordinary wit, and he wouldn't think twice about flying from Paris for a party. Benno was the historian of *le tout monde*. He and I would demonstrate the hully-gully, which was *the* dance of the moment in Paris.

To spend time with the President was the conversational equivalent of athletic competition; you had to be prepared, and always on your toes. Whenever he asked my opinion of something—"Well, Oleg, what do you think of that?"—I felt the responsibility to be clever and not boring.

There were times when the President would take the next step and actually demand that his close friends—I thought of our small group as social samurai—compete for his amusement. I remember once in Palm Beach when he said, after lunch, "Okay, everyone, push-ups!" And we hit the floor. I won the competition with sixty-five push-ups, beating Howard Oxenberg by two, because I would not allow myself to stop until I knew that everyone else had quit.

But that was how it was with the Kennedys. Competition was prized; everyone competed. There was a continuing effort on the part of the President's sisters, Pat Lawford and Eunice Shriver, to arrange a pentathlon between Bobby and me. They insisted he would beat me, even though I had bested him on several occasions at tennis and skiing. Given Bobby's passionately competitive nature, this might well have been quite a contest; unfortunately, we were never able to arrange it.

The other side of that particular coin was a fierce family loyalty. The Kennedys were a tribe, and once the word had passed from the *paterfamilias* that I was to be trusted, I became a member in good standing. This meant frequent acts of friendship by them that were well beyond the call of duty. I remember a windy, blizzardy day in Chicago when I had a fashion show scheduled at Saks; there were chairs set out for three hundred, but five minutes before the program was to start, not a single guest had arrived. We were going to cancel, when two heavily bundled figures staggered in: Pat and Eunice. Laughingly, they insisted that I give the show for them alone, and I did.

On another occasion, a dinner at the White House for Prince Rainier and Grace Kelly, which I did not attend, Eunice made sure to mention to Jackie—in a way that Grace could not avoid hearing: "Aren't Oleg's clothes just the best!"

In return, I was always more than happy to participate in the various charity functions the Kennedys arranged. Often I would provide a fashion show for their dinners, as I did in 1961, at the Caritas Catholic Charities gala in Chicago. That occasion was marked by a telegram from the President:

> Caritas should be congratulated for having chosen you to put on the fashion show this year. It assures the success of the occasion. . . . Mrs. Kennedy and I hope the supply of dresses is not exhausted so that one can be sent to her at the White House.

Joan Kennedy, the beautiful wife of Senator Ted Kennedy, invited me one year to be the entertainment for a charity event in Boston, which Cardinal Cushing sponsored and attended. It was a repeat performance of one of the Caritas shows, and was heavily attended by nuns. Strangely enough, the nuns formed the most enthusiastic support for the show, wildly applauding my creations and the commentary that went with them. This occasion was also the beginning of a special relationship with Ted, the Kennedy whom up to that time I had known the least.

The President liked to make comments about my clothes, and I would always find some way to give him reason for comment, perhaps wearing red socks with dark velvet evening slippers, along with white flannel trousers, a blue blazer, silk shirt, and red tie. I would encourage him to dress more enterprisingly, and he was quite receptive. "Mr. President, there's been only one truly elegant man in this century, the duke of Windsor," I told him. "You could be the second. I could make you as important in the world of fashion as Jackie."

He was interested and perhaps a bit intrigued. Had he lived, there might have been important developments in this area, as I was beginning to make some headway. At one point, I bought him several ties, and Jackie wrote to me: "Jack ADORES his ties—they are so perfect—thought I would never be able to get him pretty ties again, now that I can't go to my old haunts—but these are better than any I ever saw. . . ."

Of course, Jack Kennedy had a nonchalant elegance that transcended anything he wore. I saw him with holes in his socks, baggy, worn suits, frayed shirts—it didn't make a difference. He always had style and a charming fatalism that never varied, even under the heaviest pressure.

I was there in the midst of the Cuban missile crisis. A state dinner had been planned, then canceled. A small group of us were asked to stay on. Bobby and Ethel, Lee Radziwill and her husband, Stash, were there; McGeorge Bundy drifted in and out, occasionally drawing the President aside for private consultation. It was a quiet, somber evening, but the President refused to seem depressed or overwhelmed by the immensity of the moment. At one point, after Bundy told him that the Russian ships carrying the missiles had apparently stopped en route to Cuba, he said, lightly, with a twinkle and a puff on his cigar, "Well, we still have twenty chances out of a hundred to be at war with Russia."

There was always that elegant fatalism to him: "I'll do my best, in my style, and leave the rest to God."

He believed in God. "I'd better keep my nose clean, just in case He's up there," he'd say. He was so publicly devout; I wondered how he really felt about organized religion. I cited the dictum in *The Prince* about the impossibility of conforming to conventional moral dictates if one was to be a successful monarch.

"I acknowledge that," he said. "A leader has to be flexible, but there are boundaries that cannot be crossed. And the leader also has a responsibility to set an example for his people."

"You mean going to church on Sunday?" I said, and he laughed. On other occasions, I would taunt him lightly, as I had Grace Kelly, about the notion of papal infallibility and other mysteries of the faith, but he refused to take the bait. "The weakness of man should not weaken the image of God," he would say.

We often discussed morality and moral systems. I told him about the *Kama Sutra.* "It's not just the eighty-six positions—I'm convinced, by the way, that no one has ever tried all of them successfully and lived—it is a guide to the achievement of happiness through the perfect knowledge of another, and this can only be done through love."

He was very interested in this topic, and I would discuss with him the other moral systems in the ancient world, the rules that governed polygamy, the various conceptions of fidelity that varied from culture to culture. We would have these conversations, just the two of us, over brandy and cigars. He mused that Pierre Salinger had the best life: "Every other week in Paris, eating at the best restaurants, and smoking Cuban cigars." He favored long, very slim cigars, and at one point he warned me: "Oleg, better stock up—we're going to boycott Cuba."

I could have made a fortune off this tip, but of course I would never take advantage in that way, and the President knew it (I did, however, lay in a generous supply for my personal use).

One of the things he most enjoyed talking about was women. We discussed what constituted a champion. I mused, "Well, there are different sorts, Mr. President, in men and women. There are romantic personalities and erotic personalities. It is possible to be very beautiful or handsome and not at all erotic. For example Tyrone Power presented an image on the screen that was more romantic than erotic—and then there was Errol Flynn, whose image and real personality were entirely erotic."

"Is this something you're born with, like charm," he asked, "or can you acquire it?"

"You can work on it," I said, "like a quarterback works on his passes. Throughout history, the great lovers have worked on their *game*, trying to improve their techniques and appearance, with perfumes and creams and fashion. In fact, until the Industrial Revolution, men took as much care with their appearance as women did."

"Well, how would you categorize me?" he asked.

"Oh, you're definitely erotic," I said, and he laughed. "In fact, you could be right up there with the greats in history, with Don Juan and Casanova, because you have the physical attributes, and also the charm to seduce. The only thing you lack is the time. And, of course, you're married."

My evaluation amused him. We talked, on many other occasions, about the women I'd known in Hollywood and after.

"Gina Lollobrigida is erotic, I assume," he said.

"Absolutely," I agreed. "There is a quality of sexuality to everything she does, but she is more a polo pony than a Thoroughbred."

"A polo pony?"

"She is smaller than a Thoroughbred, and I think a Thoroughbred woman would be tall like the top models. And she is rounder—very much so. But you know, not only the Thoroughbreds are champions. I have known a few women who have been Amazons and absolutely gorgeous—world-champion Clydesdales."

This was a game that he and I would frequently play. We zoomorphized all our acquaintances: most were either birds or dogs of different types, although Jackie was a fawn, and there was a lawyer we knew who was a perfect toad. His father, we agreed, was an owl. Bobby, a basset hound. He thought I was a Siamese cat, and I thought he was a fine hunting dog, like a golden retriever or an Irish setter. There were other games we would play—word games and such. He enjoyed my ability to mimic others; I did my Chaplin walk for him. I saw that he was bored by those who tried to impress him with their seriousness; I hoped to entertain, not impress, and I knew that if the entertainment was sophisticated enough, he would be impressed as well.

One person who tried to impress John Kennedy with his seriousness, and whom the President enjoyed teasing in return, was Adlai Stevenson. I saw him do this one day in Newport, Rhode Island, where he and Jackie were spending a summer holiday at the Auchincloss house. The skies were particularly dark and threatening that day; the President said, "I'll tell you what I'm going to do. I'm going to get that Adlai to fly out here today."

"Mr. President," I said, "look at the skies."

"Good," he said, "he'll be airsick."

We received word that Stevenson was en route with one of his sons, and then that he had landed at an air base and was proceeding to Newport by helicopter. I remember seeing that helicopter, which seemed to stand still in the sky, fighting the winds and rain, gradually growing larger until it plopped down on the lawn and Stevenson emerged, wiping his brow, a little green at the gills, it seemed to me.

"Adlai," the President said, with a charming smile, "how good to see you. Let's go and talk."

"Wonderful, Mr. President. There are a lot of things I want to talk to you about."

"We'll go out for a sail on my boat."

"The boat?" Stevenson said, and I could see the horror in his eyes.

The boat. The seas were treacherous that day. The wind was up, it was drizzling and threatening to pour, lightning flashed in the distance. Secret Service men in coast guard cutters bobbed all around us. The President, who, of course, was quite a good sailor and used to such things, insisted Adlai sit out back with him in the two captain's chairs; Stevenson's

son and I went below. I could see the President sitting there with no coat
on, though. Stevenson, who wasn't going to wear a coat if the President
wasn't, was attempting—unsuccessfully—not to shiver in the wind and
rain. Finally, the President said, "Well, it's a little rough out today. Let's
go back in."

And as soon as we returned, the President said, "Well, Adlai, there's
your helicopter waiting."

We watched again as the little helicopter, struggling against the
storm, edged off from the house. "Mr. President," I said, "that is truly
cruel and unusual punishment."

"He could use it," the President said. "It's good for his health."

Mother died suddenly, late that summer.

She died on a September weekend in 1961, of a heart attack. She had
been gallant to the end; on the Friday preceding her death, she had insisted from her hospital bed, "No, boys, don't stay here in this gloomy
room with me. Go to the beach and I will see you on Monday." We had
been assured by her doctors that there was no imminent danger, but they
were wrong.

I was shattered and inconsolable. The loss to Igor and me was immense. Her disappearance created a gigantic hole in our lives. Gone were
her strength, her support; gone also was the fun of discussing with her
our daily happenings, our achievements or failures, large or small.

Her funeral had the air of a state occasion. It was held in a Russian
Orthodox church in New York. The church was very crowded; Mother had
been extremely popular. I tried to appear stoic, but to no avail. I cried,
for the first time in many years.

Jackie called immediately upon hearing of Mother's death. She invited
me to join them in Newport. "Come and spend some time with us," she
said. "Bring a friend."

I did bring a friend, a girl from Texas, who simply froze when confronted by the prospect of a social conversation with the First Family.
The four of us had dinner alone in the dining room, and she found herself
the focus of the President's attentions, whose conversational technique
was determinedly Socratic. I don't think she ever recovered from being
on that most prestigious hot seat. "She's very pretty," Jackie said to
me later, and then, clearly not understanding the girl's awestruck silence, added, "but certainly you can find someone more interesting than
that!"

The President confided in me frequently that summer. He asked if I knew any good Italian-Americans he could appoint to positions in his administration (I suggested a judge, whom he did not use because of a conflict of interest). We talked about appointees to ambassadorial posts, who invariably turned out to be monolingual, and I permitted myself to suggest that he'd have fewer problems overseas if he appointed ambassadors whose qualifications included something more than a sizable campaign contribution, perhaps a knowledge of the native language and customs.

"Yes," he said, "but if there wasn't the promise of some such reward, no one would ever contribute."

I visited them in Rhode Island on several occasions. I always slept badly there: the Secret Service contingent pacing the gravel drive always kept me awake. On one occasion, Jawaharlal Nehru was there for meetings. The President didn't like him very much. "That sanctimonious . . . He is the worst phony you've ever seen."

He was occasionally frustrated with Secretary of State Dean Rusk, whom he considered brilliant: "He always gives me twenty options and argues convincingly for *and* against each of them."

Secretary of Defense Robert McNamara was more decisive, he said: "He'll come in with his twenty options and then say, 'Mr. President, I think we should do this.' I like that. Makes the job easier." We were on his yacht off Newport when he said this, reviewing what seemed a flotilla of navy vessels. "You know, this job might even be fun if the world weren't such a mess."

I treasured such moments. At one point the President said to me, "I enjoy talking to you because we can go from one thing to another—from the sacred to the profane—but also because you are one of the few who aren't looking for anything from me and, most important, I can trust you. You never tell anyone anything."

This last, I suppose, was quite an odd attribute for the brother of a society columnist—especially a columnist who delighted in taking potshots at the President, much to my dismay.

There was one incident that was particularly embarrassing. It was in Palm Beach. The President and I would often go out on his yacht in the morning. Usually, he would read the newspapers as soon as he awoke, then have breakfast, and then we would go for a sail. On this particular morning, he had not yet read the papers. He carried a bunch of them out to the boat, and waving Igor's paper, the *Journal-American*, he said, "Why are you so different from your brother?"

"Mr. President, my brother is a great admirer of yours."

"He's been indiscreet to the utmost," Kennedy said, and mentioned a column he had written about an evening at the Wrightsmans'. It was supposed to have been a private evening and off the record. The President was concerned about more than the column, however, as I would soon learn.

"Your brother is impossible!" he continued, as we left the dock. "How can I invite him to the White House if he's going to write everything the next day? One Cassini is enough, believe me!"

So we went out, and the President, as was often the case, wanted to take a swim. The Secret Service warned him against it, though: "Mr. President, you'd better not go in. We've received reports of sharks."

"You coming, Oleg?"

"Mr. President," I said, "if you don't mind, I'll avoid being shark bait."

Besides, the water seemed very cold and I've never been all that much for aquatics. The President jumped in, however, and it was quite a sight: the coast guard boats circling in close, creating almost a swimming-pool-sized protective circumference in the ocean, and there, in the middle, the President, treading water and puffing a cigar. He loved the grand gesture, the successful gamble. That morning, he had played against the sharks and won—and, signaling for a line, he allowed himself to be pulled back onto the yacht, triumphantly puffing all the while.

Back on deck, he opened the *Journal-American*, turning to Igor's column. "Your brother certainly is a wonderful friend of mine! Look at the bouquet he's sent me today."

He tossed me the paper, and I read that Cholly Knickerbocker had learned, exclusively, that John Kennedy was one of the most unpopular boys at Choate thirty years earlier.

"Mr. President, what can I say?" I said. "It must be his assistants. He's away from New York now and his assistants are preparing the column."

But of course I knew that was not true. He was in New York and, more to the point, he knew damn well where *I* was and was jealous. It was a vindictive act, this item. As soon as we got back to shore, I called him, screaming, "You son of a bitch! I am a friend of the President and you try to sabotage me with this nonsense!"

"I am a newspaperman," he said, "and it is my duty to the readers."

"It is your duty to tell them that the most popular president in history was not popular in school? *Merde!* You're just being petty."

"It was my assistants," said Igor, retreating along the same route I had used. "But I stand by it."

"In the meantime you are causing me great pain," I said. "I cannot understand your mentality. I can't stand what you are doing—to him, or to me!"

Later that day, once again, the President made a comment on my loyalty to U.S. Chief of Protocol Angier Biddle Duke: "Ah, here is Oleg," he said. "One of his greatest qualities is that he can be trusted."

I did not learn until later that the President had been informed of the details of my argument with Igor . . . and, indeed, of all the conversations I had with my brother. For security reasons, all the phone lines were monitored.

The last time I saw the President was at a dinner at Stephen and Jean Smith's Fifth Avenue apartment in early November 1963. Adlai Stevenson was there, advising him—I remember this clearly—not to go on his political trip to Texas. As I left the party that night, I said to the President, "Why do you go? Your own people are saying you should not."

He shrugged, and smiled. We shook hands. I thought nothing of it; I was always asking him why he did this, and didn't do that. It was a comment made *en passant*.

A week later, I was having lunch in a little restaurant near my showroom on Seventh Avenue when someone mentioned that the President had been shot in Dallas. I did not react; I don't know why—perhaps it was just too enormous, maybe I thought it was a joke. I returned to my studio, and there everyone was listening to the radio. The President was dead. I went to my office, closed the door, and just sat there; the feeling was much the same as when Mother died—an overpowering numbness. Eventually, there would be moments when the sadness would overtake me, when I would realize how irrevocably gone the era was . . . but it was hard to believe then, and remained so. Every time I attended a Kennedy family gathering since, I felt it was, on some level, an attempt to regain the magic of that time. There were a great many of these occasions—in Hyannis Port; Palm Beach; Sun Valley, Idaho (where I once made a spaghetti dinner for thirty-eight Kennedy children and their friends). I was thrilled when Robert Kennedy took my concern about the situation of Native Americans to heart in a way his brother never really had; I was terribly shaken when he was killed. So much happened to them, and through it all, the spark, the golden memory remained and the tantalizing hope of a restoration lingered. Perhaps it was just a way to dull the pain, but it gave solace to a great many people who yearned for a return to the idealism and elegance the Kennedys symbolized. That dream lingers still.

I remained friendly with Jackie, too, although our extraordinary business relationship ended with the administration. We would have dinner together from time to time.

I was only a member of the court, but I know how strong the image of the President remained with me. He departed so abruptly that the image never had time to fade; it was there as it had been the last night I saw him at Stephen Smith's apartment. A part of me assumed I would see him again soon, and we would have our philosophical talks, and play our word games, and he would ask me about this girl or that: "What does she have, Oleg? Do you think she has it?"

He had it. He had it in spades, and we have not seen it since.

CHAPTER

12

I have never been a very good sleeper. Insomnia has proved as much a blessing as a burden, though; it is an old friend now. There are always books to be read on my night table, and a notebook, too, for those times when I am jolted awake by an image, a half-dream, an idea. I've done some of my best thinking when frustrated by the coquettish elusiveness of sleep.

At some point in the mid-1950s, I was awakened by a quotation from Dante—the opening lines of *The Inferno*—that had set off a clangorous tumult in my subconscious:

> *Nel mezzo del commin di nostra vita*
> *mi retrovai per una selva oscura. . . .*
>
> (In the middle of my life,
> I found myself in a dark forest. . . .)

I was then very much in the middle of my life, enjoying great success, but I knew that it would not be sufficient. I had designed elegant and profitable collections of ladies' clothing. I would soon have enough money to last two lifetimes, but was that all there was to it? Would Oleg Cassini be just a women's fashion designer?

I thought of Leonardo. When one is raised in Florence, the genius of Da Vinci is never far from your consciousness. Leonardo was not merely a painter or sculptor. He designed pottery, castles, weapons, a flying machine, aqueducts, parks. His only creative restriction was the limits of his imagination.

I was not Leonardo, of course. I could, however, in my modest twentieth-century manner, expand the definition of what a designer might do. I needn't be limited to dresses, even if fashion in those days was a very specialized affair. You designed dresses or hats or gloves. You designed for ladies (no one really designed for men, except tailors, whose idea of a radical departure in fashion was to change the width of a lapel a quarter-inch). You did what you did, usually for no more than seven or eight years, after which you faded into a wealthy senescence. I could name you twenty designers who were celebrated during the 1950s and 1960s but whom no one remembers now, which doesn't mean they were bad; it just means creative vision is fleeting, especially when it is restricted to a single article of clothing.

I had other ideas. I saw things in my mind. There were clothes I wanted to wear that no one was designing.

I started with ladies' coats and men's ties. It was a modest effort, in the mid-1950s, but it was the first step toward franchising. I would design the ties, using the regimental patterns I'd always loved and the English-public-school look, and they would be manufactured elsewhere. There was no reason to limit myself to coats and ties, though . . . and, in the early 1960s, I began to take steps toward realizing my goal. I moved into other forms of ladies' clothing, like swimwear, lingerie, and hats, but there was no reason to stop *there*, either. My name had a certain clout by then. I was known as the designer for Jackie Kennedy, but also a gentleman of the world, an arbiter of taste in many things. If the *Good Housekeeping* Seal of Approval meant that a domestic product had quality, why not an *Oleg Cassini* Seal of Approval—my name on a fashion product, even if it was one that I had not completely designed myself but merely edited or approved—certifying that it had style? And why limit it to clothing? Eyeglasses could be stylish or not. Luggage, perfume, sheets and towels, just about anything that was designed.

There was resistance to this at first, both in the trade press and among the large manufacturers. The latter were doing well enough on their own, and didn't believe a designer's imprimatur on their already successful products would improve sales. I saw that I would have to start with smaller, more flexible manufacturers. They soon found that "Swimwear by Oleg Cassini" had a certain cachet, and certainly a better chance of success than "Swimwear by John Doe." There were no precedents for this type of relationship, however, and it posed a difficult problem with the lawyers. I had an attorney named Arnold Biegen who became the Christopher Columbus of licensing law, charting the route to the New World. The formula we established was that the designer would receive four to ten percent of gross sales, plus a minimum guarantee, and that the manufacturer had to spend a certain percentage to advertise the product.

The biggest mistake we made early on was in the length of our contracts. We yoked ourselves to some manufacturers for as long as ten years. This became a source of regret when the big companies changed their minds about the merit of licensing, and we were unable to sign contracts with them because of our prior commitments. Sometimes we would buy back a contract. Eventually, three years became the most common length.

As always, in every business, there were failures of nerve and imagination. I remember one of the early agreements we made with a manufacturer, who had lease departments at Bonwit Teller and other fine stores, to produce a line of Oleg Cassini shoes.

"I think maybe ten percent of the line should be boots," I suggested, once the deal was completed.

"Boots?" he said, incredulous. No one had done boots for ladies before. "You mean like *army* boots? You're out of your mind. Women aren't going to buy boots."

I couldn't convince him, and so we dropped the deal. Thus, I missed participating in the most successful footwear innovation of the decade.

The early resistance from the large manufacturers and the trade press convinced me that I was going to have to go directly to the public with my idea. That had always been my forte, in any case. So now, in addition to making personal appearances in different cities, I became the first designer to appear regularly on national television—which, in the decade since my initial success, had become a major force, penetrating the entire country. In putting my imprimatur on many different products, I was looking for a larger, more diverse market than the relatively small group of women who'd bought my collections; I aimed at the sort of recognition that only television could provide.

So I adapted my road show—the models, the clothes, and, especially, the humor—to the talk-show format. I was aided in this by the fact that the most popular program of that type, *The Tonight Show* (then starring Jack Paar) was based in New York and in constant need of guests; Paar had a virtual repertory company of regulars, of whom I was one. There were other programs as well—and now, instead of going from Chicago to Cleveland to Philadelphia with my station wagon full of models, I went from Irv Kupcinet (Chicago) to Phil Donahue (Cleveland) to Mike Douglas (Philadelphia) to Merv Griffin (Los Angeles). The purpose of my appearances had changed a bit, too. It was no longer to sell a particular article of clothing. The idea was to make my name familiar to the public at large, to let people know that this Cassini fellow had a sense of humor and a sense of style, and that there was a large range of products that reflected my sensibility. Early on, well before the talk shows became the favored target of merchandisers of all sorts, I discovered that they were the ultimate American marketing tool.

I was always amazed by how large the audience actually was. Once, while presenting a fashion show for Johnny Carson's *Tonight Show*, I joked that a model with a pageboy haircut was wearing a new product I'd invented—a rainproof pomade. "You can go out in a thunderstorm or a *blizzard* with this pomade and never muss your hair," I said. "It's just like a hat."

A thousand phone calls were received from women wanting to know where they could buy this imaginary product.

There were several parallel developments of significance in my life at that time. I had sold my house on East Sixty-second Street and was now living at 525 Park Avenue. It was noisy—sleep was practically impossible there. I didn't know what to do. One day, without any encouragement from me, a real estate agent called me and said, "Mr. Cassini, I think I have the house for you, but you will have to use your imagination."

She took me to Gramercy Park. I walked into the foyer, and fell in love. It was a place unlike any other in New York, a sixteenth-century Dutch house transported brick by brick from Europe by the Wells Fargo family in the early twentieth century. There was a vaulted, twenty-foot ceiling in the living room, leaded windows, elegantly carved wood paneling in many of the rooms. It was completely bare; there was no furniture, and it was dusty, dirty. It needed a coat of paint. I was reminded of a beautiful girl who needed only a different hairstyle, or dress, to shine. But, more important, it was very reminiscent of the period and style of the house in which I'd been raised in Florence. It felt like home; I bought it on the spot, and spent the next few years decorating it. Soon the interior of the house looked exactly as I'd dreamed it would, like a sixteenth-century Florentine palazzo.

336

This inspired me in business, too, and I did something that had never been done before. I organized a coordinated sales theme for the fifteen franchises I held at the time: the Renaissance Look from the House of Cassini. The advertising campaign featured a photograph of me standing in the window of my new home, with Renaissance-inspired dresses, men's wear, gloves, shoes, jewelry, furs, hosiery, and lingerie.

And so, franchising blossomed. I was quickly followed by Pierre Cardin, whom I always considered a brilliant designer and businessman. The concept was reinforced by other designers, people like John Weitz and Bill Blass. The four of us together were cited by the *Daily News Record*, a men's-wear trade magazine, as the Founding Fathers of men's fashion franchising. The idea that a designer was merely someone who created an article of clothing—a dress, a suit, a coat—was obliterated in the mid-1960s.

The Renaissance Look and subsequent experiments redefined the profession. A designer became someone with a universal vision, an arbiter of elegance, a Renaissance man. I didn't solicit licensees; they came to me, and I rejected many more proposed products than I accepted. Licenses came and went; not every product was a winner. At times, though, I had as many as fifty licensees—and then, with seven or eight hundred products bearing my name on them, it was obviously difficult to completely design each one. I functioned like a quarterback with my design team; the genesis of each idea came from me. I initiated every move, but I did not do everything myself. Within a matter of years, I had created an empire. We were grossing as much as $350,000,000 retail. Over the years, licensees have changed for all the major designer labels; but the important labels remain the same.

In some ways, the 1960s were the most exciting years of my life; certainly they were the most active professionally and socially. Suddenly I found myself in the vanguard of the great changes that were taking place, not just in fashion, but in society as well. The old formal, black-tie social life was crumbling in New York. The Stork Club, El Morocco, all the old haunts were closing down. They were replaced by a wilder, freer nightlife, a scene that I helped create, somewhat to my surprise.

The revolution began very quietly, on a remote farm in Warren, Vermont, where I was spending several contemplative weeks one winter in the late 1950s. This was something I often did, and still do whenever possible: go off to the wilderness and gather my thoughts, take stock of my life and plan for the future. That winter, I spent many hours staring out the window of the little farmhouse, staring at a mountain where a new, single ski lift was being constructed. Eventually, I stared long enough to see something. I had this thought: if one didn't necessarily have to go to Europe for fashion, why should one have to go to Europe for skiing? The success that Agnelli had enjoyed with Sestrieres was very much on my mind, too. The Green Mountains weren't the Alps, or even the Rockies, but they were much more convenient to New York and Boston. I decided to call my brother, who was then at the zenith of his power as Cholly Knickerbocker.

"This is virgin territory," I said. "We could start something here. Between your contacts and mine, we could make this *the* place to ski in the East."

And so, Sugarbush.

It happened very quickly, and was much easier than I would have imagined. Together, Igor and I established a private club at the foot of the mountain. There were ten original incorporators, and so we called it "Ski Club Ten." They included Igor and me; Henry J. Heinz II, of the "57 Varieties"; Basil Goulandris, the Greek shipping and armaments tycoon; Hans and Peter Estin, of a wealthy Boston family (Peter was so enamored of the place that he became our first ski instructor there); George Baker, Jr., a banker who was very prominent in society; Andrew Burden, who had been a member of the U.S. national ski team; Neil A. McConnell, an heir to the Avon fortune; and Michael Butler, the dashing fellow I'd known from Palm Beach and fox hunting, a good skier and a better dresser—he had at least twenty different outfits, all coordinated (hat, sweater, pants); you never saw him wearing the same thing twice.

The Ski Club Ten lodge was more functional than elegant. It was set on a narrow piece of land, not more than two hundred yards from the lifts. It was a white clapboard building with large windows so we could sit there in comfort watching the skiers. It had one long, well-furnished room with a large fireplace and a dining area, big enough to accommodate about seventy-five people. There was also a kitchen, presided over by a Frenchman, Olivier Coquelin, who had excellent taste in food and wines. We'd often gather at the club for drinks on a Friday evening, after the long trip up from Boston and New York; on Saturday evenings, there would be an excellent dinner, often followed by dancing—sometimes a *bal masqué*.

The atmosphere at Sugarbush was informal and almost collegiate.

Every weekend seemed a breezy, high-society version of the Dartmouth Winter Carnival, with games and contests and practical jokes. A group of us built Swiss chalets in a quiet, secluded valley about a half-mile from the slopes. My neighbors there included Skitch Henderson, the bandleader; Taki Theodorokopoulos; Michael Butler; and the Estins. Each of us had friends whom we invited up; invariably, they wanted to join the ski club and build a chalet, too. Various Kennedys—Jean and Steve Smith, Pat Lawford, Eunice and Sargent Shriver, etc.—would arrive from Boston and New York, including Senator Ted Kennedy, who was one of the boldest skiers I've ever seen, taking what I thought were unreasonable risks, especially when we had downhill competitions. I remember we often had cross-country races in which men and women were paired, tied together by a rope; invariably, this would take place after a heavy lunch and several bottles of wine (invariably, too, my date for the weekend would be a model who'd never put skis together before and whom I'd practically have to carry across the finish line). Remarkably, we had crowds of people who came to watch our races and games. Word of this place "where the Jet Set skied" was spreading.

Damon Gadd had the vision to enlarge the lifts, opening new trails and runs, opening up the whole mountain; and then, adding boutiques and restaurants. Armando Orsini bought an old barn, hung crystal chandeliers, and opened the restaurant that bore his name. The great skier Stein Ericksson came to teach at the ski school and brought a group of top-flight European instructors with him. The area boomed; it was an explosive success. All the Europeans came: the Agnelli group, Benno Graziani, Vittorio de Camerana, the French contingent; the Texans, Lynne and Oscar Wyatt, Bob Sakowitz, Josephine Abercrombie; the Greeks, Goulandris and Niarchos—there were always an incredible number of beautiful, young, and rich people.

In retrospect, there was a killing to be made here—in real estate (I could have bought 7,000 acres of land for $7 an acre), hotels, food, ski equipment, even ski fashions—if my mind worked that way, but it didn't. I was just thrilled to have found a place where all my friends could get together and ski, to have a place for winter weekends when I couldn't get to Europe. It was almost as if health were a drug and I was looped on all that fresh air—thoughts of commerce did not even enter my mind. In truth, Sugarbush could never really compare with a resort like St. Anton or the other Alpine slopes. The conditions generally weren't very good: Vermont was colder than the Alps and often icier. The slopes would become rutted and treacherous, especially when the traffic became greater as time went on. Indeed, Igor's wife, Charlene, suffered a terrible fall on the ice, fracturing her ankle badly, an injury that never quite healed properly and caused a dependence on painkillers that contributed to her untimely death.

But at the time, Igor was flying high, as was I, and we soon flew even higher when we took the formula that we developed in Vermont and came up with a way to apply it in New York. Sugarbush was a great success, but it was nothing compared with the phenomenal popularity of Le Club.

One night early in the 1960s, Igor happened upon a little-known night-club near Times Square called the Peppermint Lounge. It had been known as a sailors' hangout, but that had clearly changed: the dance floor was jammed with kids doing a dance that was unlike anything we had ever seen before; it was, of course, the twist. We knew that our friends—especially those who wanted to be on top of the latest thing—would soon be seeking a place where they could twist elegantly; at least, without colliding with hyperactive teenagers. The idea was to establish a private club for the promulgation of such dancing. It would be the first private discotheque in America. It would be something entirely different: re-corded music rather than a live orchestra; informal dress rather than black tie . . . We would be taking a real chance, especially Igor, who was ready to invest large sums of his own money in the project.

We contacted our friends, the same types of people who had made Sugarbush so successful; the response was positive enough to proceed with our plans. A large, open space—formerly a photography studio—was rented on East Fifty-fifth Street near the river; Pierre Scapula was hired to create the decor, and he made it into an elegant European hunting lodge, with mounted animal heads, swords, and tapestries on the walls. There were two rooms: the first had the traditional long bar and a small dance floor in the rear; the second had tables—including one large round table just to the right of the door where I would hold forth frequently à la John Perona at El Morocco. Olivier Coquelin was imported from Sugar-bush to handle the food and wine—which were not only excellent but also inexpensive, and continued throughout the night.

We called the place simply, exquisitely, "Le Club."

Le Club was more than an immediate success; it was a social phenom-enon. Membership cost $5,000 and was limited. There were constant ef-forts to get us to expand. Everyone, it seemed, wanted to be part of our eclectic roster, which included some rather unlikely twisters, covering the social landscape from the maharajah of Jaipur (who danced in beautiful brocaded Nehru-style jackets) to the duke of Bedford, from Gianni Agnelli to Ray Stark, from Skitch Henderson to Nicholas Biddle, from Douglas Fairbanks, Jr., to Roy Cohn . . . and of course the Greeks: Niarchos, Onassis, Goulandris, Coumantaros, and the Marchessinis. We also encouraged ladies to come unescorted; beautiful models, actresses, and society girls, most of whom were members.

Occupancy at Le Club was 175, and the place was always full . . . and the street outside crowded as well most nights, with *paparazzi*, would-be guests, and just plain oglers, people who knew that this was where the biggest stars in Hollywood would come when they were in town (the doorman had implicit instructions to forget our strict entrance requirements when it seemed appropriate). Indeed, every night at Le Club seemed a summit conference of the best-known people in society, politics, and the arts.

As President-for-Life (an egregious but wonderful title), I had many official duties and also the unofficial responsibility of making sure Le Club was filled with beautiful girls. This was not a painful task: I made it my habit to engage in impromptu Pygmalionic activities, discovering new girls—stewardesses, actresses, models—dressing them up, and inviting them out for the night; there was still a certain innocence to all this. The scene had not yet degenerated into the inelegant, drug-addled profligacy that would begin in the late 1960s and continue for more than a decade.

I held forth at the round table most every night when I was in town. I would work till seven in the evening, then go home, shower, dress, and be at Le Club by nine. It was a fantasy life: Not only did I run a private nightclub, but the most popular private club in town. Part of my pleasure was to arrive with the most beautiful girl imaginable, to create a stir. Often, in those years, my date would be Ursula Andress, who always was quite conscious of the effect she had when she entered a room. In particular, I remember the party we had at Le Club celebrating her stunning debut in the first James Bond film, *Dr. No;* she arrived that night in a black jumpsuit unzipped to the waist. There were other spectacular entrances. When my old friend Marilyn Monroe came to visit with Milton Green, she made no effort to turn heads, but the impact of her arrival was decidedly seismic.

If health was the drug at Sugarbush, power was *it* at Le Club. I had very mixed feelings about this. Naturally I was pleased to have, say,

Jackie Kennedy call me to ask if I could reserve her a table for the night (as she did on several occasions). It was fun, too, to receive a summons from the doorman—this happened several times a night—and go to the gate, only to find an old friend from the Continent waiting there, desperate to get in. It was a form of power I'd never experienced before. No doubt it would have been corrupting if I'd taken it more seriously, but my purpose at Le Club was, as it had been at Sugarbush, to enjoy myself, not to make money, and certainly not to exert influence.

But then, every night seemed memorable, an adventure fueled by the music, which, in the hands of a skillful disc jockey, would increase in tempo and intensity as the night wore on. I loved to watch the crowd on the dance floor, a fashion assemblage unlike any that had ever been seen in the world before. Members could show up in leather jackets without ties, coming as they were from a weekend of skiing or whatever. There were people wearing furs, leathers, dungarees, black tie, diamonds, turtlenecks (a form of dress that was unacceptable in the better restaurants at the time, if you recall), and business suits. The heterodoxy of the crowd started me thinking; as before, my social life informed my professional life. I became more adventurous in my ideas about fashion than ever before. It was, suddenly, the 1960s . . . and anything was possible.

Actually, my most successful idea in those years was a nostalgic one. The inspiration for men's shirts in vivid colors came not from the new age but from the past. I remembered the shirts my father owned when I was a boy, silk shirts that he bought in Paris and kept till they were tattered, shirts in many colors, strong colors—reds, blues, even pumpkin orange—with a variety of collar styles. I also thought about the military look, which was something I'd always loved and had adapted to ladies' clothing—the walls of my house were covered with pictures of all sorts of uniforms, regimental colors. And then, finally, one day I had an idea. What an imposition a white shirt is upon a brown suit! Why such tyranny? Why not a green shirt, or an orange one?

I set up a meeting with executives from Van Heusen, a large shirt company. I knew the top man, because he was a member of Le Club. I sat down at the conference table with these fellows, all of them in their dull shirts. "My idea," I told them, "is really a very simple one . . ."

And I showed them some sketches I'd done: an entirely new look. Men wearing shirts of dark blue, orange, and—I went all the way—purple, combinations of orange shirts and purple sweaters. There was a palette of new colors that I had created, colors that were unimaginable to these stodgy executives. Predictably, they thought I was out of my mind.

"If I didn't know your reputation as a creative designer," said one of them, "I would call you insane. You mean to tell me you think there are men in this country who would buy shirts in these colors?"

"Yes, I believe that," I said, suffering a moment of doubt. These people were so deeply rutted, were they right? No, I was stubborn and had to press my case. "I think people are tired of your boring shirts. They are ready for something new."

They were, but the shirtmakers weren't. I took the idea to several of the biggest in the business, and the reaction was always the same. I wouldn't give up, though. I told Rubirosa of my idea—he was always one of the best-dressed men I knew—and he grew very excited. We talked about the details of our own shirts (custom-made by Hilditch & Key of London and Paris) that might be incorporated into the new idea; indeed, Rubi and I earlier had invented an interesting hybrid, a Western shirt with Prince of Wales collar, which Hilditch & Key made specially for us. Now I returned to those shirtmakers—both Rubi and I considered them the best in the world—and asked them to produce prototypes of my designs. There were three basic styles: a classic, high Prince of Wales collar (always my favorite), a straight collar, and a button-down (neater, more precise than the floppy Brooks Brothers type).

Eventually, a fellow named Barry Boonshaft manufactured the shirts. He was an executive at Eagle Shirts—the son-in-law of the owner, in fact —and even *he* wasn't convinced of the idea's merit, but he was anxious to get out on his own. He was young, with a lot of flair. He was eager to take a chance and prove his mettle. "They don't see what you see," he told me. "You'll never get them to do it. Why not give me the chance? I'll give you the best."

Well, the shirts flew out of the stores. It was instantaneous. They hit at a moment in the mid-1960s when the whole mood of the society was loosening, becoming more adventurous; they captured the spirit of the time . . . and the volume of shirt sales doubled industry-wide in the next year. My styles and colors were copied almost immediately, but we had been there first and had the greatest impact—and, of course, I was ready with ties and sweaters and suits to go with the new shirts.

There was a boom, a revolution in men's clothing at that moment, and I began to introduce men's, as well as women's, fashions in my television appearances. We had a memorable men's show on *The Mike Douglas Show* in Philadelphia. Peter Lawford was the guest host and guest model as well. Someone had forgotten to bring an evening shirt in his size, so I had him wear a white silk turtleneck with his tuxedo. The style became an instant hit, and for a time, everybody wore a turtleneck with his tuxedo.

I introduced another distinctive men's style of that period—the "Nehru Jacket." It was a short-lived trend, but successful while it lasted. The brocaded jackets *sans* lapels I'd seen the maharajah of Jaipur wearing at Le Club had made an impression on me, as had the more conservative ones I'd seen Nehru himself wear at the White House. I liked the clean, uncluttered simplicity of it. And then too, my mind was on India during that period. I'd met with Indira Gandhi in New York, and she had invited me to visit her country and start a clothing industry there. "We spin the thread—the spinning wheel is at the center of our flag," she told me. "Why should we not also make the clothing?"

This was an intriguing idea. I wish I had done it, but so many things were happening to me at that moment. I was getting all sorts of interesting offers, and the notebook on my night table was filling with all sorts of curious ideas. On *The Johnny Carson Show* one night, I made the same boast I had to the President: "I can make you the Jackie Kennedy of the men's world."

This got a good laugh. Johnny gave me one of his deadpan looks, tapping his pencil. Finally, he said, "O-kay."

But I was serious. I began to design some suits, ties, and shirts specifically for him. *Newsweek* magazine noted in 1968: "After Carson modeled an Oleg Cassini Nehru suit last February, NBC got 1,000 calls from viewers asking where the suit could be bought."

That sort of response made the next step very obvious to me. "Why not have a Johnny Carson line of clothing?" I suggested to several of my licensees. "It would be another label, in addition to Cassini."

Once again, I was considered nuts. "Johnny Carson isn't a designer," they said. "It will never sell."

"So what?" I said. "He's the king of television. Half the men in America want to dress and look like him."

They didn't understand. It took a decade, but the idea of celebrity clothing lines (including Carson's) eventually caught on. In fact, just about anything you could think of caught on for a week or two during those tumultuous times. It was a most wonderful period in which to be a designer. I was able to exorcise all my fantasies. In the same article about

"Male Plumage" in which *Newsweek* mentioned my success with Carson, I was given credit for introducing the "Cowboy Look" in 1968. I introduced it again in 1978 on *The Mike Douglas Show.* I have always believed the cowboy to be one of the best-dressed men in America. The look included one idea that I certainly should have done more with: designer jeans. There were many other "looks" as well, nearly more than I can recall.

All this seemed natural, almost unnoticeable at the time. Revolution —social, cultural, political—was in the air. In fashion, change had become an almost brutish master. In 1962, I had written an article for the *Saturday Evening Post* in which I congratulated Paris for *not* introducing a "new look" that year. This created something of a stir at the time, as I was a known critic of the Paris establishment, and it was done, in part, I must admit, for its shock value. But I had hit upon a theme that would later have resonance.

Little did I know then that the mania for the new would reach the levels it did by the late 1960s. Designers were expected to create a *revolution* with each new season. I look back at the news accounts of fashion shows of the time and remember, somewhat ruefully, the contortions we practiced to remain fresh. This, for example, is how a fashion show that Bill Blass, John Weitz, and I put on at Le Club in 1968 was reported by the correspondent of the Moline (Illinois) *Dispatch:*

> Bill Blass, who is against fads, trends and costumes, showed a functional collection including "Windsorpane" checked suits with dark shirts, a double-breasted raccoon coat and raspberry velvet at-home pants with a black and white checked sweater.
>
> Probably the most sensational outfit of his collection is a maxi military coat lined in red, which is masculine to the last degree.
>
> Mr. Cassini, who described himself as the "Earl of Sandwich" since his showing came in the middle, had a sensational display of Nehru jackets, mostly double-breasted, in every color and fabric.
>
> There was even a convertible Nehru jacket with a collar which folded down to form a lapel. Cassini also favors plaid pants for men.
>
> John Weitz displayed several blanket coat jackets, a new practical look in the male fashion field. His evening attire featured a beige dinner jacket with white binding, worn with a pink shirt and black tie, and a navy tuxedo piped in red . . .

In retrospect, it seems that my double-breasted Nehru suits were the most conservative garments on display that day. How odd, how remarkable that period was!

Nonstop revolution proved exhausting. It became a tired concept soon enough, and eventually so meaningless that the very notion of "tradition," or the absence of change, was considered a "radical" departure when it re-emerged in the 1970s.

I think that even then, as the pace of life in the 1960s began to accelerate and spin out of control (just as the music did each evening at Le Club), I was growing wary. In the midst of all the excesses and innovations, there were traditions lost; the softer, more mannered and polite lifestyle of my youth was being elbowed aside . . . and other changes, too, which gave me pause and led me to question, if nothing else, the speed at which all this was transpiring.

There were dizzying changes in my family as well, some happy, some very sad. My daughter Tina was growing up so quickly. She made her debut in Houston at the River Oaks Club. It was a gala party, presided over by Gene, who was living in Texas with her husband, Howard Lee. It was my pleasure to give the party there in Gene's new hometown.

My father died in 1968. He had been in excellent health; he choked on a piece of meat. Having survived a revolution and a total upheaval of his life, he died in a way that seemed so banal. Father had been very dear to us, and was greatly missed. It was as if another door to the past had been closed.

And there were career upheavals as well. One casualty was my dress-manufacturing business, which was poisoned by the intransigence of the unions. There was a bizarre system that was introduced at that time, a price scale in which the union charged according to the price the dress would sell for, as opposed to the amount of time that went into making it. This was madness, I believed. I sat down with representatives of the unions and pleaded for an industrial structure. The workers would be paid hourly, at one rate, regardless of the garment; the more expensive dresses usually took more time, in any case. The unions held firm, though, and so did I.

"I quit; I close," I said, and an era ended. I did not stop designing dresses, though. I stopped manufacturing them in volume in the United States for several years, creating instead a showcase line of very expensive dresses that would help set the mood for my various franchises. These were made in Italy, and so—irony of ironies—I had gone full circle: from an Italian making clothes in America, to an American making clothes in Italy.

It was at this point that I had my final confrontation with the excesses of the 1960s, which, in addition to being years of violence and social exper-imentation, were a raffish period in the business world as well: the "Go-Go Years," they were called. Fortunes seemed to be made instantaneously and lost even faster; and no one exemplified the half-crazed, disastrous dynamism of the period better than Bernard Cornfeld, who was a friend of mine—and almost became a business partner in a brief, but eventful, episode.

CHAPTER
13

Some people lead happy, uneventful lives, I am told. They work hard, achieve a measure of success, enjoy the fruits of their labor; they live on an even keel. That is the American Dream.

Others suffer tragedies. They work hard, achieve a measure of success, but then—for reasons that are often inexplicable—the bottom drops out. Life isn't meant to be fair.

Others are plain lucky. They don't work very hard, but lightning strikes and they are borne giddily on a tidal wave of success; they breeze through life.

Most people, I suspect, just muddle along.

I have done none of the above. My life has been a roller coaster. The Cassini-Loiewskis had lost two fortunes by the time I reached twenty-one. Since then, I have had my bad moments and, I would submit, grown stronger and wiser (and more wary) in the process. I think of my life this way: I am walking along the street, walking head down as I always do, thinking, reflecting, analyzing my behavior; over time, this hard contemplative work pays off. I achieve some success, perhaps a modicum of self-knowledge. I begin to feel better about myself. I walk proudly (I may even strut a bit), head held high now . . . and then, just as I cease to pay attention to the sidewalk below, life presents me with a banana peel and I go flying, and have to pick myself up; I am forced to reassemble my life and start all over again.

I have not consciously sought out these banana peels; they appear, as if by magic, in my path. I do not like the experience of slipping on them (I would have preferred a life of clear sailing), but I have come to understand this banana-peel process, and to know that I *can* pick myself up again, and start again, and succeed again. A banana peel needn't be fatal; there is a moment where you are in midair, before the crash, when it can even be fun.

Which brings me to Bernie Cornfeld.

I met him through a friend, who kept saying to me, "You gotta meet this guy." Cornfeld was very much on top then. He had built a huge financial empire in Europe through the sale of mutual funds; it was said that his company, Investors Overseas Services, was so large that its transactions represented five percent of the volume on the New York Stock Exchange. IOS was worth, literally, billions.

Cornfeld's great skill was as a salesman. He had built a sales force of thousands who were devoted to him in an almost cultlike way. Whatever Bernie said was good as gold; he had made some 130 of them into millionaires, and it had all happened so quickly. It had happened within ten years, starting from scratch, with Bernie assembling a Fund of Funds (a mutual fund that bought shares in other mutual funds) and soliciting salesmen through an ad in the *International Herald Tribune* which read: "Want to Have Fun?" At first, they had sold this fund to American servicemen on military bases abroad, but soon they branched out, and were selling busily all over the world. And Bernie's investments had branched out, too. He owned banks and insurance companies and had invested, through proprietary funds he established, in hotels, fashion, entertainment, real estate . . .

Fashion. He had bought a share in the Paris House of Guy LaRoche and was looking to expand. He was hungry for ideas, investments. Almost immediately, he made a proposal to me that only a fool could have refused.

In the beginning, though, he was a fellow with startling blue eyes, whom I met at a party. He was balding, and dressed in the most frenetic, novel styles of the times; much of his wardrobe came from Cardin at a moment when Pierre was at his most Edwardian, a surfeit of ruffles and flourishes. Cornfeld proposed that I visit him in Switzerland. I was not very interested. The stories about his fabulous lifestyle had not yet begun to appear, and I had more entertaining things to do than hang out with a hyperactive financier.

But Cornfeld was hospitable. Eventually, I did visit him in Geneva, where he lived in a spectacular villa on the lake, a palazzo that Napoleon had built for Josephine. I also visited the Château de Pelly, a thirteenth-century castle, complete with moat and working drawbridge, in Savoy, forty minutes from Geneva. He had had the castle renovated, covering all the walls in velvet—which attracted hordes of *puces* (fleas) in the summer. He lived in a manner that was barely imaginable: he had ten saddle horses at the castle, a pack of Great Danes, ocelots (which he kept in cages), and girls. There were so many girls. He kept both houses stocked with them in the same way that certain trout streams are stocked by the state. They were there to be caught; Bernie kept two or three off limits, but the rest were fair game. It was a game, though, in which I had no interest in indulging. Some of the girls were pretty, others merely proximate; but quality seemed not to be a concern of Bernie's in this and many other areas. He was interested, primarily, in consumption. He was an insatiable consumer.

He was also an Orthodox Jew, or so he claimed, who had set aside those disciplines of his faith that he found inconvenient, which was to say almost all of them. He surrounded himself with Jewish associates, though, many from his old neighborhood in Brooklyn; they were, he said, the only ones he could trust. He did like me, however. "For a non-Jew," he said, "you're not bad."

I admired his energy and sagacity. He was a very good psychologist, with a real charm and an excellent, almost blindingly fast mind. He seemed to like my sense of style, and quickly I fell into my accustomed role of arbiter of elegance, advising him on matters of quality, like furniture: "Why do you buy these silly copies of Louis the Fourteenth when you have the money to buy the real thing?" I asked him once. He laughed and replied, "You're the only one who knows the difference! Besides, I *prefer* the fakes."

Bernie had a peculiar sense of gastronomy, preferring corned beef on rye. He loved delicatessen food. He also adored Sara Lee frozen baked goods, especially the cream cheese cakes, which arrived by airplane in regular shipments. Fortunately for his guests, he had a very good chef. But even a high-quality chef meant little when he would set a dinner party (with forty or fifty guests) for eight o'clock and not arrive until midnight. "You cannot do this to your guests," I would say. "You cannot even do this to the chef."

"Okay, then, let's all go out for dinner," he'd reply. And he would then scout around for a restaurant still open that he could commandeer for the benefit of his guests. It was an astonishing way to do business, and I told him so. "I won't wait twenty minutes for a girl; I'm not going to wait four hours for you."

"I know," he said. "I have this problem."

"I have a problem, too," I said. "I'm always punctual, and I'm tired of waiting around here."

"Okay, then," he said, "let's talk business."

Boy, did this fellow know how to talk business! Within a matter of minutes he had spun out the most remarkable fantasy. He wanted to be my sole backer in a new business. It would be very, very big. The company would be part of his portfolio, part of his Fund d'Italia, since it would be based in Italy. But that was only the start. It would not only be a manufacturing operation, but would also involve marketing and sales. There would be Cassini boutiques all over the world (such a concept would later be promulgated successfully by Benetton). "We could give the franchises to the wives of my salesmen, give 'em something to do, have 'em all over, three thousand of 'em. It'll be great. These women are natural salesmen."

He was so good at talking about these things, he made it seem as if it had already happened, as if I already had $50,000,000 in the bank from the public sale of this corporation through his funds. I was seduced, to put it mildly. Bernie played me like a Stradivarius.

I spent much of the next year working on this deal. I found a partner in Italy, a manufacturer named Roberto Memmo, who controlled a great many factories in the south. He had six thousand workers ready to go, to create the Cassini line. Over the years, Memmo had been buying one of the most famous villas in Rome, the Palazzo Ruspoli, piece by piece from the Ruspoli family.

The palazzo was a magnificent structure in the very center of Rome; it had a main hall that could seat two thousand, and it was overflowing with priceless antiques. The idea was to use this marvelous building as our flagship: the Rome House of Cassini. In size and grandeur, it would dwarf all the competition. Buyers and press from throughout the world would be invited there for shows; it would be a Roman version of the *maisons de couture* in Paris. For American buyers, especially, it would have that European mystique. It had a certain mystique for me as well; I was finally doing what Jacques Fath had advised in the 1950s. I was establishing my presence as a designer of merit on the Continent, but I was doing it with a twist—in Italy (which was just coming into its own as a design center), rather than in Paris.

My return to Italy after so many years was both satisfying and disconcerting. I had been Americanized; I found it hard to adapt to Mediterranean business practices. The constant refrain was: *"Bisogna aver pazienza."* ("You must have patience.") There was a nonchalance about time, about punctuality, that was positively maddening. At the same time, though, I fell very easily into the more relaxed daily pace and into the quaint formalities of Roman society. Also, in truth, Italy had been Americanized almost as much as I. It had become more of a meritocracy. A new business class, with my old friend Gianni Agnelli at the apogee, was now ascendant; the old aristocracy, my friends and clients from the 1930s, had become superfluous and anachronistic, ornate decorations atop the layer cake of Italian society.

Meanwhile, there was Cornfeld. He called frequently, inviting me to Switzerland, asking my advice on this suit, that wine, this piece of furniture, that girl. It wasn't a nuisance; we had some memorable times. He was a very generous host. A weekend with Bernie could begin in Switzerland and end anywhere in the world. He had several jets on call at the airport in Geneva. Bernie liked to travel and to buy. There was a secretary with him at all times, carrying a briefcase with $50,000 in cash for shopping.

I remember one weekend that commenced in Geneva, with dinner for twenty-five, including a United States senator, Claiborne Pell. In the midst of it, Bernie precipitously decided, "Let's go to Cannes. I have a yacht there."

He gave orders to have a plane prepared, and, as always, it was left to the rest of us to ask pertinent questions like: "Where shall we stay? It is August. The hotels are no doubt full."

"Don't be silly," he said. "We can all stay on my yacht."

The senator seemed quite impressed. A fleet of limousines took us to the airport; another fleet was waiting for us at Cannes. We proceeded to the marina and there, as Bernie questioned the *capitaine du port*, it became apparent that he had never seen the yacht he had just bought. "A guy in New York sold me a couple of them," he explained. "This is the first time I've actually seen it."

The harbormaster told us the yacht was at the end of the second pier, and we trooped down there, an unlikely procession—Bernie, the senator, the girls, the secretary with the $50,000, me, several others. We reached the end of the pier, but there was no yacht. There was only a little house-boat. "I wonder where it can be," Cornfeld said.

"You are looking at it," said an aide, who had checked the registration numbers of the houseboat.

There were widespread groans and consternation. This was a very humble craft. "I guess," Bernie said, in cavalier fashion, "it is not as large as I had imagined. But don't worry, we'll figure out something."

Hotels were called. Nothing. We inspected the houseboat, a process that was accomplished in the blink of an eye. There were no beds, no linens, no kitchen equipment, no curtains on the windows; just a fellow who had been hired to watch the boat. "Well, we'll all just have to sleep on the floor," Bernie said.

"Not on your life," said Senator Pell, and efforts were redoubled to find him a room; eventually, he would pass the night atop the servants' quarters at the Hôtel du Cap. As it happened, Bernie was the only one who seemed pleased with the accommodations that night, telling me later he had been crawling about the floor, making love to four different girls (including his secretary), while the rest of us were trying to sleep. The sun came streaming through the curtainless windows at 5:00 A.M., and he was still at it. At six, we decided that further attempts to sleep would be fruitless and the group of us went off for breakfast at the Hôtel Marti-nique. "Bernie," I said, "we cannot spend another night like this."

"No," he said, "tonight let's go to Le Pirate," which was a popular restaurant about eleven miles outside town in the hills. "Don't worry about the accommodations. We'll work out something."

That is how he was: always optimisitic, always cavalier. After break-fast, he announced, "Let's go shopping!" And shop he did, fervently. He bought each of us a motorcycle for our trip to the disco that night, and then he decided to take his houseboat out on the open seas. The fact that it was built to sit at a dock did not affect him in the slightest; we went, ran out of gas, and had to be towed back to shore. There were times when I would lose patience with this sort of behavior, but I had made the same decision as the rest of his entourage, that the rewards, both personal and monetary, outweighed the mercurial inconveniences. But even if I didn't have many millions of dollars at stake, I think I would have enjoyed observing his peripatetic style. Every night was an adventure with him, and that evening, after we returned to port, proved truly memorable: the group of us roaring up to Le Pirate on our motorcycles, a strange band of gypsies, then roaring back to the harbor at 3:00 A.M., rather tipsy, but exhilarated. I am, in retrospect, quite happy to have had the experience.

We also had a memorable trip to Acapulco, by way of Venezuela. Bernie was scouting, and buying, hotels at the time. He looked at one in Caracas. He didn't like the hotel, but he seemed intent on buying everything else of value in town, stuffing the LearJet with clothes and assorted goods, piling them up in the bathroom, making the w.c. inaccessible for what turned out to be a very long flight to Mexico. I remember arriving in Acapulco in the middle of the night, with another large entourage, including the requisite girls and a Cornfeld lawyer. We proceeded to our hotel, which Bernie did ultimately buy, and created confusion at the desk as the poor clerk attempted to find rooms for us all. Bernie was engaged in animated conversation with the owner when two large rednecks tried to push through the throng to get their room keys. "Hey," Bernie said, "wait a minute."

At which point one of the rednecks said to the other, disgustedly, "Can you believe this arrogant little creep?"

Bernie heard it. He looked up, blinked, and said, "I'm gonna kill 'em," and took off after them, down a long corridor that led to the restaurants and cabanas. By the time I caught up with him, he literally had one of them by the throat. The guy was flailing at him, but Cornfeld had very powerful arms and the fellow couldn't get free. The other one was about to come to the rescue when I intervened, grabbing him by the lapels and tossing him against the cement wall, which he hit head on, fortuitously, and sank to the ground. Then I went to Bernie's aid, trying to separate him from the other guy before Bernie choked him to death or they both fell off the rather precarious wooden rampart they were leaning against. I gave the fellow a couple of shots to the stomach, and disengaged Bernie, who was still screaming, "I'll kill 'em, I'll kill 'em!"

"Calm down, Bernie," I said. "You've won. Stop it before you kill yourself."

Indeed, he had won. The guy I'd thrown against the wall was still down, and groggy—a very unfortunate position to be in, as the lawyer, who had been following all this from a prudent distance, suddenly approached and kicked the poor guy in the stomach with all his might, breaking his own toe.

This was a story Bernie loved to tell afterward: I took care of one, he took care of the other, and the lawyer broke his toe. No one was hurt but the lawyer. After that, too, he always wanted to have me around (I introduced him to Victoria Principal, who became part of the entourage for a while); I knew how to handle myself. And, I must admit, I did enjoy flying about, building my sand castle; together, we visited the factories in southern Italy where the Cassini boutique line would be made. Together, we made other trips as well; indeed, I was with him in Palm Springs, at the home of Ralph Stolken, when reality—huffing and puffing from the strain, no doubt—finally caught up with Bernie Cornfeld.

Reality, of course, was an unwelcome visitor in his life. He had by then lost all sense of what it was. He mentioned, lightly, in passing, that there was an important meeting taking place in Geneva. The board of IOS was in revolt against him. He was entirely unconcerned about it, of course.

"You fool," I said. "You should go there and defend yourself."

Perhaps you're right," he said, "I've got my plane here. I'll go."

But the next morning I walked in and found him in Stolken's dining room having a cup of coffee with a blonde. "What happened?" I asked. "Are you out of your mind?"

"I couldn't wake up in time," he said. "The hell with it."

The hell with it. He was kicked out by his board of directors. He had gone too far, gotten too wild with his investments, plunging into all sorts of silliness—$100,000,000 in entertainment projects that never material-ized, for example—through his poorly supervised proprietary funds. These funds, instead of the solid investments in existing mutual funds that had been the backbone of IOS, became a large part of the "assets" in the Fund of Funds. The rumors of profligacy spread; there was a mad rush by investors to redeem their shares. It all came tumbling down very quickly, a remarkable feat of self-destruction.

And the Palazzo Ruspoli, the Rome House of Cassini, the six thousand women waiting to create my boutique line?

Gone.

The banana-peel principle had struck again. I had slipped very badly. I had been absent from my New York business and staked a lot on Corn-feld; it seemed a sure thing. And now I was faced with a serious problem: I did not want to come back from Europe empty-handed. I felt I had to have a new success in addition to my existing business in Italy. I had to regroup. Life is a contest, and I had lost a round—but I would continue the fight.

I could not sleep. I walked the streets of Rome at night searching for an answer.

Luckily, I knew a very talented fellow from Milan named Mario Fer-rari. He had been a top salesman and merchandiser of clothing in Europe and was looking to expand, to go into business for himself. We talked about my situation; I asked him for advice. "You know," he said, "we may have a common interest here. You have a prestigious name in Italy. I think you are in a very good position to make a success here. The novelty of an Italo-American designer coming home is good too."

To make a long story short, I moved to Milan. I was the very first American designer to open in Milan, or Italy, for that matter. I was immediately made to feel at home by the local press, which treated my arrival in town as quite an event: Jackie Kennedy's designer had come to Milan to create a new line. But I was still plagued by post-banana-peel doubt. What would this new line be? How would it change the prêt-à-porter we had been doing?

There was a girl I knew at the time who was my conscience. I could talk better with her than with anyone; she knew my business, and understood my situation. We would take long walks and talk in great detail about what was to be done. She gave me courage. "Take a chance," she told me. "Don't just make another collection, make a *statement*. Do something unique, something you will really be proud of."

And she was right. It was a time for boldness, not caution. It was also a situation that was familiar to me. Once again, I had a good chance, one collection, to prove myself . . . just as it had been when I worked all night to get my first job at Paramount in 1940, and for my first collection in New York in 1950, and for Jacqueline Kennedy in 1960.

Now it was 1972. I was nearing my sixtieth year of struggle on the planet. Would I be able to do it again?

I reviewed my past. I thought about looks and styles and historical periods, and I realized that there was one area I'd never really exploited: my lifelong obsession with American Indians. I did not make a precipitous decision; I rolled it over in my mind. The finest fabric houses in Europe were located in Como, outside of Milan. I began to consider the possibility of a collection of fine dresses in authentic American Indian prints; it would have to be very skillfully done—if not, it might seem merely gimmicky. We would be walking a fine line. I discussed it with my associates; they seemed excited by the concept.

And so began my almost archaeological research into Indian design. I sent to New York for various materials; I collected a library of a hundred books on the subject, and I would pore over them and make sketches each day in my office. This was quite an experience. I was working with great craftsmen, master printmakers, and we were creating some of the most complex patterns imaginable, some of which required as many as fifteen or sixteen different colors. Nowhere in the world would work of this sort be possible. And I developed a renewed respect for the Italian artisan class; as a group, they had a remarkably sophisticated visual sense. I had a very young, very talented *première* named Henrietta, two sketch artists, and an excellent team of sample hands and patternmakers. The collection was moving in an ambitious direction. It would have more than 120 pieces. It would utilize only the best cotton and silk. The dresses would be priced very expensively.

I lived again with the discipline of an athlete, but an *Italian* athlete. I would awaken each morning at seven, walk twenty blocks to my ofice, and work until early afternoon. Then, in the grand Mediterranean manner, Ferrari and I—often Etro, as well—would have a sumptuous lunch at one of the many fine restaurants in Milan (a city that is unsurpassed in its cuisine); the lunch would be accompanied by wine, and long philosophical ruminations on the direction the line was taking, along with the problems and possibilities we were facing. This exhausting process would lead, inevitably, to a midafternoon nap, and then I would return to my desk and work until nine in the evening. Later I would gather a company of friends —often as many as twenty or thirty—and we would have dinner together, after which most of them would go on to a discotheque without me. I was in training, after all; I had a discipline to maintain.

Finally, the sketches were done and I was faced with an eight-week hiatus while the printer—Etro—created more than forty different prints I had designed for the collection. Rather than sit around waiting, I took the opportunity to visit the Far East for the first time. My men's collection had been produced by Mitsui in Japan, and the large Mitsukoshi department-store group had invited me over to promote it.

The welcome I received in Japan was completely overwhelming. I was met at the airport by geishas bearing bouquets of flowers. Mitsui had reserved an entire floor of the Imperial Hotel in Tokyo for me. The courtesy, the charm of these people was a revelation, and I attempted to respond in kind. I gave two shows in Tokyo, one for the press and the other for a group of top customers, and memorized a brief speech in Japanese, thanking them for the generosity of their welcome. I traveled throughout the country, sampling its many pleasures: small country inns, the traditional baths. I even participated in a Japanese golf tournament that had been arranged in my honor at the Hakone golf course on Mount Fuji.

From there, I went on to Hong Kong. A good many of my American Indian dresses required intricate beading of a sort that was not available in Italy; I'd been told Hong Kong was the place to find such material. The search for beads was successful, but took somewhat longer than I had expected. There was a meeting scheduled in Milan to review the Etro prints; I called to see if it could be postponed several days. "Impossible! We've worked night and day on this. You must return immediately."

Immediately, I returned—but not so quickly. I was booked on the ultimate puddle-jumper: my plane made fourteen stops between Hong Kong and Milan. I arrived at the office exhausted but on time. Ferrari, who had called me, wasn't there. I waited nearly an hour for him. Finally, he breezed in, nonchalant, unconcerned.

"Ah, Oleg," he said, "how nice of you to be here."

"And the prints?" I asked.

"A small delay," he said. "They won't be ready till next week."

"You must be joking!" I said, and launched into a detailed description of the fourteen airports I had visited in the previous forty-eight hours.

"Oleg," he said, *"bisogna aver pazienza."*

Bisogna aver pazienza. Bisogna aver pazienza. Eventually the prints materialized, and I thought they were glorious. My associates weren't sure, though. "Too ethnic," they mumbled. "Too different, too American, too wild, too colorful . . ."

Too bad. It was too late. They really had no choice but to go ahead now, and my fine design team and I pressed on. We worked late into the night (I might mention that the concept of "overtime" did not exist for people who worked in fashion; they were paid a salary and were willing to work until two in the morning because they had pride in what they did, and they believed in the collection).

Finally we finished. I was enormously proud of what we had accomplished. It was a complete summer collection from bathing suits to evening gowns, a very eclectic collection, as good as any work I'd ever done. One dress with a plunging V-neckline and a full floor-length skirt featured a geometric print in more than a dozen shades of red, yellow, orange, and blue, broken at the waist by a Sioux-like patterned cummerbund; the patterns were quite authentic. There were others that would be almost impossible to describe. (I later gave the entire collection to the Fashion Institute of Technology in New York; it can be see there.)

Ferrari then announced a showing: fifty of the top stores in Italy, Germany, and Switzerland responded. It was an impressive indication of initial interest, but the greatest test lay ahead. He was in a panic the day of the show, pacing back and forth, saying, "Why did I let this man convince me to do American Indian clothes in Europe?"

I did not play any games at the showing. There were no jokes. I made a brief speech: "This collection represents a major effort by some of the most talented people I've ever encountered. If these clothes are not to your liking, the fault is mine and mine alone . . . because I've never worked in more amenable surroundings for an artistic project, nor with people who had more taste or devotion."

And then the show began. The line was modeled by girls with dark hair and the somatic characteristics of Indians; one wore beads and head-dresses. Sometimes the models were barefoot, but generally they wore moccasins. It was quite an exotic presentation; the reaction was respectful, but I couldn't be sure if it was favorable. It wasn't until the end of the day that Ferrari approached me smiling. "We did it!" He had orders from almost all the major stores.

The dresses were a big hit in Italy and Germany, and later at Saks, which gave us all its display windows on Fifth Avenue. Eventually I brought the line to Japan, where it was well received. Again, somewhat to my surprise this time, I had proven that the country or city of origin meant nothing when it came to fashion; style was universal. It had no home except in the human spirit.

Ten years later, in the early 1980s, I received a similarly spectacular proposal from Imelda Marcos. She was looking for a designer to produce a line using Philippine goods—clothing, furniture, even cigars. Factories were waiting; she was arranging a tour of the islands for me. Millions were to be made; a grand future was in the offing.

I met with Mrs. Marcos several times on her frequent shopping trips to New York. She was a charming woman, and very flattering. She called me "Maestro." But I had this sense, nothing specific—I didn't know that Mr. and Mrs. Marcos would soon be a part of history. I decided to watch events take their course and by early 1986 there was no longer a need to make a decision.

With the decline of the United States as a manufacturing center, I found myself venturing to exotic places—a Marco Polo of fashion, in search of local specialties. Over the years, I visited a German printmaking village in the midst of the Brazilian jungle, Turkish leather makers (who, unfortunately, used urine as a tanning agent), and Rumanian embroiderers, a venture that the Communist government of that country encouraged. I enjoyed my visit to Rumania—I stayed in the home of tennis friend Ion Tiriac and was entertained by Ilie Nastase—but I was reluctant to make a deal for the embroidery. The workers there seemed less enthusiastic about their work (the very opposite of the proud, devoted Italians I'd worked with in Milan), and I had little confidence that the government could inspire them to meet production schedules.

Actually, the wisdom that comes from experience is one of the few accoutrements of growing older that I will acknowledge. I have been around the block a few times now, and I often think of the old wolf in the Jack London novel who had once been a young, impetuous cub but, through determination and a certain amount of luck, had managed to survive. Most young wolves didn't—the forest was a dangerous place—but this one had, and now, in his old age, he could go out into the forest each day, understanding the dangers (the lupine equivalent of banana peels), perhaps not as supple as he'd once been, but more alert, with a better chance of persevering because he had faced every danger and conquered them all.

In a business that chews up designers and spits them out every seven years on average, in a society that consumes people as if they were soft drinks, I have managed to survive and prosper for more than forty years in the business and nearly three-quarters of a century in life. I have survived a revolution, the Stock Market Crash, and several wars, in addition to the chemise and the critics. I have done this by refusing to stand still (a moving target is harder to hit), by never being satisfied, by learning from my mistakes.

I have been luckier than most, and also unluckier: the continuing death-in-life of my daughter Daria—a pretty girl who cannot recognize me or her mother. This extraordinary, ongoing tragedy has been more than a counterweight for all the luck I've ever had. On the other hand, Daria's sister, Christina, has had quite a different sort of life. She is happily married and living in Europe with her four children as if the tempestuous nature of her mother's life and mine, and the tragedy of her sister's, had led her to the very opposite conclusion about how to proceed from day to day in this world.

My own conclusions about life have changed very little over time. I still go out to fight it each day as if it were a war. I still hear my mother's words at the dock in Italy—"Always remember who you are"; the fierce pride and determination have remained with me. I have known how precarious wealth and position in society can be. I am the old wolf—more secretive in my ways than before, but still guarding my territory.

I have made this compromise with age: I am more selective now.

There was a time in my life when I had to prove myself constantly. In the 1930s, I felt almost a physical need to go to El Morocco each night and cause a ripple (and also to see who else was there, who was new in town, who was getting old). This was an obscure and exhausting malady, which I later named "discotosis," after observing Philippe Junot suffering many of the same symptoms in the elegant club Castel's in Paris in the 1960s.

In any case, I never found a cure for discotosis. It receded over time, though. I still enjoyed the company of beautiful girls, but the frantic, competitive edge to my amorous life disappeared. Now I no longer go out every night simply to go out. Sometimes I will stay home . . . and home has become a more important place. In that regard, I realized that I needed a weekend retreat that complemented my medieval home in the city; eventually, I found it in Oyster Bay, Long Island—a splendid Edwardian mansion designed by Louis Comfort Tiffany, on forty-eight rolling acres overlooking Long Island Sound. It was the sort of house that prudent people—my accountant, for example—would look at and say, "White elephant." There are moments in life, however, when prudence should be the very last thing that one considers. I knew immediately that it possessed a beauty and grace that can no longer be purchased for any price. It was enormous, and now I spend most of my time in only five of the twenty rooms; but they are so pleasing as to be invigorative, with fine marble fireplaces and intricate carved-wood paneling that had been hidden, strangely, under layers of paint. I have a kennel there, which holds my sixteen dogs, and a tennis court, a small staff, and five horses.

This is not to say that I have been totally domesticated. I have not abandoned the field. I do not assume, as so many men my age do, that young ladies will not be interested in me. So often I have heard older men use the insipid line, "If I had only met you ten years ago, I could really go for you!" They are hoping, of course, for the girl to say, "But you look so good, why don't you try?"

I do not acknowledge age in this area. I think only, *Here I am. Am I interested? If I am, then it's valid. If it's valid, I go.*

Of course, my part of the bargain has been to keep myself in proper working order. I did not really think about how well I had maintained myself until 1975, when, at the age of sixty-two, I was invited by ABC Television to participate in a "celebrity" round of the *Superstars* program.

I wasn't aware of the invitation until a week before the competition was to begin, and so I didn't have much of an opportunity to prepare. Among my opponents were Robert Duvall, Kenny Rogers, Peter Duchin,

Peter Benchley, and George Plimpton; I was more than fifteen years older than the oldest of them.

A very curious thing happened there in Florida: I more than held my own; indeed, after the first day, I was leading the competition—and the crowds, composed mostly of older people,, were cheering me on. A very emotional rapport, a bond, was developing between me and that audience; and the producers, sensing a good story, began to focus on me. O. J. Simpson, who was one of the announcers that day, said to his partner, Keith Jackson, "Can you believe a sixty-two-year-old man is doing this well?"

Actually, I thought I could have done better. I should have won the tennis, but had a bad day (in a high wind) and finished third. I had lost a step over the years, and finished a disappointing fourth in the half-mile run (although I did beat Plimpton, who was very proud of his running). My most unexpected triumph came in the rowing, a sport that was new to me. I had to ask the fellow from J. C. Penney who provided the boats, how it was done. He said to take very short strokes. I did, and finished second to Peter Duchin, who had been rowing all his life and turned in a time that nearly tied the record for the course, set by the athlete Marty Riesen. Keith Jackson was nonplussed. He asked me how I'd done it.

"It was pride," I said. "I don't know anything about rowing."

It was pride, too, that had forced me to engage in fierce combat against the subtle encroachments of age. The *Superstars* program was a turning point of sorts for me. I realized, for the first time, that I was in pretty good shape "for a man my age." After the competition, I visited several doctors in New York, who confirmed it.

All my life I had enjoyed sports more than anything else, so I decided to mix business with pleasure; I entered the major pro-am events in golf and tennis. This had the double advantage of combining competition at a very high level with an exposure that had not been gotten by any other fashion designer.

I played in the Bing Crosby Classic at Pebble Beach several times. In 1975, I had the luck to be in the foursome with Ben Crenshaw, who won that year, and Mickey Van Gerbig, his partner; we were followed by huge galleries. Apart from the golf, the atomosphere at the Delmonte Lodge, the sheer beauty of the Monterey Peninsula, and the camaraderie with people like Andy Williams, Jim Garner, Jack Nicklaus, Clint Eastwood (now the mayor of Carmel), Bing, and of course our charming hostess,

Katherine Crosby, always made the Crosby Classic a memorable tournament.

The same atmosphere prevailed at Bob Hope's Desert Classic. To play in these tournaments was the dream of every golfer; there were positively thousands of people who would have given anything to play in them, but they were by invitation only.

At the same time, I was designing golf and tennis clothing, and it was the height of the tennis boom. There were many pro-celebrity tennis tournaments, most importantly the Robert F. Kennedy Tournament in New York. It was a major event, hosted by Ethel Kennedy, Bobby's widow, and benefited the RFK Memorial Foundation. No one having the luck to be invited to such an occasion could refuse. Large contingents of celebrities from all over the country, and the top players on the circuit, would congregate in New York for the weekend. On Friday night, Ethel would give a huge party at the Rainbow Room, where the teams were picked from a hat. The party would last until late at night; the next morning, the games would begin. It was a most competitive atmosphere. Everyone wanted to win, including me. The fact is, it was really a genuine athletic event, because the play was almost uninterrupted until late in the afternoon, when the finals were held. The heat and humidity in August always made it an endurance test. The pros tried extremely hard, as there was a huge prize—a car or a motorboat or something of comparable value.

I did win in 1976 with Jaime Fillol. He received a $45,000 car, and I had the pleasure of being congratulated by Governor Hugh Carey, Howard Cosell, Jackie, and Ethel in front of twenty thousand spectators, and ABC's TV cameras, at Forest Hills.

And yet, in the eyes of the world, I was nearing retirement age. I wondered about this arbitrary barrier, the age of sixty-five—who had come up with it? How had it been determined? I made a study of it, and discovered that Bismarck had established sixty-five as the retirement age in nineteenth-century Germany for one very simple reason: he had recently made a show of granting old-age benefits, and being told by his actuarial experts that most men died by sixty-five, he set that as the mandatory retirement age at which time one became eligible for state benefits.

What did this mean in the twentieth century? Nothing. What did it mean in my particular case? Even less. I had my own company and so there was no pressure on me to pack it in, but I took it one step further, too.

There are those who say you should grow old gracefully; others say you should be "young at heart" or "rage against the dying of the light." I decided that I simply would not acknowledge any of the clichés about the aging process. I would not acknowledge the process, period.

I had stumbled upon certain fortuitous habits in diet and exercise in the course of my life, and I would continue those. And now, I still play tennis three times a week. My diet continues as always: I create a mental picture of my stomach as a pocket and I watch what I am mixing there. I am very conscious of ingesting chemicals and the varieties of garbage that often pass for food these days. I do not mix protein and carbohydrates. Often people will ask me what is true "inner" beauty, and I will joke, "Good digestion." But it is not so much of a joke. My motor has run a long way on pasta.

Actually, that is one image I often think about. If you can keep a Rolls-Royce cleaned and tuned and attended to, it will not be "old" in twenty years; it will be a "classic."

And that is another valuable secret I have discovered over the years: the importance of keeping a positive but autocritical frame of mind. I think of myself as an ageless young man with white hair. Every day, I awake ready to do battle. I feel pretty good. I feel better than yesterday. I can't wait to start the day, to win the prize. As long as I compete, I will remain alive. There is no reason, given my ancestry, that I cannot emulate the yogurt eaters from the Caucasus and live to be 120 or 130 (in which case you may consider this work an interim report).

At night before I go to sleep I meditate—but not some unintelligible gibberish. I meditate on all the things I've done wrong that day. I do not belabor them, or attack myself because of them. I think about what I might have done differently, how I will make tomorrow better. I acknowledge my humanity, and engage in a silent determination to improve upon it, knowing full well that I will be back tomorrow evening, still gloriously imperfect, still stuggling to be a little better.

These meditations have enabled me to keep things in perspective; I never let a day pass without reviewing the ethics of my behavior. I have tried to remain consistent in that regard. Despite all the ups and downs of my life, I never became bitter or vindictive. I might behave poorly at times, but I was never unkind or uncharitable. I like to think that I have not become a hard man in a hard world. Those who know me—whether they like me or not, whether they admire my work or not—know I am an honest man; honest toward life, toward the world, toward people. I have not achieved my success at the expense of others. I have competed with all my might, but in the chivalric spirit that Colonel Zboromirski brought to life for me as a child, in the spirit of my ancestors.

A few years ago, I experienced an epiphany: I was invited to be part of the *Night of 100 Stars*, the glamorous Actors Equity benefit staged in New York at Radio City Music Hall. It seemed that all the disparate parts of my life had gathered, for once, in a single place. There were many of my old friends from Hollywood, from the worlds of fashion and athletics, and from international society. It had the feeling of a homecoming. I had lunch that day with Linda Evans and Jill St. John, both of whom were old friends, and a new friend, John Forsythe. We talked about Hollywood, how it had changed since the days when I roamed Sunset Boulevard.

That evening, there was a long wait backstage. My role was to be rather limited. Like several other designers, I would merely walk onstage, flanked by two famous ladies (in my case, Janet Leigh and Gloria Loring) wearing clothes I had designed.

I sat off to the side and mused on the spectacle behind the scenes, the chaos that the public could never see. I drifted off then, into a reverie . . . back to Hollywood, the great sound stages, the blinding lights, people shouting and cursing, the magic moment of a take and, finally, the celluloid projected onto a screen—a larger-than-life illusion all too often mistaken for reality, even by those, like Gene and Grace, who were at the heart of the magic and should have known better.

Illusions. I had spent the better part of my life promulgating illusions through fashion. My goal had always been to enhance and celebrate the natural body shape, but the human form so rarely matched that ideal. The "natural" look was almost always illusion, a subtle manipulation of fabric and fantasy. The art of fashion was the appearance of ease, of effortless elegance.

And as I continued my reverie, I realized that these illusory arts of film and fashion weren't so different from the politician's trade I had observed in Washington. John Kennedy had been a master magician, hiding the intense pain of his illnesses and the agonies of office with stirring rhetoric and natural grace, creating an aura of enthusiasm, intelligence, and easy elegance that so many since have attempted to emulate and none have matched.

So much of my life—of all life in our complex, modern world—was engaged in the creation and pursuit of illusions. I wondered, fleetingly, what was real.

* * *

It is a question that has stayed with me. Recently, I participated in another one of those celebrity sporting events that are always a curious mixture of façade and genuine athletic endeavor. It was George Plimpton's Celebrity Challenge Harness Race, held in Pompano Beach, Florida. My fellow competitors included Plimpton, football players Ken Stabler and Kim Bokamper, and New York Yankees owner George Steinbrenner. Ostensibly this was all to be in good fun for worthy charities (I made the additional contribution of designing the racing silks for all the participants). We were there to enjoy a friendly sporting challenge, yet my rivals and I, all strongly competitive souls, often found ourselves jockeying for the psychological upper hand and turning to tactics of intimidation.

There we were, sizing up one another, and I knew some of these younger fellows thought my presence was merely a novelty. But I'd intended, despite my lack of experience, to give them a good run for their money.

We would alternate between mock seriousness and magnanimous words of praise for one another and bona fide belligerence. Steinbrenner, which perhaps is to be expected, was the feistiest. He was heard to say that he would "Dump the little guinea bastard" (me) in the Pompano infield pond if I presumed to get in his way during the race.

It was all I needed. I entered the silent vehemence of my ancestral soul. I had no age. I was a child confronting the caddies at Deauville with golf clubs; I was a young man confronting Belmonte on the street in Rome after he called me "only a tailor"; I was a thousand years of European history, a cossack, a member of the czar's Imperial Guard, a Knight of Malta, a *cavalleggiero di Novara*—and I would not be intimidated by anyone.

I thought back to my recurring reverie about the illusory quality of modern times and realized that if *anything* in my life was "real" it was this—this very basic fierceness, this pride, this competitiveness, this determination to come back from adversity, the determination to fight each day as if it were a war, as if I were one of my ancestors in brilliant uniform, sabre gleaming, charging into the fray, with my favorite horse and in full armor . . .

Thus, boldly, I challenged Steinbrenner and the others with all my energy. It was an exhilarating experience, controlling—no, *merging* with —the horse at those fast speeds, fending off fearsome competitors riding dangerously close. I managed to lose by just a whisker to Steinbrenner.

I do think I surprised all concerned with my credible performance.

Afterwards, Steinbrenner came up to me with sincerity and—could it be? —admiration and congratulated me on challenging him as he had never anticipated. "I know now," he said, "that you are the one to beat."

Meanwhile, as I left the field, friends and acquaintances who'd witnessed the treacherous race, who were incredulous from the moment I told them I was competing, surrounded me. "How could you do such a crazy thing?" they asked me once again. "You could have been killed. How could you do that?"

"How could I not?" I replied with a shrug, as the congratulations of ancestors coursed through my veins. "How could I not?"

INDEX